Family Observational Coding Systems

Resources for Systemic Research

Family Observational Coding Systems

Resources for Systemic Research

Edited by

Patricia K. Kerig
University of North Carolina at Chapel Hill

Kristin M. Lindahl
University of Miami

 LAWRENCE ERLBAUM ASSOCIATES, PUBLISHERS
2001   Mahwah, New Jersey   London

Lawrence Erlbaum Associates, Inc., Publishers
10 Industrial Avenue
Mahwah, New Jersey 07430-2262

Cover design by Kathryn Houghtaling Lacey

Library of Congress Cataloging-in-Publication Data

Family observational coding systems : resources for systemic
research / edited by Patricia K. Kerig, Kristin M. Lindahl.
     p. cm.
  Includes bibliographical references and index.
  ISBN 0-8058-3323-4 (cloth : alk. paper)
    1. Family—Research—Methodology. 2. Family—Ob-
servations—Methodology. I. Kerig, Patricia K. II. Lindahl,
Kristin M.
HQ728.F3218 2000
306.85'07—dc21   00-026444
                                     CIP

Books published by Lawrence Erlbaum Associates are
printed on acid-free paper, and their bindings are chosen for
strength and durability.

Printed in the United States of America
10 9 8 7 6 5 4 3 2 1

For the people who taught me most about family processes:
my father, my mother, my sisters, and my brother.

—PKK

For my parents—who taught me what it means to be a family.

—KML

Contents

Preface

PURPOSE OF THIS VOLUME

The idea for this volume arose from a series of conversations among family researchers at the meetings of the Society for Research in Child Development and the Family Research Consortium Summer Institute. On repeated occasions, colleagues expressed the wish to know more about one another's nascent coding systems, particularly those oriented toward capturing triadic or whole-family processes. Recent thinking in family research increasingly stresses the importance of investigating processes at the systemic level in order to understand how relationships develop and affect one another. Much of this research is new, and individual investigators are often faced with the task of creating coding systems that will allow them to capture their constructs of interest. However, developing an observational coding system is a difficult, complex, and time-consuming process, and evidence for reliability and validity are limited when a measure is designed for a single study or used in a single lab, as is often the case. In addition, because it is difficult for individual researchers to learn about the work going on in other labs until it is published—sometimes not until years after the work was completed—we may be frustrated to find that we have been "reinventing the wheel," struggling to operationalize constructs that have been successfully captured by colleagues with similar interests. This lack of communication limits our ability to learn from one another and to engage in a cross-fertilization of ideas. Therefore, the central purpose of this book is to provide information and resources to stimulate systemic research and to aid investigators interested in carrying out family observational coding.

The primary readership for this book is expected to include investigators, faculty, and graduate students at academic institutions and research/teaching clinics. In addition, however, we expect this work will be of interest to family clinicians. A number of the contributors to this volume are clinical psychologists, including the editors. We find that our training in coding family interactions has benefitted our clinical work by making our observations of family relationships better targeted and more acute, and by refining our understanding of the implications of these family dynamics for parent and child emotional health.

ORGANIZATION AND CONTENT OF THE CHAPTERS

The first two chapters in this volume present overviews of conceptual and methodological issues in the study of whole-family processes. The remaining chapters describe contributions to the field by 14 independent laboratories. Each chapter provides information about the conceptual underpinnings and structure of the coding system developed by the author(s), as well as evidence for its psychometric properties. In order to ease the process of comparing across systems, every chapter uniformly addresses a number of key issues, including the theoretical foundations of the measure, the strategic conceptual and methodological choices made in its development, the properties and content of the measure, the processes of coding and coder training, the evidence for reliability and validity, and the range of empirical tests to which the measure has been put. Finally, excerpts from the coding manual are provided in order to give the reader a "flavor" of the way in which the system goes about capturing the constructs of interest. Because space limitations precluded the incorporation of the entire coding manuals in this volume, these have been made available to the reader on Lawrence Erlbaum Associates' web site (www.erlbaum.com). A particular benefit to the web-based coding manuals is that contributors will be able to make modifications and refinements to them as the need arises, and therefore the reader can be assured of having access to the most up-to-date version of each coding scheme.

Due to our interest in making this volume as current, diverse, and representative of the field as possible, a range of contributions was solicited. Some of these represent well-established and widely used measures, with a significant history of research behind them. Others represent the very latest work of well-known scholars in the field, "hot off the press." Yet others are the contributions of relatively young investigators who are on the crest of the next wave of family research. Although the field is growing and changing even as this volume goes to press, it is our hope that this collection will remain pertinent and contemporary for some time to come.

ACKNOWLEDGMENTS

The editors would like to express their appreciation to Judi Amsel, whose unfailing enthusiasm about the project and personal warmth made the production process a pleasure, and to Victoria Rentz, an unfailingly helpful editorial assistant who has since expanded her horizons. A number of colleagues offered words of support and encouragement that kept the wind in our sails, including Philip and Carolyn Cowan, Mari Clements, and Lynn Fainsilber Katz. Finally, we would like to thank each of the contributors for their hard work, their patience, and, most of all, their generosity in sharing their work. Particularly for those whose chapters represent work very young in its development, thank you for letting us coax your fledglings from the nest.

—Patricia K. Kerig

—Kristin M. Lindahl

List of Contributors

Lorna Smith Benjamin, University of Utah, Department of Psychology, 390 South 1530 East, Salt Lake City, Utah 84112; E-mail: benjamin@xmission.com.

Amy Coffield, Department of Psychology, Bowling Green State University, Bowling Green, Ohio 43403-0228.

Rand D. Conger, Department of Sociology, Iowa State University, 107 East Hall, Ames, Iowa 50011; E-mail: rconger@iastate.edu.

Martha J. Cox, Frank Porter Graham Child Development Center, University of North Carolina–Chapel Hill, CB# 8180, 105 Smith Level Road, Chapel Hill, North Carolina 27599-8180; E-mail: Martha_Cox@unc.edu.

Susan Dickstein, E. P. Bradley Hospital and Brown University, 1011 Veterans Parkway, Providence, Rhode Island 02915.

Barbara H. Fiese, Department of Psychology, Syracuse University, 430 Huntington Hall, Syracuse, New York 13244-2340; E-mail: bhfiese@mailbox.syr.edu.

Paul Florsheim, Department of Psychology, University of Utah, 390 South 1530 East, Salt Lake City, Utah 84112; E-mail: florsh@freud.sbs.utah.edu.

Charles Forbes, Department of Human Development and Family Science, Oregon State University, Corvallis, Oregon 97370; E-mail: forbesc@ccmail.orst.edu.

Deborah Fravel, Department of Applied Health Sciences, Indiana University, Poplars 221, Bloomington, Indiana 47405.

Elana B. Gordis, Department of Psychology, University of California–Los Angeles, Franz Hall, Box 951563, Los Angeles, California 90095-1563; E-mail: gordis@psych.ucla.edu.

Harold Grotevant, Department of Family Social Sciences, University of Minnesota, 1985 Buford, St. Paul, Minnesota 55108; E-mail: hgrotevant@che2.che.umn.edu.

Amanda W. Harrist, Department of Family Relations and Child Development, Oklahoma State University, 333C HES, Stillwater, Oklahoma 74078; E-mail: wiginto@okstate.edu.

Olga Hervis, Center for Family Studies, University of Miami School of Medicine, Department of Psychiatry and Behavioral Sciences, Miami, Florida 33124.

Korrel W. Kanoy, Department of Psychology, Peace College, 15 E. Peace Street, Raleigh, North Carolina 27604; E-mail: kkanoy@peace.edu.

Patricia K. Kerig, Department of Psychology and Children's Psychiatric Institute, University of North Carolina at Chapel Hill, CB# 3270, Chapel Hill, North Carolina 27599; E-mail: kerigpk@unc.edu.

Blythe Kneedler, Department of Human Development and Family Science, Oregon State University, Corvallis, Oregon 97370.

Regina Kuersten-Hogan, Department of Psychology, Clark University, 950 Main St., Worcester, Massachusetts 01610.

Sam Lashley, Department of Psychology, Bowling Green State University, Bowling Green, Ohio 43403-0228.

Allison Lauretti, Department of Psychology, Clark University, 950 Main St., Worcester, Massachusetts 01610.

Terri Lewis, Department of Psychology, Bowling Green State University, Bowling Green, Ohio 43403-0228.

Kristin M. Lindahl, Department of Psychology, University of Miami, P.O. Box 249229, Psych Annex, Coral Gables, Florida 33124-0721; E-mail: KLindahl@umiami.ir.miami.edu.

Eric W. Lindsey, Department of Human Development and Family Studies, Texas Tech University, Box 41162, Lubbock, Texas 79409; E-mail: elindsey@hs.ttu.edu.

Annette Mahoney, Department of Psychology, Bowling Green State University, Bowling Green, Ohio 43403-0228; E-mail: amahone@BGNet.bgsu.edu.

Neena M. Malik, Department of Psychology, University of Miami, P.O. Box 249229, Psych Annex, Coral Gables, Florida 33124-0721; E-mail: nmalik@umiami.ir.miami.edu.

Gayla Margolin, Department of Psychology, University of Southern California, Los Angeles, California 90064-1061; E-mail: margolin@mizar.usc.edu.

James P. McHale, Department of Psychology, Clark University, 950 Main St., Worcester, Massachusetts 01610; E-mail: jmchale@clarku.edu.

Janet N. Melby, Institute for Social and Behavioral Research, 2625 North Loop Dr., Ames, Iowa 50010-8296; E-mail: jmelby@iastate.edu.

Victoria B. Mitrani, Center for Family Studies, University of Miami School of Medicine, Department of Psychiatry and Behavioral Sciences, Miami, Florida 33101.

Jacqueline Mize, Department of Human Development and Family Studies, 203 Spidle Hall, Auburn University, Auburn, Alabama 36849-5604; E-mail: mizejac@mail.auburn.edu.

Blair Paley, University of California–Los Angeles Neuropsychiatric Institute and Hospital, 760 Westwood Plaza, Rm. #58-239A; Los Angeles, California 90024; E-mail: BPaley@mednet.ucla.edu.

Gregory S. Pettit, Department of Human Development and Family Studies, 203 Spidle Hall, Auburn University, Auburn, Alabama 36849-5604, E-mail: gpettit@auburn.edu.

Michael S. Robbins, Center for Family Studies, University of Miami School of Medicine, Department of Psychiatry and Behavioral Sciences, Miami, Florida 33101; E-mail: Allapattah@earthlink.net.

Alan Russell, School of Education, Flinders University, GPO Box 2100, Adelaide SA, 5001, Australia; E-mail: alan.russell@flinders.edu.au.

Judith Saebel, School of Education, Flinders University, GPO Box 2100, Adelaide SA, 5001, Australia.

Arnold Sameroff, University of Michigan, Center for Human Growth and Development, 300 N. Ingalls- 10th Level, Ann Arbor, Michigan 48109-0406; E-mail: sameroff@umich.edu.

José Szapocznik, Center for Family Studies, University of Miami School of Medicine, Department of Psychiatry and Behavioral Sciences, Miami, Florida 33101.

Samuel Vuchinich, Department of Human Development and Family Science, Oregon State University, Corvallis, Oregon 97370; E-mail: vuchinis@ccmail.orst.edu.

Frederick Wamboldt, National Jewish Medical Research Center and University of Colorado Health Sciences Center, 1400 Jackson St., Littman 301, Denver, Colorado 80206; E-mail: wamboldtf@njc.org.

Michael A. Westerman, Department of Psychology, New York University, 6 Washington Place, 4th Floor, New York, New York 10003; E-mail: mwest@psych.nyu.edu.

Introduction and Overview: Conceptual Issues in Family Observational Research

Patricia K. Kerig
University of North Carolina at Chapel Hill

In recent decades, social scientists increasingly have come to appreciate the importance of the family context in which child development takes place. Carlson and Grotevant (1987b) referred to this as "a dramatic paradigm shift ... toward relationships rather than individuals as the unit of analysis" (p. 23). Interest in family relationships spans theoretical orientations, including behavioral, attachment, psychodynamic, and systemic. Thus, the family provides a unifying theme across theories and promises to contribute to the much needed integrative approach called for by developmental psychopathology (Achenbach, 1990; Cicchetti & Cohen, 1995). By the same token, family work has become pivotal to interventions of all types, whether cognitive behavioral (e.g., Howard & Kendall, 1996; Stark, Swearer, Kurowski, Sommer, & Bowen, 1996), interpersonal (Schwartz, Kaslow, Racusin, & Carton, 1998), or psychodynamic (Slipp, 1991). For the theorist, the researcher, and the clinician, in short, the family is the heart of the matter.

WHY OBSERVE THE FAMILY?

Observational research is uniquely suited to the study of families, providing access to the relationships among individuals rather than the characteristics of the indi-

1

viduals engaged in those relationships. Observing family processes helps us to uncover the mechanisms linking parenting and child development (P. A. Cowan & C. P. Cowan, 1990), and allows us to investigate the dynamic, reciprocal, and transactional ways in which these effects take place. Observation provides access to "the rich, nuanced, and distinctive set of interpersonal dynamics characteristic of whole-family group interaction" (McHale, Kuersten, & Lauretti, 1996, p. 5).

As Stoneman and Brody (1990) pointed out, observational research also provides data that cannot be obtained in any other manner. People behave in ways that are discrepant from their self-perceptions, and only direct observation can capture their behavior independently of their appraisals of it. The "outsider" perspective is a privileged one in its way, adding unique and independent information from that provided by those "inside" the family circle. However, saying that the observer has a unique viewpoint does not mean that it necessarily is the most valid one. Observational methods are no more purely "objective" than any other tool in the researcher's toolbox. Underlying every coding category lie choices, and every choice of behavior to code or strategy for coding it is informed by the investigator's conceptual framework. "The coding systems themselves are derived out of researchers' a priori assumptions as to what constitutes important communication differences.... Even when such differences are empirically validated, we have no way of knowing whether the differences discovered [are] the only ones, or are the most significant ones" (Margolin, 1990, p. 210).

Thus, despite the achievements and promises of research on the family system, there are a number of conceptual challenges that remain unanswered. Questions have been raised about the validity and generalizability of observational methods, as well as about the extent to which they have been meaningfully linked to theory. Other limitations noted include the fact that some significant family patterns are not amenable to observation. Given the heavy investment of time and resources required to use observational coding schemes—as many as 20 hours to code 1 hour of interaction (Gottman, 1979)—observational methods bear the onus to prove their worth, perhaps more than other methodologies. This chapter offers a review of the conceptual issues and dilemmas involved in observational research on the family system, illustrated with examples from the methodologies represented in this volume (Table 1.1 provides an overview of these coding systems and their properties).

HOW ARE WE DOING? PROBLEMS AND PROGRESS

The Role of Theory

A number of critics, including P. A. Cowan (1987), L'Abate and Bagarozzi (1993), and Grotevant and Carlson (1987a; 1987b), have decried the lack of integration between theory and method in the study of family relationships. Particularly in the early development of family observational coding systems, the focus of attention in psychology generally was on behavior rather than the inferred processes underlying it. As the prevailing conceptual framework shifted from the study of behav-

TABLE 1.1

Properties of Family Observational Coding Systems in this Volume

Coding System	Construct(s)	Level of Analysis	Coding Categories	Generalizability			
				Contexts/Tasks	Family Forms	Samples	Child Ages
Structural Analysis of Social Behavior (Florsheim & Benjamin)	Circumplex model of interdependence and affiliation	Micro or Macro	Free–forget, affirm–understand, love–approach, nurture–protect, watch–control, belittle–blame, attack–reject, ignore–neglect Assert–separate, disclose–express, joyfully connect, trust–rely, defer–submit, protest–recoil, wall off–distance	Any interaction Videotaped with verbatim transcript	Triadic and dyadic interactions	Normative and clinical, range of SES and ethnicities, couples, therapist–client interactions	infancy through adolescence
Family Narrative Consortium Coding System (Fiese et al.)	Family narratives	Macro	Coherence Narrative interaction Relationship beliefs	Any interview or story-telling task Audiotaped or videotaped with verbatim transcript	Multiple family members, couples, individual parents, school-age children	Normative and clinical; adoptive parents and youth, families with asthmatic child	school-age
Family Problem Solving Code (Forbes et al.)	Problem-solving effectiveness and contributing individual, relational, family characteristics	Macro	Positive behavior Negative behavior Relationships Coalitions Participation Problem solving	Family problem-solving interaction Audiotaped, videotaped, live	Three or more family members	Diverse social classes and family forms; clinical and community samples	8 through 19
Family Coding System (Gordis & Margolin)	Effects of marital conflict on parent–child interactions	Meso (1-min. intervals, behavior counts)	Interparental affect Parent-to-child affect and communication Child behavior Cross-generational alliance	Family discussion of child behavior problem Videotaped	Triadic family interaction	Multiethnic two-parent families	9 to 13

(Continues)

TABLE 1.1 (CONTINUED)

Coding System	Constuct(s)	Level of Analysis	Coding Categories	Contexts/Tasks	Generalizability			
					Family Forms	Samples	Child Ages
Social Events System (Harrist & Pettit)	Context and meaning of naturally occurring family interactions	Molar (meso)	Control Teaching Reflective listening Social contact	Naturalistic live family interactions Live, narrative description	Multiple family members, family subsystems (parent–child dyad, siblings, parent–child–sibling triad)	Euro-American and African-American two-parent and single-parent families	infancy to adolescence
System for Coding Interactions and Family Functioning (Lindahl & Malik)	Family functioning in each subsystem	Macro	Family: emotion, cohesiveness, focus of problem, structure Marital communication Parent: rejection, coercion, withdrawal, triangulation, emotional support Child: affect and behavior	Family problem-solving discussion Videotaped	Triadic, multichild, and dyadic parent–child interactions	One- and two-parent families, diverse ethnicities	5 to 12
Parent–Child Mutuality Coding System (Lindsey & Mize)	Mutuality	Micro (event-based)	Mutual play initiation/dyadic initiation imbalance Mutual compliance/dyadic compliance imbalance	Parent–child or parent–peer play Videotaped	Dyadic mother–child, father–child, child–peer interactions	Largely White, middle-class, community families	preschool; but relevant to any age
Meso-Analytic Behavioral Rating System for Family Interactions (Mahoney et al.)	Parent, child, and coparental behaviors related to child externalizing symptoms	Meso (1-min. intervals)	Parent: positive attention, hostility, involvement, controllingness, ambiguous or coercive control, permissiveness Child: overt noncompliance, antisocial, prosocial	Triadic play or forced-compliance activities Videotaped	Triadic family interactions	White, middle-class families from suburban-rural community	4 to 7

Instrument	Construct	Level	Dimensions/Codes	Task	Interaction type	Sample	Age range
Coparenting and Family Ratings Scales (McHale et al.)	Coparenting	Macro	Coparental competition, cooperation, verbal sparring; Child vs. adult centeredness; Family warmth; Discrepancies in parenting	Structured teaching tasks and unstructured play; Videotaped	Triadic family interactions	Largely White, middle-class, community samples	infancy to preschool
Iowa Family Interaction Rating Scales (Melby & Conger)	Behaviors and relationship processes	Macro	Individual characteristics; Dyadic interaction; Group interaction; Parenting; Individual problem solving; Family problem solving	Discussion or problem solving; Videotaped	Triadic; dyadic parent–child, couple, sibling, peer interactions	Diverse ethnicities, social classes, and family forms	2 to young adulthood
Whole Family Interaction Coding (Paley, Cox & Kanoy)	Systemic and attachment influences on children's emotional development	Macro	Family: sensitivity, positive affect, negative affect, detachment, intrusiveness, stimulation of cognitive development, parental confidence, family alliances; Child: anger, compliance, enthusiasm	Family building task; Videotaped	Triadic family interaction	Normative, largely White and lower middle- to middle-class	2 to 3
Structural Family System Ratings (Robbins et al.)	Family functioning	Macro	Structure; Disengagement, enmeshment; Developmental stage; Identified patienthood; Conflict resolution	Family discussion; Videotaped	Triadic, single-parent, and extended family interactions; adult parent–child	Diverse ethnicities and family forms, clinical and community samples	6 to adulthood
Parent–Toddler Play Coding Scheme (Russell et al.)	Horizontal and vertical dimensions of parent–child interaction	Macro–micro (1- to 4-min. interval behavior ratings)	Parental play roles: director, facilitator, coplayer; Specific behaviors/qualities; Child's enjoyment of play, mutual enjoyment, level of conflict	Play in naturalistic home setting; Videotaped	Mother–child and father–child	Predominantly White, low- to middle-class community families	toddlers
Triadic Coordination Scales (Westerman)	Triadic coordination	Macro	Participation, attempts to involve, uninvolved, agreement/support, elaboration, disagree, constructive disagreement	Structured problem solving; Videotaped	Triadic family interaction	Largely White, middle-class community samples	5 to 12

ior to appreciation of the relational context in which behavior develops, systems theory offered a number of important concepts that could be meaningfully applied to the family (Bertalanffy, 1968). The systemic perspective differs from the behavioral one in that it views interactions within the context of a larger, circular system, in which cause and effect are mutual, reciprocal, and bidirectional. Thus, in contrast to social learning theory, the systemic approach looks for recurrent processes and interprets their meanings (Margolin, 1990). As Carlson and Grotevant (1987b) stated, "theoretical conceptualizations regarding family interaction concern patterns, whereas family interaction research has examined, for the most part, rates of behavior" (p. 24).

In the present day, the rift between theory and method in family observational research appears to be narrowing. For example, the majority of the contributions to this volume are explicitly informed by theory, and even advance family theory in new directions. It is noteworthy that, of all the theorists to apply systemic concepts to the study of the family, Salvador Minuchin (1974) made some of the most significant and enduring contributions. Minuchin's structural perspective is cited as a conceptual inspiration by many of the contributors to this volume, including Paley, Cox, and Kanoy; Gordis and Margolin; Lindahl and Malik; McHale, Kuersten, and Lauretti; Robbins, Hervis, Mitrani, and Szapocznik; Russell, Mize, and Saebel; and Westerman.

The way in which coding systems are informed by theory differs across the contributions to this volume. Some contributors focus explicitly on a particular systemic theory, furthering its development by testing its precepts (e.g., Robbins et al.) or updating it with newer thinking in the family field, such as attachment theory (e.g., Paley et al.). Other contributors derive broad, general qualities of family relationships through integrating systemic theory and other perspectives, such as social learning (e.g., Forbes, Vuchinich, & Kneedler; Gordis & Margolin; Lindahl & Malik; Mahoney, Coffield, Lewis, & Lashley) or narrative development (Fiese et al.). Some coding systems are designed to tap a specific construct (e.g., McHale et al.; Westerman) derived from an integration of different family theories. Yet other measures are empirically derived and expansive in scope, designed to capture transtheoretical aspects of family interaction (e.g., Harrist & Pettit; Melby & Conger). Despite these different approaches, it seems fair to say that it is the exception than the rule for theory to be neglected completely.

What Is the "Whole" Family?

A more difficult problem to resolve has been a basic definitional question regarding the phenomenon under study: the "whole" family. One of the central tenets of systemic theory is that the family gestalt represents something above and beyond the individual relationships that comprise it. As Bertallanffy (1968) expressed it, "The meaning of the somewhat mystical expression, 'the whole is more than the sum of parts' is simply that constitutive characteristics are not explainable from the characteristics of isolated parts" (p. 55). Thus, the study of dyads cannot act as a proxy for the study of the family as a unit (P. Minuchin, 1985). Observation of the whole family also allows us to assess more complex and subtle transactions than can be detected in dyadic relationships, such as the ways parents affect children indirectly through affecting behavior of their partner toward the child (Parke, 1990). Moreover, the systemic family environment has a unique and independent influence on children's adjustment. As Brody and Flor (1996) argued, processes involving the relationships among all family members—such as cohesiveness, engagement and harmony—are essential for optimal child development:

> [The whole-family environment creates] an arena of comfort for children and parents alike that fosters a sense of security and serves as a buffer against stressful life events. For children, this emotional comfort provides a springboard from which they can explore and shape their environment. (p. 79)

Research also supports the view that the family whole is not equivalent to its summed parts. A clear example of this is the finding that the roles and behavior of family members change as they move from dyadic to triadic interaction (e.g., Gjerde, 1986). "Dyads are fluid and the interpersonal dynamics of dyadic interactions often change when a third family member joins in" (Brody & Flor, 1996, p. 89). For children, interacting with both parents together means coping with the dynamics of the marital relationship, which, whether positive or negative, have a profound effect on child development (Cummings & Davies, 1994; Grych & Fincham, in press). In turn, for adults, moving from the dyad to the mother–father–child triad means a change of role demand from that of parent to that of parent/spouse, and "thus the parent–child dyad is transformed into a family system" (Gjerde, 1986, p. 297).

Family-level research also redresses a particular shortcoming in the study of child development, that is the tendency to ignore fathers. As P. Minuchin (1985) chided, "Psychological researchers created the single-parent family long before it was a characteristic of American society" (p. 296). Including fathers in the study of the family has contributed in major ways to our understanding of family processes and their effects on child development, as is attested to by a large body of research in general (e.g., Belsky, 1989; P. A. Cowan, Cohn, C. P. Cowan, & Pearson, 1996; Lamb, 1997) and the present volume in particular (e.g., Paley et al.; McHale et al.; Gordis & Margolin).

However, nowhere in the literature is there more contention than over the definition of the family "whole" or the methods necessary to measure it. "The operationalization of family systems theory continues to be the source of methodological challenges" (Carlson & Grotevant, 1987b, p. 42). For example, P. A. Cowan and C. P. Cowan (1990) pointed out that, although the concept of the "enmeshed family" seems sound, in normative families, one enmeshed parent–child relationship is usually counterbalanced by detachment in the other dyads. "How, then, are we to describe *the family*?" (p. 42). McHale (this volume) makes a helpful differentiation between "whole-family" and "family-level" concepts. Whole-family concepts describe characteristics of the family gestalt, which are global, abstract, and difficult to access. Family-level concepts, in contrast, describe processes occurring when the family is together as a group, and are more specific, operationalizable, and amenable to observation. However, conceptual and methodological problems still arise in the study of family-level processes. It is quite challenging to capture characteristics of the family unit as distinct from the individuals or dyads that make it up.

To address these problems, we need to construct models of the family that take into account the complex and interacting patterns among the individuals and subsystems that comprise it. Rutter (1988) argued that despite the fact that the "functioning of the whole is qualitatively different from the sum of its parts ... the properties of the family as a whole derive from the properties of relationships between the individuals in the family" (p. 333). Gjerde (1986) echoed this point, stating that the systems perspective "implies more than mutual interdependence among family members; it entails interdependence among *relationships*. That is, the quality of one relationship influences and is, in turn, influenced by other relationships" (p. 297).

For example, despite the fact that parent–child relationships change across dyadic and triadic settings, children interact with each parent in both dyadic and triadic contexts, and are influenced by all subsystems in the family. In turn, all of these subsystems are interdependent on one another (Sroufe & Fleeson, 1988). In Parke's (1990) words:

> It is insufficient to trace only the individual—whether parents or child; it is also necessary to trace the development of dyads (mother–child; father–child as well as the husband–wife dyad), and larger units, such as families over time. Each of these units may show a partially independent trajectory and the interplay across the trajectories of different units (individual, dyad and family) provides a more complete picture of the context in which the individual of interest is embedded. (p. 182)

Moreover, it is possible, even usual, for dynamics relevant to the family triad to take place at the dyadic level. Belsky, Putnam, and Crnic (1996) offered a definition that acknowledges this, suggesting that "Whole family dynamics include events and processes that involve all family members together *or a family subsystem (parent–child or husband–wife) that affects and is affected by the other subsystems in the family* [emphasis added]" (p. 46). In this regard, we need only to look again to the rich literature investigating the influence of one specific dyad—the couple—on the interactions between the parent and child. The fact that mother–child and father–child interactions may be differentially affected by the quality of the marital relationship (e.g., Hayden et al., 1998; Kerig, P. A. Cowan, & C. P. Cowan, 1993; McHale, 1995) argues in favor of attending to these dyads in the context of the family triad.

Another premiere example of a dyadic family-level interaction is covert coparenting hostility (McHale, 1997). For example, if a parent disparages the spouse when alone with the child, the child is ensnarled in a triangle despite the fact that not all members of the triad are present. To take another example, consider Fivaz-Depeursinge, Frascarolo, and Corboz-Warnery's (1996) concept of the triadic alliance, the three-way synchrony and coordination that allows each family member to maintain a balanced, simultaneous engagement with the other two members of the triad. This process, too, can occur in the dyad. A child might challenge the triadic alliance by coaxing permission from one parent when the other has said no, or a parent might tip the scale by fostering a special bond with the child that implicitly excludes the other parent. The ability of mothers and fathers to parent in ways that are consistently supportive of and coordinated with one another—*especially* when apart from one another—may provide the child the most convincing demonstration of the firmness and security of the marital alliance.

Attention to dyadic interactions within the family can also help to elucidate different forms of triadic relationships (see Katz & Gottman, 1996). In this regard, a crucial distinction concerns who is "driving" the interaction (Kerig, 1999). For example, McHale et al. (1996) and McConnell and Kerig (1999) noted the difference between the family in which "hostile-competitive" coparenting is the product of one parent's behavior versus the family in which both parents contribute to the process. In a similar vein, there is a distinction to be made between family processes that are "child-driven" from those that "parent-driven": Triangulation in interparental conflict takes a different form when the child attempts to intervene out of a misplaced sense of responsibility as opposed to when parents actively entangle the child in their quarrel (Kerig, in press).

Finally, it is important to recognize that our definition of "family" must not be limited to the stereotypical nuclear group. Single parents and their children constitute a valid and prevalent family form and, therefore, coding systems generalizable to these families are needed. For example, of particular interest are the interactions between single parents and their children concerning the absent parent, usually a father: Is the child permitted to miss him and express affection for him, or is this construed as a betrayal or as a threat to the mother–child bond (Kerig, 1992)?

In sum, it could be said that whole-family data cannot stand as a proxy for individual or dyadic data. As P. A. Cowan (1987) stated:

> Perhaps we have been swayed too much by the argument of family theorists … that analyses of individual data will not allow us to arrive at systemic conclusions. It may not be necessary to choose between individual and family system perspectives. Family functioning may be a combinative product of events in individual, dyadic, triadic, and outside-the-family domains. (p. 49)

However, it is both perplexing and intriguing that there is often little correspondence among data derived from individuals, dyads, and triads (e.g., Hayden et al., 1998; Paley et al., this volume); and this is worthy of further study in its own right. Like the blindfolded sages each attempting to describe an elephant based on a single body part, each point of view may describe a limited, but essential, piece of the family whole. Still needed in the study of the family is systematic investigation of the independent, relative, and interactive effects of each family domain so that, as P. A. Cowan and McHale (1996) suggested, we may put Humpty Dumpty together again.

What will help to advance the field is for investigators to expand our own "triadic capacity" (Klitzing, Simoni, & Burgin, 1999) by thinking systemically about all forms of family relationships, whether assessed through individual, dyadic, or triadic data. Intrapsychic life and dyadic interactions occur in a larger web of family relationships that weaves them together and lends them meaning (P. A. Cowan, 1997; Kerig, 1995). Therefore, we might add to McHale and colleagues' (1996) distinction between whole-family and family-level concepts a third category, "family-dynamic" processes, referring to interactions that have implications for family-level functioning even when they do not take place in the presence of all family members.

In conclusion, there is still a place for the study of dyads within the family, as is attested to by a number of contributions to the present volume. For example, Russell and colleagues focus on dyadic parent–child interactions, as do Lindsey and Mize, whereas other contributors study dyadic interactions in the presence of a third party (e.g., Mahoney et al., Westerman). Yet others include dyadic parent–child coding in their triadic systems (e.g., Florsheim & Benjamin; Lindahl & Malik).

Proliferation Versus Integration

Another problem that has hindered progress and cohesion in the field concerns the continual development of new coding systems. Though it is sometimes necessary for researchers to construct a new measure in order to tap unique constructs of interest, redundancy also exists. Given the significant time, expense, and energy required to construct a new coding system, the benefits of utilizing existing coding systems are clear, including the opportunity to compare across samples and sites, and the accumulation of evidence for validity and reliability. A structure of knowledge will be built only as we add bricks to an existing foundation, rather than repeatedly erecting new scaffolding across the landscape.

Because most of the existing coding systems have been used in a very few studies, often conducted in the same laboratory, there are serious limitations to what we know about their generalizability, reliability, validity, and utility (Coyne, 1987). L'Abate and Bagarozzi (1993) went so far as to call for a "moratorium" on the development of new family process measures:

It is probably time to take stock of what is available to us, to refrain from creating additional measures that only give the field more of the same, and to concentrate efforts on the improvement and refinement of those theoretically derived instruments and procedures that are already in existence. (p. 250)

Copeland and White (1991) echoed that point:

> There is certainly a lot to be said for researchers using systems already in the literature. Only in this way can we start to develop a database in which results from various studies can be compared. Using a published system saves each researcher the enormous task of developing and standardizing a new system, and keeps the literature relatively free of studies with small sample sizes and limited psychometric support. The more researchers use the same systems, the more valuable information about their validity and reliability accrues, making them, in turn, even more useful for future research. (p. 59)

Simultaneous application of different coding systems to the same data would also illuminate what the systems have in common and what they do not (Carlson & Grotevant, 1987a). However, though accrual of knowledge will undoubtedly benefit from synthesis among coding systems, here, too, there are a number of caveats regarding generalizability to be considered. These issues concern us next.

HOW FAR CAN WE GENERALIZE?

Generalizability of Constructs

In some cases, similar constructs are tapped by different coding systems, enabling them to be compared and integrated in meaningful ways. For example, in this volume, Westerman operationalizes triadic coordination in terms of how spouses cooperate with one another as they interact with the child, whereas McHale and colleagues tap a congruent construct in the study of coparenting. However, other coding systems are not equivalent or comparable. Although there may be considerable overlap in the behaviors coded by family observational systems, the underlying constructs these codes are intended to tap may be quite discrepant (Grotevant & Carlson, 1987a). Some constructs are viewed differently through the lenses of a specific theoretical orientation (e.g., a supportive statement would be conceived as an index of permeability in one system, or of positive affect in another). Other constructs take on a different cast when the investigator's focus is on normative versus pathological family processes (e.g., positive responses may comprise part of an "enmeshment" code in a system designed to tap such problematic family dynamics). In addition, the same behavior may take on a different meaning when it is construed at an individual level or at a relational level. In sum, "because of the theoretical diversity represented in the family interaction codes, comparisons of research findings using the different coding systems must be made with caution" (Grotevant & Carlson, 1987a, p. 59).

Level of Analysis

Another source of diversity among coding systems concerns the level of analysis at which coding takes place (e.g., micro-, macro-, or mesoanalytic). This is a methodological issue (see Lindahl, this volume) but also is inextricably linked to the problem of conceptualization. The concept under study may be at a high order of inference, such as when an investigator attempts to tap the underlying meaning and coherence of behaviors, requiring macrolevel or molar codes (e.g., Fiese, Sameroff, Grotevant, Wamboldt, Dickstein, & Fravel). In turn, the construct of interest may be more concrete, focusing on specific behaviors and their sequential ordering, requiring molecular or micro codes (e.g., Lindsey & Mize). In addition, as Grotevant and Carlson (1987b) noted, macro ratings are most valuable for studying behaviors that are stable over time and context, as well as those that are highly salient but occur infrequently. Micro codes, in turn, are required for studying contingencies in the immediate interpersonal environment (see also Lindsey & Mize, this volume). In addition, as Mahoney and colleagues (this volume) point out, there are distinct advantages to coding at the midrange, or meso, level, which allows the investigator to navigate between the two hazards of under- and overelaboration.

Carlson and Grotevant (1987a) argued that macro codes may be ideally suited to the study of family processes. Macro coding is able to take into account the larger context in which behavior occurs (see also Westerman, this volume) and to "incorporate the interdependence of behavior in relationships into the rating process" (Carlson & Grotevant, 1987a, p. 26), thus capturing qualities that are "essential to the description of stable relational patterns or dimensions of the family system" (p. 25). However, macro coding systems require a priori choices about what to code, which are sometimes agonizing to make, and run the risk of lumping conceptually distinct constructs together (Carlson & Grotevant, 1987a; Mahoney et al., this volume). Further, though it is an advantage that human beings are uniquely able to process multiple sources of data, synthesize them and extract meaning from them, this is also a cognitively taxing process fraught with many threats to reliability and validity. In sum, each level of analysis may contribute something valuable to the study of family interaction, but none can be recommended as the sole method of choice. P. A. Cowan's (1987) advice remains appropriate: "It is premature to put all of our eggs in one methodological basket" (p. 50).

Dimensions of Interaction

Coding systems may also target dimensions of family relationships that are not readily comparable. Copeland and White (1991) likened these to the qualities of a song: One can describe the tune, the lyrics, or the sentiment. The "tune" refers to the structure of interaction among family members (e.g., timing, sequencing, domination), the "lyrics" refer to the content of what is said (e.g., acceptances vs. negations), and the "sentiment" refers to the affective undercurrents to what is said (e.g., sarcasm, playfulness, or competitiveness). Each of these dimensions requires a different level of inference, with conceptual as well as pragmatic implications, and each provides useful information not captured by other descriptors.

Is Observational Coding Ecologically Valid?

The thorniest conceptual issue concerns the ecological validity of observational coding: the generalizability of observed interactions to the "real world." The representativeness of observations may be affected by participant reactivity, and there may be limitations to generalizability across contexts, settings, tasks, samples, and family forms.

Participant Reactivity

Observed interactions may be unrepresentative of the family for a number of reasons, one of which is the reactivity of participants to being observed. As Hooper and Hooper (1990) put it, "We can hope to develop theories of observed human development and interaction, but, probably, not of what goes on when 'no one' ... is looking" (p. 292). Reactivity may emerge in general ways (e.g., families may be stilted or self-conscious) or in specific ways (e.g., families may attempt to present a favorable impression; Copeland & White, 1991). Interestingly, however, studies show that families are more successful in "faking bad" than "faking good," and this is especially true for disturbed families. Therefore, it may be possible to observe negative processes even when families are reluctant to display them. Families who do not know how to resolve conflicts amicably, for example, are unable to simulate doing so. As Copeland and White stated: "People cannot profoundly change their behavior ... just by trying to do so" (p. 50).

In addition, a number of steps can be taken to reduce the reactivity of family participants to the procedure as well as to the setting (see Harrist & Pettit, this volume). For example, Copeland and White (1991) suggested that tasks will be more representative of family functioning if they are interesting and engaging, and if they are perceived by family members themselves as valid and reasonable. The tasks chosen can also be designed to be less artificial, for example, by asking family members to discuss an actual conflict episode rather than generating one in the lab (e.g., Gordis & Margolin). In addition, Margolin (1990) recommended observing interactions over a number of episodes, including both naturalistic and structured tasks, in order to obtain more representative sample of behavior (e.g., Mahoney et al.).

Generalizability Across Contexts

Jacob, Tennenbaum, and Krahn (1987) differentiated between two aspects of the context, the setting and the task. Each of these is vulnerable to threats concerning representativeness and reactivity.

Setting.   The setting in which observations take place is by necessity artificial. This artificiality is most apparent when observations take place in the laboratory. For example, Baldwin (1967) argued that studies based on laboratory interactions have created a "mythology of childhood" in which artificial effects observed in the laboratory are assumed to take place in natural contexts. But, as implied earlier in the section on reactivity, even in the home the presence of the camera and the researcher-defined procedure detract from the natural spontaneity of the observed behavior. Thus, in a similarly pessimistic vein, Forehand (1990) argued that, "what we have obtained by direct observational assessment is a small, rather biased, picture of the parent–child interaction" (p. 18).

Among the studies that have compared home and laboratory observations, a widely replicated finding is that interactions at home elicit more negative behavior and negative reciprocity than do those in the laboratory. However, not much empirical evidence has been brought to bear on this issue. As Brody and Stoneman (1990) stated:

> Family researchers in general have not investigated whether the behavioral samples collected in either naturalistic or laboratory contexts are actually representative of family behavior as it normally occurs for the subjects under investigation. An implicit assumption appears to be driving family process research; any context that elicits behavior from family members can be assumed to evoke behavior representative of the typical interaction patterns in that family. This assumption has led researchers to confuse the occurrence of behavior with its representativeness. (p. 208)

Neither the laboratory nor the home setting is necessarily right for all research questions; again, strategic choices must be made. As Grotevant and Carlson (1987) argued, investigations focused on parent socialization would benefit from home observation (e.g., Russell et al.), whereas studies of pathological family processes might better observe families under the stressful conditions of the laboratory or clinic environment (e.g., Robbins et al.).

Task.   The task to which each coding system is applied, and to which it is best suited, varies significantly. Coding systems in the present collection have been design to assess tasks involving free play or naturally occurring behavior (e.g., Harrist & Pettit; Lindsey & Mize; Russell et al.), conversation (e.g., Fiese et al.), structured play (e.g., McHale et al.), and structured problem solving (e.g., Forbes et al.; Melby & Conger; Robbins et al., Westerman). Some coding systems span a variety of contexts (e.g., Florsheim & Benjamin; Lindahl & Malik), whereas others are designed to be relevant to a specific task (e.g., Fiese et al., Gordis & Margolin) but may be useful for other tasks, as well (e.g., Paley et al.).

The choice of activity to code has implications for the structure of the coding system, as well as its generalizability to other tasks and contexts. Benefits to assigning a structured task include the fact that it can be tailored to elicit the kind of interaction that will best tap into the researcher's construct of interest. In addition, if reactivity causes the parent and child to be on their "best behavior" (Forehand, 1990), the investigator may have few opportunities to observe problematic interactional styles. A more structured task can overcome this tendency by directing behavior toward the kind of challenge the investigator wants to assess, for instance, by requiring parents to set limits on children's behavior (e.g., Mahoney et al.; Paley et al.).

The choice of tasks is a crucial one that should reflect the purposes of the research. Thus, as Copeland and White (1991) noted, if the main interest is in conflict resolution strategies, an appropriate task would be to ask families to discuss a recent disagreement, whereas decision making is best elicited by asking families to plan an activity, and patterns of domination would be most likely to emerge if family members were offered choices as to leadership of the interaction. On the other hand, Markman and Notarius (1987) argued that, in order to allow comparability across studies, researchers should include at least one task identical to that used in other laboratories. This task is likely to be relatively nonspecific in order to be relevant across conceptual and methodological contexts.

Generalizability Across Samples

The samples to which coding systems have been applied, and to which they are applicable, also vary widely. Samples may be clinical (e.g., Forbes et al.; Robbins et al.), normative (e.g., Gordis & Margolin; Lindsey & Mize; Paley et al.; Russell et al.), or both (e.g., Florsheim & Benjamin; Forbes et al.; Melby & Conger). However, an important sampling issue that has not received sufficient attention concerns the age range of the children to be included in the family interaction, and to whose behavior the coding system applies. In the present collection, age ranges may span all of childhood (e.g., Florsheim & Benjamin; Harrist & Pettit) or else may be constrained to one developmental period (e.g., Paley et al., Russell et al.).

However, though we often refer to "the child," there is a significant difference between the child at preschool age, school age, and adolescence. The child's developmental stage affects her or his status in the family and ability to engage in the task. The child's age is also a critical factor in determining what comprises a typical parent–child interaction (Margolin, 1990); for example, parenting of preschool children calls for more structure than is appropriate for adolescents. By the same token, stage-salient issues at different developmental periods challenge the parent–child relationship in new ways, such as children's proximity seeking in the 2nd year and autonomy strivings in the 3rd (Carlson & Sroufe, 1995; see Paley et al., this volume). In addition, the appropriateness and frequency of particular behaviors changes over development, to the extent that it may be problematic to use the same code for both child and parent. The meanings of certain actions—for example, whining, thumb sucking, shrieking with glee—are strikingly different at different developmental periods, and may represent "negative" behavior for adults while representing "positive" behavior for children. Some systems deal with this issue by providing coders with guidelines for interpreting behaviors according to their context and developmental appropriateness (e.g., Florsheim & Benjamin;

Robbins et al.), whereas others provide separate codes for parent and child contributions to the interaction (Russell et al., Lindahl & Malik; Mahoney et al).

In addition, it is interesting to note that various coding schemes differ in terms of whether they view parents and children as coparticipants in family interactions (e.g., Florsheim & Benjamin; Lindsey & Mize) versus whether they weight parents' contributions more heavily (e.g., Harrist & Pettit; Westerman). However, apart from the quantity of parents' and children's participation, there is the matter of quality. Children's contributions to the family process differ in meaningful ways from those of adults. In this regard, Russell and colleagues (this volume) make the important distinction between horizontal and vertical influences in family interaction. Whereas children's peer interactions are largely symmetrical and egalitarian, parent–child interactions normally include dimensions that are asymmetrical and complementary. Thus, it is sometimes appropriate for parents to be directive of the interaction, particularly when children are attempting to solve a problem beyond their ken, just as parents normatively engage in nurturing of their children. However, such behaviors take on different, and less adaptive implications, when displayed by a child toward a parent, suggesting role reversal or boundary dissolution (Brown & Kerig, 1999). Coding systems need to capture—but not equate—interactional qualities appropriate to different developmental periods.

Moreover, it is not only children who develop; adults do as well. For example, men who become fathers later in life are more involved with parenting their children (Parke, 1990). Thus, the nature of parent–child interaction changes as a function of both parents' and children's age. As P. Minuchin (1985) stated, families are "natural units composed of people at different stages of development whose live are constantly interwoven" (p. 295).

Ethnic Diversity.   A specific concern in regard to generalizability is that of the limited ethnic diversity typical of participants in family observational research. Because most of the samples recruited for such research are middle-class and Euro-American, hesitation is needed before coding systems are applied to other ethnic groups. Some behaviors have different meanings in different cultural contexts. For example, Lindahl and Malik describe how their category of autocratic parenting is informed by an understanding of Hispanic culture, in which such parenting is normative rather than problematic. In addition, Robbins et al. are explicitly concerned with developing a coding system applicable to diverse cultural groups, whereas Melby and Conger cite accumulating evidence regarding the validity of their coding systems across samples and cultures, as do Florsheim and Benjamin. Thus, the issue of ethnic diversity is in the forefront of many cutting-edge investigators' thinking about the constructs and methods necessary to do family observational research.

It is noteworthy that consideration of ethnic diversity has long been pivotal to the very theoretical perspective that informs many of the contributions to this volume, Salvador Minuchin's (1974) structural family theory. Thoughtful pieces have been written about adapting the structural perspective to therapeutic work with African-American (Boyd-Franklin, 1989), Asian (Ho, 1989), Hispanic (Kurtines & Szapocznik, 1996), and Native-American (Napoliello & Sweet, 1982) populations. The insights these authors provide in the clinical realm might contribute to the development of more cross-culturally sensitive—and thus, more powerful—research methods.

Family Forms

Whereas some coding systems assess global constructs that are applicable across various family constellations (e.g., Lindahl & Malik; Melby & Conger), others are designed to capture dynamics specific to two-parent families (e.g., McHale et al.; Westerman). There is certainly a need for both. Though interparental conflict is a powerful influence on child development in two-parent families, single-parent families also exist. Yet other family forms are commonly seen in culturally diverse groups, such as the mother–grandmother–child constellation. On the other end of the extreme, many families extend beyond the triad. Coding interactions among more than three families members is extraordinarily challenging, requiring longer strings and more complex data analytic procedures. However, Brody and Stoneman (1990) pointed out that siblings experience different within-family environments, and thus it is important to be able to assess family interactions in which more than one child is present. By the same token, extended families may be comprised of multiple adult caretakers (e.g., Robbins et al.), each of whom has a role in the socialization of the child. In sum, each of these constellations comprises a legitimate family form, for which we need to have some suitable devices in our methodological toolkit.

Does Observational Coding Have Clinical Utility?

Another quality on which observational coding systems can be rated is their utility for practitioners engaged in clinical work with children and families. Although not all contributors to this volume are concerned with the application of their methods of clinical work with children and families, many are; indeed, the majority of us are clinical psychologists by training. There is a natural complementarity to clinical practice and family observational research. For example, empirical methods can contribute to the development of theory-based treatments and standardized assessments, can help to detect problematic interactional patterns, and can be used to measure therapeutic change or the lack thereof (L'Abate & Bagarozzi, 1993):

> [Direct observations] are tied more closely to the identification of specific behaviors that could be targeted for intervention.... Such data can contribute to the development of theoretical hypotheses and allow for the testing of specific models and the evaluation of treatment outcomes in a scientifically rigorous manner. (Hops, Davis, & Longoria, 1995, p. 194)

However, those concerned with applying family research to the clinical setting often find fault with the instruments developed in the laboratory. For example, L'Abate and Bagarozzi (1993) created a rating scale for evaluating the clinical utility of family instruments, the application of which led them to conclude that, although observational coding systems provide the best measures on offer, "the best is not good enough" (p. 224). In addition to citing weak links to theory and poor psychometric properties of the measures, the authors criticized macrolevel coding systems for failing to provide the kind of detailed information about family structure, transactional patterns, and individual family relationships that might lead to the development of a specific treatment plan.

Perhaps in the intervening half-decade, the "not-good-enough" has gotten better. As noted earlier, the observational systems in this collection overall feature clear links to theoretical concepts and have undergone careful psychometric evaluation. Further, particular contributions to this volume represent the much needed integration of theory, research, and clinical relevance. A premier example is Robbins and colleagues' programmatic research assessing change brought about by the application of structural family therapy.

Another limitation of the utility of observational coding to clinical work is its unwieldiness and expense, particular regarding microanalytic systems. Grotevant and Carlson (1987), however, made an intriguing suggestion. Programmatic and systematic research on a given coding system may lead to identification of those particular dimensions of family interaction that are most relevant and predictive of particular outcomes. In this way "clinical versions" or "short forms" of family observational coding systems with greater clinical utility might be developed.

SUMMARY AND CONCLUSION

"It is much easier to criticize the state of the art than to improve upon it" (Stoneman & Brody, 1990, p. 37). Although this statement is undeniably true, it also is the case that criticism can improve the state of the art. This review of the literature suggests that family investigators have responded to the cogent critiques of a decade ago, and that progress has been made in the field. In general, as the contributions to this volume attest, family observational coding systems are better informed by theory, and advances have been made in the development of methods that are generalizable across tasks, samples, and settings. In particular, it is encouraging that systems have been developed that are sensitive to ethnic diversity, developmental differences, and the multiplicity of family forms. There also is significant diversity among the coding systems themselves, in terms of the constructs they assess, the level of analysis they rely on, and the purposes they are meant to serve. Despite the call for greater integration and generalization in the field, such diversity may be a necessary evil given the range of family types and research questions to be answered. As noted previously, the well-equipped methodological toolkit may require measures of various shapes, sizes, and functions. On the other hand, there continues to be a need for greater collaboration and synthesis among family observational researchers. By informing investigators in the field about the process and progress going on in other laboratories, the contributors to this volume promise to advance the development of the field.

REFERENCES

Achenbach, T. M. (1990). Conceptualization of developmental psychopathology. In M. Lewis & S. M. Miller (Eds.), *Handbook of developmental psychopathology* (pp. 3–14). New York: Plenum.

Baldwin, A. (1967). *Theories of child development.* New York: Wiley.

Belsky, J. (1989). The developing family system. In M. R. Gunnar & E. Thelen (Eds.), *Minnesota symposia on child development: Vol. 22. Systems and development* (pp. 119–166). Hillsdale, NJ: Lawrence Erlbaum Associates.

Belsky, J., Putnam, S., & Crnic, K. (1996). Coparenting, parenting, and early emotional development. In J. P. McHale & P. A. Cowan (Eds.), Understanding how family-level dynamics affect children's development: Studies of two-parent families. *New Directions for Child Development, 74,* 45–55.

Bertalanffy, L. von (1968). *General systems theory: Foundations, development, applications.* New York: Braziller.

Boyd-Franklin, N. (1989). *Black families in therapy: A multisystems approach.* New York: Guilford.

Brody, G. H., & Flor, D. L. (1996). Coparenting, family interactions, and competence among African American youths. In J. P. McHale & P. A. Cowan (Eds.), Understanding how family-level dynamics affect children's development: Studies of two-parent families. *New Directions in Child Development, 74,* 77–91.

Brody, G. H., & Stoneman, Z. (1990). Sibling relationships. In I. E. Sigel & G. H. Brody (Eds.), *Methods of family research: Biographies of research projects* (pp. 189–212). Hillsdale, NJ: Lawrence Erlbaum Associates.

Brown, C. A., & Kerig, P. K. (1999, April). *Boundary dissolution in single-parent families: The effects of role-reversal and gender on the relationship between maternal and child adjustment.* Presentation at the meeting of the Society for Research in Child Development, Albuquerque, NM.

Carlson, C. I., & Grotevant, H. D. (1987a). A comparative review of family rating scales: Guidelines for clinicians and researchers. *Journal of Family Psychology, 1,* 23–47.

Carlson, C. I., & Grotevant, H. D. (1987b). Rejoinder: The challenges of reconciling family theory with method. *Journal of Family Psychology, 1,* 62–65.

Carlson, E., & Sroufe, L. A. (1995). Contribution of attachment theory to developmental psychopathology. In D. Cicchetti & D. J. Cohen (Eds.), *Developmental psychopathology: Vol. 1. Theory and methods* (pp. 581–617). New York: Wiley.

Cicchetti, D., & Cohen, D. J. (Eds.). (1995). *Developmental psychopathology: Vol. 1. Theory and methods.* New York: Wiley.

Copeland, A. P., & White, K. M. (1991). *Studying families.* Newbury Park, CA: Sage.

Cowan, P. A. (1987). The need for theoretical and methodological integrations in family research. *Journal of Family Psychology, 1,* 48–50.

Cowan, P. A. (1997). Beyond meta-analysis: A plea for a family systems view of attachment. *Child Development, 68,* 601–603.

Cowan, P. A., Cohn, D. A., Cowan, C. P., & Pearson, J. L. (1996). Parents' attachment histories and children's externalizing and internalizing behaviors: Exploring family systems models of linkage. *Journal of Consulting and Clinical Psychology, 64,* 53–63.

Cowan, P. A., & Cowan, C. P. (1990). Becoming a family: Research and intervention. In I. E. Sigel & G. H. Brody (Eds.), *Methods of family research: Biographies of research projects. Vol. I: Normal families* (pp. 1–51). Hillsdale, NJ: Lawrence Erlbaum Associates.

Cowan, P. A., & McHale, J. P. (1996). Coparenting in a family context: Emerging achievements, current dilemmas, and future directions. In J. P. McHale & P. A. Cowan (Eds.), Understanding how family-level dynamics affect children's development: Studies of two-parent families. *New Directions for Child Development, 74,* 93–106.

Coyne, J. C. (1987). Some issues in the assessment of family patterns. *Journal of Family Psychology, 1,* 51–57.

Cummings, E. M., & Davies, P. (1994). *Children and marital conflict: The impact of family dispute and resolution.* New York: Guilford.

Fivaz-Depeursinge, E., Frascarolo, F., & Corboz-Warnery, A. (1996). Assessing the triadic alliance between fathers, mothers, and infants at play. In J. P. McHale & P.A. Cowan (Eds.), Understanding how family-level dynamics affect children's development: Studies of two-parent families. *New Directions for Child Development, 74,* 27–44.

Forehand, R. (1990). Families with a conduct problem child. In G. H. Brody & I. E. Sigel (Eds.), *Methods of family research: Biographies of research projects. Vol. II: Clinical populations* (pp. 1–30). Hillsdale, NJ: Lawrence Erlbaum Associates.

Gjerde, P. F. (1986). The interpersonal structure of family interaction settings: Parent–adolescent relations in dyads and triads. *Developmental Psychology, 22,* 297–304.

Gottman, J. M. (1979). *Marital interaction: Experimental investigations.* New York: Academic Press.

Grotevant, H. D., & Carlson, C. I. (1987). Family interaction coding systems: A descriptive review. *Family Process, 26,* 49–74.

Grych, J. H., & Fincham, F. (in press). *Child development and interparental conflict.* New York: Cambridge University Press.

Hayden, L. C., Schiller, M., Dickstein, S., Seifer, R., Sameroff, A. J., Miller, I., Keitner, G., & Rasmussen, S. (1998). Levels of family assessment: I. Family, marital, and parent–child interaction. *Journal of Family Psychology, 12,* 7–22.

Ho, M. K. (1989). Applying family therapy theories to Asian/Pacific Americans. *Contemporary Family Therapy, 11,* 61–70.

Hooper, F. H., & Hooper, J. O. (1990). The family as a system of reciprocal relations: Searching for a developmental lifespan perspective. In I. E. Sigel & G. H. Brody (Eds.), *Methods of family research: Biographies of research projects. Vol. I: Normal families* (pp. 289–316). Hillsdale, NJ: Lawrence Erlbaum Associates.

Hops, H., Davis, B., & Longoria, N. (1995). Methodological issues in direct observation: Illustrations with the living in familial environments (LIFE) coding system. *Journal of Clinical Child Psychology, 24,* 193–203.

Howard, B. L., & Kendall, P. C. (1996). Cognitive-behavioral family therapy for anxiety-disordered children: A multiple-baseline evaluation. *Cognitive Therapy and Research, 20,* 423–443.

Jacob, T., Tennenbaum, D. L., & Krahn, G. (1987). Factors influencing the reliability and validity of observation data. In T. Jacob (Ed.), *Family interaction and psychopathology: Theories, methods, and findings* (pp. 297–328). New York: Plenum.

Katz, L. F., & Gottman, J. M. (1996). Spillover effects of marital conflict: In search of parenting and coparenting mechanisms. In J. P. McHale & P.A. Cowan (Eds.), Understanding how family-level dynamics affect children's development: Studies of two-parent families. *New Directions for Child Development, 74,* 57–75.

Kerig, P. K. (1992, August). *Effects of marital discord on child development: Implications for developmental psychopathology.* Invited talk, Mount Hope Family Center, University of Rochester, Rochester, NY.

Kerig, P. K. (1995). Triangles in the family circle: Effects of family structure on marriage, parenting, and child adjustment. *Journal of Family Psychology, 9,* 28–43.

Kerig, P. K. (1999, April). "Put a sock in it!" Predictors and consequences of children's interventions into interparental conflict. In G. Harold (Chair), *Gender-differentiated processing of family conflict.* Symposium conducted at the meeting of the Society for Research in Child Development, Albuquerque, NM.

Kerig, P. K. (in press). Coping with interparental conflict. In J. H. Grych & F. Fincham (Eds.), *Child development and marital conflict.* New York: Cambridge University Press.

Kerig, P. K., Cowan, P. A., & Cowan, C. P. (1993). Marital quality and gender differences in parent–child interaction. *Developmental Psychology, 29,* 931–939.

Klitzing, K. von, Simoni, H., & Burgin, D. (1999, April). Mother, father, and the infant: The triad from pre-natal representations to post-natal interactions. In J. A. Talbot (Chair), *Transitions of parenthood revisited: Pre-birth precursors of coparenting and family-level dynamics.* Symposium conducted at the meeting of the Society for Research in Child Development, Albuquerque, NM.

Kurtines, W. M., & Szapocznik, J. (1996). Family interaction patterns: Structural family therapy within contexts of cultural diversity. In E. D. Hibbs & P. S. Jensen (Eds.), *Psychosocial treatments for child and adolescent disorders: Empirically based strategies for clinical practice* (pp. 671–697). Washington, DC: American Psychological Association.

L'Abate, L., & Bagarozzi, D. A. (1993). *Sourcebook of marriage and family evaluation.* New York: Brunner/Mazel.

Lamb, M. E. (Ed.). (1997). *The role of the father in child development.* New York: Wiley.

Margolin, G. (1990). Marital conflict. In G. H. Brody & I. E. Sigel (Eds.), *Methods of family research: Biographies of research projects. Vol. II: Clinical populations* (pp. 191–225). Hillsdale, NJ: Lawrence Erlbaum Associates.

Markman, H. J., & Notarius, C. I. (1987). Coding marital and family interaction. In T. Jacob (Ed.), *Family interaction and psychopathology: Theories, methods, and findings* (pp. 329–390). New York: Plenum.

McConnell, M., & Kerig, P. K. (1999). *Inside the family circle: Coparenting and adjustment in a school-age sample.* Manuscript submitted for publication.

McHale, J. P. (1995). Coparenting and triadic interactions during infancy: The roles of marital distress and child gender. *Developmental Psychology, 31,* 985–996.

McHale, J. P. (1997). Overt and covert coparenting processes in the family. *Family Process, 36,* 183–210.

McHale, J. P., Kuersten, R., & Lauretti, A. (1996). New directions in the study of family-level dynamics during infancy and early childhood. In J. P. McHale & P. A. Cowan (Eds.), Understanding how family-level dynamics affect children's development: Studies of two-parent families. *New Directions for Child Development, 74,* 5–26.

Minuchin, P. (1985). Families and individual development: Provocations from the field of family therapy. *Child Development, 56,* 289–302.

Minuchin, S. (1974). *Families and family therapy.* Cambridge, MA: Harvard University Press.

Napoliello, A. L., & Sweet, E. S. (1982). Salvador Minuchin's structural family therapy and its application to Native Americans. *Family Therapy, 19,* 155–165.

Parke, R. D. (1990). In search of fathers: A narrative of an empirical journey. In I. E. Sigel & G. H. Brody (Eds.), *Methods of family research: Biographies of research projects. Vol. I: Normal families.* (pp. 153–188). Hillsdale, NJ: Lawrence Erlbaum Associates.

Rutter, M. (1988). Functions and consequences of relationships: Some psychopathological considerations. In R. A. Hinde & J. Stevenson-Hinde (Eds.), *Relationships within families: Mutual influences* (pp. 332–353). Oxford, England: Clarendon.

Schwartz, J. A., Kaslow, N. J., Racusin, G. R., & Carton, E. R. (1998). Interpersonal family therapy for childhood depression. In V. B. Van Hasselt & M. Hersen (Eds.), *Handbook of psychological treatment protocols for children and adolescents* (pp. 109–151). Mahwah, NJ: Lawrence Erlbaum Associates.

Slipp, S. (1991). *The technique and practice of object relations family therapy.* New York: Aronson.

Sroufe, L. A., & Fleeson, J. (1988). The coherence of family relationships. In R. A. Hinde & J. Stevenson-Hinde (Eds.), *Relationships within families: Mutual influences* (pp. 27–47). Oxford, England: Oxford University Press.

Stark, K. D., Swearer, S., Kurowski, C., Sommer, D., & Bowen, B. (1996). Targeting the child and the family: A holistic approach to treating child and adolescent depressive disorders. In E. D. Hibbs & P. S. Jensen (Eds.), *Psychosocial treatments for child and adolescent disorders* (pp. 207–238). Washington, DC: American Psychological Association.

Stoneman, Z., & Brody, G. H. (1990). Families with children who are mentally retarded. In G. H. Brody & I. E. Sigel (Eds.), *Methods of family research: Biographies of research projects. Vol. II: Clinical populations* (pp. 31–58). Hillsdale, NJ: Lawrence Erlbaum Associates.

2

Methodological Issues in Family Observational Research

Kristin M. Lindahl
University of Miami

Increasingly, researchers are turning to observational data to understand the development and functioning of family systems and to identify family interaction patterns that reliably differentiate problem from nonproblem families. The burgeoning interest in observational methods stems in large part from the emphasis of family systems theoretical orientations on the interdependency of individuals and relationships within the family and on the need to capture the nature of complex systemic interactions scientifically. Observational research is costly and labor-intensive, yet it offers investigators the opportunity to collect reliable and valid data unavailable through traditional assessment strategies. From a methodological perspective, whereas self-report measures are useful when one is interested in family members' perceptions of family functioning (e.g., satisfaction with roles within the family), observational data are preferred for more complex aspects of family functioning. For example, observational methods can capture patterns of interaction, including responses that are difficult to describe such as behavior rates, affective expression, nonverbal behavior, and events that participants may be unwilling to report or else may distort as a function of the event's social undesirability or of the effort required for adequate description (Hartmann & Wood, 1992). Direct observational methodology may be particularly useful for studying families with young children who do not have the language skills to re-spond to questionnaires or interviews. In addition, direct observations have high face validity and good generalizability and are less susceptible to confounding in-fluences (Jacob, Tennenbaum, & Krahn, 1987). Data gathered through the direct observation of behaviors without an intermediary questionnaire or other instru-ment reflect those behaviors directly. It therefore requires relatively little concep-tual inference to connect the data to the phenomenon (Suen & Ary, 1989).

LEVEL OF ANALYSIS

Whether one chooses a microanalytic, mesoanalytic, or macroanalytic coding pro-cedure depends on the nature of the research question, the type of raw observa-tional data available, and the resources of the researcher. The coding of interactional data is essentially a data reduction procedure, with microanalytic systems involving smaller coding units and hence ' ; data reduction, and macroanalytic systems involving larger coding units ana more inference to assign a code and thus more heterogeneous coded behavior (Markman & Notarius, 1987). Microanalytic systems are often the approach of choice when hypotheses concern specific sequential patterns of interaction. Because of their low levels of inference, they are viewed as less susceptible to bias. Of course a limitation of microanalytic systems is their significant cost in terms of time required to code an interaction, with the time and complexity increasing dramatically as the number of observed participants increases. If sequential analyses are to be performed, then an exten-sive sampling of behavior is needed as well as a behavioral pattern that occurs with some frequency, in addition to a highly reliable coding system (Coyne, 1987). The difficulty in establishing conditions adequate for such sequential analyses is a ma-jor reason they are not more frequently used (Coyne, 1987). Of the coding systems reviewed in this volume, just one is truly microanalytic in nature, the SASB (Struc-tural Analysis of Social Behavior). Although it is the more "macro" codes of the SASB that receive attention in this chapter, most of the codes contained in the SASB system are microanalytic. The SASB is a well-established coding system wherein every interpersonal event in an interaction is coded along three dimen-sions. The behavioral units to be coded are never longer than a complete sentence, and may be as short as a grunt or gesture.

Macroanalytic systems use large coding units that require coders to synthesize the interaction and apply a global judgment, often involving considerable infer-ence. An advantage of macroanalytic systems is that they typically require less coder training and less coding time than microanalytic systems. In addition, they allow the larger context of the interaction to be considered, a factor that is often im-portant when trying to capture meaning in family interactions (Parke, 1990; see also chaps. 11 and 14, this volume). This purpose is clearly illustrated when inter-active processes, relational concepts, or family-level dynamics are of interest to the investigator. In each of these cases, by definition, specific behaviors cannot be examined without context. Examples of macroanalytic codes described in this volume that refer to contextualized behaviors include triadic coordination (Westerman), coalitions and alliances (Forbes, Vuchinich, & Kneedler; Lindahl & Malik; Gordis & Margolin), detachment (Paley, Cox, & Kanoy), conflict resolution and problem solving (Melby & Conger; Robbins, Hervis, Mitrani, & Szapocznik), competition (McHale, Kuersten-Hogan, & Lauretti), and control (Harrist & Pettit). One way in which macroanalytic systems (and also mesoanalytic systems described later) are able to capture the context in which a behavior is embedded is by incorporating the intensity and affective valence of a relational exchange or behavior, and most of the coding systems contained in this volume utilize affect related codes.

Mesoanalytic systems attempt to capitalize on elements of what is useful about both microanalytic and macroanalytic coding systems. Rather than coding very small, specific behaviors over small units of time (e.g., every 15 seconds) or global ratings about qualitative aspects of an interaction over longer periods of time (e.g., 10 minutes), mesoanalytic systems operate in between the two. For example, the Family Coding System (Gordis & Margolin) and the Mesoanalytic Behavioral Rating System (Mahoney, Coffield, Lewis, & Lashley) specify that behaviors are rated each minute, and the system described by Russell and his colleagues and codes within the SASB Global Coding Scheme (Florsheim & Benjamin) are assessed every 2 minutes. As summarized by Mahoney and her colleagues (chap. 13, this volume), meso-analytic systems have the advantages over microanalytic systems of containing individually analyzable codes (without having to resort to summary codes) and of being less susceptible to problems associated with low base rate behavior. In contrast to macroanalytic systems, meso-level systems allow the researcher to examine changes in behavior over time (though not at the level of sequential contingencies as afforded by microanalytic systems).

An alternative to a time-based approach for determining when ratings should be made is event-based coding. Event-based coding allows the investigator to target discrete behaviors and the their associated contingencies. An important advantage of event-based systems is that they permit sequences of behaviors to be revealed and complex chains of interactional events can be identified. For example, The Social Events System (Harrist & Pettit) targets parent–child interactions that fall into one of four categories (teaching, control, social contact, reflective listening) and records antecedents and consequences of these social events. The coding system developed by Lindsey and Mize selects initiations and responses to initiations between parents and their children.

RELIABILITY

Most measurements in the behavioral sciences involve measurement error, but judgments made by humans are especially prone to this problem. Reliability has been defined in various ways in the literature, but it is generally agreed upon that a reliable instrument is one with small errors of measurement, and one that shows consistency and stability of scores on the behavior being evaluated (Mitchell,

1979). The establishment of reliability of family interaction data is essential if we are to have faith in the conclusions drawn from those data. There are many different methods for computing reliability. With respect to observational data, reliability is most commonly thought of in terms of the extent to which two observers, working independently, agree on what behaviors are occurring, and this is a quite reasonable place to start. Less commonly applied to observational data is Cronbach's theory of generalizability, which refers to the extent to which the coding system is representative across conditions as well as across coders (Cronbach, Gleser, Nanda, & Rajaratnam, 1972). For example, it will be important for future investigations to determine whether family coding systems are reliable across different socioeconomic groups, across different cultural, ethnic, or racial groups, across home and lab settings, and across clinical and nonclinical samples.

Family process coding systems, including most of the coding systems reviewed in this book, report interobserver reliability, or reliability coefficients that demonstrate that two or more observers watching the same behavior at the same time will record the same data (Mitchell, 1979). Three statistical indices have been most commonly used to estimate interobserver agreement: percent agreement, Cohen's kappa (Cohen, 1968), and correlation. These statistical procedures are quite useful though they only provide information about a specific type of reliability. They give us confidence that the data are consistent across a number of independent observers but do not provide information about intraobserver reliability (the consistency of data should a single observer observe the same behavior over and over again) or reliability across conditions (Suen & Ary, 1989). It also has been argued that interobserver agreement may not represent accuracy of measurement unless the observations are compared to some established standard (Jacob et al., 1987).

Percent agreement and Cohen's kappa are recommended for categorical scores, with Cohen's kappa being the preferred index of the two as it corrects for chance agreement by coders. Yet another option is to use a weighted kappa, which gives partial credit for codes that are closely related and subtracts credit for codes that are quite disparate (chap. 8, this volume).

Interobserver reliability of interval-scaled data is often estimated with a product–moment correlation coefficient. It has many advantages including its familiarity to most audiences and ease and flexibility of use. Product–moment correlations, however, are insensitive to differences in level between two observers (Jacob et al., 1987). If one observer consistently records a higher level of a behavior than the other observer, then a high correlation would be obtained, even though the observers actually rarely were in agreement. A highly skewed distribution of a behavior within a data set also can inflate correlational reliability estimates (Jacob et al., 1987). Thus, the insensitivity of product–moment correlations to level differences and their sensitivity to frequency and range distributions at times make interpretation difficult.

As noted by several contributors to this volume (e.g., Florsheim & Benjamin; Gordis & Margolin; Mahoney and colleagues, Melby & Conger; and Robbins and colleagues), when calculating interrater reliability among multiple coders, intraclass correlation, which is a type of generalizability coefficient, is often a preferred alternative to correlation. Intraclass correlation provides a means of estimating interobserver reliability within the framework of a factorial design (Jacob et al., 1987) and is designed to assess for the rate of agreement between two or more raters on a continuous scale or interval data, while controlling for any systematic bias among raters (Shrout & Fleiss, 1979). Intraclass correlations also have the capacity to inform about intraobserver reliability (temporal stability). A substantial amount of duplicate coding is required, however, for a generalizability study, far more than would need to be collected for a traditional reliability check (Jacob et al., 1987). Minimum levels for accepted reliability have been set at .70 for percent agreement, .60 for Cohen's kappa, and .60 for correlation (Hartmann, 1982).

VALIDITY

Reliability, of course, is only a precondition for good data quality. By itself, it does not show that the data are adequate representations of particular behaviors. To accomplish this, validity must also be assessed (Suen & Ary, 1989). Validity is the degree to which a set of data represents what it purports to represent. Validity is more difficult to measure or "prove" than reliability, as it is inferred from circumstantial evidence that an observed score is or is not a credible representation of the behavior of interest. To gather evidence of validity, the existence of a theory or a reasonable conceptual framework is critical (Suen & Ary, 1989). With a theory at hand, three main types of evidence of observational data validity can be obtained: content validity, construct validity, and criterion-related validity. Content validity is the extent to which a measure reflects the theoretical domain of interest and is often assessed merely by having others review the coding system and judge whether it appears to survey the intended theoretical domain. It is usually one of the first steps in the development of a coding system but is not sufficient in and of itself to establish a coding system as valid.

Construct validity is concerned with how well a measure reflects a construct. It involves gathering evidence to show that a coding system does indeed reflect the construct of interest. In other words, does the coding system measure what it purports to measure? Construct validity is commonly assessed by correlating the observational scores with other measures of the same construct (convergent validity) or verifying that the observational scores are unrelated to dissimilar constructs (discriminant validity), with the former being more popularly examined than the latter. For example, Lindsey and Mize's system for coding parent–child mutuality has been found to correlate positively with measures of parent–child synchrony, a related construct. Ratings of balanced involvement from the Coparenting and Family Rating System (McHale) correlate with self-report measures of engagement in parenting, and codes from the Iowa Family Interaction Rating Scales have been shown to be associated with numerous self- and other-report measures of the constructs assessed in the observational system (Melby & Conger). Parent report of family conflict, family cohesion, and parenting style have been shown to correlate with observational measures of similar constructs from the System for Coding Interactions and Family Functioning (SCIFF; Lindahl & Malik).

Criterion validity is concerned with how well a set of scores obtained from a particular measurement procedure relates to a chosen criterion (Suen & Ary, 1989). One way to demonstrate evidence in support of criterion validity is when the results derived from a coding system can be used to identify membership in a known group (concurrent validity). For example, as described in later chapters in this volume, the SCIFF (Lindahl & Malik) has been shown to distinguish control families from families with a child with a disruptive behavioral disorder (Lindahl, 1998), and the scales developed by the Family Narrative Consortium (Fiese et al.) distinguish depressed from nondepressed mothers. Predictive validity, whereby observational codes are able to predict a later outcome, is discussed for several coding systems. For example, the Family Problem Solving Code (Forbes, Vuchinich, & Kneedler) was found to correlate with parental report of family cohesion and adaptability 1 year later.

CODING PROCESS

As summarized by Markman and Notarius (1987), the decision to record the interaction or to use live observation will to a large degree depend on the complexity of the coding system. When coding systems are more complex, having a permanent interactional record is essential. The information-processing demands for coders using a complex coding system is simply too great for coders to assess family interaction in real time. The development of a coding system is an evolutionary process, and for this reason, it is advantageous to have a permanent interactional record so data can be recoded if necessary. A permanent interactional record also facilitates establishing reliability as coders are able to review segments repeatedly to make careful judgments and to recode if necessary. Using videotaped recordings rather than live interactions also reduces training time for observers, as they need less extensive training to run subjects (Stoneman & Brody, 1990). Disadvantages to videotaping include the restrictions placed on participants (they must stay within camera range) and the longer time lag between data collection and coding when compared to live coding (Stoneman & Brody, 1990). Coding live reduces the technological demands required and allows investigators often to study families more easily in more naturalistic settings. However, live coding typically requires a greater number of coders (as many as one per person in the family) and therefore can be quite disruptive. Observers must be trained to be nonreactive to the family's behaviors and the level of reactivity families show to observer presence is not well understood. Virtually all of the coding systems described in this volume were developed with the use of videotaped data. Exceptions include the multidimensional approach to examining family processes and family narratives described by Fiese and her colleagues that combines videotaped or audiotaped data with the use of transcripts, and the Social Events System described by Harrist and Pettit, which employs written narratives recorded from live interactions naturally occurring in the home.

CHOICE OF TASK AND SETTING
FOR OBSERVATION

Clearly one of the most important decisions that one makes in deciding to conduct interaction-based research is what task the families will complete and where they will do it. Observational research is expensive to do and, for this reason, laboratory situations are often created or structured so as to maximize the chance that the family will display behaviors of theoretical interest to the investigator. Task structure restricts the behavior of the participants to varying degrees depending on the purpose of the research endeavor. Tasks used by investigators in this volume range from relatively unrestricted, as in a free-play situation such as used by Cox, Lindsey, and Mize, and Russell, Mize, and Saebel, to relatively specific, as in focused problem discussions as illustrated in chapters by Forbes, Vuchinich, and Kneedler; Gordis and Margolin; Lindahl and Malik; Robbins, Hervis, Mitrani, and Szapoznik; and Westerman. Thus, the investigator who believes that family problem solving is important is likely to present families with a problem-solving task and to observe how they handle this task, rather than placing families in the laboratory and hoping that the family will naturalistically display problem solving (Markman & Notarius, 1987). When the structure of the task is closely related to the behaviors observed (e.g., a revealed differences task is used to examine conflict resolution skills within the family), the general finding in the literature appears to be that increased task structure leads to a greater likelihood of observing group differences (Jacob et al., 1987). Similarly, researchers interested in behaviors or patterns of interaction that might have a low baserate of occurrence due to social desirability issues (e.g., family conflict, noncompliance) may need to devise structured tasks that are likely to elicit the behavior of interest. Employing a consistent and specific task demand also facilitates comparisons across families.

If the decision is made to use a structured task, then taking care to establish sufficient external validity for the task becomes an important consideration. It has been argued that who is present should be considered as a criterion for the ecological validity of what observations are obtained (Coyne, 1987). In the end, the task that is designed may be less natural for some families than others. For example, context may particularly affect father–child interactions if the task chosen is not one fathers often engage in with their child (Parke, 1990). As Coyne pointed out, many, if not most, crucial family interactions may occur without all family members present. If most discussions about how to implement a reward chart at home occur between mother and child when they are alone with each other, then observing and coding their discussions may provide a more valid characterization of how the family adapts to child behavior problems than a discussion with the father present. Many of the tasks selected for use by the investigators contributing to this volume leave it up to the family to determine who will partake in the task. For example, the Structural Family Systems Ratings (chap. 12, this volume) can accommodate as many family members as desired, and the family narratives task employed by Fiese et al. would not appear to constrain participation. Most of the other systems, however, are at the point in their development that they are best suited for dyads and triads.

In addition to the type of task, the setting for the task must also be given consideration. For most investigations, the choice is between a home-based observation and a lab-based observation. Data collected in laboratory settings have been criticized on grounds of ecological invalidity (Bronfenbrenner, 1974). To the extent that interactional data are influenced by the context in which they are collected, the generalizability of these findings to other, presumably more representative, contexts of family interaction is potentially compromised. Data collected in the laboratory may be questioned for several reasons. The laboratory is a novel setting and likely to be less comfortable for family members than their own home. In fact, studies have demonstrated how the physical setting can influence the nature of observed family and marital interactions. There is more of a tendency on the part of adults to be on "good behavior" when in the laboratory when compared to their behavior at home. Nevertheless, the behaviors and patterns that discriminate distressed from nondistressed couples in the laboratory are generally the same ones that are apparent in the home. What does differ across the two settings is the magnitude and the number of differences in the home relative to a less naturalistic situation (Jacob et al., 1987).

Home-based observations have their advantages and disadvantages. Observations conducted in the home have the obvious advantage of high ecological validity. In addition, scheduling a home visit is invariably easier for families than coordinating members' schedules to come into the lab. Therefore, obtaining a representative sample may be more easily accomplished if home-based visits are conducted. Although most of the coding systems in this volume involved videotaped lab-based situations, the Social Event System (see Harrist & Pettit) was specifically designed to capture family interaction patterns at home. Home-based observations are not, however, without their limitations. Due to the lack of experimental control and resulting variability in interaction contexts and persons present, naturalistic observations usually require longer periods of observation in order to gather stable patterns of behavior and also leave open the question as to whether differences in interaction are due to selection of different interactive contexts (Stoneman & Brody, 1990). Naturalistic observations also tend to be more costly in terms of the number of observers needed and the time required to complete the observation. In addition, observations in homes tend to be more intrusive and thus potentially more likely to cause reactivity on the part of the participants. Although subject reactivity may affect the interpretation of observational data in many ways, a primary concern is its threat to the external validity of the study. For an extensive discussion of issues related to reactivity, the reader is referred to Jacob et al. (1987).

PARTICIPANTS

Decisions about which family members to include in an observational task vary by the behavioral constructs of interest to the investigators as well as the complexity of the coding system. Options include observing dyads (e.g., husband–wife, father–child, mother–child), triads (mother–father–child), or larger units (e.g., parents and all children and, perhaps, grandparents). Although studying whole families has much to merit, in doing so the data-analytic burden and the requisite complexity of a coding system designed to manage such a task increase significantly as the number of observed family members increases. Particularly for investigators interested in sequencing interactional events, the logistics of keeping track of parallel conversations and reciprocal interactions among four or more participants is daunting (Markman & Notarius, 1987). For this reason, most of the coding systems described in this volume, and in general most family researchers have chosen to, limit their observations to triads. The Structural Family Systems Ratings is described in chapter 12 of this volume and is a notable exception that can accommodate larger family constellations.

SUMMARY AND CONCLUSIONS

Given the complexity and the differing benefits and costs associated with various types of coding systems, the prospect of choosing a coding system for a particular study may seem daunting. The flexibility of direct observational methodology, however, is one of its significant strengths. There are numerous decisions to make, for example, micro-, meso-, or macrolevel coding systems and home- or lab-based data collection. What choices are made will likely depend on the construct of interest. Indeed, to make the most out of observations, researchers must carefully determine the phenomena under investigation and consider each issue involved in coding, including the level of analysis of the system, reliability, validity, live or videotaped coding, and the setting, including the choice of task and the participants for the observational procedure. Very few methodologies in the behavioral sciences afford the flexibility and capture the temporal and heuristic complexity of interpersonal interactions as well as direct behavioral observation, and the chapters in this volume reflect numerous carefully derived methods to examine a variety of important family constructs

REFERENCES

Bronfenbrenner, U. (1974). Developmental research, public policy, and the ecology of childhood. *Child Development, 45,* 1–5.

Cohen, J. (1968). Weighted kappa: Nominal scale agreement with provision for scaled disagreement or partial credit. *Psychological Bulletin, 70,* 213–220.

Coyne, J. C. (1987). Some issues in the assessment of family patterns. *Journal of Family Psychology, 1,* 51–57.

Cronbach, L. S., Gleser, G. C., Nanda, H., & Rajaratnam, N. (1972). *The dependability of behavioral measures.* New York: Wiley.

Hartmann, D. P. (1982). Assessing the dependability of observational data. In D. P. Hartmann (Ed.), *New directions for the methodology of behavioral sciences: Using observers to study behavior* (pp. 51–65). San Francisco: Jossey-Bass.

Hartmann, D. P., & Wood, D. D. (1992). Observational methods. In A. S. Bellack, M. Hersen, & A. E. Kazdin (Eds.), *International handbook of behavior modification and therapy* (pp. 107–138). New York: Plenum.

Jacob, T., Tennenbaum, D. L., & Krahn, G. (1987). Factors influencing the reliability and validity of observational data. In T. Jacob (Ed.), *Family interaction and psychopathology* (pp. 297–328). New York : Plenum.

Lindahl, K. (1998). Family process variables and children's disruptive behavior problems. *Journal of Family Psychology, 12,* 420–436.

Markman, H. J., & Notarius, C. I. (1987). Coding marital and family interaction: Current status. In T. Jacob (Ed.), *Family interaction and psychopathology* (pp. 329–389). New York : Plenum.Mitchell, S. K. (1979). Interobserver agreement, reliability, and generalizability of data collected in observational studies. *Psychological Bulletin, 86,* 376–390.

Parke, R. D. (1990). In search of fathers: A narrative of an empirical journey. In I. E. Sigel & G. H. Brody (Eds.), *Methods of family research: Biographies of research projects. Vol. I: Normal families* (pp. 153–188). Hillsdale, NJ: Lawrence Erlbaum Associates.

Shrout, P. E. & Fleiss, J. L. (1979). Intraclass correlation: Uses in assessing rater reliability. *Psychological Bulletin, 86,* 420–428.

Stoneman, Z., & Brody, G. H. (1990). Families with children who are mentally retarded. In G. H. Brody & I. E. Sigel (Eds.), *Methods of family research: Biographies of research projects. Vol. II: Clinical populations* (pp. 31–58). Hillsdale, NJ: Lawrence Erlbaum Associates.

Suen, H. K., & Ary, D. (1989). *Analyzing quantitative behavioral observation data.* Hillsdale, NJ: Lawrence Erlbaum Associates.

3

The Iowa Family Interaction Rating Scales: Instrument Summary

Janet N. Melby
Rand D. Conger
Iowa State University

The *Iowa Family Interaction Rating Scales* (IFIRS; Melby, R. D. Conger et al., 1998) is a global or macrolevel observational coding system designed to measure behavioral and emotional characteristics of individuals, the nature of behavioral exchanges from one family member to another and between family members, and attributes regarding overall family processes. The IFIRS initially was developed to code behavioral processes in discussion and problem-solving interactions in families with adolescents (see Lorenz & Melby, 1994). However, the system has been used extensively to score interaction in young-adult dyads and was recently adapted for scoring behaviors of parents and young children (2–8 years of age) engaged in activity-based interactions (Melby, R. D. Conger et al., 1998). Although developed using a sample of European-American families, the scales subsequently were used successfully for scoring interactions in Native-American and African-American families.

THEORETICAL FOUNDATIONS

This observational coding system primarily draws on social interactional, behavioral, or social contextual theories in assessing displays of behaviors and relationship processes at the individual, dyadic, and group levels (R. D. Conger, 1997; R. D. Conger, Rueter, & Elder, 1999; R. D. Conger & Simons, 1997; Gottman, 1979a; Patterson, 1982; Patterson, Reid, & Dishion, 1992). Observed behaviors and interactions are considered part of an ongoing dynamic system wherein patterns of behaviors and ways of relating to one another develop over time. The video-recorded interaction segment viewed by observers captures a sample of behavior at a particular point in time and has an influence on individual adjustment and relationship quality. To a trained observer, the behaviors displayed during this segment provide information on relatively stable, and sometimes traitlike characteristics of the individuals and their relationships with one another.

With two exceptions (e.g., Physically Attractive, Rater Response), scales are defined in terms of specific behavioral indicators. Observers are trained to avoid making assumptions about motivation or intent of the person observed ("focal") when determining ratings and to base scores on what actually is seen and/or heard rather than on inference, conjecture, or imputed motivation. Along with frequency of behaviors, context and affect are of key importance in determining how to categorize observed behaviors and relationship processes; intensity and proportion also are considered in determining ratings. As opposed to more molecular, event-based observational system, an advantage of macrolevel observational coding systems such as the IFIRS is that observers assess the "gestalt" of the interaction (see also Hetherington, 1994). This advantage is also a limitation, however, in the sense that analyses of rates per minute, actual frequency, or duration cannot be generated from the coding procedures.

This system incorporates developmental considerations, yet is designed for application in a consistent manner across focal persons and interaction contexts. Because this system was designed for use in longitudinal studies, across diverse age groups (e.g., early adolescents, young adults, middle-aged adults), and with multiple types of relationships (e.g., parent–child, husband–wife, siblings, friend pairs), an attempt was made to devise scales containing consistent standards of measurement. In other words, an action judged to be hostile if displayed by a focal in one type of dyad should be judged similarly if it occurred in another type of dyad. However, the system recognizes that certain behavioral indicators may occur more frequently in some dyads or contexts than in others. For example, affectionate touching may occur more frequently between young adult romantic partners than between sibling pairs; however, if this behavior occurs in either type of pair, it should be scored as an indicator of Warmth/Support. Similarly, aversive physical contact may occur more frequently between adolescent sibling pairs than between husband–wife pairs; however, even though such contact is somewhat normative in the sibling dyad, the behavior is not excused. In other words, the level or "characteristicness" of the assigned rating is neither reduced nor elevated based on the type of dyad or type of interaction being assessed. This feature of the coding system creates the opportunity for comparisons of behaviors across dyads of different types, for example, spouses compared to siblings. Of the many possible behavioral indicators for each scale, those displayed vary slightly from one person or situation to the next. Only some of many possible indicators need to be exhibited in order to score a focal as showing evidence of the behavior on the overarching scale. Final score decisions are based on frequency and intensity of observed behaviors.

DEVELOPMENT OF THE IFIRS

Populations Assessed

This rating system was developed at Iowa State University's Institute for Social and Behavioral Research (ISBR) for use in a 4-year panel study of the relationship between economic hardship and specific developmental outcomes, including the psychological well-being of individual family members and the quality of family relationships (see R. D. Conger & Elder, 1994). This study of 451 primarily lower- or middle-class intact families living in rural areas of a midwestern state included a married couple, a seventh-grade target child, and a sibling within 4 years of age (older or younger) of the seventh-grader. A similar 3-year panel study investigated these processes in single-parent families with an eighth- or ninth-grader (see Simons, 1996). Subsequently, youth from these two samples were combined into the Family Transitions Project and followed for 4 years as they interacted with parents (Year 1) or a friend or romantic partner (Years 2 and 4) (R. D. Conger, Elder, Lorenz, Simons, & Whitbeck, 1993).

Results of the initial panel studies served as the basis for two intervention studies aimed at teaching parenting skills to parents of young adolescents in one- and two-parent households in Iowa. The studies involved 600 families in Project Family (Spoth & Redmond, 1996, 1998) and 700 families in Capable Families and Youth (Spoth & Redmond, 1997).

The IFIRS recently was adapted for scoring interactions in activity-based tasks involving youth and their young children (2–8 years of age) from Iowa (R. D. Conger et al., 1999) and New York (Thornberry, Smith, Krohn, Lizotte, & Rodriguez, 1997). Other applications have been to 40 parents and their adopted adolescents (Ge, R. D. Conger, Cadoret et al., 1996), a pilot study of Native-American families in the Midwest (Hoyt, 1994), a pilot sudy of African-American families (R. D. Conger & Simons, 1990), and a longitudinal study of 800 African-American families in Iowa and Georgia (R. D. Conger, Gibbins, Cutrona, & Simons, 1995).

Researchers at other sites have used or adapted parts of the IFIRS in studies of patients with Alzheimer's disease and their caregivers (Algase et al., 1996), mothers of premature infants and their spouse or support person (Pridham, 1995), parent–child relations (Brody, 1994), and family conflict (Stone & Buehler, 1997). The IFIRS also was used to study families in California and inner-city, economically disadvantaged families in Rochester, New York, and Chicago. Evidence to date suggests that the rating scales produce meaningful assessment across these diverse settings.

Interaction Tasks

The rating scales have been used to score behavioral processes occurring in various types of interaction tasks. Although sometimes collected in laboratory settings, most projects collect videotapes in homes of study participants.

Discussion-Based Tasks.   The ratings scales were initially developed for scoring interaction in discussion-based tasks. For these interactions, interviewers provided instructions, set up and started the video equipment, gave family members a set of cards containing discussion questions, and then left the room so as not to hear the recorded discussion. Family members not involved in the task completed questionnaires in a separate room where they would not hear the discussion.

The type and number of interaction tasks vary from one Institute research project to the next. In *parent–child discussion tasks* (15, 20, or 30 minutes; two parents and one or two children, or one parent and one or two children) participants discuss topics such as what they enjoy doing together, parental rules and expectations, and the child's biggest accomplishment or disappointment in the past year. For *family problem-solving tasks* (12 or 15 minutes; two parents and one or two children, or one parent and one or two children) members discuss and try to resolve problems regarding 3 of 18–25 possible topics selected for them based on questionnaires completed earlier. The interviewer selects issues that family members agree generate the greatest conflict in their family. Topics include children fighting, chores, respect among family members, and use of free time. *Couple problem-solving tasks* (15 minutes; young adult and friend, significant other, or spouse) are similar in format and topics include future plans, time use, sexual behavior, and activities with friends. *Sibling interaction tasks* (15 minutes; adolescent and near-age brother or sister) include topics such as the most fun thing done together during the past few weeks, the last thing they fought or disagreed about, and different ways and the fairness of how parents treat each child. *Marital interaction task* (20, 25, or 35 minutes; husband and wife) topics include the extent of agreement about childrearing, satisfaction with employment, and what the couple found most rewarding and their biggest disagreement during the past year. *Couple interaction tasks* (20 or 25 minutes; young adult and friend, significant other, or spouse; primary caregiver and secondary caregiver) ask how the pair spends time together, similarities and differences in their goals, and relationships with each other's families.

Activity-Based Tasks.   The system recently was adapted for scoring interactions of parents and young children (2–8 years of age) in activity-based tasks. For these tasks, materials are left for the young child and parent to use in the manner designated by the interviewer. A camera operator is present due to the greater likelihood of participants moving out of camera range.

The types of activity-based tasks rated by observers include a *parent–child teaching task* (5–10 minutes, one parent and one child) in which the child is given a puzzle or other activity that generally is too difficult to complete independently.

The parent is instructed to assist the child in any manner deemed appropriate. In the *clean-up task* (5–10 minutes, one parent and one child), the child first plays with and later is told by the interviewer that it is time to pick up and put away in appropriate containers a number of small toys or objects (e.g., blocks, plastic animals, doctor kit items, etc.). The parent is told to provide whatever assistance he or she feels the child needs.

IFIRS Revisions

To date, there have been five revisions of the coding system. The first edition (Melby et al., 1989) contained 53 scales and was based largely on experiences coding video-recorded interactions of 76 families who participated in a pilot study (Iowa Youth and Families Pilot Study; R. D. Conger et al., 1987, 1988) using rating systems developed by Hetherington and Clingempeel (1986) and Forgatch and Wieder (1981). After coding pilot tapes but prior to completing the first edition of the manual for use with the panel study families, several other coding systems were reviewed in an effort to make the IFIRS definitions and examples as universally representative and consistent with other theoretically relevant observational coding systems as possible. Following considerable recoding of videotapes using scales and definitions from several other observational coding systems, the scales used in the pilot study were adapted, modified, and expanded into the set of scales included in the first edition (Melby et al., 1989). Although the first and later editions drew extensively on systems developed by Hetherington and Clingempeel and by Forgatch and Wieder, the IFIRS also incorporated dimensions of several other schemes for rating family interaction processes (i.e., R. D. Conger, 1984; Dishion et al., 1987; Gottman, 1979b; Hops et al., 1988; Julien, Markmann, Lindahl, Johnson, & Van Widenfelt, 1987). Many scale definitions and coding conventions included in the third edition (Melby, R. D. Conger et al., 1993) were developed based on a careful review of these other coding systems. The fifth edition (Melby et al., 1998) added scales for scoring interactions involving young children, including some adapted from Cox (1997). See Appendix A for a list of scale names used in Editions 1–5.

The first two editions (Melby et al., 1989; Melby et al., 1990) employed a 5-point scoring system and, except for the addition of five new scales in the second edition, were alike in terms of rating scales and definitions. The third edition (Melby et al., 1991) also used a 5-point rating system, but added four more behavioral scales. The fourth edition (Melby et al., 1993) contained 55 scales, introduced a 9-point rating system, and made a number of other changes: 10 scales were dropped, 5 transformed, 1 split into 2 separate new scales, 1 expanded, and 1 added. The fifth edition (Melby, R. D. Conger et al., 1998) updated and clarified existing definitions based on extensive experience applying the scales to interactions among several thousand family members and friendship pairs participating in multiple research studies. In addition, this edition incorporated minor modifications in scale definitions, adapted existing scales for use in scoring behaviors of

young children, introduced several new scales designed to code interaction in activity-based rather than discussion-based tasks involving young children and their
parents, and included an appendix listing all scales appearing in previous editions.
A summary of scale changes across the various editions appears in the fifth edition.
The authors were the same for each of the first four editions; the fifth edition lists as
authors the persons who made substantive contributions to the manual throughout
the history of its development and use and who also contributed to the new scales
introduced in this latest edition.

DESCRIPTION OF THE IFIRS

This global system was developed in an effort to capture relatively stable qualities
of individuals and relationship processes across a large number of research participants and projects (see Lorenz & Melby, 1994). In general, macrolevel rating
scales such as these, compared to more fine-grained, microanalytic codes, are
more appropriate for assessing ongoing characteristics of individuals and relationships and less appropriate for evaluating counts, sequences, and durations of behaviors. They also are less costly than microanalytic observational systems in
terms of labor and time. However, initial and ongoing training costs may be higher
due to the need for trained observers to make discriminating judgments. For most
scales in this macrolevel system, both frequency and intensity of observed behaviors influence ratings. For example, one extremely intense hostile act (e.g., physical aggression) may produce the same rating for Hostility as several less serious
behaviors (e.g., low-level complaints about the other interactor's activities during
the previous day). Observers also consider contextual cues when determining ratings, being careful to focus on observed behaviors rather than making inferences
regarding the motivation or intent of research participants. Thus, careful initial
training, ongoing training, and reliability assessments are particularly important
aspects of quality control for this and other macrolevel systems.

Ratings

Nearly all of the 60 behavioral scales in the fifth edition of the manual are rated on
a scale from 1 to 9, with the odd-numbered points defined and the even-numbered
points described only as "between the two other points." In this system, most behavioral or relationship process scales are scored as: *1 = not at all characteristic, 3
= mainly uncharacteristic, 5 = somewhat characteristic, 7 = moderately characteristic,* and *9 = mainly characteristic* of the individual, dyad, or larger group being evaluated. Final ratings of "characteristicness" are based on combinations of
frequency and intensity, with strong consideration given to affect, context, and
proportion. A few scales are scored based on counts of behaviors. Some scales use
1 = negative, 5 = neutral or mixed, and *9 = positive.* It is important to note that the
scales in this system are viewed as neither mutually exclusive (i.e., a behavior can
be used as evidence for more than one scale) nor exhaustive (i.e., some behaviors
demonstrated in social interactions fit into none of the scales).

Measurement Levels

This system rates behaviors and interaction processes at four levels. *Individual characteristic scales* separately rate each focal person on specific behaviors or dispositions, regardless of the other interactor (e.g., Humor or Sadness displayed by the father). *Dyadic interaction scales* rate each focal's behavior toward one specific other person in the interaction (e.g., Hostility or Warmth/Support of the mother toward the child; wife's Hostility toward husband); separate ratings are assigned for the behavior of each focal to each other interactor. *Dyadic relationship scales* rate process characteristics of each dyad's relationship that cannot be scored at the individual level (e.g., Silence/Pause between father and mother or the Relationship Quality of the father–child pair). *Group interaction scales* characterize processes and relationships that transcend individuals and dyads to tap into dimensions describing processes involving all interaction participants (e.g., Group Enjoyment or Agreement on Problem Description).

Scale Categories

Scales are divided into three categories, each including one or more of the four measurement levels described previously. The largest category, *General Interaction Rating Scales*, contains 35 scales that rate behavioral interactions in all types of tasks and include each of the four levels described earlier. Although most ratings are based on observed behaviors only, two general scales document coders' subjective impressions of individuals assessed (i.e., Physical Attractiveness and Rater Response). Two other scale categories rate interactions in specific types of interaction tasks; these scales are called "specialty scales." *Parenting Scales* (15 scales) rate parents' observed and reported childrearing behaviors as displayed during parent–child interaction tasks; both parent and child reports are considered when rating these behavioral categories. All parenting scales are assessed at the dyadic interaction level. *Problem-Solving Scales* (10 scales) measure observed problem-solving behaviors displayed during a family or group problem-solving task; they include individual- and group-level ratings.

The total number of scales rated varies with the type of interaction task being scored. For example, the marital interaction task typically employs 33 separate scales, the discussion-based problem-solving interaction uses 43 scales, and the parent–child discussion task uses 45 scales. For activity-based tasks involving parents and young children, up to 31 scales are used for the clean-up task and 35 scales for the puzzle task. Many scales will be rated for each focal person or dyad, thus increasing the total number of scores recorded for a given interaction task.

Sample Items

Examples of each combination of scale category and measurement level follow. These examples also illustrate exceptions to the 9-point scoring system.

Positive Mood is a general interaction rating scale that rates an individual characteristic. It assesses the focal individual's expressions or demonstrations of contentment, happiness, and optimism toward self, others, or things in general. Other such scales include Humor, Sadness, Anxiety, Whine/Complain, and Externalized Negative.

Solution Quantity is a problem-solving scale measured at the individual characteristic level. It assesses the number of specific proposals and/or ideas for an action or change in behavior suggested by a focal as a means for reaching a goal or solving a problem. Ratings are based on the number of solutions proposed, from *1 = no solutions* to *9 = 10 or more solutions*. Other individual-level problem-solving scales include Solution Quality, Effective Process, Disruptive Process, and Negotiation/Compromise.

Rater Response is a general interaction rating scale measured at the individual characteristic level. It assesses the observer's subjective reaction to or emotional feelings regarding the focal. Ratings are from *1 = negative* to *9 = positive*, with *5 = neutral or mixed*. The one other subjective scale in this system is Physically Attractive, with four possible scale points.

Hostility is a general interaction rating scale measured at the level of dyadic interaction. It rates the extent to which hostile, angry, critical, disapproving, or rejecting behaviors are directed by one focal toward another interactor's behavior, actions, appearance, or personal characteristics. Some other scales of this type include Warmth/Support, Dominance, Lecture/Moralize, Interrogation, Assertiveness, Listener Responsiveness, Communication, Prosocial, Antisocial, and Avoidant.

Child Monitoring is a parenting scale measured at the dyadic interaction level. It rates the extent to which a parent demonstrates specific knowledge and information concerning the child's life and daily activities, including the extent to which the parent accurately tracks the behaviors, activities, and social involvement of the child. Some other scales in this category are Neglecting/Distancing, Positive Reinforcement, Quality Time, Harsh Discipline, Consistent Discipline, Consistent Discipline, Inconsistent Discipline, Inductive Reasoning, and Easily Coerced.

Group Enjoyment is a general interaction rating scale measured at the group interaction level. It rates the presence of fun, enjoyment, and/or satisfaction evident in the interaction of group members.

Agreement on Solution is a problem-solving scale measured at the group interaction level. It rates the extent to which the group resolved and/or reached agreement on a problem they discussed. Ratings are on a scale from *1 = no one stated a solution* to *9 = all agreed and seemed pleased or satisfied with the agreement reached*. Other group-level problem-solving scales are Family Enjoyment, Agreement on Problem Description, Implementation/Commitment, and Problem Difficulty.

CODER TRAINING

Staff hired as Family Interaction Analysts ("coders") at the Institute for Social and Behavioral Research generally have a minimum of a bachelor's degree in social science, humanities, literature, or education. They must display good verbal ability, attention to detail, interest in human behavior, ability to apply standardized ratings, and excellent auditory and visual memory skills. Although many coders are employed on an hourly basis, some are graduate research assistants.

Once hired, coders are expected to remain in the position for a minimum of 2 years. Due to the intense nature of the work, employees work no more than 20 hours per week in this capacity. Time requirements and the need for continuity of staff across multiple years and projects have precluded hiring undergraduate students. All staff sign agreements promising to protect the confidentiality of the research participants.

New-coder training typically lasts approximately 10–12 weeks, at 20 hours per week (a total of 200–240 hours). Trainees study the coding manual; attend small-group, new-coder training meetings; participate in weekly ongoing training meetings with experienced observers; view videotaped examples of specific behaviors and how they should be scored ("behavioral spots"); code practice videotapes; take written tests on scale definitions and coding conventions; and complete viewing tests on criterion tapes that have been prescored. Trainee ratings of these tapes allows comparison of their scoring with a known standard or criterion. The first four to five weeks of new-coder training are devoted to learning the *General Scales*. Depending on the task the coder will eventually code, the next 4 weeks of training may focus on learning one of the two sets of specialty scales (*Parenting Scales* or *Problem-Solving Scales*). The final segment of training consists of scoring practice tapes until the criterion is reached on two consecutive tapes. There is an additional period of training for coders who specialize in observing interaction between parents and young children in activity-based tasks.

To successfully complete training and be accepted into the pool of regular observers, all written tests must be passed with at least 90% correct responses. All viewing tests and final criterion tapes must be passed at the level of 80% perfect match or within a one-step match on a 9-point scale, with fewer than 10% of scales scored two steps or more from the criterion score; percentages are based on approximately 63 to 168 score decisions, depending on the type of task and number of focal persons in the task.

To the extent possible, coders are trained using tapes similar in task type, age of participants, length, and so on, to the tapes they will score after completing their initial training. In addition, they participate in weekly meetings involving the entire coding staff during which they gain experience scoring all types of interaction tasks and research participants currently being studied at our Institute. This helps ensure stability in definitions and coding conventions across various projects and years.

The hours in a coder's typical workweek are divided into a variety of activities. In addition to meetings of the entire coding staff (2.0 hours per week), all staff participate in weekly meetings of their specialty groups (1.5 hours). Meetings are devoted to discussing coding questions, coding practice tapes, focusing in depth on current coding difficulties, and group-building activities. Each coder spends approximately 2 hours each week in consensus meetings during which pairs of coders reconcile discrepancies in scores on tapes randomly selected for reliability checks. They do not see their original scores until reaching mutual agreement on score decisions. The remainder of their time is devoted to independently coding videotapes.

Researchers wishing to learn the IFIRS are encouraged to contact the first author at the Institute for Social and Behavioral Research to make arrangements that will best meet their needs while at the same time maintaining the integrity of the coding system. Some researchers may be interested in learning details about or being trained on only part of the observational system, whereas others may wish to learn the complete system. To date, a variety of training models have been followed, as described later. For an initial introduction to the rating system, a copy of the most recent edition of the manual may be obtained by contacting the first author. We charge a nominal fee for the manual to cover copying and postage costs will be assessed. The manual should be reprinted only with permission of the first author. This coding system is abstracted in Touliatos, Perlmutter, & Holden (in press) and has been deposited with the National Auxiliary Publication Services.

A set of videotapes containing verbal explanations and discussion of scales presented during actual new-coder training meetings also is available on a restricted basis. Although no videotapes involving research participants are available for use off site due to confidentiality agreements, it is possible to obtain a basic understanding of the coding system using the verbal-explanation tapes in conjunction with the manual. Interested persons should plan to spend some time on site where they can participate in ongoing training sessions, view behavioral spots, and view tapes of family interactions that are limited to onsite use only.

Two other options are available. First, experienced coders from the Institute for Social and Behavioral Research can provide criterion scores on tapes collected by researchers conducting projects at other institutions. These criterion scores can then be used at researchers' own sites with members of their staff. Second, experienced observational training staff at the Institute can consult on location with researchers at other sites. These types of services require funding for time, materials, travel, and so on. Contact the first author to inquire about such arrangements.

THE CODING PROCESS

An observer using the IFIRS makes global judgments about video-recorded interactions after viewing a tape several times. The initial viewing provides an overview of the content. Next, the observer randomly selects one interactor as the first focal person and views the tape twice focusing on that person. During these viewings, the observer makes notations about this focal's behaviors, pausing or replaying the tape at any point but being careful not to lose the flow or context of the interaction. Before proceeding to the second focal, the observer indicates on a score sheet numerical ratings for each scale that apply to the first focal. Each participant in the interaction task is rated using this procedure. For tasks where specialty scales (parenting or problem solving) are rated, at least one additional tape viewing is necessary.

In the process of determining ratings on a particular task, an observer can modify initial scores based on more complete information obtained in subsequent viewings. Whereas initial observations about behaviors and score decisions are recorded on a note sheet, final score decisions are transferred to a rating form or grid containing categories for scoring the various combinations of focals and behaviors in a given task. Observers score all interactors present in a task, but score only one task per family or group. They complete all ratings for one assigned task for a family or group prior to proceeding to the next family or group they are to assess. Because this system involves considerable judgment by trained observers in order to arrive at global ratings, paper-and-pencil techniques are preferred for note taking and for documenting final scores.

The amount of time required to score a task depends on the number of focals present and the length and type of task. Generally, it is necessary to allow double the time required for all viewings. For example, a 15-minute task with three family members would require seven viewings (one general viewing and two viewings for each family member) and approximately 3.5 hours to complete all ratings. If this task contains specialty scales, one additional viewing would be permitted, bringing the time for scoring the tape to about 4 hours on average.

RELIABILITY

Each interaction task is independently rated by a randomly assigned primary observer who has been trained to criterion level. To assess reliability, a portion of all videotapes is selected at random for consistency checks and independent rating by a second observer. The proportion of double-coded tapes has ranged from 12% (for the 1st year of the Iowa Youth and Families Project) to 100% (the African-American Families Pilot Project), with the percentage being 25% for most projects. Interobserver agreement has been assessed using interclass correlations or generalizability coefficients (see Booth, Mitchell, & Solin, 1979; Shrout & Fleiss, 1979; Suen, 1989) and confirmatory factor analysis procedures (Kenny & Kashy, 1992: Melby, R. Conger, Ge, & Warner, 1995). Intraobserver reliability (internal consistency) also has been evaluated for summary constructs.

Intraclass correlations have been obtained for single scales and for summary constructs used with each project and wave of data collection. In general, intraclass correlations for observer ratings of single scales range from .55 to .85 for the scales used in most analyses. For example, in the Iowa Youth and Families Project during 1992, the intraclass correlation for father-to-child behaviors during the family discussion task was .82 for Hostility and .77 for Warmth/Support. Usually, however, theoretically related behavioral ratings are summed to create composite measures that reflect a wider range of behaviors. For example, the ratings of Hostility, Antisocial, and Angry Coercion load heavily on a hostility construct in confirmatory factor analyses and, thus, normally are combined to create a composite scale or latent construct. Because they reduce restrictions in range, intraclass correlations for composite measures tend to be higher than for single ratings. For instance, a reliability coefficient of, for example, .86 is obtained for husband-to-wife behavior for a summary construct consisting of Hostility, Angry Coercion, Antisocial, and Escalate Hostile rated during the marital discussion task. These levels are acceptable for these types of data (see Kenny, 1991; Mitchell, 1979). A study by Ge, Best, R. D. Conger, and Simons, (1996) demonstrates acceptable interobserver reliability, internal consistency, and test/retest reliabilities for composite measures of three types of parental behaviors (warmth, hostility, and discipline). The extent of rater bias associated with this observational system was assessed using generalizability analyses. Results based on data from multiple projects and waves indicated that rater main effects did not constitute a prominent portion of the total observed variance for most scales (Becker, 1999).

VALIDITY

The observational scales have been validated against reports from self and other family members (spouse, child) using correlational and confirmatory factor analytic procedures (see Kashy & Kenny, 1990). Using these types of analyses, ratings of marital hostility/coercion demonstrated reliability and validity (Melby, R. Conger et al., 1995). Observational assessments of marital warmth/prosocial behaviors (Warmth/Support, Communication, Listener Responsiveness, Assertiveness, and Prosocial) supported the reliability of global ratings and illustrated the importance of task context in evaluations of validity (Melby, Ge, R. D. Conger, & Warner, 1995). Ratings of adolescent behaviors were validated against self, sibling, and parent reports of behaviors and evaluations of the relationship. Age of sibling (younger or older than adolescent) and type of task context (parents present or absent) were important considerations (Melby, Conger, & Puspitawati, 1999).

An exploratory investigation of ethnicity and training effects on ratings of European-American and African-American parent–child dyads by African-American and European-American trainees found that inter-observer agreement increased with training and that systematic bias was mainly absent. None of the observer effects was large, thus they do not raise concerns about the basic validity of the IFIRS (Melby, Bryant, & Hoyt, 1998). Taken together, the evidence reviewed in this chapter suggests that the IFIRS provides a useful set of measures for studying social processes and individual development.

STUDIES USING THE IFIRS

Observer ratings provide a trained outsider perspective on behaviors and interaction processes that may be difficult for participants to assess objectively. Whereas family members are likely the best source of information on events that do not occur in the presence of an observer or on their own thoughts and feelings, outside observers provide valuable information on family processes and relationships. If used in conjunction with self- and family-member reports, observer ratings enable researchers to employ multi-informant techniques in testing hypotheses, thus reducing method-variance problems (see Lorenz & Melby, 1994).

IFIRS ratings have been used as single scales, in composite observational measures, as indicators of latent constructs, and combined with self- and other-family-member reports. Depending on the focus of the analyses, they have served as predictor, moderating, mediating, and outcome variables. Although extensive discussion of research findings is beyond the scope of this summary, in this section we illustrate various ways these observational scales have been used and some key results in selected areas of research.

Economic Stress.   In a study of the link between family economic stress and the adjustment of male adolescents, observer reports were used as one of three indicators for the latent factor of depressed mood for fathers and for mothers; the other two indicators were self- and spouse-report. Marital conflict was assessed by a single indicator formed by summing observer reports of each spouses' Hostility, Angry Coercion, Antisocial, and Transactional Conflict toward the other spouse in the problem-solving and marital interaction tasks. Three indicators for nurturant/involved parenting were created based on observer ratings of the parent–child discussion task: (a) involved/warm parenting (eight scales), (b) low hostility (four scales), and (c) consistent discipline (two scales). Economic conditions were related to parents' emotional distress and behaviors through their perceptions of increased economic difficulties. These perceptions were associated with parental depression and demoralization, which was related to marital conflict and disruptions in skillful parenting. Disrupted parenting mediated the relations between earlier steps in the stress process and adolescent competence (e.g., school performance) and maladjustment (e.g., antisocial behavior) (R. D. Conger et al., 1992). Similar results were found for female adolescents. Parents' depressed mood and disrupted childrearing behaviors directly affected girls' adjustment (R. D. Conger et al., 1993).

The role brothers and sisters play in the family economic stress model was examined by K. J. Conger, R. D. Conger, and Elder (1994). Latent constructs of mother's and father's hostile behaviors as well as sibling hostile and warm behaviors were measured with reports from seventh-graders, older siblings, and observers. Family economic pressure was related to parents' hostility toward their children. Mother's and father's hostility were linked to adolescent externalizing behaviors primarily through hostility in the sibling relationship. Based on seventh-grader perception, warmth and support from an older sibling moderated the relationship between mother's and father's hostility and seventh-graders' externalizing feelings and behaviors. Hostile behaviors by parents and older siblings increased internalizing and externalizing symptoms of early adolescents.

Simons, Lorenz, Wu, and R. D. Conger (1993) looked at the way spouse support (self-report and observational measures) moderated relationships among economic strain, depression, and quality of parenting (self-report and observational measures) by reducing the relationship between economic strain and depression, as well as the relationship between depression and quality of parenting.

Marital Instability.   In a prospective, longitudinal study, observer ratings predicted divorce over and above variability accounted for by spouse and self-reports (Matthews, Wickrama, & R. D. Conger, 1996). Observer ratings captured important dimensions of family interaction not revealed in family member reports. Economic stress increased marital instability, but observer ratings of marital support and problem solving buffered the impact of stress on marriage (Conger, Rueter, & Elder, 1999).

Adoptive Parenting.   Observer ratings, parent self-reports, and adolescent reports were used in a study of youth adopted at birth (Ge, R. D. Conger, Cadoret, 1996). Half of the adoptees had biological parents diagnosed with substance or other adjustment problems at the time of the child's birth. Psychiatric disorders of biological parents were significantly related to adoptee's antisocial/hostile behaviors and to adoptive parents' nurturant/involved and harsh/inconsistent behaviors toward adolescents. Results showed relatively high convergence among report sources for each type of parental behavior.

Adolescent Problem Behaviors.   Fathers' and mothers' harsh/inconsistent parenting composite observational measures were associated with higher adolescent tobacco use, both directly and indirectly through peer associations. Observed nurturant/involved parenting was associated with lower adolescent tobacco use, directly for both parents and indirectly through peers for mothers only (Melby et al., 1993).

A study of family processes and characteristics related to adolescent alcohol use and problems examined harsh/inconsistent parenting (three subfactors: harsh discipline, hostility, and inconsistent discipline) and nurturant/involved parenting (four subfactors: standard setting, behavior tracking or monitoring, positive reinforcement, and warmth/support) (R. D. Conger, Rueter, & K. J. Conger, 1994). Each subfactor aggregated standardized scores from four informants: parent self-report, spouse report, observer report, and adolescent report. Mothers' alcohol problems had a direct influence on adolescent alcohol use and problems, as well as an indirect effect through her harsh/inconsistent parenting. Mother's alcohol problems also had a significant, negative effect on her nurturant/involved parenting, which in turn increased adolescent risk for alcohol use and problems. When either parent was above the median on harsh/inconsistent discipline practices, older sibling drinking was significantly and positively related to seventh-grader drinking. When parents were low, compared to high, on nurturant/involved parenting, older sibling drinking was significantly related to seventh-grader alcohol use; the difference was significant for mothers, marginal for fathers. These analyses demonstrate that IFIRS may reveal family processes that either promote resilience to or increase risk for adolescent problem behaviors.

Observer ratings across two tasks and three waves of data collection were summed to create composite scales for parental warmth (Warmth/Support, Listener Responsiveness, Prosocial, Communication, Assertiveness, and Quality Time), hostility (Hostility, Angry Coercion, and Antisocial), and discipline (Consistent Discipline, Child Monitoring, Positive Reinforcement, Parental Influence, Inductive Reasoning, and Harsh Discipline-reverse coded). These measures predicted the occurrence and co-occurrence of adjustment problems among 10th-graders after controlling for 7th-grade depressive symptoms and delinquent behavior (Ge, Best et al., 1996).

A 4-year longitudinal study used the composite observational measure of hostility directed by fathers toward daughters. When compared to on-time and late-maturing peers, early-maturing girls were more vulnerable to prior psychological problems, deviant peer pressures, and fathers' hostile behaviors (Ge, R. D. Conger, & Elder, 1996).

A test of latent trait versus life course perspectives on the stability of adolescent antisocial behavior supported a life course explanation for the stability of antisocial behavior from late childhood through adolescence. Oppositional-defiant behavior (observational ratings and parent report measures) during late childhood predicted target-reported reductions in quality of parenting and school commitment and increased affiliation with deviant peers. These changes, in turn, predicted conduct problems during adolescence. When the effect of parenting, school, and peers was taken into account, there was no association between childhood antisocial behavior and adolescent conduct problems (Simons, Johnson, R. D. Conger, & Elder, 1998).

Community disadvantage (census data) indirectly increased the chances of adolescent conduct problems and psychological distress (both target report) by reducing quality of parenting (observational measures) while increasing affiliation with deviant peers (parent report) (Simons, Johnson, Beaman, R. D. Conger, & Whitbeck, 1996). These results demonstrate the sensitivity of the IFIRS measures to multiple levels of influence in developmental processes.

Academic Performance.   Measures created by combining parent, adolescent, and observer reports of parenting behaviors were used as indicators of latent constructs that predicted change in the adolescents' school performance. Parenting practices fostered change in academic accomplishment across time. Setting and positively reinforcing appropriate behavioral standards (parent management) increased academic performance, whereas hostility (negative emotional affect) decreased academic performance (Melby & R. D. Conger, 1996).

Physical Health.   Observer ratings of spouses' Relationship Quality were used as an indicator of marital integration in a paper examining physical health. Marital integration mediated the effect of occupational quality on sense of control and on health risk behaviors of husbands and wives (Wickrama, Lorenz, R. D. Conger, & Elder, 1997). Observed parental support influenced change in adolescent physical health through adolescents' perceived parental support. In addition, initial level of observed parent behavior to the adolescent in 7th grade had a direct effect on change in adolescent physical health between 8th and 12th grades (Wickrama, Lorenz, & R. D. Conger, 1997). Observer ratings of father–adolescent and mother–adolescent Relationship Quality mediated the effect of parental health risk behaviors and education on adolescent health-risk behaviors (Wickrama & R. D. Conger, 1998).

Sibling Relationships.   The influence of differential parental hostility during early and middle adolescence on changes in differences in siblings' delinquency by middle to late adolescence was examined using observer and adolescent reports in a series of two-wave two-variable models. Observers rated parent hostility to siblings; youth reported on delinquent behaviors. Mother's and father's differential hostility had a significant effect on sibling differential delinquency at Time 2 after controlling for Time 1 differences in delinquency. The sibling treated in the most hostile fashion demonstrated relatively more delinquent behaviors at Time 2. The findings were mixed regarding the influence of sibling differential behavior on parental hostility across time (R. D. Conger & K. J. Conger, 1994).

An investigation of the influence of divorce on sibling relationships used a measure of inept parenting formed from self-report, adolescent report, and observer report of four dimensions of parental behavior: hostility, low monitoring, inconsistent discipline, and harsh discipline. Latent constructs for sibling hostility and sibling warmth each included observer ratings as one of the three indicators. Divorced status, family stress, and maternal personality characteristics were related to sibling behavior indirectly through parenting (R. D. Conger & K. J. Conger, 1996).

Problem-Solving Behaviors.   Observer ratings of Solution Number, Solution Quality, and Effective Process served as single indicators along with observer ratings of Hostility, Warmth/Support, and Communication. They predicted family's report of their problem-solving effectiveness in a cross-sectional study by Rueter and R. D. Conger (1992).

Three papers assessed the relationship between observed problem solving and interactions among family members. Constructive problem solving was assessed using three indicators: Effective Process, Solution Number plus Solution Quality, Negotiation/Compromise plus Prosocial. Destructive problem solving also was assessed using three indicators: Destructive Process, Denial, and Antisocial. Individual's general interaction style predicted their problem-solving behavior (Rueter & R. D. Conger, 1995b). A family's general interaction style predicted their problem-solving behavior (Rueter & R. D. Conger, 1995a). A reciprocal relationship was found between an adolescent's problem-solving behavior and parental behavior (Rueter & R. D. Conger, 1998).

Problem solving, measured as a combination of both spouses' Solution Number and Solution Quality scores summed across three waves of data collection, moderated the relationship between marital conflict and marital instability. The relationship was weakest among couples exhibiting high levels of problem-solving effectiveness (Conger, Rueter, & Elder, 1999).

Intergenerational Transmission of Behaviors.   Preliminary prospective investigations of relationship processes demonstrated intergenerational transmission of affective behaviors. Observed warm-supportive behaviors by parents toward their children during early and middle adolescence predicted observer ratings of the same behaviors by the youth at age 22 years to a romantic partner (spouse, cohabiting, or dating relationship). Furthermore, these behaviors were strongly related to reports of relationship satisfaction in this dyad (Bryant & R. D. Conger, in press).

Observer ratings of hostile and coercive behaviors by parents toward adolescents during the 9th and 10th grades significantly correlated with the subsequent cognitive development and adaptive temperament of the grandchild, except when sensitive parenting was statistically controlled. Results demonstrate that observable qualities of parenting during adolescence affect the youth's parenting during early adulthood which, in turn, influences their child's development (Scaramella, R. D. Conger, & Simons, 2000).

Intervention Studies.   Family intervention outcome studies conducted by Spoth and colleagues at ISBR used both self-report and observational methods. One study examined directly targeted outcomes (e.g., rewarding competence regarding child compliance with rules about substance use) and more general protective parenting outcomes (e.g., child monitoring, rewarding, disciplining). Analysis of Variance results showed significant intervention effects on both measures. Results also indicated that parents' level of intervention attendance, expressed readiness for parenting change, and parent self-efficacy were predictors of targeted parenting outcomes. The targeted parenting outcomes significantly affected general child management outcomes (Spoth, Redmond, Haggerty, & Ward, 1995).

In another study, 33 rural schools were randomly assigned to one of three conditions: family competency training, parenting training, or minimal contact. Structural equation modeling used latent parenting constructs to assess three parenting outcomes: intervention-targeted parenting behaviors (parent report), general child management (parent report and observer ratings), and parent–child affective quality (parent report and observer ratings); models controlled for measurement method effects. Both interventions found direct intervention effects only on intervention-targeted parenting behaviors and indirect effects on affect quality and general management (Spoth, Redmond, & Shin, 1998).

In summary, the IFIRS have been used to rating behaviors and relationships of family members in a variety of population types. The obtained ratings have been formed into diverse constructs and analyzed in relation to a wide range of predictor and outcome measures for both basic and applied research. Strengths of the system include the use of observers trained to assess behavioral processes that participants may find difficult to assess.

EXCERPTS FROM THE IFIRS MANUAL

The length of the IFIRS manual precludes inclusion of complete descriptions of sample scales. To give the reader an overview of the scales contained in the manual (Melby, R. D. Conger et al., 1998), abbreviated versions of two scale definitions are presented here, one general interaction rating scale scored at the dyadic inter-action level (Verbal Attack) and one parenting scale scored at the dyadic interac-tion level (Positive Reinforcement). Please note that although only odd-numbered scale levels are defined, raters use the complete 1–9 range in actual scoring:

Verbal Attack

Verbal Attack (VA) is a specific form of Hostility that assesses personalized and unqualified disapproval of another interactor. Look for the presence of unkind statements that appear intended to demean, hurt, or embarrass the other person. Such statements include put-downs, personally derogatory adjectives, criticisms of the other person, comments that are overwhelming and demeaning of another's personal characteristics, and sarcasm directed toward the other person as a person. The negative evaluation must attribute *ongoing* and *global* aversive or negative characteristics to the recipient of the behavior. Use only observed in-task behaviors for scoring.

1 - *Not at all characteristic.* The focal displays *no signs* of personalized and unquali-fied attack of the other interactor.

3 - *Minimally characteristic.* The focal *infrequently* shows evidence of personalized and unqualified attack toward the other interactor. However, such behavior is of low frequency and intensity.

5 - *Somewhat characteristic.* The focal *sometimes* expresses personalized and un-qualified attack toward the other interactor. Such behavior is of low to moderate frequency or intensity. Even one instance of VA may be scored '5' if it is of moder-ate intensity.

7 - *Moderately characteristic.* The focal *fairly often* expresses personalized and un-qualified attack toward the other interactor that is of low to moderate intensity. Even one instance of VA may be scored '7' if it is of relatively high intensity.

9 - *Mainly characteristic.* The focal *frequently* expresses personalized and unquali-fied attack toward the other interactor. Such behavior is of quite high intensity. However, even one instance of extremely intense VA may be scored '9'.

Clarifications for scoring Verbal Attack: (a) VA statements refer to global characteristics of another person applicable across people, situations, and time. They suggest that a characteristic is pervasive (e.g., "You are stupid," or "I think you are stupid") rather than specific only to the focal (e.g., "I hate you" or "You never help me"). (b) Rate unqualified personalized attacks, criticisms, name-calling, and specific humiliation of the recipient as VA. (c) Comments must relate to characteristics that exist at the present time to score under VA. If they relate to characteristics that existed only in the past, score under Hostility, Angry Coercion, etc. (e.g., "You were stupid when you did that"). (d) Synonyms for VA include *personalized* forms of accusation, character assassination, contempt, criticism, disapproval, disgust, indictment, insult, mocking, name-calling, negative attribution, and scorn. (e) Some statements that appear to contain qualifiers (e.g., "sort of ... " "kind of", and "pretty ... ") do not necessarily make less global negative characterizations. Such phrases may still be coded as VA if they ascribe ongoing, global negative attributions or labels to the recipient (e.g., "You're really sort of stupid, you know that").

Positive Reinforcement

Positive Reinforcement (PO) assesses the extent to which the parent's contingent responses to the child include the use of praise, approval, rewards, special privileges, warm smiles, or hugs. Such responses are contingent upon 'appropriate child behavior' or upon child behavior that meets specific parental standards (stated *or* implied rules, regulations, and expectations). For positive responses by the parent to a child's behavior during the video task, also code as Warmth/Support. Score using both observed and reported behaviors.

1 - *Not at all characteristic.* Contingent parental responses to desired child behavior are *never* affirming or positively reinforcing.

3 - *Minimally characteristic.* Contingent parental responses to desired child behavior are *rarely* affirming and positively reinforcing. The parent's responses to the child's behavior may be mildly positive, e.g., infrequently offering praise and positive reinforcement.

5 - *Somewhat characteristic.* Contingent parental responses to desired child behavior are *occasionally* affirming and positive. Some evidence of positive reinforcement, e.g., praising and positively reinforcing comments.

7 - *Moderately characteristic.* Contingent parental responses to desired child behavior are *fairly often* affirming and positive. More intensive affirmation is evident and displayed to a fairly high degree.

9 - *Mainly characteristic.* Contingent parental responses to desired child behavior are *frequently* affirming and positive. Such responses are very affirming and positive.

Clarifications for rating Positive Reinforcement: (a) 'Appropriate child behaviors' are those that comply with specific parental standards (stated *or* implied rules, regulations, and expectations). These behaviors generally are thought desirable, e.g., doing well in school, doing a good job on chores, getting along with others, etc. (b) Pay particular attention to the context in determining whether or not the behavior is merely Warmth/Support ("You're nice", "I love you") or is both PO and Warmth/Support ("You chose a nice shirt to wear," "That was a great answer"). If a behavior observed during the interaction task is coded as PO, it also is evidence of Warmth/Support; however, the reverse is not necessarily true. (c) If a parent is consistent in giving positive rewards, score this under PO, not under Consistent

Discipline. (d) Frequency is more important than consistency in determining the score level for PO (e.g., if the parent consistently follows through on promised rewards, but only rarely makes such promises, keep the score lower than if they always say "good job," "thank you," etc., for doing chores). (e) Promised rewards or bribes with evidence of no follow through on the part of the parent do not count as PO (e.g., "If you pick up your toys you can have ice cream"); consider such behavior when scoring Consistent Discipline, Inconsistent Discipline, and Parental Influence.

ACKNOWLEDGMENTS

This summary is based on a series of collaborative research efforts at the Institute for Social & Behavioral Research and the Center for Family Research in Rural Mental Health supported by grants from the: Bureau of Maternal and Child Health (MCJ-109572), Iowa Agriculture & Home Economics Experiment Station, Ames, IA (Projects #2931 & #3320), MacArthur Foundation Research Network on Successful Adolescent Development Among Youth In High-Risk Settings, National Institute for Child Health and Human Development (HD27724), National Institute on Drug Abuse (DA05347, DA07029), National Institute of Mental Health (MH00567, MH19734, MH43270, MH48165, MH49217, DA07029, MH51361, MH56486).

REFERENCES

Algase, D., Beck, C., Kolanowski, A., Whall, A., Berent, S., Richards, K., & Beattie, E. (1996). Need-driven dementia-compromised behavior: An alternative view of disruptive behavior. *American Journal of Alzheimer's Disease, 11,* 10–19.

Becker, M. R. (1999). *Rater bias in observational data: A generalizability analysis.* Unpublished maters thesis, Iowa State University, Ames.

Booth, C. L. , Mitchell, S. K., & Solin, F. K. (1979). The generalizability study as a method of assessing intra- and interobserver reliability in observational research. *Behavior Research Methods and Instrumentation, 11,* 491–494.

Brody, G. (1994). *Observational Coding Manual for the Adolescent Development Research Project.* Unpublished manuscript, University of Georgia, Athens.

Bryant, C. M., & Conger, R. D. (in press). The DEARR model of romantic relationship development. In H. T. Reiss, M. A. Fitzpatrick, & A. L. Vangelisti (Eds.), *Stability and change in relationship behavior.* New York: Cambridge University Press.

Conger, R. D. (1984). *Social Interaction Scoring System Coder Manual.* Unpublished manuscript, Iowa State University, Ames.

Conger, R. D. (1997). The social context of substance abuse: A developmental perspective. In E. B. Robertson, Z. Sloboda, G. M. Boyd, L Beatty, & N. J. Kozel (Eds.), *Rural substance abuse: State of knowledge and issues* (NIDA Research Monograph No. 168, NIH Publication No. 97–4177, pp. 6–36). Washington, DC: National Institute on Drug Abuse.

Conger, R. D., & Conger, K. J. (1994). Differential parenting and change in sibling differences in delinquency [Special issue on siblings]. *Journal of Family Psychology, 8,* 287–302.

Conger, R. D., & Conger, K. J. (1996). Sibling relationships. In R. L. Simons (Ed.), *Understanding differences between divorced and intact families* (pp. 104–121). Thousand Oaks, CA: Sage.

Conger, K. J., Conger, R. D., & Elder, G. H., Jr. (1994). Siblings relations in hard times. In R. D. Conger & G. H. Elder, Jr. (Eds.), *Families in troubled times: Adapting to change in rural America* (pp. 235–252). New York: Aldine de Gruyter.

Conger, R. D., Conger, K. J., Elder, G. H., Jr., Lorenz, F. O., Simons, R. L., & Whitbeck, L. B. (1992). A family process model of economic hardship and adjustment of early adolescent boys. *Child Development, 63,* 526–541.

Conger, R. D., Conger, K. J., Elder, G. H., Jr., Lorenz, F. O., Simons, R. L., & Whitbeck, L. B. (1993). Family economic stress and adjustment of early adolescent girls. *Developmental Psychology, 29,* 206–219.

Conger, R. D., & Elder, G. H., Jr. (Eds.). (1994). *Families in troubled times: Adapting to change in rural America.* New York: Aldine de Gruyter.

Conger, R. D., Elder, G. H., Jr., Lorenz, F. O., Simons, R. L., & Whitbeck, L. B. (1993). *Critical transitions in rural families at risk.* Funded by National Institute of Mental Health grant (MH51361) to the Institute for Social and Behavioral Research, Iowa State University, Ames.

Conger, R. D., Gibbins, F., Cutrona, C., & Simmons, R. (1995). *Center for family research in rural mental health.* Funded byNational Institute on Mental Health grant (MH48165) to Iowa State University, Ames.

Conger, R. D. (principal investigator), Lasley, P., Lorenz, F. O., Simons, R. L., Whitbeck, L. B., & Elder, G. H., Jr. (Co-principal investigators). (1988). *Rural family resilience to economic stress.* Funded by National Institute of Mental Health grant (MH43270) to the Social and Behavioral Research Center for Rural Health, Iowa State University, Ames.

Conger, R. D., Rueter, M. A., & Conger, K. J. (1994). The family context of adolescent vulnerability and resilience to alcohol use and abuse. *Sociological Studies of Children, 6,* 55–86.

Conger, R. D., Rueter, M. A., & Elder, G. H., Jr. (1999). Economic and resilient couples. *Journal of Personality and Social Psychology, 76,* 54–71.

Conger, R. D. (principal investigator), Simons, R. L., & multiple co-investigators. (1990). Center for family research in rural mental health. Funded by National Institute on Mental Health grant (MH48165) to Iowa State University, Ames.

Conger, R. D., & Simons, R. L. (1997). Life-course contingencies in the development of adolescent antisocial behavior: A matching law approach. In T. P. Thornberry (Ed.), *Advances in criminological theory (Vol. 7,* (pp. 55–99). New Brunswick, NJ: Transaction.

Conger, R. D., Simons, R. L., Lorenz, F. O., Rueter, M., Wickrama, K. A. S., Conger, K. J., & Melby, J. N. (1998). *Critical transitions in rural families at risk.* Funded by National Institute of Mental Health grant (MH51361) to the Institute for Social and Behavioral Research, Iowa State University, Ames.

Conger, R. D. (principal investigator), Simons, R. L., Whitbeck, L. B., & Lasley, P. (Co-principal investigators). (1987). *Rural family economic stress and adolescent drug use.* Funded by National Institute on Drug Abuse grant (DA05347) to the Social and Behavioral Research Center for Rural Health, Iowa State University, Ames.

Cox, M. (1997). *Qualitative ratings: Parent/child interaction at 24–36 months of age.* Unpublished manuscript, University of North Carolina, Chapel Hill.

Dishion, T., Gardner, K., Patterson G., Reid, J., Spyron, S., & Thibodeaux, S. (1987). *The Family Process Code: A multidimensional system for observing family interaction.* Unpublished manuscript, Oregon Social Learning Center, Eugene.

Forgatch, M. S., & Wieder, G. B. (1981). *Parent Adolescent Negotiation Interaction Code (PANIC).* Unpublished manuscript, Oregon Social Learning Center, Eugene.

Ge, X., Best, K. M., Conger, R. D., & Simons, R. L. (1996). Parenting behaviors and the occurrence and co-occurrence of adolescent depressive symptoms and conduct problems. *Developmental Psychology, 32,* 717–731.

Ge, X., Conger, R. D., Cadoret, R. J., Neiderheiser, J. M., Yates, W., Troughton, E., & Stewart, M. A. (1996). The developmental interface between nature and nurture: A mutual influence model of child antisocial behavior and parenting. *Developmental Psychology, 32,* 574–589.

Ge, X., Conger, R. D., & Elder, G. H., Jr. (1996). Coming of age too early: Pubertal influences on girls' vulnerability to psychological distress. *Child Development, 67,* 3386–3400.

Gottman, J. (1979a). *Marital interaction: Experimental investigations.* New York: Academic Press.

Gottman, J. (1979b). *Rapid Couple Interaction Scoring System.* Unpublished manuscript, Department of Psychology, University of Washington, Seattle.

Hetherington, E. M. (1994). Siblings, family relationships, and child development: Introduction. *Journal of Family Psychology, 8,* 251–253.

Hetherington, E. M., & Clingempeel, W. G. (1986). *Behavior Rating Scales of Family Interaction.* Unpublished manuscript, Department of Psychology, University of Virginia, Charlottesville.

Hops, H., Biglan, A., Arthur, J., Warner, P., Holcomb, C., Sherman, L., Oostenick, N., Osteen, V., & Tolman, A. (1988). *Living in Family Environments (LIFE) Coding System.* Unpublished manuscript, Oregon Research Institute, Eugene.

Hoyt, D. (1994). *Pilot study of Native American families.* Unpublished research results, Institute for Social and Behavioral Research, Ames, IA.

Julien, D., Markman, H., Lindahl, K., Johnson, H., & Van Widenfelt, B. (1987). *Interaction Dimensions Coding System.* Unpublished manuscript, University of Denver, Colorado.

Kashy, D. A., & Kenny, D. A. (1990). Analysis of family research designs. *Communication Research, 17,* 462–482.

Kenny, D. A. (1991). A general model of consensus and accuracy in interpersonal perception. *Psychological Review, 98,* 155–163.

Kenny, D. A., & Kashy, D. A. (1992). Analysis of the multitrait-multimethod matrix by confirmatory factor analysis. *Psychological Bulletin, 112,* 165–172.

Lorenz, F. O., & Melby, J. N. (1994). Analyzing family stress and adaptation: Methods of study. In R. D. Conger & G. H. Elder, Jr. (Eds.), *Families in troubled times: Adapting to change in rural America* (pp. 21–54). Hawthorne, NY: Aldine.

Matthews, L. S., Wickrama, K. A. S., & Conger, R. D. (1996). Predicting marital instability from spouse and observer reports of marital interaction. *Journal of Marriage and the Family, 58,* 641–655.

Melby, J. N., Bryant, C. M., & Hoyt, W. T. (1998, February). Effects of observers' ethnicity and training on ratings of African American and Caucasian parent–youth dyads. In A. M. Cauce (Chair), *Issues in multi-cultural/multi-ethnic observational research.* Symposium conducted at the seventh biennial meeting of the Society for Research on Adolescence, San Diego.

Melby, J. N., & Conger, R. D. (1996). Parental behaviors and adolescent academic performance: A longitudinal analyses. *Journal of Research on Adolescence, 6,* 113–137.
Melby, J. N., Conger, R. D., Book, R., Rueter, M., Lucy, L., Repinski, D., Ahrens, K., Black, D., Brown, D., Huck, S., Mutchler, L., Rogers, S. Ross, J., & Stavros, T. (1989–1993). *The Iowa Family Interaction Rating Scales (editions 1–4).* Unpublished manuscript, Center for Family Research in Rural Mental Health, Iowa State University, Ames.
Melby, J. N., Conger, R. D., Book, R., Rueter, M., Lucy, L., Repinski, D., Rogers, S. Rogers, B., & Scaramella, L. (1998). *The Iowa Family Interaction Rating scales* (5th ed.). Unpublished manuscript, Institute for Social and Behavioral Research, Iowa State University, Ames.
Melby, J. N., Conger, R. D., Conger, K. J., & Lorenz, F. O. (1993). Effect of parental behavior on tobacco use by young male adolescents. *Journal of Marriage and the Family, 55,* 439–454.
Melby, J. N., Conger, R., Ge, X, & Warner, T. (1995). The use of structural equation modeling in assessing the quality of marital observations. *Journal of Family Psychology, 9,* 280–293.
Melby, J. N., Conger, K. J., & Puspitawati, H. (1999). Insider, participant observer, and outsider perspectives on adolescent sibling relationship. In F. M. Berardo (Series Ed.) & C. L. Shehan (Vol. Ed.), *Contemporary perspectives on family research: Vol. 1. Through the eyes of the child: Re-visioning children as active agents in family life* (pp. 329–351). Stanford, CT: JAI Press.
Melby, J. N., Conger, R. D., Rueter, M. Lucy, L. Repinski, D., Rogers, S., Rogers, B., & Scaramella, L. (in press). The Iowa Family Interaction Rating Scales [Abstract]. In J. Touliatos, B. Perlmutter, & G. Holden (Eds.), *Handbook of family measurement techniques, Vol. 2.* Thousand Oaks, CA: Sage [Instrument has been deposited with National Auxiliary Publication Services].
Melby, J. N., Ge, X., Conger, R. D., & Warner, T. D. (1995). The importance of task in evaluating positive marital interactions. *Journal of Marriage and the Family, 57,* 981–994.
Mitchell, S. K. (1979). Interobserver agreement, reliability, and generalizability of data collected in observational studies. *Psychological Bulletin, 86,* 376–390.
Patterson, G. R. (1982). *Coercive family process.* Eugene, OR: Castalia.
Patterson, G. R., Reid, J. B., & Dishion, T. J. (1992). *Antisocial boys.* Eugene, OR: Castalia.
Pridham, K. F. (1995). *Support of mothers and family members in feeding an extremely low birthweight premature infant at risk for chronic lung disease.* Funded by March of Dimes Birth Defects Foundation grant (FY96–0467) to the University of Wisconsin, Madison.
Rueter, M. A., & Conger, R. D. (1992). The relationship between family problem solving interaction and family problem solving effectiveness. *Family Perspective, 26,* 331–360.
Rueter, M. A., & Conger, R. D. (1995a). Antecedents of parent–adolescent disagreements. *Journal of Marriage and the Family, 57,* 1–14.
Rueter, M. A., & Conger, R. D. (1995b). The relationship between interaction style and family problem solving effectiveness. *Child Development, 66,* 98–115.
Rueter, M. A., & Conger, R. D. (1998). The interplay between parenting and adolescent problem solving: Reciprocal influences. *Developmental Psychology, 34,* 1470–1482.
Scaramella, L. V., & Conger, R. D. (1998, May). *Like parent like child like grandchild? The intergenerational transmission of angry and sociable behaviors.* Paper presented at the American Psychological Society Conference, Washington DC.

Scaramella, L. V., Conger, R. D., & Simons, R. L. (2000). *Three generations of influence on the competence and maladjustment of young children*. Manuscript in preparation.

Shrout, P. E., & Fleiss, J. L. (1979). Intraclass correlations: Uses in assessing rater reliability. *Psychological Bulletin, 86,* 420–428.

Simons, R. L. (in collaboration with Conger, R. D., Elder, G. H., Jr., Lorenz, F. O., & Whitbeck, L.) (1996). *Understanding differences between divorced and intact families.* Thousand Oaks, CA: Sage.

Simons, R. L., Johnson, C., Beaman, J., Conger, R. D., & Whitbeck, L. B. (1996). Parents and peer group as mediators of the effect of community structure on adolescent problem behavior. *American Journal of Community Psychology, 24,* 145–171.

Simons, R. L., Johnson, C., Conger, R. D., & Elder, G. H., Jr. (1998). A test of latent trait versus life-course perspectives on the stability of adolescent antisocial behavior. *Criminology, 36,* 217– 244.

Simons, R. L., Lorenz, F.O., Wu, C., & Conger, R. D. (1993). Social network and marital support as mediators and moderators of the impact of stress and depression on parental behavior. *Developmental Psychology, 29,* 368–381.

Spoth, R., & Redmond, C. (1996). *Rural family and community drug abuse prevention project.* Funded by National Institute on Drug Abuse grant (DA07029) to the Institute for Social and Behavioral Research, Iowa State University, Ames.

Spoth, R., & Redmond, C. (1997). *Rural families competencies building project.* Funded by National Institute on Drug Abuse grant (DA07029) to the Institute for Social and Behavioral Research, Iowa State University, Ames.

Spoth, R., & Redmond, C. (1998). *Rural youth at risk: Extension based prevention efficacy.* Funded by National Institute on Mental Health grant (MH49217) to the Institute for Social and Behavioral Research, Iowa State University, Ames.

Spoth, R., Redmond, C., Haggerty, K., & Ward, T. (1995). A controlled parenting skills outcome study examining individual differences and attendance effects. *Journal of Marriage and the Family, 57,* 449–464.

Spoth, R., Redmond, C., & Shin, C. (1998). Direct and indirect latent-variable parenting outcomes of two universal family-focused preventive interventions: Extending a public health-oriented research base. *Journal of Consulting and Clinical Psychology, 66,* 385–399.

Stone, M. G., & Buehler, C. (1997, November). *Preliminary development of a covert conflict observational rating scale.* Paper presented at the annual meeting of the National Council on Family Relations, Arlington, VA.

Suen, H. K. (1989). Agreement, reliability, accuracy, and validity: Toward a clarification. In H. K. Suen, & D. Ayr, (Eds.), *Analyzing quantitative behavioral observational data* (pp. 99–189). Hillsdale, NJ: Lawrence Erlbaum Associates.

Suen, H. K., & Ary, D. (1989). *Analyzing quantitative behavioral observation data (chapters 5, 6, & 7, pp. 99–189).* Hillsdale, NJ: Lawrence Erlbaum Associates.

Thornberry, T. P., Smith, C. A., Krohn, M. D., Lizotte, A. J., & Rodriguez, M. L. (1997). *Intergenerational transmission of antisocial behavior.* Funded by National Institute of Mental Health grant (MH56486) to Hindelang Criminal Justice Research Center at the University at Albany, State University of New York.

Touliatos, J., Perlmutter, B., & Holden, G. (Eds.) (in press). *Handbook of family measurement techniques, Vol. 2.* Thousand Oaks, CA: Sage.

Wickrama, K. A. S., & Conger, R. D. (1998). *Family influences on adolescent health risk behaviors: Mediational processes and gender moderating effects.* Manuscript submitted for publication.

Wickrama, K. A. S., Lorenz, F. O., & Conger, R. D. (1997). Parental support and adolescent health: A growth curve analysis. *Journal of Health and Social Behavior, 38,* 149–163.

Wickrama, K. A. S., Lorenz, F. O., Conger, R. D., & Elder, G. H., Jr. (1997). Linking occupational conditions to men's health outcomes: Mediational processes. *Journal of Health and Social Behavior, 4,* 363–375.

APPENDIX A:
IOWA FAMILY INTERACTION RATING SCALES
AT A GLANCE*

Individual Characteristic Scales
PA   Physically Attractive
HU   Humor/Laugh
SD   Sadness
AX   Anxiety
WC   Whine/Complain
EX   Externalized Negative
PM   Positive Mood
IP   Indulgent/Permissive
DF   *Defiance*
CP   *Compliance*
RR   Rater Response
PH   Physical Movement**
FM   Facial Movement**
IN   Internalized Negative**
EH   Escalate Hostile**
EP   Escalate Positive**
IS   Intellectual Skills**

Dyadic Interaction Scales
HS   Hostility
VA   Verbal Attack
AT   Physical Attack
CT   Contempt
AC   Angry Coercion
EH   Escalate Hostile
RH   Reciprocate Hostile
DO   Dominance
LM   Lecture/Moralize
IT   Interrogation
DE   Denial
WM   Warmth/Support
ED   Endearment
AF   Physical Affection
EW   Escalate Warmth/Support
RW   Reciprocate Warmth/Support
AR   Assertiveness
LR   Listener Responsiveness
CO   Communication
PR   Prosocial
AN   Antisocial
AV   Avoidant
VI   Verbally Involved**
BT   Body Toward**
BA   Body Away**

Dyadic Relationship Scales
SP   Silence/Pause
RQ   Relationship Quality

Group Interaction Scales
GE   Group Enjoyment
GD   Group Disorganization**

Parenting Scales
ND   Neglecting/Distancing
QT   Quality Time
PI   Parental Influence
CM   Child Monitoring
ID   Inconsistent Discipline
CD   Consistent Discipline
HD   Harsh Discipline
PO   Positive Reinforcement
IR   Inductive Reasoning
EI   Encourages Independence
EC   Easily Coerced
NT   *Intrusive*
CC   *Sensitive/Child Centered*
SC   *Stimulates Cognitive Development*

Individual Problem-Solving Scales
SN   Solution Quantity
SQ   Solution Quality
EF   Effective Process
DS   Disruptive Process
NC   Negotiation/Compromise

Group Problem-Solving Scales
FE   Family Enjoyment
AP   Agreement on Problem Description
AS   Agreement on Solution
IC   Implementation Commitment
PD   Problem Difficulty

* Scales especially relevant to coding
behaviors of parents and young children in
activity-based tasks are presented in
italicized type.

** Rated for projects using Edition 1,2, 3, or 4
only, but also defined in Edition 5 appendix.

4

Assessing Families With the Family Problem Solving Code

Charles Forbes
Sam Vuchinich
Blythe Kneedler
Oregon State University

The Family Problem Solving Code (FAMPROS) provides a comprehensive, efficient observational assessment of family problem-solving characteristics. It can be used to evaluate global family functioning, or specific features of problem solving. It includes multiple-item scales for individual-, relationship-, and family-level characteristics. The code was designed to capture characteristics of family interactions involving three or more family members. It may be applied in a variety of settings where family discussions take place.

Coding can be done from audiotapes, videotapes, or live observations. The system has been successfully applied with a variety of family types including stepfamilies, foster families, ethnic minority families, families in treatment for psychological disorders, low-income families, as well as middle-class, biological-parent families. The code yields an overall score on the effectiveness of problem solving, as well as scale scores for individual, relationship, and family characteristics that contribute to problem-solving effectiveness. Ratings are made on the following dimensions: positive behavior, negative behavior, relationships, coalitions, participation, and four aspects of problem solving. The system can be applied in families with children ranging in age from 8 years old and older.

THEORETICAL FOUNDATIONS

One of the things that families must do is cope with the inevitable problems that arise in the course of family life. These may be traumatic life-changing crises, or relatively minor ongoing irritations. Because of the intertwined nature of family life, problems with individual family members or relationships usually have direct consequences for other members of the family. A family's social and emotional survival depends on managing these difficulties. Families that fail in this regard typically deteriorate into cycles of conflict, coercion, or withdrawal. These cycles have short- and long-term negative consequences (e.g., Patterson, Reid, & Dishion, 1992; Robin & Foster, 1989). Families that effectively resolve their problems typically provide a healthy environment for the growth and development of all family members.

Family problem solving has sometimes been conceptualized as a rather limited specific set of skills (e.g., define the problem, generate possible solutions, etc.) that need be applied only when a major family problem arises. But it is becoming increasingly apparent that the elements of problem solving permeate many aspects of family life. Indeed problem solving is increasingly viewed as an expression of a fundamental characteristic of a family (Forgatch & Patterson, 1989; Reiss, 1981; Reiss & Klein, 1989; Robin & Foster, 1989; Vuchinich, 1999; S. Vuchinich, Wood, & Angelelli, 1996). Family problem solving is an arena in which basic dimensions of family cohesion, adaptability, and communication (e.g., Olson, 1986) are displayed in an observable, measurable setting.

Family problem solving represents an important point of convergence between behavioral (Falloon, 1988; Forgatch & Patterson, 1989) and family systems approaches (e.g., Robin & Foster, 1989) to psychosocial treatment (e.g., Hibbs & Jensen, 1996). Sequential patterns of positive and negative reinforcement, such as coercive family process (e.g., Patterson, 1982), are linked to family systems concepts such as hierarchy and coalition (Robin & Foster, 1989; S. Vuchinich, Wood, & R. Vuchinich, 1994), as well as cohesion and adaptability (Olson, 1986). Indeed both behavioral and family systems approaches recommend family training in family problem solving for family-based treatment of a variety of disorders (Forgatch & Patterson, 1989; Hibbs & Jensen, 1996; Robin & Foster, 1989; Vuchinich, 1998; S. Vuchinich, Wood, & Angelelli, 1996).

The FAMPROS is theoretically based on this convergence between behavioral and family systems theory. Several of the FAMPROS coding categories focus on assessing who displays positive and negative behavior toward whom. This allows identification of individual family members with extreme reinforcement tendencies, in either the positive or negative domain. Because these codes are directional, they can be used to assess positive or negative reciprocity.

Family systems theory is the basis for two types of codes. One is the coalition code, which indicates the extent to which two family members "gang up" on a third family member. This code identifies patterns such as triangulation and detouring (e.g., S. Vuchinich et al., 1994). The other type of code focuses on dyadic relationships that make up subsystems within the family. Thus the quality of the mother–father relationship is assessed separately from the mother–child relationship.

The remaining codes are based on research and theory in family problem solving (Vuchinich, 1999). Participation levels of each family member are rated and can be used as indicators of power distribution or democratic participation. The extent of family perspective taking is assessed in a problem-solving process code that indicates whether family members consider the needs, feelings, and opinions of each other during problem solving (e.g., Selman, Beardslee, Schultz, Krupa, & Podorefsky, 1986; S. Vuchinich, Wood, & Angelelli, 1996). In addition, the extent to which the problem was clearly defined, completely resolved, and the quality of the proposed solutions are each rated separately. These codes provide a detailed profile of the mechanics of a family's problem-solving style.

Many quantitative approaches to coding family problem solving have been used since the early pioneering efforts almost 50 years ago (e.g., Strodtbeck, 1954; see Markman & Notarius, 1987, for reviews). Even though there is overlap among many of these coding systems, none has emerged as the "gold standard" observational family coding system. Computer technology and statistical advances have motivated some changes in coding methodology. But beyond that, most research and clinical efforts have always seemed to have some particular, unique focus that required a special coding system. There has always been a generous borrowing of codes and procedures. The FAMPROS continues this tradition. Some form of all the codes in this system have been part of previous coding systems. The FAMPROS was especially influenced by the Family Process Code (Dishion, Gardner, Patterson, Reid, & Thibodeaux, 1982), and the Solving Problems in Families Codes (Forgatch, Fetrow, & Lathrop, 1984) from the Oregon Social Learning Center, and by Hetherington's Family Process Code (Hetherington & Clingempeel, 1992).

DEVELOPMENT OF THE FAMILY PROBLEM SOLVING CODE

The FAMPROS emerged from research efforts to understand how coalitions within the family were related to antisocial behavior in preadolescents (S. Vuchinich, 1987; S. Vuchinich, Emery, & Cassidy, 1988; S. Vuchinich, R. Vuchinich, & Wood, 1993; S. Vuchinich et al., 1994). One key study examined videotapes of three types of families: those in therapy to treat the child's diagnosed conduct disorder, families at risk for behavior problems, and a comparison group of middle-class two-parent families (S. Vuchinich et al., 1994). The study began using only a sequential code that assessed every overt behavior by any family member. This proved to be a valuable, but time-consuming process. Because funding was limited, high coding costs would have curtailed the sample size, and thus the statistical power available for analysis. A different, more efficient, coding strategy was needed. The solution was found with a system that used a 10-minute family session as the coding unit, rather than a single behavior at one point in time. Thus, for example, one code rated a mother's positive behavior toward the child across the 10-minute period. This is sometimes known as a "global" code. A sequential code could assess the same construct by counting how many times the mother was "positive" toward the child. Coding costs were cut in half. Although the global code did not capture all the temporal information included in the sequential code, it provided a transformation of that information that was even more useful for that research project. It opened up new research insights that led to several further studies.

Two features distinguish the FAMPROS from previous family coding systems. First, it focuses on family problem solving as a central part of family functioning. It provides a global score of family problem-solving effectiveness, and provides quantitative details on what contributes to that level of effectiveness in terms of individual behavior, dyadic family relationships, and coalitions. For example, it could identify a conflictual relationship between father and son that derails effective problem solving. Or it could locate the aggressive or withdrawing tendencies of a mother that inhibit progress toward resolution of difficulties. Furthermore, codes may be used together to construct measures of important family characteristics. For example, the positive behavior codes of mother, father, and child may be summed to create a composite scale of positive supportive family behavior.

Second, the FAMPROS was designed to streamline the coding process so that accurate coding could be done quickly and efficiently. A number of strategic choices were made to promote these features as the code was constructed. Family interactions over problems can become extremely complex. The FAMPROS was developed to allow coders to focus on key target behaviors and avoid getting lost in the complexity of secondary multiperson dynamics. This facilitates the training process and promotes higher levels of reliability. Three features contribute to this efficiency:

1. Each code is defined in terms of easily identified behaviors with clear indication of who is doing what to whom. For example, the code "negative behavior father to child" is rated on a scale from 1 to 7. It refers to how much behavior of the following type the father directs toward the child: criticizing, anger, accusing, reprimanding, disagreeing, complaining, insulting, negative commands, negative affect. A score of 1 on this scale indicates virtually none of this behavior. A score of 7 indicates high levels of this behavior. The coder's task is to determine how much of a specific behavior type is observed. These codes are "nondiagnostic" in the sense that the coder is not required to infer the presence of complex family or individual traits such as cohesion, adaptability, coercion, and so on. An advantage of this approach is that coders are not required to have advanced degrees or clinical experience. Undergraduates are able to learn and use the code with relatively brief training periods.

2. The FAMPROS is designed to be used with videotapes, audiotapes, or live observation. Typically coders can rate a 10- to 20-minute family interaction with one viewing. Coding time is usually about 10 minutes. The full FAMPROS has 25

codes, all rated on a 7-point scale. Some especially complex interactions may require an additional viewing of the tape, but this is rarely needed.

3. The code was developed for use in situations where family members are trying to resolve a problem they have chosen. Many of the codes are applicable to other settings. The full system is tuned to provide a comprehensive assessment of a family's problem-solving style. For example, there are specialized codes for how clearly a problem is defined, the quality of solutions proposed, and the extent to which a resolution was achieved. Some FAMPROS codes, such as those for negative behavior, apply to any family interaction (e.g., family dinners, play situations, general family discussion). But these specialized codes are relevant only in conflict- or problem-solving tasks.

Thus far, the FAMPROS has been used primarily in two settings. One is in the family's own home; the other has been in a community research and family therapy center. The coding system performed equally well in both settings. As has been found in past research, structured family problem-solving sessions can be used to collect valid and reliable information about families. This coding system has also been used in other settings such as family dinners. However, not all the codes are relevant for all settings. For example, most naturalistic family dinners include positive and negative behavior, but little in the way of problem-solving behavior. Thus the problem-solving codes could not be used in the family dinner setting.

Another consideration is the age of the children in the family. Our research has found that children in the 8- to 19-year-old range can participate actively in this kind of problem-solving task. But some children younger than that tend to participate less or are easily distracted from problem-solving activities. We recommend using the coding system in families with children from age 8 through 19 years.

FAMPROS has been used successfully with a variety of family types. This includes families with the child diagnosed with behavior problems, families with children at risk for antisocial behavior, stepfamilies, two-biological-parent families, and foster families. It has been used with low-income families as well as affluent families. The ethnicity of the families used in the published studies was more than 90% White. However, one unpublished study applied the system successfully to a sample of 26 Native-American families (Kawamoto, 1996). An important issue in such applications is the background of the coders and their familiarity with the culture from which the sample is drawn. Coders must be able to understand the linguistic patterns of the sample families in order to provide accurate codes.

DESCRIPTION OF THE FAMPROS CODES

There are six coding domains in the FAMPROS: positive behavior, negative behavior, participation, relationships, coalitions, and problem solving. Each domain includes several specific codes. The *positive behavior* codes assess how much positive behavior each family member directs toward each other family member. Positive behavior refers to displays of affection, warmth, agreement, support, or understanding. A score of 1 indicates none, or almost none of this behavior. A score of 7 indicates a very high level of this behavior. If there are three family members (mother, father, child) in the session, there are six positive behavior ratings made: mother to father, mother to child, child to mother, and so on.

Negative behavior refers to displays of criticism, anger, disagreement, complaining, rejection, and the like. The same 7-point scale is used to rate how much of this behavior each person directs to each other person. Thus in a three-person family, six negative behavior ratings are made. The positive and negative codes can be used to assess the overall tone of family interaction, and to identify sources and targets of reward and punishment. Combinations of these codes can be used as sociometric assessments of relationships, reciprocity, and coercion.

The *participation* code rates how active each person is in the interaction. In a three-person family, there are three ratings on the 7-point scale. This code is used to identify families in which one person dominates or where one person is withdrawn or excluded. An even distribution of participation is an index of democratic family process. Low overall participation indicates low engagement or avoidance.

The *relationship* code rates the amount of interpersonal closeness displayed for each dyad in the session. This is a bidirectional code in that the support and affiliation must be reciprocated for a score to increase. This is distinguished from the positive and negative behavior codes, which are each unidirectional. As for all the codes, a 7-point scale is used with 1 indicating no apparent relationship, and 7 indicating an "exceptionally close" relationship.

The *coalition* code indicates the extent to which two family members "gang up" on a third family member (e.g., S. Vuchinich et al., 1988). In a three-person family group, there are three coalitions rated (mother–father against child, mother–child against father, father–child against mother). A rating of 1 indicates no evidence of a coalition at all. A 7 indicates that the coalition was displayed throughout the interaction.

There are four specific *problem solving* codes, which refer to specific aspects of the family's problem-solving performance. *Definition* assesses the extent to which a problem was clearly defined. *Extent of resolution* rates how close to family came to an overt resolution of the problem. *Quality of proposed solutions* evaluates the solutions offered in terms of how practical they were, whether they dealt adequately with the problem, and how creative they were. And finally, the *problem solving process*, or perspective-taking, code assesses the extent to which participants work together toward a solution, whether they take each other's viewpoints into account, and whether they use higher order processing such as compromise or building on the suggestions of others. A 1 here indicates an extremely poor problem-solving process; a 7 indicates an extremely good process.

The 25 codes include all the main domains of family problem solving. However, specific research projects may need only a subset of these codes, depending on purpose of the research. A brief summary of all the coding categories is provided at the end of this chapter.

CODER TRAINING

Both undergraduate and graduate students have been successfully trained as coders using the FAMPROS. The code is designed to rely on the basic social skills available to coders as part of their social competence. Coders with some background in behavioral science, developmental psychology, family studies, and similar majors typically learn the codes and procedure quickly. No diagnostic evaluation of complex family problems or patterns is involved. Graduate students have been trained in the FAMPROS code, but there is some tendency for them to "overanalyze" families, and infer complex characteristics. If such tendencies can be curbed, graduate students make reliable coders.

Once coders have been selected, training begins with the goal of achieving intercoder reliability and validity. Coders are given a general introduction to the procedures used in coding. Typically coders must be kept "blind" to the hypotheses guiding the research. Various approaches can be taken to keep coders blinded.

Training occurs in three phases: the group-meeting phase, the repeated viewing phase, and the final calibration phase. In the group-meeting phase, an experienced coder will watch a tape with new coders on two separate occasions, describing coding-relevant behaviors as they arise. This is the beginning step toward reliability. Some dissonance often exists between the naive coder's appraisal of family behavior and the master codes. The goal in this phase is to start bringing new coders' decisions into line with the master coders. During these discussions, the coding system as a whole is presented and described through examples.

In the repeated viewing phase, trainees take three tapes and view each twice before rating families. Following this viewing process, a meeting is held with the experienced coder. New coders present their ratings, and again discuss any variance between their codes and the master codes. This should require two to three sessions of three videotapes each.

The final calibration phase is typified by trainees honing their coding proficiency after only one viewing of a family. This final phase continues until a preset level of reliability is found between the new coders' scores and the master codes. During this process, coders-in-training can be supplied with the master codes in order to evaluate their own progress. Weekly meetings should still be held in order to discuss progress. Although there will be variability in the amount of total training time necessary per coder, expect at least 40 hours of training.

Extensions in training time may also be necessary depending on the family type under investigation. For more complex family situations, such as stepfamilies, foster families, or families with serious problems, coders may need additional time to come to grips with the variations in family interactions present in diverse family types.

Following training, tapes that have master code ratings can be inserted into the coder's workload. This will serve as a check on coder drift and accuracy. Also, regular meetings should still be continued as a forum for questions and to discuss issues as they arise.

Training requires the brief coding manual, and a few calibration tapes. Coding materials are available for a small fee from Professor Sam Vuchinich (Oregon State University). Consultation is also an option, and can be arranged when the materials are ordered.

CODING PROCESS

The typical family problem-solving session used in our research is 25 minutes in duration and made up of a total of three sections. In the first 5 minutes, families are asked to plan a fun family activity. This activity helps families become comfortable in a new situation and prepares them for the next phase by encouraging discussion. Following are two 10-minute problem-solving sessions. For one of the 10-minute periods, the child selects the problem for discussion. For the other, the parents choose the issue. Other procedures could be used as well.

Because it is a warm-up, the fun family activity is usually ignored in our coding. Coders view one of the 10-minute problem-solving sessions and rate it immediately after viewing the videotape. The coder can take down notes during the video, as well as stop and restart the tape if necessary. It takes approximately 10–15 minutes for an experienced coder to rate a 10-minute problem-solving session. Also, although there are exceptions, each problem-solving session typically needs to be viewed only once.

The numerical ratings for each coding category are written on a scoring sheet that has each category listed in the far-left column. The individual positive and negative behaviors are coded first, followed by the family-level codes. Coders go through all codes in an initial pass with minimal reflection. While observing the tape, mental notes are made that usually give the coder a good sense of the appropriate rating. At this time they write down scores for those codes that were most clear in the session. Typically this completes all but two or three codes. The less apparent codes are rated with more reflection in which the coder takes time to recall details of behavioral events and their frequency. In some particularly complex family sessions, the coder may still be uncertain about one or more codes. In that case the videotape is played again, with a focus on the few codes that need scores.

The coding process emphasizes verbal behavior, and part of the training requires coders to cite specific statements, or patterns of statements, that are evidence for specific ratings that are made. Coders must take into account all the variations in speech and expression (e.g., intonation, tone of voice, facial gestures, body gestures, etc.) as well as frequency of behavioral types when making ratings. These involve the same basic skills of interpersonal perception that any socially competent person uses. Because modes of expression can vary across cultures it is important that coders have similar cultural background to the families being coded.

RELIABILITY

Interrater Reliability.   The global family problem-solving coding system has been used in several studies. Pearson correlation coefficients were calculated to test for interrater reliability between independent ratings of the same 10-minute session. S. Vuchinich et al. (1993) tested 20% of the data coded by the team of five coders. The correlations were an average of 0.74 for individual behaviors (with a range of 0.61 for mother–father [MF] coalition to 0.86 for MF negative; S. Vuchinich et al., 1993). S. Vuchinich et al., (1994) found that reliability coefficients averaged 0.72 for individual behaviors (with a range of 0.61 for parental coalition to 0.83 for father–child [FC] coalition. S. Vuchinich, Angelelli, and Gatherum (1996) tested intercoder reliability on 20% of their data. The mean correlation was 0.77 across the three individual positive behavior ratings, 0.72 across negative, and 0.82 for participation (S. Vuchinich et. al., 1994). For family-level variables, the correlations have been no less than 0.65 for quality of solutions , 0.62 for extent of resolution (S. Vuchinich et al., 1993, 1994; S. Vuchinich, Angelelli, 1996). Additionally, the correlations for perspective taking were 0.76 and 0.78 (S. Vuchinich et al., 1993; S. Vuchinich, Angelelli et al., 1996), and 0.76 for overall problem-solving process (S. Vuchinich et al., 1994). The Cronbach's alpha for total score of effectiveness (sum of quality, extent, and perspective taking/ process) was 0.86, 0.88, and 0.88 (S. Vuchinich et al., 1993, 1994; S. Vuchinich, Angelelli, 1996).

Point-by-Point Agreement. Exact agreement between different coders has also been examined. S. Vuchinich et. al. (1993) calculated a point-by-point check on scores (i.e., comparing one coder's code with another coder's code). The average percentage agreements were 92.8 (the range was from 85.7 for father–mother [FM] negative, to 100 for FM positive). S. Vuchinich et al. (1994) calculated Cohen's (1968) weighted kappa, which counts agreement if ratings were within 1 point. The weighted kappas (with corresponding percentage agreements in parentheses) were: 0.71 (91) for FC positive, 0.64 (87) for mother–child (MC) positive, 0.81 (96) for FC coalition, 0.86 (96) for MC coalition, 0.70 (89) for MF coalition, 0.68 (89) for quality of solution proposed, 0.76 (97) for extent of resolution, and 0.71 (88) for overall quality of problem solving. S. Vuchinich, Angelelli et al. (1996) also calculated Cohen's (1968) weighted kappa. The kappas (with corresponding percentage agreements in parentheses) were: 0.68 (89) for quality of solutions proposed, 0.76 (92) for extent of resolution, 0.71 (88) for perspective taking in problem solving, 0.72 (90) for positive behavior, 0.69 (85) for negative behavior, and 0.81 (90) for participation. The kappas for exact agreement were 0.59 for quality, 0.64 for extent, 0.63 for perspective taking, 0.65 for positive behavior, 0.62 for negative behavior, and 0.73 for participation (S. Vuchinich, Angelelli et al., 1996).

Test–Retest Reliability. Test–retest reliability has been evaluated two ways. Short-term reliability correlations were calculated between the two 10-minute family problem-solving sessions undertaken within the same wave of assessment (one parent-selected problem and one child-selected problem per wave of assessment). For long-term reliability, the ratings of two waves taken 2 years apart were compared. For each wave, scores for the two 10-minute problem-solving sessions were combined. Short-term reliability comparisons have been calculated at 0.70 (S.

Vuchinich et al., 1993) and 0.73 (S. Vuchinich, Angelelli et al., 1996). Long-term reliability correlations have been calculated at 0.50 (S. Vuchinich et al., 1993) and 0.55 (S. Vuchinich, Angelelli et al., 1996). All of these correlations were highly significant and of at least moderate magnitude.

Researchers who use family problem-solving sessions must be concerned that a single 10- or 20-minute session may not give a true reflection of family characteristics. Different topics may trigger different aspects of a family. To guard against this, more than one session from the same family can be coded. S. Vuchinich et al. (1996) calculated stability correlations between problem-solving sessions using different numbers of sessions at each point in time 2 years apart. Time 1–Time 2 correlations of problem-solving scores with one session was 0.28, for two sessions it was 0.41, for three sessions it was 0.54, and for four sessions it was 0.55. The correlations demonstrated support for the psychometric viability of the problem-solving measure, and suggest three sessions may be needed to accurately capture a family's enduring profile of problem-solving effectiveness (S. Vuchinich et al., 1996).

Internal Consistency.   To examine the internal consistency of the family problem-solving measure, S. Vuchinich, Angelelli et al. (1996) calculated a correlation matrix of the subscales (extent of resolution, quality of resolution, and perspective taking) for each of the cells of the basic design. The mean correlation between extent and perspective taking was 0.66, between extent and quality it was 0.72, and between quality and perspective taking it was 0.82. The correlations were consistent with a single underlying concept with varying domains represented by each indicator (S. Vuchinich, Angelelli et al., 1996).

VALIDITY

Predictive validity has been assessed in many studies. S. Vuchinich, Angelelli et al. (1996) used correlations between the family problem-solving measure (using mean scores of the parent-selected and preadolescent-selected sessions at Time 1) and two well-known measures: Family Adaptability and Cohesion Scales–III (FACES–III; Olson, 1986), and Family Environment Scale (FES; Moos & Moos, 1981). The two self-reporting family scales were collected from each parent separately 1 year prior to the second wave assessment. The correlations were comparable between the mother reports and the father reports, with the father reports a little lower. Correlations between family problem-solving scores and mother reports of family characteristics were for 0.35 ($p < .001$) Cohesion, 0.22 ($p < .10$) for Adaptability, -0.45 ($p < .0001$) for Conflict, and -0.29 ($p < .05$) for Control (S. Vuchinich, Angelelli et. al., 1996). There were similar findings for the observational measures of positive and negative behavior, but not for participation. The correlations, overall, support the predictive validity of the problem-solving measure (S. Vuchinich, Angelelli et al., 1996).

In 1995, Vuchinich and Angelelli explored the connection between coalitions in the family and effectiveness of family problem solving. The study used two systems of coding: global (different coders watched an entire session then made ratings about the families) and sequential (each behavior in a session was determined to be positive, negative, or other. This system included both the sociometric and side-taking methods (see S. Vuchinich & Angelelli, 1995, for details). Correlations with family problem-solving effectiveness, child antisocial behavior, and child externalizing were used to assess the predictive validity of the coalition measures. Correlations showed stronger MF coalitions were associated with less effective family problem solving (−0.56 for MF coalition global, and −0.59 for MF coalition sociometric) and having a more antisocial son (0.40 for MF coalition global and .41 for MF coalition sociometric; see Table 6.2 of S. Vuchinich & Angelelli, 1995, for complete data).

Evidence for discriminant validity comes from the S. Vuchinich and Angelelli (1995) study of coalitions and family problem-solving effectiveness. The correlations (previously discussed) could have been due to the presence of increased conflict in families with stronger coalitions instead of the coalitions themselves. To assess that possibility, Vuchinich and Angelelli conducted a multiple regression analysis with effectiveness of family problem solving as the dependent variable. This alternative was not supported. Conflict frequency was found to have no effect on problem solving ($rs = .01$ and $.01$; S. Vuchinich & Angelelli, 1995). With correlations of −0.05 for MF coalition global, 0.56 for MF global sociometric, and −0.35 for antisocial child, it was concluded that MF coalitions could be validly assessed in that context and was associated with problem-solving effectiveness and child antisocial behavior (see Table 6.3 of S. Vuchinich & Angelelli, 1995, for complete data).

STUDIES USING THE FAMPROS

S. Vuchinich et al. (1993) examined how well 68 family triads (mother, father, and preadolescent son) resolved parent–child problems that are often issues at home, in association with the quality of parental relationship. Using regression analysis, four aspects of the parental relationship were assessed (marital satisfaction, parental agreement, conflict during problem solving, and parental coalitions) while controlling for family structure (intact vs. stepfamilies) and child externalizing. The design was longitudinal, with two waves of assessment. The families were assessed when the son was in fourth grade (mean 9.7 years) and 2 years later. Although parental agreement enhanced family problem solving, strong parental coalitions against the preadolescent son inhibit family problem solving. Thus although parental agreement facilitates problem solving, when that agreement takes the form of a coalition, problem solving is inhibited (S. Vuchinich et. al., 1993).

S. Vuchinich et al. (1994) examined the association of coalitions (MF, PC, and parental warmth expressed) with family problem solving in 188 family triads (mother, father or stepfather, and preadolescent son or daughter), 564 participants total. Families either were referred for treatment of behavior problems, had a child at risk for conduct disorder, or were a comparison family. Problem solving was less effective in referred and at-risk families. Strong interparental coalitions were associated with low levels of family problem solving in at-risk and referred families. This effect on family problem solving shows one specific way that family coalitions contribute to deteriorated family functioning. Parental warmth (a composite of mother and father positive behavior toward child FAMPROS codes) was strongly associated with better family problem solving (S. Vuchinich et al., 1994).

S. Vuchinich, Angelelli et al. (1996) longitudinally assessed 63 two-parent families with a preadolescent child when the child was about 9.5 years of age, and again 2 years later. Using structured discussions in the home, links between contextual ecological factors and family problem solving (using coded family sessions and self-report family scales) were examined. The quality of family problem solving declined markedly during preadolescence, in association with changed father and preadolescent participation and affective behavior. When parents chose the topic, problem solving was worse, though not less effective. Alternatively, when the preadolescent chose the topic, both the parents and the adolescent displayed productive participation and affective behavior. Changes in family problem solving, associated with preadolescent autonomy striving, were specified, thereby clarifying the nature of the parent–child relations during that ambivalent time (S. Vuchinich, Angelelli et al., 1996).

The FAMPROS has already proven to be a useful research tool in advancing our understanding of how family interaction develops over time and how it is related to child psychopathology. It is a coding system that promotes the empirical integration of behavioral, family systems, and group process approaches to understanding families. It was designed to be flexible and efficient while retaining good psychometric properties. The challenges of assessing family-level characteristics in family interaction are considerable. The coding systems described in this book demonstrate how these challenges can be met.

EXCERPTS FROM THE FAMPROS BRIEF CODING MANUAL

1–6 POSITIVE BEHAVIOR

Overall, how positive was ...

1. the mother to the son?	1-virtually none
2. the son to the mother?	2-low
3. the father to the son?	3-some
4. the son to the father?	4-moderate
5. the mother to the father?	5-more often than not
6. the father to the mother?	6-high
	7-very high

One type of positive behaviors (A) include, but are not limited to: showing positive affect, warmth, smiling, and displays of affection, giving compliments, displays of high enthusiasm, appearing interested in the other, and so forth.

Positive behaviors (B) also include supporting another, as well as defending or siding with another. Also included is demonstrating generally cooperative behavior, complying with requests/commands, participating, bringing up ideas, and so forth.

Note that the type of behaviors listed in B are, in general, less overtly positive and are scored lower than most type A behaviors.

For example, a child who is demonstrating generally acquiescent behaviors would be scored a 2 or 3 depending on factors such as frequency and sincerity. A child displaying more direct and active cooperativeness and like behaviors could be scored a 4. To get to the 5–6 and 7 range, you need more initiative with sincerity.

For example, a parent's supportive behavior of another parent would be scored a 3 if it generally occurred throughout the interaction. If the parent showed consistent active support for his/her partner (e.g., agreeing with the other, picking up where the other left off), then you would score the parent's [sic] a 4. To get higher than a 4, there must be other direct behaviors.

Note that these behaviors should be directed to another person. For example, a child having a "good time" laughing and joking is not necessarily a positive behavior to the mother or the father.

7–12 NEGATIVE BEHAVIORS

Overall, how negative was …

7. the mother to the son?	1-virtually none
8. the son to the mother?	2-low
9. the father to the son?	3-some
10. the son to the father?	4-moderate
11. the mother to the father?	5-more often than not
12. the father to the mother?	6-high
	7-very high

Negative behaviors include, but are not limited to: showing negative affect, displaying anger, criticizing, accusing, swearing, reprimanding, disagreeing, arguing, complaining, insulting, negative teasing, leading questions, refusing to allow another the opportunity to talk, and negative directive commands. Pay attention to coverbal behaviors such as tone (e.g., neutral vs. harsh, clarifying vs. accusatory).

Negative behaviors also include displaying noncompliant or refusal behaviors (verbal or nonverbal) and demonstrating in general uncooperative behaviors (such as inappropriate responses, inappropriate changes of topic, inappropriate resistance behavior), displaying agitation, aggravation, and so forth. Inappropriate aloofness is coded neg.

Physical displays of aggression (e.g., hitting and kicking) and some physical or coverbal behaviors (e.g., kicking in space, heavy sighing directed toward another, stomping feet) are also considered negative.

19–21 COALITION

Overall, how much were …

19. mother and father in a coalition against the son?	1-not at all
	2-occasionally
20. mother and son in a coalition against the father?	3-sometimes
	4-regularly
21. father and son in a coalition against the mother?	5-more often than not
	6-usually
	7-almost always

Coalition behaviors include: siding with one against the other, supporting one member, agreeing with one member but not the other. The high end of the scale represents examples of coalition behaviors *against* the other. The low end of the scale may reflect some siding-with behaviors more than overt siding against behaviors. Ratings may take into account the frequency or intensity of coalition behaviors. Look for behavioral evidence of a coalition. However the final rating includes your overall impression of the strength of a coalition between two participants against a third. Oppositional behavior against the third party may involve overt disagreement or more subtle behaviors. Active exclusion of the third party from the interaction may involve ignoring their comments, interrupting them, or other subtle tactics.

For example:

a 1   indicates no evidence of a coalition between these two participants.

a 2   indicates that the parties did occasionally agree with each other or were "in synch" for a substantial amount of time.

a 3   a. the two parties sometimes side with each other against the third, or,
b. the two parties each oppose the third person, but don't necessarily agree with each other overtly.

a 4   a. two parties regularly siding with each other against the third person, or,
b. two parties siding with each other while actively excluding the third person.

a 5   frequent agreement between two parties which sometimes opposes the third person.

a 6   consistent agreement between two parties which often opposes the third person.

a 7   very consistent agreement between two parties which almost always opposes the third person.

22–25 PROBLEM SOLVING

22. How was the problem defined:

1. Totally unclear.

2. Somewhat unclear, not defined in session, and while some seemed to understand, others did not.

3. No definition in session, but they all seemed to have same understanding of the problem.

4. Problem was defined some in session: there was some checking to see if all had same understanding.

5. Very well defined.

23. Extent of resolution:

1. No resolution, total disagreement.

2. No resolution, little or no attempt to solve problem.

3. No resolution; tried, but poor skills.

4. No resolution, not enough time (did work towards solution).

5. Somewhat resolved; valid solution(s) proposed.

6. Fairly well resolved.

7. Agreed; problem resolved.

24. Quality of proposed solution(s):

1. No solution(s) proposed. <solution vs. resolution>

2. Very poor solution(s) proposed.

3. Poor solution(s) proposed.

4. Fair solution(s) proposed.

5. Good solution(s) proposed.

6. Very good solution(s) proposed.

7. Excellent solution(s) proposed.

25. Quality of the overall problem solving process:

1. extremely poor

2. very poor

3. poor

4. moderate

5. good

6. very good

7. extremely good

Overall, how well did the participants work towards a solution? Did they define the problem and spend most of the time on the problem? Did they discuss possible solutions to the problem? Was everyone involved in the process? Were the participants receptive to others' views, feelings, and so forth?

ACKNOWLEDGMENTS

The research basis for this coding system was supported by the National Institute of Mental Health through grants to Sam Vuchinich (MH-45073), Gerald R. Patterson (MH-37940), and John Reid (MH-38730). Additional support was provided by the Administration for Children and Families, U.S. Department of Health and Human Services through a grant to Clara Pratt and Claudia Hatmaker (90-CW-1090). The authors also thank the staff of the Family Study Center at Oregon State University.

REFERENCES

Cohen, J. (1968). Weighted kappa: Nominal scale agreement with provisions for scaled disagreement or partial credit. *Psychological Bulletin, 27,* 213–220.

Dishion, T. J., Gardner, K., Patterson, G. R., Reid, J. B., & Thibodeaux, S. (1983). *Family process code.* [Unpublished coding instrument]. (Available from OSLC, 207 E. 5th, Suite 202, Eugene, OR 97401)

Falloon, I. R. H. (1988). Prevention of morbidity in schizophrenia. In I. R. H. Falloon (Ed.), *Handbook of behavioral family therapy* (pp. 316–394). New York: Guilford.

Forgatch, M. S., Fetrow, R., & Lathrop, M. (1984b). *SPI-FI coder impressions* [Unpublished assessment instrument]. (Available from OSLC, 207 E. 5th, Suite 202, Eugene, OR 97401)

Forgatch, M. S., & Patterson, G. R. (1989). *Parents and adolescents living together: Part 2. Family problem solving.* Eugene, OR: Castalia.

Hetherington, E. M., & Clingempeel, W. G. (1992). Coping with marital transitions. *Monographs for the Society for Research in Child Development, 57* (Serial No. 227).

Hibbs, E. D., & Jensen, P. S. (1996). *Psychosocial treatments for child and adolescent disorders: Empirically based strategies for clinical practice.* Washington, DC: American Psychological Association.

Kawamoto, W. (1996). *Marital satisfaction and maternal involvement in Native American and European endogamous families.* Unpublished doctoral thesis, Department of Human Development and Family Sciences, Oregon State University, Corvallis.

Markman, H. J., & Notarius, C. I. (1987). Coding marital and family interaction: Current status. In T. Jacob (Ed.), *Family interaction and family psychopathology: Theories, methods, and findings* (pp. 329–390). New York: Plenum.

Moos, R. H., & Moos, B. S. (1981). *Family environment scale manual.* Palo Alto, CA: Consulting Psychologists Press.

Olson, D. H. (1986). Circumplex model VII: Validation studies and FACES III. *Family Process, 25,* 337–351.

Patterson, G. R. (1982). *Coercive family process.* Eugene, OR: Castalia.

Patterson, G. R., Reid, J. B., & Dishion, T. J. (1992). *Antisocial boys.* Eugene, OR: Castalia.

Reiss, D. (1981). *The family's construction of reality.* Cambridge, MA: Harvard University Press.

Reiss, D., & Klein, D. (1989). Paradigm and pathogenesis: A family-centered approach to problems of etiology and treatment of psychiatric disorders. In T. Jacob (Ed.), *Family interaction and psychopathology: Theories, methods, and findings* (pp. 203–258). New York: Plenum.

Robin, A. L., & Foster S. L. (1989). *Negotiating parent–adolescent conflict: A behavioral-family systems approach.* New York: Guilford.

Selman, R. L., Beardslee, W., Schultz, L. H., Krupa, M., & Podorefsky, D. (1986). Assessing adolescent interpersonal negotiation strategies: Toward the integration of structural and functional models. *Developmental Psychology, 22,* 450–459.

Strodtbeck, F. L. (1954). The family as a three person group. *American Sociological Review, 19,* 23–29.

Vuchinich, S. (1987). Starting and stopping spontaneous family conflict. *Journal of Marriage and the Family, 49,* 591–601.

Vuchinich, S. (1999). *Problem solving in families: Research and practice.* Thousand Oaks, CA: Sage.

Vuchinich, S. & Angelelli, J. (1995). Family interaction during problem solving. In A. Vangelisti & M. A. Fitzpatrick (Eds.), *Perspectives on family communication* (pp. 177–205). Thousand Oaks, CA: Sage.

Vuchinich, S., Angelelli, J., & Gatherum, A. (1996). Context and development in family problem solving with preadolescent children. *Child Development, 67,* 1276–1288.

Vuchinich, S., Emery, R. E., & Cassidy, J. (1988). Family members as third parties in dyadic family conflict: Strategies, alliances and outcomes. *Child Development, 59,* 1293–1302.

Vuchinich, S., Vuchinich, R., & Wood, B. (1993). The interparental relationship and family problem solving with preadolescent males. *Child Development, 64,* 1389–1400.

Vuchinich, S., Wood, B., & Vuchinich, R. (1994). Coalition and family problem solving with preadolescents in referred, at-risk, and comparison families. *Family Process, 33,* 409–424.

Vuchinich, S., Wood, B., & Angelelli, J. (1996). Coalitions and family problem solving in the psychosocial treatment of adolescents. In E. D. Hibbs & P. S. Jensen (Eds.), *Psychosocial treatments for child and adolescent disorders: Empirically based strategies for clinical practice* (pp. 497–520). Washington DC: American Psychological Association.

5

The System for Coding Interactions and Family Functioning

Kristin M. Lindahl
Neena M. Malik
University of Miami

The purpose of the System for Coding Interactions and Family Functioning (SCIFF) is to behaviorally assess family functioning across multiple ethnic groups, integrating both family systems and social learning perspectives. Originally developed for a multiethnic study of externalizing behaviors in school-age boys, the SCIFF assesses universal aspects of family functioning and is applicable with a wide range of populations. It has been found to be reliable with one- and two-parent families, as well as with a variety of ethnic groups, including

Euro-American, Hispanic-American, and African-American families. The SCIFF was designed to code family problem discussions but also has been used successfully to code family play interactions (Kitzmann, 1998).

THEORETICAL FOUNDATIONS

Theoretical foundations for this coding system primarily are systemic family theory (e.g., Boscolo, Cecchin, Hoffman, & Penn, 1987), structural family theory (e.g., Minuchin, 1974), and social learning theory (e.g., Baumrind, 1989;

Patterson, 1982). One of the goals of this system is to operationalize in terms of observable behavioral patterns those aspects of family functioning that have been deemed theoretically important to child mental heath outcomes. In the coding system, therefore, there is a mix of codes ranging from an overall affective and structural or organizational sense of family relationships (to answer more family systems–oriented questions) to specific frequency counts of behaviors hypothesized to be part of sequential or reciprocal patterns of dysfunction, such as parental coerciveness and child oppositionality (relating to questions that are more social learning focused).

The SCIFF codes were developed to assess functioning in each family subsystem: the family as a whole and each parent–child dyad. Additionally, because of the focus of our work on child behavioral and emotional outcomes, five codes are specific to the child's behavior in the interaction. Across triadic, dyadic, and individual child codes, a strong focus on capturing the affective climate of the family exists. Both the tenor and range of affect demonstrated by family members within a problem-oriented discussion are important to understanding how a family copes with stress (albeit stress simulated by a laboratory-based discussion). A highly negative interaction or an interaction with a restricted range of affective expression likely indicates poor adaptability and restricted communication in the face of stress, which has been linked theoretically to a family being stuck in maladaptive interactional patterns (see Hoffman, 1981).

In addition to the assessment of the emotional climate of the family, the SCIFF includes codes that relate to the overall structure and organization of the family, tapping into the flexibility–rigidity dimension of functioning, as well as the set of rules that govern family communication and decision making. Though clear and appropriate boundaries distinguishing family subsystems from one another and clear rules that govern behaviors are thought to be critical for healthy family and child development (Minuchin, 1974), it is also important that these boundaries or rules do not become so rigid (or so loose) that the individuality of family members becomes compromised (Minuchin, Rosman, & Baker, 1978). Evidence of flexibility within a homeostatic range of functioning (operationalized in the SCIFF by, e.g., a rating of "balanced" in the Alliance Formation code) indicates the potential for adaptability hypothesized to be necessary for continued development and healthy functioning for all organisms, including families (e.g., Bateson, 1972).

In addition to being guided by structural and systemic family theories, the SCIFF also incorporates specific behaviors hypothesized by social learning theory to be related to maladaptive patterns of family and parent–child interactions, such as coercive, rejecting, and triangulating behaviors on the part of parents and oppositionality/defiance on the part of children (Patterson, 1982). Examining how these specific behaviors (in addition to the affective climate of the whole family) occur within family interactions allows the simultaneous evaluation of the relative predictive utility of both triadic and dyadic family system factors and child functioning.

DEVELOPMENT OF THE SCIFF

The original study for which the SCIFF was developed assessed family functioning in the following manner. Parents and one of their children between 7 and 12 years of age were instructed to discuss a recent family argument that involved all three family members (or two, if it was a single-parent family). If there was more than one child in the family between the ages of 7 and 12, parents chose which child would participate. The SCIFF was developed for use with two parents and one child but also may be used in single-parent families or families where more than one child participates in the discussion. Topics were chosen by the family before videotaping began. Families were instructed to review the topic of the conflict, what each person's role in the conflict was, and how they would like to resolve similar disagreements in the future. Discussions lasted 10 to 12 minutes.

A problem discussion was selected, as opposed to an unstructured task, for several reasons. Given the extensive evidence found in the marital and parenting literatures of the ability of negative affect and negative behavioral exchanges to predict to or correlate with clinical phenomena (e.g., Cummings & Davies, 1994), and our interest in understanding better which family processes are related to child maladaptation, a task that had the potential to elicit negativity was required. In addition, an effort was made to develop a task with high ecological validity, and we expected that a family discussing a problem might more closely mirror naturally occurring interactions in the home than a play task, for example.

DESCRIPTION OF THE SCIFF

One of our goals in writing in the SCIFF was to develop an observational system that would capture the richness of family interaction without resorting to a microanalytic level or a series of individual or dyadic codes only. With that goal in mind, we created both family-level triadic (mother–father–child) codes as well as dyadic (marital) and individual (mother, father, child) codes. Verbal and nonverbal elements of communication are incorporated in the codes of the SCIFF.

The Family Codes

The SCIFF contains six family-level codes: Negativity/Conflict, Positive Affect, Cohesiveness, Focus of Problem, Parenting Style, and Alliance Formation. The first four of these variables are rated on a 5-point Likert-type scale where 1= very low and 5= high, and the latter two are categorical codes. Negativity/Conflict and Positive Affect assess the overall affective valence of the family interaction. Negativity/Conflict assesses the level of tension in the family and includes clear expressions of anger and hostility, as well as more subtle forms of negative affect including undercurrents of tension and behaviors such as a slightly raised voice, impatience, and annoyance. Positive Affect reflects the overall positive emotional tone in the family, and includes expressions of happiness, affection, and contentment. Cohesiveness represents the sense of unity, togetherness, and closeness within a family. Cohesiveness also represents a sense of respect and reciprocity among family members. Focus of Problem evaluates the focal point of the family discussion, ranging from child centered or family centered. That is, the family may characterize the problem as exclusively resulting from the child's behavior, or responsibility for the problem may be spread among multiple family members.

Parenting Style and Alliance Formation are categorical variables that assess family structure, including communication, decision making, and the interrelationships among the subsystems within the family. Parenting Style assesses the process of decision making between parents and child, the type of authority maintained by parents, and the extent to which each family member has the opportunity to contribute to the family discussion. There are four different parenting styles: Democratic, Hierarchical/Autocratic, Lax, and Inconsistent. In a democratic family, each family member feels free to offer opinions, and it appears that for the most part, each member's opinions are listened to and considered by other family members. In a hierarchical or autocratic family, one or both parents unmistakably hold authority. Other family members are respectful of the authority figure(s) and rarely interrupt or persistently challenge the authority figure. A lax parenting style is one in which it appears that there is no one in clear control, or one in which the child seems to be in control. An inconsistent family pattern of interaction is identified by clashing parenting styles in which parents undermine or contradict each other's parenting efforts, or by significant inconsistency or unpredictability in the parents' behaviors.

It is important to note that the Hierarchical/Autocratic rating has been written to include a range of behaviors consistent with a hierarchical family structure but excludes certain negative behaviors traditionally described in the literature as hierarchical or autocratic, such as harsh, domineering, and unresponsive parenting (e.g., Maccoby & Martin, 1983). A strong emphasis in the development of this coding system was on understanding cultural variations in family structure and interrelationships among family members. With literature indicating that

Hispanic-American families may be more likely to have hierarchical family structures (e.g., Vega, 1990), it was important to ensure that the assessment of family structure and other aspects of family functioning would be appropriately captured within the codes without any ethnicity bias. As such, the SCIFF separates affective and structural family codes and is written so that, for example, a democratic and a hierarchical family may be coded as equally cohesive.

Alliance Formation assesses the nature of the alliances in the family (i.e., marital, mother–child, father–child). A family is either "Balanced" or it is one of four choices, Marital (Detouring-Attacking), Parent–Child (either father/child or mother/child), or Disengaged. In balanced families, although the parents maintain a degree of authority, no one dyad has disproportionately more influence or power in the interaction than any other dyad. In families with a Marital/Detouring-Attacking alliance, the marital dyad is clearly the most powerful, influential dyad in the interaction. The parents may seem to start getting into conflict themselves, but they reroute the conflict toward the child. In families with a Parent–Child Alliance, the primary alliance appears to be between one of the parents and the child. The parent (mother or father) and child appear notably closer and/or more affectionate with each other. There is a degree of enmeshment between one parent and the child, and the other parent appears almost to be a "third wheel." In families with Disengaged Alliances, it is difficult to identify any strong alliances. There is little closeness among family members.

The Dyadic and Parent Codes

In addition to the aforementioned family-level assessments, the SCIFF also includes one dyadic (marital) and five individual parent codes. The marital dyad is coded for the quality of communication that occurs. This code assesses the degree to which the marital partners are able to express their feelings and opinions (e.g., self-disclose) in a constructive, nonjudgmental, and respectful manner. Being attuned and emotionally responsive to each other is also considered to be part of good communication. Given that the focus of the discussion is the whole family, marital communication may well center on the child. Therefore, good marital communication statements are supportive with regard to parenting, even if there is disagreement (e.g., "I have to admit that I totally disagreed with how you handled _____ yesterday, but what you did does make sense to me now. I know we both do our best with the kids").

There are five parent codes, Rejection/Invalidation, Coerciveness, Triangulation, Withdrawal, and Emotional Support, and mothers and fathers are rated separately for each code. (If more than one child is present, each parent should be rated on each code for each child.) Parental Rejection/Invalidation is primarily a content code based on the frequency and intensity with which a parent makes critical, insulting, blaming, rude, or insensitive statements to the child. Coerciveness is a content code that is based on the frequency with which a parent makes threatening or manipulative statements to the child, bullies the child, or uses a threatening tone or body language. For example, a parent can be coercive by making statements such as, "Only babies fight over toys with their brother. You don't want to be a baby, do you?"

Triangulation is a content code that is based on the frequency with which a parent tries to convince the child to side with him or her (and against the other parent), or when a parent tries to obtain support and sympathy from the child when in conflict with the other parent. A good example of triangulation is when one parent says to the other parent, "I won't listen when you yell" and turns to the child and says, "Your mother is impossible to listen to when she yells, isn't she?" Withdrawal assesses the degree to which a parent seems to be evasive, retreat into a shell, become detached, back off, or shut down, physically or emotionally. Emotional Support assesses parental emotional support and affective attunement or sensitivity, and the parent's ability to recognize and meet the child's emotional needs.

The Child Codes

There are five individual child codes, three of which assess the child's affective state (Anger and Frustration, Sadness, and Positive Affect), and two of which assess the child's behavior (Withdrawal, see the adult code previously discussed, and Opposition/Defiance). Anger and Frustration assesses verbalizations, overt behavior, and emotional expressions indicative of anger, tension, or frustration. Sadness assesses the overall quantity of sadness, anguish, pain, regret, and remorse displayed by the child. Positive Affect reflects the degree to which the child seems happy or satisfied, or expresses warmth. Opposition/ Defiance assesses the degree to which the child displays oppositional, noncompliant, or belligerent behavior.

CODER TRAINING

When undertaking observational procedures in research, one of the most important decisions facing researchers is deciding who will do the coding. We have found undergraduates students to be reliable coders in using the SCIFF. If one has the luxury of choosing between undergraduate and graduate coders, the preference would in most cases be the graduate students, as it has been our experience that they require less training time. In order for undergraduates to be reliable, extensive training and supervision are necessary. Training lasts as long as it takes to get coders up to adequate reliability (correlations of .70 or higher with the gold standard tapes). Typically, undergraduates need to code a total of 10 to 12 tapes before they are considered reliable on every code in the manual. Graduate students usually require fewer training tapes, about six.

When doing research with a multiethnic group of families, it is important to ensure that the group of coders is multiethnic, as well. In addition, the ethnicity of the coders as much as possible should reflect the ethnicity of the study participants, which will vary by subject population and geographical location. For example, the original study for which the SCIFF was developed took place in Miami, Florida, where the population is primarily Hispanic, with the next highest ethnic group consisting of Anglos, then African Americans. Within the Hispanic ethnic group, the majority of the population is Cuban American, with smaller groups of South American and other Hispanic groups. The ethnicity of the subjects in the study generally matched the demographics of the population. As such, the coders for the original study were Anglo and Hispanic primarily, with Cuban-American as well as other Hispanic-American groups represented in the group of coders. As some of the families in the study were bilingual, several coders were bilingual, as well. By including a multiethnic team of coders, any cultural nuances in family interactions are more likely to be better understood and more accurately coded.

In our laboratory, training has involved the following. First, the manual (Lindahl & Malik, 1996) is reviewed in detail to familiarize coders with the codes. The manual provides a one- to two-paragraph general overview of each code as well as detailed descriptions of each of the five anchor points on the 1–5 scale used for the continuous codes and detailed paragraphs describing each of the Parenting Style and Alliance Formation types. Second, four or five previously rated videotaped interactions are reviewed, item by item, with the trainees (these are our "gold standard" tapes used with all trainees). Third, as a group, trainees code two to three criterion tapes with one of the authors of the coding system present (or a graduate student who is reliable). All codes are discussed and incorrect answers are analyzed to clarify misunderstandings about the codes. Fourth, trainees are assigned four to five criterion tapes to code individually, and coding mistakes are discussed at a weekly coding meeting. Trainees are instructed to watch each tape at least three times. While in training, trainees are required to justify their ratings in writing for each code. They must supply verbatim quotes or detailed behavioral observations from the tape to justify each of their ratings, and thus typically, there is significant starting and stopping of the tape while coding. It is not unusual for coders in training to take over an hour to code one 10-minute interaction. After coders achieve an adequate level of reliability, coders are assigned two to three tapes per week. Once training is completed, weekly meetings are used to review disagreements and to prevent observer drift.

As with most coding systems, the safest way to ensure that coders from other labs are using the SCIFF reliably, meaning that they are using the system in the same way we have, is to have consultation from our lab. Though some other labs have used the SCIFF coding system with audiotapes, we do not recommend this, as this procedure makes it much more difficult to code affect. We do not currently have training tapes that we make available outside our own coding lab, but we do consult with others using the SCIFF and have offered to code tapes from others' labs to assist them in establishing reliability. Training can also be done by just using the manual, which some other labs have done. With this approach, though it is difficult to know whether interlab reliability exists, our colleagues have reported being able to obtain reliability within their own lab (M. Clements, personal communication, November, 1998).

THE CODING PROCESS

The process of coding for an experienced coder is similar to the procedure described earlier for training, except that coding takes less time. As stated previously, coding is conducted from videotapes of family problem discussions. The SCIFF is probably too complex of a coding system with which to do live (real-time) coding (Markman & Notarius, 1987), unless just a very few codes are used. Each 10- to 12-minute interaction takes an experienced coder between 35 and 45 minutes to code if all codes are used. Coders watch the tape and take notes on important quotes or behaviors, stopping and starting the tape as necessary. We require coders to watch each tape a minimum of three times if all of the codes are being used, but they are permitted to watch each tape as many times as they like. An experienced coder does not need to take notes that are as detailed as when in training (mostly because an experienced coder is more "expert" at discriminating the most important elements of the interaction). After each viewing, coders make all the ratings they feel they have the information to make. The tape is then watched a third time to verify the coding or to watch specifically for whatever codes are still uncertain (for most families no more than one to three codes are left at this point). We do not specify the order in which raters need to evaluate the codes, as different codes stand out for different families. When disagreements arise between coders, they are discussed at the weekly coding meeting and a group decision is made regarding the most appropriate code to use for data analysis.

RELIABILITY

To evaluate reliability and validity parameters of the SCIFF, a validation study of 70 families was conducted (38 Hispanic-American families, 25 Euro-American families, and 7 African-American families). Good interrater reliability was found for most of the SCIFF codes. Reliability analyses were initially calculated separately for the Euro-American and Hispanic-American families in the validation study. As similar reliability figures were found for both ethnic groups, only the overall analyses are presented here. Pearson correlations indicated adequate interrater reliability for Negativity/Conflict $r = .77$), Positive Affect $r = .70$), Cohesiveness $r = .74$), Marital Communication $r = .72$), Parental Rejection $r = .75$ for fathers, $r = .80$ for mothers), Parental Coerciveness $r = .72$ for fathers, $r = .77$ for mothers), Emotional Support $r = .70$ for fathers, $r = .71$ for mothers), Father Withdrawal $r = .73$), and marginal interrater reliability for Parental Triangulation $r = .60$ for fathers, .65 for mothers) and Mother Withdrawal $r = .50$). Satisfactory interrater reliability was found for the child codes ($rs = .65$ to .80). The categorical variables of Parenting Style and Coalition Formation also were coded reliably (kappas = .75 and .74, respectively).

We did not design the coding system with a priori hypotheses about summary or composite codes, and in general, the SCIFF codes are not highly interrelated (Pearson correlations range from $r = .03$ to $r = .66$, with a mean $r = .38$). The codes that tend to be most highly interrelated are: Cohesiveness and Negativity/Conflict $r = -.66$) and Cohesiveness and Parental Support $r = .60$ for mothers and $r = .64$ for fathers).

VALIDITY

Evidence for concurrent and construct validity for the family (triadic) and parenting codes comes largely from comparisons made between the SCIFF codes and parents' self-report of various marital and family processes. In the validation study, in addition to the 10-minute family (triadic) problem-solving discussion, couples were also observed during a 10-minute marital problem-solving discussion. This marital discussion was coded using the System for Coding Interactions and Dyads (Malik & Lindahl, 1996), which is a companion system to the SCIFF for marital dyads. Parents completed a measure of whole-family functioning, the Family Functioning Scale (FFS; Bloom, 1985), as well as measures of marital distress and conflict, including the Marital Satisfaction Inventory (Snyder, 1981) and the Marital Agendas Protocol (MAP; Notarius & Vanzetti, 1983).

To assess concurrent validity for the SCIFF codes of Negativity/Conflict, Positive Affect, Cohesiveness, and Parenting Style, parents completed the family conflict, cohesion, Authoritarian Parenting, Democratic Parenting, and Laissez-Faire Parenting subscales from the FFS. Both mothers' and fathers' report of the level of whole-family conflict and family cohesion at home correlated significantly (and in predicted directions) with the SCIFF triadic codes of negativity (conflict: $rs = .35$ and .54; cohesion: $rs = -.37$ and $-.42$), positive affect (conflict $rs = -.33$ and $-.40$; cohesion: $rs = .35$ and .45), and cohesiveness (conflict: $rs = -.45$ and $-.56$; cohesion $rs = .46$ and .50).

Multivariate analysis of variance (MANOVA) indicated the four SCIFF Parenting Styles (Democratic, Hierarchical, Lax, or Inconsistent) to differ significantly on the FFS parenting scales (Authoritarian, Democratic, and Laissez-Faire) ($F(6, 176) = 3.82, p < .001$). A series of follow-up post hoc comparisons indicated that fathers from families coded as Hierarchical described their families as more authoritarian than did fathers in Lax families ($p < .01$); both mothers and fathers from SCIFF-rated Democratic families described their families as more democratic than either Lax or Inconsistent families ($p < .05$ to $p < .01$); and fathers from Lax and fathers and mothers from Inconsistent families reported greater levels of Laissez-Faire parenting than parents from families coded as Hierarchical or Democratic ($p < .01$ to $p < .001$).

In the validation study, concurrent measures for assessing family coalitions or of the parenting dimensions of rejection, coercion, triangulation, withdrawal, or support were not included, in large part due to a concern regarding a potential bias in self-reporting on these dimensions given the strong social desirability bias for some of them, in addition to the inherent difficulty for parents to describe ongoing interactional processes. For these codes, we assessed construct validity by examining whether the SCIFF ratings were related to other marital and family measures in a theoretically meaningful way. Due to a relatively small number of father–child coalitions, we grouped the mother–child and father–child coalitions together for the validity analyses, thus creating four coalition types: balanced, marital, parent–child, and disengaged.

MANOVA indicated that the four SCIFF Alliance Formation types differ significantly on self-report measures of marital distress and marital conflict and observational measures (SCID) of marital conflict and cohesion ($F(6, 176) = 5.45, p < .001$). Follow-up comparisons indicated that mothers and fathers from families with Parent–Child or Disengaged alliances experienced clinically significant levels of marital distress and were more maritally distressed than parents from families with balanced or marital alliances ($p < .05$ to $p < .001$). Mothers and fathers from families with Parent–Child or Disengaged alliances were also found to report more marital conflict on the MAP than parents from families with balanced or marital alliances ($p < .05$ to $p < .001$). Mothers and fathers from families with Disengaged alliances were also found to report more conflict over childrearing than parents from families with balanced, marital, or parent–child alliances ($p < .05$ to $p < .001$). Observed marital cohesion was significantly higher, and observed marital conflict and negative escalation were significantly lower, in families with balanced alliances than in families with marital, parent–child, or disengaged alliances ($p < .05$ to $p < .001$).

For the five parenting codes, as hypothesized, mothers' and fathers' reports of family conflict were significantly positively related ($rs = .23$ to $.47$) to rejection (fathers), coercion (mothers and fathers), triangulation (mothers and fathers), and withdrawal (fathers), and negatively related ($rs = -.33$ to $-.50$) to emotional support (mothers and fathers). Mothers' and fathers' reports of family cohesion were found to be significantly negatively related ($rs = -.21$ to $-.44$) to rejection (fathers), coercion (fathers), triangulation (mothers and fathers), and withdrawal (mothers and fathers), and positively related ($rs = .23$ to $.40$) to emotional support (mothers and fathers).

STUDIES USING THE SCIFF

The SCIFF has been used in several studies. Lindahl (1998) studied marital, parent–child, and family-level processes for four groups of 7- to 12-year-old boys and their families: boys with no behavioral problems (control), boys with behavioral problems consistent with Attention deficit hyperactivity disorder (ADHD), boys with behavioral problems consistent with Oppositional defiant disorder (ODD), and boys with behavioral problems consistent with ADHD and ODD. Using measures of marital functioning and the SCIFF family codes, a discriminant analysis was able to correctly classify families into one of the four behavior problem groups with nearly 90% accuracy. The combination of SCIFF coercive parenting and conflictual family relationships separated the control group from the three clinical groups, whereas it was the combination of SCIFF family cohesiveness and SCIFF lax and inconsistent parenting that best distinguished the three clinical groups from one another.

Lindahl and Malik (1999a) used self-report and observational measures to explore associations among marital conflict, triadic family processes (as assessed by the SCIFF), and child adjustment in Hispanic-American, Euro-American, and biethnic families. One hundred and thirteen families with a school-age son participated. A family problem-solving discussion, following the format described earlier in this chapter, was used to assess family functioning. A hierarchical parenting style was found to be maladaptive for Euro-American families, but not for Hispanic-American families. Marital and disengaged family alliances were associated with externalizing behavior for all ethnic groups. Ethnicity was not found to moderate the relationship between marital conflict and family functioning. Greater levels of marital conflict were associated with disengaged family interactions and also with lax/inconsistent parenting across all ethnic groups.

Couples' means of resolving marital conflict was found to be related to how parents related to their child during the triadic family discussion (Lindahl & Malik, 1999b). Destructive forms of marital conflict were associated with the SCIFF parenting codes (e.g., rejection, coercion) for fathers. If fathers were unhappy in their marriage, then marital conflict also was found to be correlated with lower levels of emotional support and paternal withdrawal. Euro-American mothers also tended to withdraw from their children when marital conflict was highly aversive. Fathers who were in marriages characterized by a struggle between the spouses for control over decision making were also coercive with their children.

Lindahl, Clements, and Markman (1997) assessed longitudinally whether couples' dysregulated negative affect before parenthood was predictive of conflict, as well as diminished affective quality, in family relationships 5 years later. Observations of 25 couples' marital communication were made before parenthood and again 5 years later, when data also were collected on parent–child and family interactions. Family interactions were coded using a precursor to the SCIFF. Husbands' prechild marital behavior and couples' prechild negative escalation were predictive of husbands' conflict and triangulation of the child into marital conflict. Alliance formation in the family was predicted by prechild negative escalation.

EXCERPTS FROM THE SCIFF CODING MANUAL

Two family codes, Cohesiveness and Parenting Style, and one parent code, Triangulation, are included here to give the reader a better sense of the codes contained in the SCIFF:

Cohesiveness

Cohesiveness represents the sense of unity, togetherness, and closeness within a family. The degree of cohesiveness in a family is related to the extent to which family members are affectionate, respectful, and warm with each other. For highly cohesive families, there is a sense of mutual appreciation between the family members as they work together toward a common goal. Family members will either appear to be comfortable, unified, and close with one another, or the family interaction will be marked by interpersonal distance, awkwardness, and stiffness. In such families, members will often appear disengaged and disconnected from one another.

1 - *Very Low.* In this code, all of the family members appear disengaged from one another; interpersonal distance, aloofness, stiffness, or awkwardness characterize the relationships within the family. Little warmth or closeness is seen in most of the interaction, such that rarely do family members demonstrate physical or verbal affection with one another. There is a sense that the individuals in the family are having difficulty working together and functioning together as a unit while discussing a family problem.

2 - *Low.* For the most part, the family appears fragmented, rather than cohesive. There are moments when the family appears unified, but these moments are infrequent and do not characterize the interaction. This code may also be given if it appears

that there is interpersonal distance, aloofness, or awkwardness in at least one or two of the dyads, but not all of three of them (e.g., mother and child appear close, but there is distance in the father/child and/or marital dyad(s)). There may be brief moments when family members clearly "connect" with one another.

3 - *Moderate.* For this code, in each of the three dyads (i.e., mother/child, father/child, and marital) there must be observable moments of closeness, unity, and cohesion. However, there are times when the family appears fragmented, rather than cohesive. Moments of interpersonal distance, stiffness, and/or awkwardness may be observed. The main difference between a code of 2 and a code of 3 is that for a family to achieve a code of 2, it should appear that the family is basically fragmented but has moments of cohesion, and for a 3, it should appear that the family basically appears to function as a unit, but the depth of the connection among family members is lacking or difficulty to ascertain.

4 - *Moderately High.* Family members generally appear connected and to function well as a unit, though on rare occasions, moments of awkwardness or interpersonal distance may be observed. These difficult moments never reach a level that would be labeled fragmented. The interaction may not always be smooth, but the spirit of unity and togetherness among family members is relatively consistent. The family members appear generally to be comfortable and close with one another, and appear to have an underlying connection, even when discussing difficult topics.

5 - *High.* Family members are connected and function very well together as a unit. They appear to be comfortable and close with one another and to clearly be working toward a common goal in their discussion. The strength of the connection between them is obvious. Family members remain strongly connected even when discussing difficult topics. The interaction likely runs very smoothly. This rating should be given if the above are true, with the understanding that the interaction may not always be positive given the difficult nature of the task.

Parenting Style

This code assesses the process of decision-making between parents and children and the nature of communication patterns among family members. This code also measures the type of authority maintained by parents in the interaction. Part of this code includes the extent to which each family member has a role in or contributes to the family discussion. Each family is assigned one of four different parenting styles (autocratic/hierarchical, democratic, lax, or inconsistent). If a family is assigned the autocratic code, who is exerting authority in the family (i.e., mother, father, or both parents) must also be indicated on the scoring sheet.

Hierarchical Parenting Style. In a hierarchical family one or both parents unmistakably hold authority. The child clearly has less influence in the discussion than his parent(s). Though the opinions of others may be carefully attended to, the parent(s)' opinions are clearly the most important. With a hierarchical family style, parents maintain their authority and are responded to as an authority figure by the rest of the family. That is, other family members tend to be respectful to the authority figure and rarely interrupt or persistently challenge the authority figure, though they may complain or voice dissent. Rules and punishment tend not to be arrived at through consensus.

Democratic Parenting Style. In a democratic family, all family members work together to identify a problem and discuss possible solutions. Each member plays a part in the decision-making process. It appears that each family member feels free to offer opinions, and it appears that for the most part, each member's opinions are respected and considered by other family members. In a democratic family, even when one or two members seem to be in control, they elicit the opinions of others. Democratic parents may maintain a certain level of authority, but rules and punishments are discussed as a family and may be arrived at through consensus. *Note*: It is appropriate that parents have more power than their children. Parents must maintain a certain level of authority if they are to be effective in teaching their children appropriate behavior. Taking this into account, this code reflects the extent to which a child is given a voice in issues that are discussed and decisions that are made.

Lax Parenting Style. A lax family style is one in which it appears that there is no one in clear control, or one in which the child seems to be in control. There are several reasons why a family may be coded as lax. Parents may neglect to exert authority over a child who is misbehaving, disrespectful, or off-task in the interaction. Parents' attempts to assert authority, if they exist, are ineffective and/or disregarded by the child, but not undermined by the other parent. Parents may make few demands for appropriate behavior, allowing their child to regulate his/her own actions. Parents may appear to be passive or somewhat hapless in attempting to structure the discussion or obtain their child's cooperation. The child may be disruptive of the discussion or bring up unrelated topics, thus disorganizing the discussion. The child often is inappropriately controlling the discussion.

Inconsistent Parenting Style. An inconsistent family pattern of interaction is identifiable by clashing parenting styles in which parents are likely to undermine each other's parenting efforts. For example, one parent may attempt to exert authority, but the other parent ignores or thwarts this effort. Parents may also contradict each other (e.g., have different opinions about appropriate discipline or how much a particular problem is the child's fault). An inconsistent family style can also include situations in which parents contradict themselves or meet criteria for two or more categories. For example, a parent(s) may start out in a very lax manner, but become increasingly more directive and strict with the child as the interaction progresses. There is an element of unpredictability to a parent or parents' behavior.

Parent Triangulation

This is a content code that is based on the frequency with which a parent tries to bring the child over to his/her side of an argument. Triangulation describes family communication patterns in which the parents appear to be in conflict with each other, and each tries to obtain support and sympathy from the child. The parental conflict may be obvious or subtle (overt or covert), but the purpose of the triangulation by the parent is to get the child to be on their side against the other parent. The child may appear to be torn between one parent and the other and may exhibit signs of distress in being forced to choose one parent or the other. For example, a parent may say something such as, "I don't think I did that at all. (Child), have you ever seen me do anything like that?"). Statements such as, "You never want to do anything with me, you always want to do things with your mother," "(Child's name), I never punish you like that, do I?" and, "You do the same thing with (child's name), as you do with me, and it doesn't work with either of us, does it (child's name)?" are other examples of triangulation.

1 - *Very Low*. The parent does not make any triangulating statements.

2 - *Low*. The parent makes 1 triangulating statement.

3 - *Moderate*. The parent twice is observed to make triangulating statements.

4 - *Moderately High*. The parent 3 times is observed to make triangulating statements.

5 - *High*. The parent 4 or more times is observed to make triangulating statements.

ACKNOWLEDGMENTS

Funding for the research described in this chapter was provided by a General Research Support Award from the University Research Council at the University of Miami and by Grant MH54631 R03 from the National Institute of Mental Health.

REFERENCES

Bateson, G. (1972). *Steps to an ecology of mind*. New York: Ballantine Books.

Baumrind, D. (1989). Rearing competent children. In W. Damon (Ed.), *Child development today and tomorrow* (pp. 349–378). San Francisco: Jossey-Bass.

Bloom, B. L. (1985). Factor analysis of self-report measures of family functioning. *Family Process, 24*, 225–239.

Boscolo, L., Cecchin, G., Hoffman, L., & Penn, P. (1987). *Milan systemic family therapy: Conversations in theory and practice*. New York: Basic Books.

Cummings, E. M., & Davies, P. T. (1994). *Children and marital conflict: The impact of family dispute and resolution*. New York: Guilford.

Hoffman, L. (1981). *Foundations of family therapy: A conceptual framework for systems change*. New York: Basic Books.

Kitzmann, K. (1998, March). *Disruptions in parenting observed immediately after negative marital exchanges in a laboratory setting*. Paper presented at the Conference on Human Development, Mobile, AL.

Lindahl, K. M. (1998). Family process variables and children's disruptive behavior problems. *Journal of Family Psychology, 12*, 1–17.

Lindahl, K. M., Clements, M., & Markman, H. J. (1997). Predicting marital and parent functioning in dyads and triads: A longitudinal investigation of marital processes. *Journal of Clinical Family Psychology, 11*, 139–151.

Lindahl, K. M., & Malik, N. M. (1996). *System for Coding Interactions and Family Functioning (SCIFF)*. Unpublished manual, University of Miami, Miami, FL.

Lindahl, K. M., & Malik, N. M. (1999a). Marital conflict, family processes, and boys' externalizing behavior in Hispanic American and European American and families. *Journal of Clinical Child Psychology, 28*, 12–24.

Lindahl, K. M., & Malik, N. M. (1999b). Observations of marital conflict and power: Relations with parenting in the triad. *Journal of Marriage and the Family, 61*, 320–330.

Maccoby, E. E., & Martin, J. A. (1983). Socialization in the context of the family: Parent–child interaction. In P. H. Mussen (Series Ed.) & M. Hetherington (Vol. Ed.), *Hand-*

book of child psychology: Vol. 4. Socialization, personality, and social development (4th ed., pp. 1–101). New York: Wiley.

Malik, N. M., & Lindahl, K. M. (1996). *System for Coding Interactions in Dyads (SCID)*. Unpublished manual, University of Miami, Coral Gables, FL.

Markman, H. J., & Notarius, C. I. (1987). Coding marital and family interaction: Current status. In T. Jacob (Ed.), *Family interaction and psychopathology* (pp. 329–390). New York: Plenum.

Minuchin, S. (1974). *Families and family therapy.* Cambridge, MA: Harvard University Press.

Minuchin, S., Rosman, B. L, & Baker, L. (1978). *Psychosomatic families.* Cambridge, MA: Harvard University Press.

Notarius, C. I., & Vanzetti, N. (1983). The marital agenda protocol. In E. Filsinger (Ed.), *Marital and family assessment* (pp. 209–227). Beverly Hills, CA: Sage.

Patterson, G. R. (1982). *Coercive family process.* Eugene, OR: Castalia.

Snyder, D. K. (1981). *Marital Satisfaction Inventory (MSI).* Los Angeles, CA: Western Psychological Services.

Vega, W. A. (1990). Hispanic families in the 1980s: A decade of research. *Journal of Marriage and the Family, 52*, 1015–1024.

6

Coding the Social Dimensions of Parent–Toddler Play From a Vertical/Horizontal Perspective

Alan Russell
Flinders University, Australia

Jacquelyn Mize
Auburn University

Judith Saebel
Flinders University, Australia

The parent–toddler play coding scheme (PTPCS) outlined here was developed to code videotaped observations of parent–toddler play under relatively naturalistic conditions in the home setting. The PTPCS is based on a view of parent–child interactions as containing vertical and horizontal components. The scheme places particular emphasis on horizontal aspects of parent–child play. The observations for which the PTPCS was developed were collected as part of a short-term longitudinal study of family influences on children's peer skills and social competence. Underlying the research aims and design was a family systems approach (P. Minuchin, 1985; S. Minuchin, 1974). A component of this approach is the view that the dyadic play of children and their parents is influenced by both the characteristics of the child and by the characteristics of the parent with whom the child is playing (Bell & Harper, 1977; Kochanska, 1997; Kuczynski, Marshall, & Schell, 1997; A. Russell & G. Russell, 1992; Stevenson, Leavitt, Thompson, & Roach, 1988). In other words, the play behavior of the parent and the child is part of a reciprocal, bidirectional system.

In each family, the play of three parent–toddler dyads was observed: the child playing with his or her mother, his or her father, and the mother of a same-age playmate. Collecting observation data for the child with three play partners in this way permits subsequent analyses to investigate parent and child contributions to the observed behavior. Although there might be some scope for adapting the PTPCS to nonplay contexts and to play with older children, the design of the scheme was shaped substantially by both the age group of the children (toddlers) and the context (parent–child play). In this sense, no special claims are being made for the generalizability of the scheme to other types of parent–child interactions.

THEORETICAL FOUNDATIONS

The observations for which the PTPCS was developed were undertaken as part of a larger project investigating links between the family and peer systems. Previous studies examining these links have concentrated on questions about the origins of children's peer skills and social competence, and possible effects of family socialization experiences on these (Parke & Ladd, 1992). The notion guiding the present research was that for young children, their peer skills and competence are mainly displayed in play contexts with peers. The peer-play context as the site for the use of social skills is probably important even for toddlers, but is certainly paramount by the ages of 3 to 4 years. When considered in this way, the question of how children acquire peer skills and competencies resolves into how children learn "play skills," referring here in particular to the *social behaviors* appropriate in play contexts. The present research was guided by a view that parent–child play can provide opportunities for children to learn and practice social behaviors appropriate to the play context with peers. Accordingly, it will be seen that the coding scheme focused on aspects of parent–child play that could potentially assist the child's development, learning, or practice of play and social skills.

To aid the development of a coding scheme directed to the link between the family and peer systems, we turned first to the literature on children's peer relationships, and determined the extent to which aspects of parent–child relationships display qualities similar to those of child–peer relationships (A. Russell, Pettit, & Mize, 1998). Child–peer relationships are typically considered to be mainly horizontal (symmetrical/between equals), whereas parent–child relationships are viewed mainly as vertical, the latter being based on asymmetrical and complementary behavior from parent and child (Hartup, 1989; Youniss, 1980). In contrast, qualities such as mutuality, synchrony, and power sharing (e.g., via collaboration and negotiation) suggest that parent–child relationships can also contain qualities usually attributed to child–peer relationships. These qualities often occur in parent–child play. The vertical/horizontal distinction had a fundamental influence on the design of the present coding system. This meant firstly that codes had to be developed to assess "peerlike" (horizontal) qualities in parent–child play.

In addition to coding for horizontal qualities, however, vertical aspects of parent–child play also were assessed. Two contrasting kinds of vertical qualities were taken into account in the scheme. In the first case, parents can be in charge by using their authority to direct the child and the interaction (although this authority may often be challenged by the child). In the second type of vertical behavior, however, the parent is child centered and acts to facilitate the child's behavior. In the latter case, parent and child are in complementary roles, with the parent attempting to be responsive and sensitive to the child's needs, interests, and behavior.

DEVELOPMENT OF THE PTPCS

The system was developed through several stages. The first stage involved a clarification of the vertical/horizontal distinction as it applied to child–peer and parent–child relationships. The second stage involved the examination of the play skills (especially the relevant social skills) of young children, and the literature on the coding of parent–child interactions and parent–child play, especially for preschool and toddler-age children (e.g., Fiese, 1990; Kerig, P. A. Cowan, & C. P. Cowan, 1993; Lytton, 1980; MacDonald, 1987; O'Reilly & Bornstein, 1993; Pine, 1992; Ross, 1982; Youngblade & Belsky, 1992). Influential in the overall conceptualization of the coding scheme was the work of Lindsey and colleagues (Lindsey, Mize, & Pettit, 1997b), with its particular focus on initiations in parent–child play, and the play roles scheme outlined by Gonçu (1987). Systems for the coding of general parent–child interaction for preschool or early school-age children, such as by P. Cowan and C. Cowan (undated document) provided sources for some codes that were then adapted for the parent–toddler context.

Pilot data were collected from videotaping parent–toddler toy play and parent–toddler physical play in nine families. These families were White, and from low- to middle-SES (socioeconomic status) categories. The pilot observations were used during the process of developing the coding manual. The first codes developed were for three general play roles, then attention turned to codes dealing with more specific behaviors. The roles and specific behaviors observed in the nine pilot families guided the development of the codes (i.e., there was an iterative process consisting of consulting existing literature while at the same time working with the videotaped observations). Codes and ideas from the existing literature were selected to cover both vertical and horizontal elements of the interactions. Adaptation of existing codes was usually required for present purpose, partly because the children were toddlers, and partly because of the play context. The project director (AR) managed the development of the coding manual, which occurred in conjunction with three principal coders (who assisted in the development of the scheme, and then undertook much of the coding).

The development of the system through the pilot work also involved decisions about the time unit to be used and whether to rate or code behaviors. Because the principal codes related to general roles played by parents, the most appropriate strategy was to make integrative or overall judgments about the presence of these roles and the degree to which they were used, rather than to attempt to event-count statements or behavior indicative of each role. The roles were conceived in terms of a general strategy or approach to the play situation, rather than in specific behavioral terms. Integrative judgments in the form of ratings were also chosen for the specific behaviors, partly for the sake of time efficiency (Elliot, Busse, & Gresham, 1993), and in keeping with the increasing use of rating scales for the measurement of the types of behavior of interest in the research (see earlier references given to previous observational schemes for the investigation of parent–child interactions).

DESCRIPTION OF THE PTPCS:
PLAY ROLES AND SPECIFIC BEHAVIORS

The PTPCS has two groups of codes. The first, the principal codes, relate to general parental play role. The second group covers more specific dimensions or elements of behavior. The two groups of codes are completed on separate passes through the tapes, and analyses are based on data from different coders for the two groups of codes.

Parental Play Roles

The codes relating to the parent's general play role assess the parent's ways of organizing the play, and his or her style of interacting with the child. Three overall play roles that the parent can take on are coded, first for their presence and then for their prominence. The three roles are as follows:

1. *Director*: The parent organizes the play, takes charge and assumes responsibility for the play. The parent's ideas and wishes therefore determine the content and style of the play.
2. *Facilitator*: The parent validates and supports the child's activity, and encourages the child's ideas by allowing, assisting, and encouraging the child to explore or expand his or her ideas so that the direction of the play is shaped mostly by the child. At times, this role is reflected in the parent allowing the child freedom to choose and act, by not hindering the child's play, and observing without interfering. When the parent watches without any effort to change the direction of play and with few or no comments, the parent is assumed to be tacitly approving the child's activities. Through the focus of attention and smiles or other forms of recognition, the parent may show interest and approval in such cases.

3. *Coplayer:* The parent engages with the child as a playmate, so that the play is jointly constructed by parent and child, with a high degree of equality between parent and child in terms of attention to each other's interests and initiations for the play. As noted earlier, the Director and Facilitator roles are considered to be vertical, with the Coplayer role being defined as primarily horizontal.

As already indicated, the parental play roles are considered to be *general* in nature, being reflected over time in a combination of behaviors, intentions, strategies, responses, and so on. For this reason, the three roles need to be coded over larger (minutes) rather than shorter (seconds) blocks of time. Further, because roles might change throughout a play session (e.g., parents could be more directive early in a play session and engage in less directive roles as the play is established), the coding procedure was designed so that parents' roles in the first minute of play were coded, and thereafter the roles were coded in 4-minute periods. Coders first determined whether or not the parent's play contained any of the role, that is, whether or not in the time segment the particular play role was observed. In addition, coders rated the relative salience or prominence of each of the roles. One possibility was that a single role was prominent and the other two were less prominent or not present at all. But, it was also possible that two (or three) of the roles could be judged to be equally salient or characteristic of the parent's play.

Specific Behaviors and Qualities

In addition to the general roles, the coding system also examined more specific behaviors used by both parents and children during the play, and qualities of the play. Because of their more specific nature, these behaviors are coded in shorter time periods, in this case for the first minute of play and then for each subsequent 2-minute period. The specific behaviors are rated on 5-point Likert-type scales, with the exception of Coldness-Warmth, which is rated on a 7-point scale.

Most of the specific behaviors were also selected to fit the vertical/horizontal framework. In this regard, parent and child initiations (Lindsey, Mize, & Pettit, 1997a) were central in the scheme, with initiations classified either as *play leads* (more horizontal) or as *play directives* (more vertical). Interactions coded as high in the Director role were expected to contain higher rates of parental initiations (leads and directives). Interactions coded as the Facilitator type were expected to contain few parental initiations. A greater balance in parental and child initiations (especially play leads) was expected to characterize a horizontal style. In addition to initiations, the scheme also codes *parent and child responses to the other's initiations*, defined in terms of the extent to which they react positively, apparently accept, or comply with the initiation, versus ignoring or rejecting the initiation. *Parental encouragement of the child's autonomy* is another important behavior characteristic of the horizontal style that is coded. In contrast, *parental overstimulation* is coded as a characteristic with a vertical quality. Several characteristics that are not peculiar to any particular play style are also coded. These non-style-specific codes include *responsiveness, coldness/warmth, parental interactiveness,* and *parental use of questioning.*

Finally, the system codes the *child's enjoyment of play, mutual enjoyment of the interaction,* and *level of conflict.* The two enjoyment codes were included mainly to enable an examination of the styles of play and types of behavior that were associated with higher/lower levels of enjoyment in play (enjoyment in the case of the child, e.g., focused on the amount of positive spontaneity). The coding of conflict examined both low- and high-level conflict situations, with an emphasis on the amount of conflict and the source of the conflict. Low conflict could arise from parent and child playing in parallel, jointly constructing the play, or either partner accepting the wishes of the other. High conflict could arise from either partner objecting to the direction that the other is attempting to impose (e.g., parent attempts to direct, and the child objects), or because they each tend to disagree with the other.

CODER TRAINING

We believe that both senior undergraduate students with psychological or child development training and graduate students are appropriate coders. In the case of undergraduates, however, the coders we have used so far have been specially selected for their interest and academic performance.

Training is based on (a) initial discussion and clarification of the scheme and the codes described in the manual, and (b) practice coding on nine pilot study families. After the scheme had been developed, representative samples (totaling 30 minutes) of parent and child behaviors (coded by three experienced coders) were selected to provide a training tape and data. Using the training tape, practice coding occurs first alongside an experienced coder, and then shifts to independent coding. At all times, there are follow-up discussions with the experienced coders about disagreements. The completion of training is based on the mastery of the scheme as demonstrated through reaching a consistent reliability at around 70% agreement with existing codes on the training tapes. Generally, it can be expected that coders-in-training would need to code at least three of the training families, and possibly up to eight or nine families, depending on the coder. After training, we continue to monitor disagreements, with over half the play sessions coded by more than one coder and disagreements discussed. Following these discussions, an individual coder is free to change his or her initial response. At times coders will accept disagreement about a particular coding, because some play segments can be ambiguous with respect to a given code.

We do not believe that training could occur using the manual alone. Training would be facilitated by access to training tapes and the associated codes. It would be helped also by opportunities to discuss codes with members of the laboratory. Training tapes are available together with the coding manual and coded interactions for these tapes, although costs need to be covered for their provision.

THE CODING PROCESS

As already indicated, each play period is divided either into three (1 min + 4 min + 4 min) or five (1 min + 2 min + 2 min + 2 min + 2 min) segments for coding, depending on which scale is to be applied. Consistent with this, the coding form is a two-part document. On page 1, there are all codes that have to be applied to the longer play segments, whereas scales on the remaining pages are for the shorter segments. Our experience has shown us that it is better to code the two sections of coding separately; for example, do the longer segments first, then rewind the tape and do the series of shorter segments next. The time required to view and then code a 9-minute play period depends on the coder, the target child, and the parent, but generally, is completed within 30–45 minutes. Repeated viewing of a play segment is sometimes required, including intensive consideration of particular interactions. At other times, coding can be completed after a single viewing of a play segment. Coding is intensive and demanding, and short breaks are required to rest. The number of codes, together with the complexity of some of the behaviors contained in the PTPCS, means that it would not be possible to use the complete scheme for coding in real time.

Given the complexity and number of scales in the scheme, it can be used only with videotapes. Furthermore, because the codings/ratings are to a large extent based on nonverbal behavior of both the parent and the child, coding from transcripts is not advised. On the other hand, note taking while watching a tape is recommended in situations where the coder is unsure of his or her decision and wants to later discuss the matter with other coders or the project director. In some situations, it helps to have a VCR (videocasette recorder), which allows viewing frame by frame, so that every action can be examined. The frame-by-frame viewing enables, for example, the determination of whether a play partner is taking away or offering a toy. Sometimes, only by viewing the tape frame by frame is it possible to see who is doing the talking (from lip movements).

RELIABILITY

A number of coders have been used, but three coders have conducted the main coding to this time. Reliability was calculated among these coders. In order to counter drift in coding interpretations, and to improve reliability, a considerable degree of double and triple coding of the observations was undertaken. After initial, naive coding, coders check against the other coder(s). Discussions about substantial disagreements are undertaken, and coders are free to modify their code. Based on data from 89 families (with each play period of about 9 minutes divided into separate time segments for coding), we calculated reliabilities for naive coding and then for the results after cross-checking and discussion.

For the overall play roles, there were two aspects to the reliability. The first concerned the coding of presence or absence for each of the roles in the play segment. The second focused on the coding of the degree to which the play role was prominent in the play (coded as 1 = *prominent,* 2 = *present but not prominent,* and 3 = *least prominent*; a code of 3 was often used because the role was not observed in the segment). These data were used to rank the prominence of each of the three play roles.

For the presence versus absence data, kappas between the individual pairs of the three coders were calculated using the procedure outlined by Rae (1984). They ranged from .32 to .81 (all $ps < .01$, $M = .58$) for naive coding and from .38 to .81 (all $ps < .01$, $M = .62$) after cross-checking. These kappas should be considered in the context of evidence that kappas are lower when there are fewer codes and their simple probabilities variable (Bakeman, Quera, Mcarthur, & Robinson, 1997). The percentage of agreement among the coders for presence/absence was over 75% ($M = 87\%$) for naive coding and over 80% ($M = 89\%$) after checking. For the rankings of the three play roles, the reliabilities were calculated using Spearman correlations and were between .48 ($p < .001$) and .80 ($p < .001$) for naive coding ($M = .69$), and .44 ($p < .001$) and .82 ($p < .001$) after checking ($M = .73$). The lowest reliabilities were recorded for the Coplayer role and also differed according to which coders were being compared (one pair of coders had lower reliability).

The reliabilities for the codes for specific behaviors were calculated using Finn's *r*. They were generally above .70 ($M = .82$) for naive coding and above .80 ($M = .83$) after checking and discussion. The lowest reliabilities occurred for codes dealing with parental play leads, parental play directives, child initiations, and mutual enjoyment of the interaction.

Summary.   The reliabilities ranged from relatively low to moderately high, with the lowest reliabilities occurring for coding of the Coplayer role, whether each of the roles was present or not in the play, and the specific behaviors of parental play leads and directives, and child initiations. The reliabilities differed according to which pairs of coders were being compared, and according to the measure of reliability. For example, in terms of the presence or not of each play role, the kappas were low to moderate, but the percentage of agreement values were acceptable. The latter data showed that coders agreed more than 80% of the time about whether a given role was present or not in the play.

The reliabilities improved following cross-checking and discussion, as would be expected. It is evident from the reliabilities and our experience of the coding process that there is a degree of interpretation involved in many of the codes, with genuine levels of uncertainty about some behavior, and that these factors are responsible for many disagreements. The uncertainty is likely when one coder judges that a role is present, barely, whereas another coder judges that the role is absent. Coders are more likely to agree that a role was prominent or not. In addition, it was apparent from the coding experience that a small proportion of parent–child dyads posed problems for coding, in that considerable difficulty was generated in coding even after extensive cross-checking and discussion. It was also evident that the Coplayer role created some difficulties in coding because coplaying can take a variety of forms and contain behaviors that are involved in both the Director and Facilitator roles. An implication of our experience with this coding scheme is that the coding of coplaying benefits from cross-checking between coders and relatively frequent discussions about the interpretation of coplaying.

The specific behaviors involving parental play leads and directives, and child initiations are central to the concept of horizontal interactions. These behaviors likewise posed some difficulty in reaching high reliability. Again, it is evident that there is a degree of interpretation involved in the coding of these behaviors and some uncertainty at times about whether or not a behavior is an initiation to change the direction of the play.

VALIDITY

Issues about both content validity and construct validity are examined. The data referred to here (and in the studies reported in the discussion that follows) relate to a study of 89 Australian families. These families are White and from low to middle SES.

Content Validity. The division of parent roles into Director, Facilitator, and Coplayer is based on the scheme proposed and developed by Gonçu (1987) and O'Reilly and Bornstein (1993). Gonçu identified three roles that the adult might take in playing with children. He labeled them the *Director, Spectator,* and *Coplayer* roles. The present Director and Coplayer codes overlap considerably with Gonçu's notion. Our code for Facilitator implies a more active role in encouraging the child's agenda than being a Spectator, although much of what we mean by facilitator is contained in Gonçu's idea of Spectator, with parents who act as spectators being coded within the Facilitator role.

There is a considerable literature on parental directiveness/intrusiveness, with research in this area often including scales that extend from parent-centered behavior at one extreme to facilitative/responsive/child-centered behavior at the other (Ainsworth, Bell, & Stayton, 1971; Rose-Krasnor, Rubin, Booth, & Coplan, 1996; A. Russell & G. Russell, 1996). The definitions of the Director and Facilitator roles are broadly consistent with the way in which parental directiveness/intrusiveness has been conceptualized. Further, the Facilitator role as coded in PTPCS overlaps considerably with the style recommended in The Child's Game, as described and used by Parpal and Maccoby (1985), and with ideas of child-centered play therapy (Ginsberg, 1989; Guerney & Guerney, 1989).

We assumed that if coplaying occurred, parents would be especially influential in creating and sustaining this type of interaction. However, children have to participate appropriately in terms of initiating, and responding to parental initiatives. In this way, coplaying overlaps with what has been coded as synchrony in parent–child interactions (Harrist, Pettit, Dodge, & Bates, 1994; Mize & Pettit, 1997), and it has links with the notions of coconstruction and bidirectionality (Kuczynski et al., 1997; Pettit & Lollis, 1997; A. Russell, Pettit et al., 1998).

As already indicated, the specific behaviors coded in the PTPCS were largely selected from the literature and adapted to suit the coding of parent–child play and the toddler age group. Overall, therefore, we believe that the present scheme has a firm foundation in current research and theory concerning parent–child interactions, play competencies, and links between the parent–child and child–peer systems.

Construct Validity.   Construct validity was examined using the data from the study for which the coding scheme was developed, that is, a study in which toddlers (aged between 24 and 29 months) were videotaped playing separately with their mother, with their father, and with the mother of a friend of theirs. The play sessions were conducted in the home and involved three periods each of about 10 minutes. In the first period, the play was with toys that the parent and child chose; the second period used a set of toys provided by the researchers that were likely to promote pretend play. The set contained animals, cars, planes, building blocks, and home furniture. During the third period, the parent and child were provided with a large soft inflatable ball and hand puppets, and asked to play physically together. The coding of each play period was divided into separate segments, as already outlined. For the play roles, there were three segments; the 1st minute, minutes 2–5, and minutes 6–9. For the specific behaviors, there were five segments; the 1st minute, and then every 2 minutes for a total of 9 minutes of play (some play periods did not run the full 9 minutes).

From previous evidence (Milke, Simon, & Powell, 1997; A. Russell, Aloa, et al., 1998), it was expected that fathers would engage in more coplayer and director behavior than mothers, and that mothers would engage in more facilitator-type behavior. The evidence on gender-based differences in parent–child interactions (e.g., A. Russell, Aloa et al., 1998) also suggested that the Director role would be used more with boys than with girls, and that the Facilitator role would be used more with girls than with boys. Analyses based on data from 89 mothers and 89 fathers, each with three play periods and three play segments (with some missing data), comparing mothers, fathers, and play with boys versus girls confirmed these expectations. In 36.4% of play segments, fathers were coded as using only the Director role, whereas this occurred in 27.0% of segments for mothers. In contrast, fathers were coded as using only the Facilitator role in 48.9% of segments, whereas the percentage for mothers was 66.4. Parents used the Director role as the only role in 35.0% of play segments with boys and in 25.7% of play segments with girls. In contrast, parents used the Facilitator role by itself in 63.1% of play segments with girls and in 52.0% of segments with boys. Each of these gender comparisons was significant at $p < .05$ (using chi-square).

The main emphasis in the discussion of construct validity is on an examination of the internal constructs, especially in order to show how behaviors and qualities associated with each of the three roles of Director, Facilitator, and Coplayer support the validity of these roles. The data used for these analyses were (a) mean prominence rankings of the three play roles for each subject (mother, father, and other mother) over the whole play period, with each subject participating in three play periods of own toys, pretend toys, and physical play, and (b) on the mean ratings of the specific behaviors and qualities over the whole play period, again separately for each play period.

These analyses were restricted to data involving separate coders for the play roles and for the specific behaviors and qualities. In total, the analyses contained 466 play periods taken from 52 families. Correlations were calculated between the mean rankings of the play roles (one coder) and the mean ratings for the specific behaviors (another coder). The findings were most clear-cut for the Director and Facilitator roles, and provide sound support for the validity of these play roles. For example, the higher parents were ranked for the Director role the greater the score for parental play directives, parental interactiveness, frequency of questions, and conflict, whereas the reverse applied for parents ranked high for the Facilitator role. Further, parental sensitivity/responsiveness and acceptance of child autonomy, and levels of child initiations were higher the more parents used the Facilitator role and lower if they used the Director role.

The results for the Coplayer role suggested differences between the Coplayer and Director roles were similar to the differences between the Director role and the Facilitator role. However, the results for parental play leads, parental interactiveness, child initiations, and mutual enjoyment provide support for the Coplayer role being somewhat distinct. First, in the Coplayer role, parents engaged in significantly more play leads whereas this did not occur for either the Director role or the Facilitator role. Correlations were positive and significant between parental interactiveness and salience of both the Director role and the Coplayer role whereas there was a negative correlation between interactiveness and salience of the Facilitator role. This indicates higher interactiveness in both of the former roles. The Coplayer role was not associated with higher levels of child initiations, whereas this was the case for the Facilitator role. The latter suggests that in the Facilitator role parents encourage child initiations whereas in the Coplayer role there is less of a focus on child initiations. As might be expected, there were higher levels of mutual enjoyment of play associated with the Coplayer role, with this association not evident for either of the other two roles.

Overall, these results provide support for distinctness of the three general play roles. The two extremes of Director and Facilitator roles showed the most separation, as expected. The Coplayer role clearly contains elements of both of the other two roles, but nevertheless emerged as distinct.

STUDIES USING THE PTPCS

Coding of the full data set for which the PTPCS was developed has just been completed, and an article based on these results is in preparation (A. Russell, Pettit, & Mize, 2000). Preliminary data from a subset of the sample (a predominantly White, lower-middle to middle-class sample in Australia) were presented at the Society for Research in Child Development conference, Washington, DC, in April

1997 (A. Russell & Saebel, 1997). In the latter paper, individual differences in parent–child play styles were examined, and their links with children's play behavior were explored. In addition to data on parent–toddler play, the Russell and Saebel report also included subsequent observations of the toddler during about an hour-long free-play session with peers in a playgroup setting outside the home. Results also were taken from a questionnaire, which examined parents' beliefs about the importance of social skills for children. The findings reported by Russell and Saebel were consistent with the validity data provided in the present chapter in that they showed the comparable links between the general play roles and the specific behaviors and qualities in the coding scheme, using a different analysis procedure and subset of the sample from the research for which the PTPCS was developed. In addition, Russell and Saebel reported that the Director role was used more in physical play than in toy play, whereas the Facilitator role was used more in toy play than physical play. Parents who were classified as having mainly a Director role were found to rate social skills as more important for children than parents classified as having mainly a Facilitator role. There were a number of associations between parents' observed play role and the ratings of children during peer play. If parents used the Facilitator role more with their children, children were rated as higher on "enthusiasm/self-esteem," "playfulness," "assertiveness," and "cheerfulness" during peer play than were children whose parents used the Facilitator role to a lesser degree. If the Director role was more salient in the behavior of parents, children were rated as lower on "autonomy," and on "directing attention to the other" during peer play.

A. Russell et al. (2000) examined (a) differences in the use of the parental roles for toy play and physical play, (b) gender differences (mother vs. father, and boys vs. girls) in play roles and behavior, and (c) differences in children's play and social behaviors as a function of their play partner. The observations for the research were conducted on toddler play with their mother, with their father, and with the mother of a friend, as indicated earlier. The aim in this paper was to disentangle child and parent effects on parental roles and behavior during play, and to focus on gender differences.

In considering these studies, it needs to be remembered that the data were obtained from a primarily White sample in Australia. Caution should always be exercised about assuming generalizability of findings to other samples. Parents from different socioeconomic, cultural, or ethnic backgrounds could differ from the sample used here in terms of such things as attitudes and beliefs about appropriate play styles and behaviors with children.

EXCERPTS FROM THE PTPCS MANUAL

The following are excerpts from the PTPCS manual to illustrate the definitions and coding strategy for the three general play roles of Director, Facilitator and Coplayer:

The parent's overall play behavior in each of the 3 segments (1 min + 4 min + 4 min) is to be examined in relation to the three roles of "Director," "Facilitator," "Co-player," and then the extent to which the parent engaged in each of the roles is to be recorded by ranking their use of the 3 roles . That is to say, the most salient role will get a ranking of 1, while the least salient will get a ranking of 3. In addition, each play role is to be coded as 1 = *observed*, or 0 = *not observed*.

If the parent displays only 2 of the 3 roles during a segment, the third play role will receive the lowest ranking and will also be coded as 0 = *not observed*. If the parent engages in 1 play role only, the ranking for that role will be 1; the remaining 2 play roles will receive a ranking of 2 each, but they also will be coded as 0 = *not observed*. However, 2 or 3 play roles may receive the same rank if their use is considered equal. For example, if "Director" and "Facilitator" are the most typical play roles, and "Coplayer" is somewhat less obvious, then the latter receives a ranking of 2, while the first two play roles will be ranked as 1; all 3 play roles will also be coded as 1 = *observed*. On the other hand, if "Coplayer" is the most salient play role and the other 2 roles are less but equally typical of the parent's play, then "Coplayer" is to receive a ranking of 1, while "Director" and "Facilitator" are to be ranked as 2.

In addition, the start of the first (i.e., the 1-min) segment is to be coded according to the play style the parent adopts when he/she is trying to get the play going (D, F, C). That is, the coder is to indicate which one of the 3 play styles the parent chooses as his/her strategy in beginning the play. If it is the child who starts the play, the parent style is coded as 0. Also, each of the three sections is to be assessed on the Child's Enjoyment Scale (described in a later section of this manual).

Definitions (descriptions) of the 3 play roles

Director Role

The "Director": structures the play for the child by providing props, and is primarily responsible for maintaining roles and the action. When playing with the child, the "Director" usually gets involved and is active in the situation, possibly making suggestions or directing the child about what he/she might do, or drawing the child's attention to what the adult is doing. For example, the "Director" might build his/her own block tower and then ask the child to look at it, or select toys and draw the child's attention to them ("Look at this!"), or have the child watch while the "Director" does something (e.g., suggesting that child looks on while the parent demonstrates how to drive a car around an imaginary track). Sometimes, the "Director" may not be involved in the play at all, but because of their excessive demand on the child's attention, away from the child's own agenda, they practically prevent the child from taking any initiative. For example, the "Director," upon seeing the child picking up some toy animals, may start to 'test' the child about animal sounds, names, etc. The intrusive manner (e.g., urgency, rate and length of questioning) in which the questions are thrown at the child prevent the latter from realizing any ideas of their own.

The "Director" is an organiser, he/she takes responsibility for the play, and sometimes tries to help the child's learning, i.e., he/she may use the play to teach something to the child. On the other hand, the "Director" may take over the play completely, clearly disregarding the child. In all cases, the "Director" is in an adult role; he/she runs the agenda of the play, shaping its direction and outcomes. The "Director" owns the play, not like the "Facilitator" who supports the child in his/her activity, or "Coplayer" who constructs the activity jointly with the child.

When assessing how salient the director play style was for the parent, instances where clearly the parent was managing the child's behavior are not to be taken into account (e.g., when a parent has to discipline the child, or when he/she has to issue commands in an attempt to bring the child back into the camera view).

Facilitator Role

The "Facilitator": supports the child's activity, validates the child's activity (ideas) by allowing, assisting, and encouraging the child to explore and/or expand on his/her own ideas so that the direction of the play/activity is shaped mostly by the child. This may happen in a number of ways: The "Facilitator" watches what the child does, comments on it, or asks relevant questions intended to facilitate and encourage the child's activity. The parent in the role of "Facilitator" is child centered, i.e., he/she is entirely in tune with the child's line of play. In so doing he/she is expanding or exploring an idea or activity that is the child's, i.e., that is initiated/owned by the child (in contrast to the "Director" play style where it is the parent's ideas that are at the core of parent–child interaction). Like the "Director," the "Facilitator" too may provide play opportunities for the child, but will allow the child choice (e.g., "There're lots of toys here, which ones would you like to play with now?"), as opposed to the "Director" who might say, "Look at these beautiful cars, you could build a garage for them with these blocks." The "Facilitator" does not join in as an active partner, but allows the child to do their own thing, although at times, he/she may provide a little practical assistance within the child's activity (e.g., steadying a swaying tower of blocks, opening a tight lid on a box, etc.).

Coplayer Role

The "Coplayer": engages in play with the child as a playmate, being a child with the child, having fun as an equal to the child, being like a child, at times doing the same things the child does. Being a coplayer also means that the child feels and behaves like he/she has an equal partner in play. For example, both the parent and the child might make suggestions about the play, and the direction of the play is shaped jointly by the parent and the child.

To assess how salient this play style was for the parent, mainly look at the degree of equality occurring between the parent and child, whether in play or in communication during a play segment. (Note that a play segment may in fact consist of play only, conversation about toys/play materials only, or a mixture of both.) If there is reciprocity, the "power" balance in terms of who is shaping the interaction does not seem to favor either of the partners. That is to say, a play activity may have originally been started by the parent, for example, but during its course, the parent and the child will several times swap the roles of leader and follower.

Possible signs indicating a high degree of equality in parent–child interaction:

1. Easy flowing conversation/dialogue, i.e., it is a circular as opposed to one-sided process, maintained voluntarily by both participants. The questions, comments,

etc., will frequently but not always follow from the other's activities, utterances, etc. The emphasis here is on "sharing the floor" so to speak, regardless of the level of sophistication of the child's language.

2. Turn-taking (e.g., feeding each other an imaginary cake, catching and throwing a ball to each other).

3. Both the parent and the child seem to need each other as partners in the interaction; they expand on each others' contributions, regardless of who has initiated them (i.e., the parent might participate in a child's activity, and vice versa). This interdependence is also indicated by their body language: most of the time, the play partners face each other squarely; they make eye contact frequently, especially when talking to the other. In general, the parent and the child seem to be in tune with each other.

ACKNOWLEDGMENTS

The coding scheme described here was developed as part of research supported by a grant from the Australian Research Council to Russell, Mize, and Pettit.

REFERENCES

Ainsworth, M. D. S., Bell, S. M. V., & Stayton, D. J. (1971). Individual differences in Strange Situation behavior of one-year-olds. In H. R. Schaffer (Ed.), *The origins of human social relations* (pp. 17–52). London: Academic Press.

Bakeman, R., Quera, V., Mcarthur, D., & Robinson, B. F. (1997). Detecting sequential patterns and determining their reliability with fallible observers. *Psychological Methods, 2,* 357–370.

Bell, R. Q., & Harper, L. V. (1977). *Child effects on adults.* Hillsdale, NJ: Lawrence Erlbaum Associates.

Cowan, P., & Cowan, C. (undated). *School children and their families project: Description of parenting styles ratings.* University of California, Berkeley.

Elliot, S. N., Busse, R. T., & Gresham, F. M. (1993). Behavior rating scales: Issues of use and development. *School Psychology Review, 22,* 313–321.

Fiese, B. H. (1990). Playful relationships: A contextual analysis of mother–toddler interaction in symbolic play. *Child Development, 61,* 1648–1656.

Ginsberg, B. G. (1989). Training parents as therapeutic agents with foster/adoptive children using the filial approach. In C. E. Schaefer & J. M. Briesmeister (Eds.), *Handbook of parent training: Parents as co-therapists for children's behavior problems* (pp. 442–478). New York: Wiley.

Gonçu, A. (1987). The role of adults and peers in the socialization of play during the preschool years. In G. Casto, S. Ascione, & M. Salehi (Eds.), *Current perspectives in infancy and early childhood research* (pp. 33–41). Logan, UT: Early Intervention Research Institute Press.

Guerney, L., & Guerney, B. (1989). Child relationship enhancement: Family therapy and parent education. *Person Centered Review, 4,* 344–357.

Harrist, A. W., Pettit, G. S., Dodge, K. A., & Bates, J. E. (1994). Dyadic synchrony in mother–child interaction: Relations with children's subsequent kindergarten adjustment. *Family Relations, 43,* 417–424.

Hartup, W. W. (1989). Social relationships and their developmental significance. *American Psychologist, 44,* 120–126.

Kerig, P. K., Cowan, P. A., & Cowan, C. P. (1993). Marital quality and gender differences in parent–child interaction. *Developmental Psychology, 29,* 931–939.

Kochanska, G. (1997). Mutually responsive orientation between mothers and their young children: Implications for early socialization. *Child Development, 68,* 94–112.

Kuczynski, L., Marshall, S., & Schell, K. (1997). Value socialization in a bidirectional context. In J. E. Grusec & L. Kuczynski (Eds.), *Parenting and children's internalization of values: A handbook of contemporary theory* (pp. 23–50). New York: Wiley.

Lindsey, E. W., Mize, J., & Pettit, G. S. (1997a). Differential play patterns of mothers and fathers of sons and daughters: Implications for children's gender role development. *Sex Roles, 37,* 643–661.

Lindsey, E. W., Mize, J., & Pettit, G. S. (1997b). Mutuality in parent–child play: Consequences for children's peer competence. *Journal of Social and Personal Relationships, 14,* 523–538.

Lytton, H. (1980). *Parent–child interaction: The socialization process observed in twin and singleton families.* New York: Plenum.

MacDonald, K. (1987). Parent–child physical play with rejected, neglected, and popular boys. *Developmental Psychology, 23,* 705–711.

Milke, M. A., Simon, R., & Powell, B. (1997). Through the eyes of children: Youths' perceptions and evaluations of maternal and paternal roles. *Social Psychology Quarterly, 60,* 218–237.

Minuchin, P. (1985). Families and individual development: Provocations from the field of family therapy. *Child Development, 56,* 289–302.

Minuchin, S. (1974). *Families and family therapy.* Cambridge, MA: Harvard University Press.

Mize, J., & Pettit, G. S. (1997). Mothers' social coaching, mother–child relationship style, and children's peer competence: Is the medium the message? *Child Development, 68,* 312–332.

O'Reilly, A. W., & Bornstein, M. H. (1993). Caregiver–child interactions in play. In M. H. Bornstein & A. W. O'Reilly (Eds.), The role of play in the development of thought. *New Directions for Child Development, 59,* 55–66.

Parke, R. D., & Ladd, G. W. (Eds.). (1992). *Family–peer relationships: Modes of linkage.* Hillsdale, NJ: Lawrence Erlbaum Associates.

Parpal, M., & Maccoby, E. E. (1985). Maternal responsiveness and subsequent child compliance. *Child Development, 56,* 1326–1334.

Pettit, G. S., & Lollis, S. P. (1997). Reciprocity and bidirectionality in parent–child relationships: New approaches to the study of enduring issues. *Journal of Social and Personal Relationships, 14,* 435–440.

Pine, J. M. (1992). Maternal style at the early one-word stage: Re-evaluating the stereotype of the directive mother. *First Language, 12,* 169–186.

Rae, G. (1984). On measuring agreement among several judges on the presence or absence of a trait. *Educational and Psychological Measurement, 44,* 247–253.

Rose-Krasnor, L., Rubin, K. H., Booth, C. L., & Coplan, R. (1996). The relation of maternal directiveness and child attachment security to social competence in preschoolers. *International Journal of Behavioral Development, 19,* 309–325.

Ross, H. S. (1982). Establishment of social games among toddlers. *Developmental Psychology, 18,* 509–518.

Russell, A., Aloa, V., Feder, T., Glover, A., Miller, H., & Palmer, G. (1998). Sex-based differences in parenting styles in a sample with preschool children. *Australian Journal of Psychology, 50,* 89–99.

Russell, A., Pettit, G. S., & Mize, J. (1998). Horizontal qualities in parent–child relationships: Parallels with and possible consequences for children's peer relationships. *Developmental Review, 18,* 313–352.

Russell, A., Pettit, G. S., & Mize, J. (2000). The role of parent–toddler play in children's development of social competence: Parenting effects, child effects or bidirectional processes? Manuscript submitted for publication.

Russell, A., & Russell, G. (1992). Child effects in socialization research: Some conceptual and data analysis issues. *Social Development, 1,* 163–184.

Russell, A., & Russell, G. (1996). Positive parenting and boys' and girls' misbehavior during a home observation. *International Journal of Behavior Development, 19,* 291–307.

Russell, A., & Saebel, J. (1997). Individual differences in parent–child play styles: Their nature and possible consequences. *(ERIC Document Reproduction Service No. ED 406010.)* Baltimore, MD: National Information Services Corporation.

Stevenson, M. B., Leavitt, L. A., Thompson, R. H., & Roach, M A. (1988). A social relations model analysis of parent and child play. *Developmental Psychology, 24,* 101–108.

Youngblade, L. M., & Belsky, J. (1992). Parent–child antecedents of 5-year-olds' close friendships: A longitudinal analysis. *Developmental Psychology, 28,* 700–713.

Youniss, J. (1980). *Parents and peers in social development: A Sullivan–Piaget perspective.* Chicago: University of Chicago Press.

7

The Family Coding System: Studying the Relation Between Marital Conflict and Family Interaction

Elana B. Gordis
University of California-Los Angeles

Gayla Margolin
University of Southern California

We developed the Family Coding System (Margolin & Gordis, 1992) as part of a larger project examining the effects of marital conflict on children. We developed this system to capture triadic family interactions involving mother, father, and child during a discussion about a behavior of the child's that is of concern to the parents and about which the parents experience some disagreement with each other. The task thus has the potential to evoke two types of conflict, that between parents and between parents and child. The discussion occurs while the family eats a snack, simulating a family meal. We have used the task and coding system with a multiethnic sample of two-parent families with a child age 9 to 13. We have used the procedures with families of girls and boys.

This coding system is currently a work in progress. Our goal in presenting this chapter is both to share codes that we have found to be reliable, as well as to make suggestions for how to improve and refine the coding system.

THEORETICAL FOUNDATIONS

This coding system was developed by researchers examining the effects of marital conflict on child adjustment and development. The underlying theoretical foundations are most broadly those of family systems and structural family theory and of social learning theory. In addition, theories more specific to the research question of how marital conflict affects children guided our development of the coding system.

Family systems theory in general and structural family theory more specifically provide primary theoretical foundations for this coding system. These theories emphasize the importance of how various family subsystems relate to each other and the boundaries that exist between them (Hayden et al., 1998; Margolin, 1981; S. Minuchin, 1974). Relevant to the question of how marital conflict affects children is the belief that to function in a healthy way, a boundary exists between the parent subsystem and the child. One measure of the health of the family functioning is the extent to which parents keep their own marital and interparental conflicts restricted to their relationship. According to structural family theorists, in problem families, the boundary between parent and child subsystems may be blurred. Parents may engage the child into an inappropriate alliance or coalition to the exclusion or opposition of the other parent, or the child may intervene to try to subdue the marital conflict (Gilbert, Christensen, & Margolin, 1984; P. Minuchin, 1985; S. Minuchin, 1974). We believed that having the parents discuss a conflictual topic about the child together with the child would allow us to examine the strength of the boundary between the parental subsystem and the child. We were especially interested in coding the conflict between parents that the child observes, as well as ways that the boundary between the parental subsystem and the child may become blurred in the face of interparental conflict.

Family systems theorists emphasize that family relationships are bidirectional and nonlinear (Margolin, 1981). Thus, one cannot look only at how the parents affect the child but how all members and family subsystems affect each other over time (Hayden et al., 1998). Although this coding system does not allow for sequential analyses and thus direct addressing of questions of causality, the goal is to obtain a picture of family interaction with the understanding that family subsystems are affecting each other, and that observing only dyads interacting cannot provide a full picture of the dynamics of family relationships. We wanted to observe the process as it unfolds even though we would not be disentangling causal directions of influence with these procedures.

The other major theoretical foundation of this coding system is social learning theory (e.g., Bandura, 1974; Patterson, 1982). Social learning theorists apply behavioral learning principles to social interaction (Jacobson & Margolin, 1979; Patterson, 1982). They maintain that social interaction, for example within the family, provides reinforcement and punishment for an individual's behavior, and thus that behavior is learned through interaction with others in an individual's environment. Perhaps most relevant to the coding system is the emphasis on modeling, such that individuals learn through observing others (Bandura, 1974). We were interested in whether children observe problematic interactions between their parents and then experience similar dynamics in their relationships both within and beyond the family. Observing these behaviors in combination with information about the child's functioning in other domains should provide useful information about the potentially maladaptive behavior patterns that the child may learn from the family and exhibit in other arenas.

Theories more specific to the investigation of the effects of marital conflict on children informed this coding system as well. Researchers have theorized that marital conflict affects children both through children's direct exposure to marital conflict as well as through the impact of marital conflict on the parent–child relationship. Researchers emphasizing direct mechanisms argue that children from conflictual homes become sensitized to conflict and are particularly upset by subsequent conflict both within and beyond the family (Davies & Cummings, 1994; Gottman & Katz, 1989). With our coding system, we aimed to capture children's apparent discomfort during a conflictual interaction with parents. Combined with information about conflict levels in the home, we hoped to find evidence for this sensitization process when the child interacted with both parents together. Researchers emphasizing indirect routes for the effects of marital conflict argue that marital conflict affects the child through its impact on the parent–child relationship (Burman, John, & Margolin, 1987; Fauber, Forehand, Thomas, & Wierson, 1990; see Erel & Burman, 1995, for a meta-analysis of this effect). We were interested in the relation between interparental and parent–child conflict in light of theories that marital conflict can compromise the parent–child relationship.

Observing how interparental and parent–child conflict interrelate in a triadic family setting is particularly important in light of research indicating that the presence of one parent seems to have an impact on the way the other parent treats the child (Gjerde, 1986). Thus, observing triadic interactions is necessary to having a complete picture of the impact of the marital conflict on the parent–child relationship.

DEVELOPMENT OF THE FAMILY CODING SYSTEM

We developed the following task and the Family Coding System with the aim of learning more about how marital conflict relates to the functioning of larger family systems and to child behavior. As noted earlier, we selected a task that we hoped would evoke conflict in both marital and parent–child domains.

Selection of Task

Our goal was to have parents discuss, together with their child, issues regarding the child's behavior about which the parents were concerned, and about which the parents experienced some interparental disagreement. Toward this end, we had parents complete a checklist of issues regarding the child's behavior that may have been of concern to the parents. For each item, parents rated, on a scale of 0 (not at all) to 4 (a lot) the extent to which they were concerned about the child's behavior regarding that item, and also on the same 0 to 4 scale the extent to which they disagreed with the spouse regarding how to handle the situation. We scored the checklist by multiplying the two ratings per item. Items with the highest product were those behaviors with higher levels of parent concern and higher levels of interparental disagreement. We worked independently with each parent, with the aid of the scored checklist, to identify a topic for the discussion. Each parent chose a topic, for a total of two topics per family. Before the family discussion, parents had 12 minutes to discuss the topics by themselves to work toward some type of agreement regarding how to present the topics to the child. In families with greater marital discord, we supposed that the task of coming to such an agreement would be more difficult, and we expected them to be more conflictual with the child.

After their 12-minute marital discussion, parents were seated around a table and were asked to discuss the same topics together with their child over a snack. A camera was set up at an angle wide enough to record activity around the table. We then brought the child into the room and seated him or her between the parents, directly facing the camera. We placed three snacks, three drinks, and three napkins on the table. We structured the task around a snack for several reasons. First, we wanted to simulate mealtime, which we supposed would be a likely time for the parents and child to be engaged together in conversation. Second, having food available provided a more naturalistic environment in which to have their discussion. We reasoned that when family members engage in conflict at home, they are unlikely to be free of distracting objects. The snacks gave family members objects to fuss with, much as they might have in their own homes. Indeed, the snack seemed to work as a distraction, apparently making participants less conscious of the cameras and laboratory setting around them.

Development of Coding Constructs and Coding Process

One set of variables of interest emerged from theories about direct effects of exposure to conflict. Researchers have found that children who are exposed to interparental conflict become sensitized to conflict. However, few studies have examined how children behave in the context of marital conflict (exceptions include Davis, Hops, Alpert, & Sheeber, 1998; Easterbrooks, Cummings, & Emde, 1994; and Vuchinich, Emery, & Cassidy, 1988). Thus, we were interested in detecting interparental conflict to which the child is exposed as well as the child's behavior during the conflict. We were particularly interested in hostile affect expressed between parents, and we designed the task to maximize the likelihood of evoking negative affect. We drew from the marital literature in developing the interparental Hostility codes (e.g., Gottman, 1993). In addition to interparental Hostility, we included codes for interparental Warmth/Empathy to detect positive affect between parents as well. We were also interested in capturing the child's discomfort during this interaction and thus included the codes of child Withdrawal, Anxiety, and Distraction.

Next, we were interested in examining the relation between marital variables and the ways that parents treat their child in order to examine possible indirect routes linking marital conflict to parents' behavior toward their child. We were interested in this link regarding both conflict observed during the triadic discussions as well as marital conflict measured through other marital assessments. We aimed to capture the affective tone of parents' communications to their child in the context of this discussion. Researchers have identified parental warmth toward the child and an absence of parental hostility and rejection of the child as possible ways that children are buffered from the effects of marital conflict (Harold, Fincham, Osborne, & Conger, 1997; Katz & Gottman, 1997). We believed that studying these variables in the context of family interaction during marital conflict would provide important information regarding the indirect routes by which marital conflict affects children. The affective dimension was captured by the Parent-to-Child Hostility and Parent-to-Child Warmth/Empathy codes. In addition, we were interested in the styles of communication that parents use in discussing the child's behavior with the child. Given links in the literature between marital aggression and power-assertive parenting styles (Holden & Ritchie, 1991; Jouriles & LeCompte, 1991), we were particularly interested in whether parents with higher levels of marital conflict and aggression are more controlling and domineering with their child. We developed the category of Controlling to detect a more dominant way of discussing the problem with the child. In contrast, the code Seek Information/Seek Help reflects the extent to which parents were interactive and collaborative with the child. In line with the idea of detecting more constructive problem solving, we included Mother, Father, and Child Assert Solution as well.

We were also interested in processes viewed as maladaptive according to family systems and structural family theories. Specifically, we wanted to detect cross-generational alliances, which represent a blurring of the functional boundary between the parental family subsystem and the child (S. Minuchin, 1974). We believed that this task would evoke these alliances in families with these blurred boundaries and included codes to detect this phenomenon.

Once we had decided on the constructs of interest, we drafted definitions of codes and held focus discussions with undergraduates to learn what they could detect as they viewed tapes. These discussions provided us with information to help us know what types of codes were communicable to undergraduate coders.

We designed the coding system so that the parents and child were all coded on the same behaviors. For several reasons, we present codes as specific to family members here. First, we found that certain family members exhibited certain codes with very low frequency. These codes appear to be more appropriate for some family members than for others. For example, although parents were coded on the dimensions Withdrawal, Anxiety, and Distraction, they exhibited extremely low base rates of these behaviors. Not only is it difficult to analyze these behaviors as parent codes, but adequate reliability as measured by the intraclass correlation coefficient is nearly impossible to achieve with low variance across the sample on the behaviors. Thus, we present these codes as child codes. The advantage to having each family member coded on the same categories and then analyzing the relevant codes later is that it may be simpler for coders to learn one set of codes and apply them. However, given that certain codes seem be more relevant for either the parents or the child, it may save time to instruct coders to code only relevant codes for each family member. In this chapter, we present the relevant codes for each family member to highlight the theoretical foundations and importance of the categories.

To establish the time unit for coding, again we experimented with different periods, from 15 seconds to 2 minutes. We found that in intervals of less than 1 minute, coders had difficulty categorizing participants' behaviors. In intervals of greater than 1-minute, there were too many overlapping and changing states. Thus, we settled on 1-minute intervals. This interval length also made the coding project feasible, with each 10-minute videotaped interaction requiring approximately 1½ hours for coding.

DESCRIPTION OF THE FAMILY CODING SYSTEM

The Family Coding System is a global system in which coders rate participants on a set of affective states and behaviors during each minute of the interaction. Each code is rated as present or absent for each participant for each minute of interaction. Scores are averaged across the 10 minutes of interaction for each of the behaviors. Codes are not mutually exclusive—a participant may exhibit many of these codes during a given minute of interaction. There are advantages and disadvantages to this type of system. A key benefit is that one can detect as many behaviors as are relevant at a time. Often, with more microanalytic coding systems in which coders are required to choose one code for a particular floor switch or interval, information may be lost because several behaviors may actually be happening at the same time. In these cases, the investigator has determined which behavior is the priority. Even if the coder can record more than one, data analysis often requires choosing one code. A second benefit to this system is the potential for analysis of which codes tend to co-occur. In addition, this system is often less costly in terms of time and resources. Transcribing is not necessary. The drawbacks of this system include the preclusion of conducting sequential analyses as well as the inability to determine the order of events happening within each minute of interaction.

Certain codes require coders to indicate the target of the behavior whereas others are intransitive and do not require indication of target. We organize codes into broad categories of Interparental Affect, Parent-to-Child Affect and Communication Style, Child Behavior, and Family Alliance Codes.

Interparental Affect Codes

Interparental Affect codes aim to detect the affective tone and presence of conflict between parents. These codes include Hostility and Warmth/Empathy directed to spouse. Hostility (Mother-to-Father and Father-to-Mother) is a summary code comprised of hostility/contempt/criticism, self-defense/argumentative, and blame toward the spouse. Warmth/Empathy (Mother-to-Father and Father-to-Mother), a summary code comprised of warmth/caring and empathy/encouragement/praise to the spouse, detects parents' warmth and caring behaviors toward each other during the discussion.

Parent-to-Child Affect and Communication Style Codes

These codes detect the affective tone of parents' communication with their child as well as the style they use to address the problems with the child. Parent-to-Child Affect Codes include Hostility to the child (comprised of hostility/contempt/criticism, self-defense/argumentative, and blame) and Warmth/Empathy to the child (comprised of warmth/caring and empathy/encouragement/praise to the child). Parents' communication style to the child was coded with the codes Controlling Child (comprised of lecture/laying down the law and leading questions), designed to detect more authoritarian and domineering behavior, and Seek Information/Help of child, reflecting more collaborative and interactive behavior. The code Assert Solution captured parents' offering possible solutions to problems during the discussion. This code was not coded with target but reflected a constructive contribution to the discussion.

Child Behavior Codes

In line with theories that children are sensitized to interparental conflict, we included codes designed to reflect children's discomfort. These included children's Withdrawal, Anxiety, and Distraction. Note that these do not necessarily refer to clinical syndromes. Rather they reflect coders' judgments of what are at times subtle indicators of children's discomfort. Drawing from social learning theory, we were also interested in detecting children's hostility to their parents to see if in families with higher levels of interparental hostility, children seem to exhibit higher levels of hostility directed toward parents. Parallel to the other Hostility codes, Child-to-Mother and Child-to-Father Hostility are comprised of hostility/contempt/criticism, self-defense/argumentative, and blame toward the parent. Coders also rated children on the code Assert Solution, parallel to the parents' code, to capture their ability to offer solutions during the discussion.

Cross-Generational Alliance Codes

Family members were rated on the extent to which they appeared to be engaged with another family member into a cross-generational alliance or coalition to the exclusion of the other participant. For each minute, coders indicated whether each participant did or did not engage in such an alliance. Thus, the each participant was coded on the same code. Because of low base rates for most of these codes, they are treated as dichotomous, having occurred or not occurred over the course of the discussion.

CODER TRAINING

Undergraduate and master's-level graduate students can serve as coders. They appear to be able to achieve reliability with many of the key constructs of the system. However, due to the poor reliability of some of the codes of interest, it may be beneficial to have only master's-level students code, due to their greater maturity, experience with relationships, and understanding of and training in family systems and social learning theories.

Coder training takes place over the course of several weeks. Coders study manuals containing definitions, descriptions, and examples of codes and attend weekly training meetings to discuss the codes and view tapes. During the meetings, coders watch segments of tapes together with the investigators. They code the tapes in writing during the meeting, and then discuss their coding decisions as a group with guidance from the investigator. Coders code five to eight practice tapes. Once they demonstrate an understanding of the codes through their practice coding and participation in the meetings, they can begin to code data. Ongoing weekly or biweekly meetings, in which the coding group and investigator view tapes together and discuss coding decisions, continue during the coding period to prevent coder drift and continue to clarify confusion regarding particular codes.

For training purposes, inter-rater agreement can be assessed on individual tapes for each minute of interaction. Because the coding system ultimately produces ratings based on the mean across minutes for the codes, this minute-by-minute agreement is more stringent than would be required from the perspective of data analysis but would be useful for training purposes (see Bakeman & Gottman, 1986, and Margolin et al., 1998, for discussions of reliability for training vs. data analysis).

This training procedure is adequate for many of the codes, including interparental hostility, children's behavior, and several of the parent-to-child codes. However, refinement of code definitions and more intensive training may lead to improved reliability on other codes. In general, those interested in using this coding system are encouraged to consult with the authors regarding refining the system.

THE CODING PROCESS

Coders view each tape four times in total. They watch each discussion without pausing or interrupting the playback. Next, they watch the tape three additional times, once for each discussion participant. These three times, the playback is paused after each minute to allow the coder to rate the participant on each behavior category for that minute. This first viewing is necessary because coders code one participant at a time. Were they to code the first participant without having viewed the tape through, the experience would be very different when coding the other participants because they would know how the discussion proceeded. Thus, in order to minimize the differences in stimulus exposure between the different participants coded, coders view the tape once straight through without interrupting the playback. In addition, to address potential order effects, the order of coding of the participants is counterbalanced randomly, so that mother, father, and child are coded first, second, and third with about equal frequency. In order to code the 1-minute intervals, a timer should be visible on the recording, and a beep should sound to signal the beginning and end of each minute. An assistant in the room should pause the machine after each minute so that the coders can be free to concentrate on the coding process. A mean score is taken across minutes for each code.

Certain codes in the coding system are transitive, meaning that the coder must indicate a target participant. For example, if a coder rates that the father is hostile, she or he must indicate if the father is hostile toward the mother, toward the child, or toward both. Other codes are intransitive, meaning that no target is indicated. For example, Withdrawal and Anxiety are codes that do not require indication of target.

A minimum of two coders should code each interaction in order to calculate intraclass correlation coefficients. Additional coders would help address reliability issues for those codes for which intraclass correlation coefficients are calculated.

RELIABILITY

Reliability for all codes except Cross-Generational Alliance codes was assessed using intraclass correlation coefficients (ICC; Shrout & Fleiss, 1979). Interobserver agreement for the dichotomous Cross-Generational Alliance codes was calculated with kappa coefficients (Cohen, 1960). The sample included 90 two-parent families with a child age 9–13 (45 with boys and 45 with girls). The sample was predominantly White (70%) with a substantial number of African-American families as well (21.1%). For further details regarding the sample, please see Gordis, Margolin, and John (1997).

We found that although many of the main constructs of interest were coded reliably, certain codes were not. A possible reason were low base rates of certain codes, resulting in low reliability as measured by intraclass correlation coefficients or kappa coefficients. Thus, whereas some of the reliability issues may be resolved through refining the code definitions, selecting coders with more experience in the field, and making training more rigorous, other codes may be unreliable because they are less frequently observed or are less relevant behaviors for a particular family member. The low base rate factor was particularly true for interparental Warmth/Empathy codes and Cross-Generational Alliance codes.

Interparental Affect Codes

Coders more reliably coded negative affect between parents than they did positive affect. Intraclass correlation coefficients were acceptable for interparental hostility codes of Mother-to-Father Hostility (ICC = .90), Father-to-Mother Hostility (ICC = .91). Coefficients were lower for positive affect codes of Mother-to-Father Warmth/Empathy (ICC = .37), Father-to-Mother Warmth/Empathy (ICC = .46), possibly in part due to low baserates.

Parent-to-Child Affect and Communication Style Codes

Intraclass correlation coefficients were variable for these codes. Mother-to-Child Hostility had an ICC of .77 and Father-to-Child Hostility had an ICC of .21. Parent-to-Child Warmth/Empathy had moderately acceptable coefficients. Mother-to-Child Warmth/Empathy had an ICC of .68 and Father-to-Child Warmth/Empathy had an ICC of .70. Parent-to-Child Controlling had moderate coefficients. Mother-to-Child Controlling had an ICC of .69; Father-to-Child Controlling had an ICC of .60. Parents' Assert Solution had moderate to acceptable coefficients. Mother Assert Solution had an ICC of .75, and Father Assert Solution had an ICC of .68.

Child Behavior Codes

Codes aimed at detecting children's discomfort had adequate intraclass correlation coefficients. Child Anxiety had an ICC of .72. Child Withdrawal and Child Distraction each had coefficients of .70. Child Hostility had lower coefficients. Child Hostility to Father had an ICC of .64; Child Hostility to Mother had an ICC of .59. Child Assert Solution had an ICC of .83.

Cross-Generational Alliance Codes

Cross-Generational Alliance codes are scored as present at all or absent across the 10-minute interaction. Thus, this score is a dichotomous code, and interobserver agreement is estimated with coefficient kappa. Kappas for these alliance codes were quite low, suggesting that this code needs further refining. As noted earlier, one cause of the low kappas may have been the low base rates, which resulted in high chance agreement (Spitznagel & Helzer, 1985). For example, Father-to-Child Alliance had a kappa coefficient of .21, and Mother-to-Child Alliance had a kappa coefficient of .45, despite greater than 80% agreement on both of these codes. When coders were rating the child, the child was rarely coded as initiating or being involved in alliances with parents. Child-to-Father Alliance had a kappa of .36, and Child-to-Mother Alliance had a kappa coefficient of .64, despite greater than 90% agreement on both of these codes. The low baserates for these Cross-Generational Alliance codes may have been partially due to this being a community sample. A clinic sample may have higher base rates of these patterns.

VALIDITY

The reader is referred to the next section, in which validity is suggested by the expected relation between codes and other measures of family conflict.

STUDIES USING THE FAMILY CODING SYSTEM

Two studies have been published using the Family Coding System. Both present evidence for the relation between marital aggression and family interaction in nonclinic families recruited from a large urban community. Gordis et al. (1997) examined the relation between parents' reports of marital aggression and children's observed behavior during triadic family interaction in a sample of 90 two-parent families from the Los Angeles area. The goal of the study was to examine whether previous exposure to marital aggression and parents' observed hostility toward each other and toward the child would be associated with children's behavior during the conflictual family discussion. Families were recruited via public announcements and advertisements for payment for participation in a study about family relationships. The majority of families in the study were White (70%), although there were a substantial number of African-American families as well (21%). In 45 of the families, the family triad being studied included a son, and in 45 families the triad included a daughter. Children's ages ranged from 9.4 to 13.4 years, with an average age of 11.4 for boys and 11.2 for girls. Families had an average gross monthly income of $4,700 (range = $700 to $12,000).

Consistent with theories that children are sensitized to interparental conflict, higher levels of physical marital aggression during the previous year were associated with higher levels of observed Withdrawal, Anxiety, and Distraction among boys during the observed triadic discussion, and with higher levels of Distraction among girls during the triadic discussion. Moreover, in families of boys reporting physical marital aggression during the previous year, higher levels of observed Parent-to-Child Hostility were associated with higher levels of boys' Anxiety and Distraction, providing additional support for the sensitization model.

Margolin, John, Ghosh, and Gordis (1996) examined family communication behaviors associated with marital aggression. Specifically, they examined the relation between parents' reports of physical and emotional marital aggression and family members' observed behavior during triadic family interaction in approximately the same sample as Gordis et al. (1997). These authors found significant relations between physical and emotional marital aggression and certain interparental and parent-to-child behaviors. For example, among families with boys, fathers' physical marital aggression and mothers' and fathers' emotional marital aggression were positively correlated with observed Father Controlling Child during the triadic interaction. Among families with girls, they found that fathers' emotional marital aggression was positively associated with observed Father-to-Mother Hostility during the triadic discussion. In addition, among families with girls, fathers' emotional marital aggression was positively correlated with Mother-to-Child Alliance and Father-to-Child Alliance. Finally, in addition to the positive association between physical marital aggression and children's observed Withdrawal, Anxiety, and Distraction, the authors found that mothers' emotional marital aggression was positively correlated with boys' Withdrawal during the triadic discussion. This study suggests that physical and emotional marital aggression are related to more subtle, observable family interaction patterns that may actually be more frequent and pervasive features of a child's environment.

A potential limitation to the generalizability of the aforementioned studies is the nonclinic status of the families. It is possible that the findings would not generalize to families recruited from a clinic setting. However, we believe that detecting relations between marital aggression and observed family interaction even in a nonclinic sample, in which one would expect lower levels of maladaptive behavior patterns, is important. In addition, another potential limitation involves the ethnic composition of the sample. Because of sample size limitations, we were unable to examine different patterns of family interaction among families of different ethnicities.

EXCERPTS FROM THE FCS MANUAL: EXAMPLES OF CODES AND SUMMARY CATEGORIES

Interparental and Parent–Child Affect Codes

Interparental, Parent-to-child, Child-to-parent Hostility reflects hostility, defensive, and blaming behaviors. Comprised of the three codes defined below:

Hostility/contempt/criticism: reflects direction of anger, contempt, exasperation, or frustration at another person. The other person is seen as the root of the problem. This category is coded when one person is feeling frustrated or angry with another. In extreme cases, the goal of the behavior is to hurt the other person, to even the score, or to be cruel. This code applies when a person expresses frustration, irritation, or annoyance with the other person . For example, a child might say, "I do try to do my homework!" The defining quality here is affect—the person feels exasperated. Extreme verbal examples include statements of revulsion or rejection, "You make me sick" "Why did I ever marry you?" as well as name calling and personal attack, "You're crazy, just like your family" "Don't be an asshole" "You don't know anything" "You used to be really beautiful." Other extreme forms of hostility/frustration are found in threats, either direct or veiled, "If you want some peace tonight, you better shut up" or "You're really going to get it when we leave here." or "That's classic! You've really done IT now."

Self-Defense/Argumentative: used when one participant is trying to wear down/defend against the other's point of view. Defending one's position, pointing out discrepancies in the other's statements, debating the details of what really happened or what was said are examples. This category is done with an "I'm right!" attitude and is to be distinguished from attempts at clarification. Nonverbal signs include pointing at another when making a statement, counting off the problems/issues.

Blame: This code indicates that one person is placing responsibility for the problem on another person. For example, one parent might blame the conflict on the other parent because the first parent doesn't believe there is a problem.

Interparental and Parent-to-Child Warmth/Empathy: This code seeks to capture one participant's positive affect and support toward another. This code is an aggregate of two specific codes:

Warmth/Affection: This code includes verbal and nonverbal expressions of caring and affection. Nonverbal signs would be an affectionate touch, or gesture such as a smile. Verbal signs would be expressions or respect, regard, liking, or concern.

Empathy/Encouragement/Praise: This category reflects verbal signs of appreciation, attempts to understand the other's perspective, or to validate the person or the person's point of view. Positive comments, expressions of empathy, understanding of what the other has said or attempted to do are included. Statements of affirmation "That's a reasonable fear", empathy "That must be difficult for you", or appreciation "I realize that you've been trying" appear here. These are the verbal expressions.

Parent-to-Child Communication Style

Parent Controlling Child: This code indicates that the parent is dominating the child during the interaction. The code is an aggregate of two specific codes:

Lecture/Laying Down the Law: This category is used when one person demands an action from the other or puts forth a plan that allow no room for negotiation or discussion. It does not matter if the other person attempts discussion or even is successful in changing that person's viewpoint. The behavior is coded on the basis of the demanding and overbearing quality with which a recommendation is put forth. This category also is coded when one person gets in a lecture mode, particularly if that lecture includes "morality lessons", that is, the "shoulds" and "musts" and generalized advice giving that is irrelevant to the individual involved and are a "soap-box" speech. This generally conveys a patronizing/condescending attitude, e.g. an attitude of "I know better or I know more than you." This category also is coded if the giving advice spins off into irrelevant and intellectualized or repetitive discourse. In summary, the person could either be making a command or demand for action that allows no room for discussion, or engaging in some lecture.

Leading Questions: This code indicates that one person is asking questions to another when the person who is doing the asking really knows the answers already, or knows that no answer is going to be satisfactory. They are proceeding with a line of questions in order to make a point rather than in order to acquire information.

Parent Seek Information/Help From Child: This category reflects that the parent requests further information, more details from the child or the child's help in solving the problem. The request generally will be direct, "Can you tell me what happened" "Do you have any ideas?"

Child Behavior Codes

Withdrawal: This code is indicated when the child makes himself or herself inaccessible to the other people. The retreat could be due to disinterest, frustration, disdain, hopelessness, self-consciousness or discomfort. Signs of withdrawal include turning the chair away from the other person, folding arms tightly across chest, pivoting body away from other person, not looking at the other person while speaking, addressing comments to one's lap, or making no eye contact while listening. Withdrawal can be coded with hostility if affect seems to be the cause of the withdrawal. Coded alone, it might indicate disinterest or boredom. The key is that the child is making him or herself inaccessible in some way, whatever the reason.

Anxiety: This code conveys a sense of self-consciousness or discomfort. It could be expressed as a sense of having one's personal space invaded, or it could be expressed as making excuses, changing the topic, replying evasively, or joking. The nonverbal cues include looking away, sheltering one's face, and expressions of discomfort.

Distraction: This code is indicated when one person distracts or diverts attention from the topic of discussion. Examples would include a child who engages in some silly type of behavior while a parent is talking about a problem, or a child who plays with or offers a parent food while the parent is addressing an issue with the child.

ACKNOWLEDGMENTS

This work was supported by NIMH Grants F31 10947 and R01 36595.

REFERENCES

Bakeman, R., & Gottman, J. M. (1986). *Observing interaction: An introduction to sequential analysis*. New York: Cambridge University Press.

Bandura, A. (1974). Behavior theory and the models of man. *American Psychologist, 29*, 859–869.

Burman, B., John, R. S., & Margolin, G. (1987). Effects of marital and parent–child relations on children's adjustment. *Journal of Family Psychology, 1*, (91–108).

Cohen, J. (1960). A coefficient of agreement for nominal scales. *Educational and Psychological Measurement, 20*, 37–46.

Davies, P. T., & Cummings, E. M. (1994). Marital conflict and child adjustment: An emotional security hypothesis. *Psychological Bulletin, 116*, 387–411.

Davis, B. T., Hops, H., Alpert, A., & Sheeber, L. (1998). Child responses to parental conflict and their effect on adjustment: A study of triadic relations. *Journal of Family Psychology, 12*, 163–177.

Easterbrooks, M. A., Cummings, E. M., & Emde, R. N. (1994), Young children's responses to constructive marital disputes. *Journal of Family Psychology, 8*, 160–169.

Erel, O., & Burman, B. (1995). Interrelatedness of marital relations and parent–child relations: A meta-analytic review. *Psychological Bulletin, 118*, 108–132.

Fauber, R., Forehand, R., Thomas, A. M., & Wierson, M. (1990). A mediational model of the impact of marital conflict on adolescent adjustment in intact and divorced families: The role of disrupted parenting. *Child Development, 61*, 1112–1123.

Gilbert, R., Christensen, A., & Margolin, G. (1984). Patterns of alliance in distressed and nondistressed families. *Family Process, 23*, 75–87.

Gjerde, P. F. (1986). The interpersonal structure of family interaction settings: Parent–adolescent relations in dyads and triads. *Developmental Psychology, 22*, 297–304.

Gordis, E. B., Margolin, G., & John, R. S. (1997). Marital aggression, observed parental hostility, and child behavior during triadic family interaction. *Journal of Family Psychology, 11*, 76–89.

Gottman, J. M. (1993). A theory of marital dissolution and stability. *Journal of Family Psychology, 7*, 56–75.

Gottman, J. M., & Katz, L. F. (1989). Effects of marital discord on young children's peer interaction and health. *Developmental Psychology, 25,* 373–381.

Harold, G. T., Fincham, F. D., Osborne, L., & Conger, R. (1997). Mom and Dad are at it again: Adolescent perceptions of marital conflict and adolescent psychological distress. *Developmental Psychology, 33,* 333–350.

Hayden, L. C., Schiller, M., Dickstein, S., Seifer, R., Sameroff, A. J., Miller, I., Keitner, G., & Rasmussen, S. (1998). Levels of family assessment: I. Family, marital, and parent–child interaction. *Journal of Family Psychology, 12,* 7–22.

Holden, G. W., & Ritchie, K. L. (1991). Linking extreme marital discord, child rearing, and child behavior problems: Evidence from battered women. *Child Development, 62,* 311–327.

Jacobson, N. S., & Margolin, G. (1979). *Marital therapy: Strategies based on social learning and behavior exchange principles.* New York: Brunner/Mazel.

Jouriles, E. N., & LeCompte, S. H. (1991). Husbands' aggression toward wives and mothers' and fathers' aggression toward children: Moderating effects of child gender. *Journal of Consulting and Clinical Psychology, 59,* 190–192.

Katz, L. F., & Gottman, J. M. (1997). Buffering children from marital conflict and dissolution. *Journal of Clinical Child Psychology, 26,* 157–171.

Margolin, G. (1981). The reciprocal relationship between marital and child problems. In J. P. Vincent (Ed.), *Advances in family intervention, assessment, and theory* (pp. 131–182). Greenwich, CT: JAI.

Margolin, G., & Gordis, E. B. (1992). *The Family Coding System.* Unpublished manual, University of Southern California, Los Angeles.

Margolin, G., John, R. S., Ghosh, C., & Gordis, E. (1996). Family interaction process: An essential tool for exploring abusive relations. In D. Cahn & S. Lloyd (Eds.), *Family violence: A communication perspective* (pp. 37–58). Newbury Park, CA: Sage.

Margolin, G., Oliver, P. H., Gordis, E. B., Garcia O'Hearn, H., Medina, A., Ghosh, C. M., & Morland, L. (1998). The nuts and bolts of behavioral observation of marital and family interaction. *Clinical Child and Family Psychology Review, 4,* 195–213.

Minuchin, P. (1985). Families and individual development: Provocations from the field of family therapy. *Child Development, 56,* 289–302.

Minuchin, S. (1974). *Families and family therapy.* Cambridge, MA.: Harvard University Press.

Patterson, G. R. (1982). *Coercive family process.* Eugene, OR: Castalia.

Shrout, P. E., & Fleiss, J. L. (1979). Intraclass correlations: Uses in assessing rater reliability. *Psychological Bulletin, 86,* 420–428.

Spitznagel, E. L., & Helzer, J. E. (1985). A proposed solution to the base rate problem in the kappa statistic. *Archives of General Psychiatry, 42,* 725–728.

Vuchinich, S., Emery, R. E., & Cassidy, J. (1988). Family members as third parties in dyadic family conflict: Strategies, alliances, and outcomes. *Child Development, 59,* 1293–1302.

8

The Structural Analysis
of Social Behavior
Observational Coding Scheme

Paul Florsheim
Lorna Smith Benjamin
The University of Utah

The Structural Analysis of Social Behavior (or SASB) Observational Coding Scheme (Benjamin, 1974; Benjamin, Giat, & Estroff, 1981; Humphrey & Benjamin, 1989) is a circumplex-based model for describing observed interpersonal behaviors. As we explain in this chapter, the SASB is well suited for family process coding for four specific reasons. First, because the SASB model is based on a well-validated theory of personality, interpersonal diagnosis, and clinical intervention, clearly delineated clinical implications can be derived from most SASB-based research findings, helping to bridge the gap between research and clinical practice (Benjamin, 1994, 1996a; Henry, 1996; Leary, 1957; Sullivan, 1953). Second, the SASB model is designed to be sensitive to variations in the nuance and meaning of behavior across different contexts. As such, SASB is particularly apt for studies designed to assess and compare family processes across groups thought to engage in interpersonally distinct mode of communication (Florsheim, Tolan, & Gorman-Smith, 1996). Third, the flexibility of the SASB model enhances its utility for developmental research. That is, because the underlying dimensions are related to interpersonal processes occurring across the life span, the SASB model can be used to assess stability and change in interpersonal behaviors at various stages of family development. Fourth, the SASB model provides a conceptually coherent, detailed, and comprehensive assessment of observed family behavior. Rather than focus on a select set of specified behaviors, or describe family interaction in molar, global terms, SASB is designed to produce a highly descriptive and thorough account of family interaction. The comprehensiveness and specificity of the SASB approach helps researchers to address sharply defined research questions and examine post hoc hypotheses more efficiently.

THEORETICAL FOUNDATIONS

The SASB is a circumplex-based model of interpersonal and intrapsychic processes derived from the work of Sullivan (1953), Murray (1938), Leary (1957), and Schaefer (1965). The original interpersonal circumplex (IPC) was based on the orthogonal axes of affiliation (love–hate) and control (dominance–submission). On the basis of these two dimensions, a person's behavior or personality type could be mapped onto the IPC. For example, a person who is both controlling and hostile would be described as competitive, or in more extreme cases, as sadistic on Leary's circumplex model. However, as noted by Benjamin (1974), the primary problem with Leary's model is that it lacks a vocabulary for describing behavior that is either autonomy taking or autonomy giving.

Benjamin (1974) refined Leary's (1957) IPC in two ways. Benjamin wanted to develop a model of interpersonal process that includes a vocabulary for describing both enmeshment and differentiation. This required the inclusion of two axes for describing interdependence: one in which the opposite of dominance is autonomy granting and another in which the opposite of submission is differentiation or autonomy taking. Related to this major reformulation of Leary's theory, Benjamin also introduced the concept of interpersonal focus, providing a mechanism for describing the target of interpersonal processes. Benjamin's model included three circumplex surfaces, described as "focus on other," "focus on self," and "intrapsychic focus." Consistent with Leary's IPC, on all three surfaces the horizontal axis describes degree of affiliation, ranging from extremely attacking or rejecting, on the left, to extremely approaching or loving on the right.

The first SASB circumplex surface, "focus on other," describes transitive actions that are directed outward toward another individual. The vertical dimension of the first surface ranges from extremes of control, at the bottom, to freeing or autonomy granting, at the top. From the perspective of the actor, other-focused codes describe actions done to, for, or about another person, and are prototypically "parentlike." For example, when a mother says "Stop hitting your sister," her statement would be coded as "other focused" because her attention is directed toward her son and is about his behavior.

The second surface, "focus on self," describes intransitive behaviors, which are generally reactive to another person. The vertical dimension of the second surface ranges from submission, at the bottom, to separation or autonomy taking, at the top. From the perspective of the actor, self-focused codes describe actions that are related to or about the self, and are prototypically "childlike." For example, when a child says to his mother "I need help," his statement would be considered self-focused because attention is drawn toward the self, and for the sake of self.

The third surface, "introject," derives from Sullivan's idea of the self as the reflexive appraisal of others (Sullivan, 1953). That is, the introject surface describes actions directed by the self toward the self, and represents the internalization of behaviors directed toward the self by important others (such as attachment figures). The vertical dimension of this surface runs from control, at the bottom, to freeing, at the top. For example, a child who responds to his mother admonishment by saying "I am such an idiot," would be coded as engaging in introject-focused behavior (self-blaming). Conversely, a toddler who completes a puzzle, and delightedly shouts "Great job!" would be coded as self-affirming on the introject surface. Although this third surface is critical to coding individual psychotherapy sessions, in which clients often make self-referential statements, it is infrequently used when coding family interactions, which tend to be either self- or other focused.

Principles of Interpersonal Process.   Based on the analysis of SASB-coded interactions, a relational process can be described as complementary, concordant, oppositional, or antithetical. Complementarity describes process in which one person's behavior complements the behavior of another in the three dimensions of affiliation, interdependence, and focus. For example, a child who trusts his mother when she behaves protectively is engaged in a complementary process. Concordance (or similarity) describes the process through which a person replicates how he or she has been treated by another. For example, a husband's blaming behavior may be matched (concordantly) by his wife's blaming behavior. An antithetical interpersonal process is the opposite of a complementary process, exemplified by a son who reacts to his father's controlling behavior by separating and asserting. Antithetical processes tend to occur in unstable relationships, in which the participants are engaging in behavior that reflects very different personal agendas. Finally, an oppositional process occurs when a person engages in behavior that is the direct opposite of how he or she has been treated. For example, a young father who was abandoned by his own father, and pledges to care for his son as he wishes he had been cared for, is engaged in an oppositional process, relative to his own father's behavior.

These principles of interpersonal process are not exclusive to the SASB model, and have been described by other interpersonally oriented researchers (Carson, 1969; Kiesler, 1983). However, the SASB model is uniquely equipped to guide efforts to apply these behavioral principles to the study of family functioning. That is, the comprehensiveness of the SASB model allows researchers (and clinicians) to describe all potential configurations of complementary, concordant, antithetical, and oppositional family processes.

For example, several researchers have recently identified the demand–withdraw process as being associated with marital distress, and predictive of marital dissatisfaction (Heavey, Christiansen, & Malamuth, 1995). Using SASB language, this pattern of behavior would be described as an antithetical interpersonal process because one partner's controlling or blaming behavior is matched or responded to by the other's walling-off. Researchers interested in devising an approach for treating couples mired in this process could utilize the SASB model to help identify antidotal processes. For example, the SASB-based positive correlate of the "demand–withdraw" pattern would be described as "nurture and express." In this case, the process of formulating the positive SASB-based correlate to the demand-withdraw pattern involved (a) holding focus and interdependence constant and (b) looking for the closest friendly combination of cluster codes. As a more general clinical tool, this process might involve helping a client to recognize problematic patterns of behavior, and then working with him or her to identify friendlier ways of communicating similar interpersonal statements. Thus, it could be hypothesized that a treatment program designed to promote nurturance in the demanding partner, and expressive behavior (or perhaps assertive behavior) in the withdrawing partner, would diminish the potentially deleterious effects of demand–withdraw processes.

The Problem of Applying a Uniform Definition of "Normality" Across Diverse Contexts.
Family process researchers often struggle with the dilemma of establishing parameters of normality while remaining sensitive to context-bound variations in communication style and interpersonal expectations. For theoretical reasons, researchers tend to describe behavior as either positive (usually defined as health promoting) or negative (usually defined as growth inhibiting). That is, most well-established theories of development (e.g., attachment theory, family systems theory) have clear mechanisms for determining whether a particular behavior is healthy or pathological. Without such a reference point for determining psychological health, the process of assigning meaning to behavior is prone to becoming hopelessly obscure.

On the other hand, family process researchers must remain sensitive to context-specific and developmentally specific variations in what one might be considered "positive" or "negative" behaviors. There are some contexts in which typically maladaptive behaviors (attack) would be appropriate and necessary for survival, and some contexts where typically adaptive behaviors (nurturing, loving behavior) would be potentially harmful. Similarly, there are some phases in the developmental life cycle when high levels of enmeshment would be considered adaptive and health promoting (a parent caring for an infant or an adult caring for an elderly parent), and other phases when high levels of enmeshment might be considered growth inhibiting (a father trying to control his grown child's career choice). The SASB model addresses this problem by providing coders with a clear set of guidelines for interpreting the interpersonal meaning of a behavior, based on well-established principles of psychological well-being, while encouraging coders to remain sensitive to contextually based variations in adaptive functioning.

Recognizing that what qualifies as normal or abnormal behavior is often contextually and developmentally dependent, the SASB model does not advocate a rigid definition of normality and abnormality. Nonetheless, the SASB model postulates that normatively heath-promoting interpersonal processes, which tend to be affiliative, are *qualitatively* distinguishable from normatively health-diminishing interpersonal processes, which tend to be hostile (Benjamin, 1996b). Moreover, the SASB model endorses an *absolute* distinction between positive (warm) and negative (hostile) interpersonal behavior, and cautions coders against coding behavior relative to a particular family's baseline characteristic. For example, though it makes sense to view a reduction in hostile behavior as a positive indicator, it is important to clearly distinguish between behavior that is "less hostile" and behavior that is warm.

However, experience has taught us that when coders are not familiar with local idioms and context-specific modes of expression, they are prone to misinterpret the meaning of behaviors. As such, the SASB observational coding system requires coders to utilize context-bound interpersonal cues when deciding how a particular behavior should be coded. "Context" may be defined by the children's age, the number of caregivers present, and/or social environmental circumstances of the family. How to interpret a mother's effort to restrict and monitor her son's behavior may depend on whether the child is 6 or 16 years old, or whether the family lives in an affluent suburb or a crime-ridden inner-city neighborhood. For example, Florsheim et al. (1996) reported that one of the mothers in their study of inner-city families told her son that he was getting *too old* to be out on the streets by himself. Such a statement makes sense in the context of a neighborhood where gangs target adolescent boys but tend to leave younger (preadolescent) boys alone. Out of context, this statement might come across as incomprehensible or overprotective (1–5); in context, it is protective (1–4).

Because the SASB model is flexible, the SASB observational coding scheme can be used in any setting (in the lab, in the home, in the therapist's office, etc.) in which two or more people are engaged in an interpersonal exchange. Because the SASB coding scheme is able to make use of interpersonally relevant data that are communicated verbally and nonverbally, it can be used to assess families engaged in almost any sort of activity and at any stage of development, provided that interpersonal processes can be inferred. Generally family researchers using the SASB model tend to provide families with a 15- or 20-minute interaction task, asking them to engage in a play activity, plan a family outing, discuss a discipline issue, or resolve a recent disagreement. Researchers interested in specific issues may want to design a task that "pulls" for relevant interpersonal data. For example, a developmental researcher studying the role of family process in adolescent separation-individuation may ask families to renegotiate household rules regarding curfew. Interaction tasks should always be videotaped in order to preserve nonverbal communications. For the purposes of family therapy research, the SASB coding scheme can be used to code therapy sessions (see Benjamin, 1977).

DEVELOPMENT OF THE SASB

The original purpose of developing the SASB model was to have a way of operationally defining object relations and the connection between internal psychological events and actual interactions with significant others, including family members. The plan was to develop a conceptually coherent, empirically validated set measures to describe a broad array of interpersonal and intrapsychic events in terms of the three underlying dimensions described earlier. These measures were designed to be useful to clinicians and researchers working from various theoretical orientations. The generality of model was intended to facilitate comparing and contrasting different ways of conceptualizing and treating mental disorders.

The SASB was initially constructed around instances of observed behaviors in monkeys, infants, children, college students, psychiatric patients, and various other sources. With the help of Earl Schaefer's model of parenting behavior and knowledge of field primatology, the initial poles of sexuality, power, aggression, and territory were defined. From there, the dimensional names, the two interpersonal surfaces, and the categories within them were derived logically.

Throughout the early phases of developing the SASB model, Benjamin referred to the literature on interpersonal and intrapsychic processes for guidance and inspiration. Schaefer (1965, 1971) had proposed a circumplex model of parenting behavior that placed love and hate as opposites on one dimension and control and emancipation as opposites on the other. Previously, Leary (1957) had placed love and hate on a horizontal axis and control and submit as opposites on the vertical axis. Benjamin (1974) suggested that dominance and emancipation are opposites, as Schaefer claimed, whereas dominance and submission are complementary or matching behaviors. Emancipation also has its complement in the SASB model, which is separate. One important consequence of using emancipate as the opposite of control is the ability to describe giving and taking of autonomy, which is marked in the clinical literature by Mahler's important observational work (1968) on separation individual in toddlers. The third SASB surface reflected the thinking of Harry Stack Sullivan, who conceptualized intrapsychic processes in terms of internalized interpersonal relations (Sullivan, 1953). The descriptors associated with each of the 108 data points outlined in the full SASB model (see Fig. 8.1) were based on Benjamin's efforts to concretely define the various points at which the affiliation and interdependence dimensions intersect within each of the circumplex surfaces. The process of selecting terms to describe these specific points was guided by the principles of symmetry, balance, and complementarity described earlier.

In addition to the observational coding scheme described in this chapter, Benjamin (1998) developed several SASB-based questionnaires for assessing interpersonal process and their intrapsychic correlates. These questionnaires can be used to rate oneself or others. Using the array of SASB-based technologies, behavioral observations can be systematically compared to self-rated subjective experi-

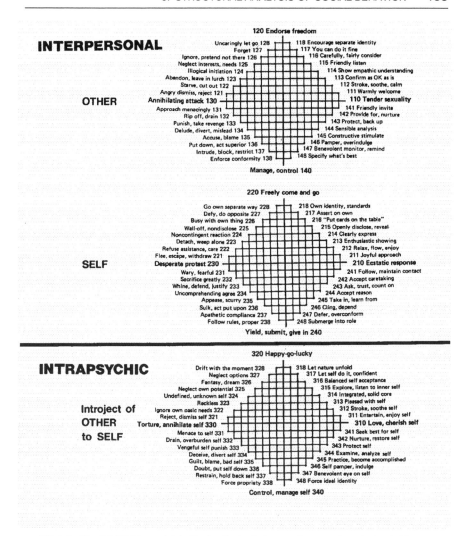

FIG 8.1. The full SASB model. In Benjamin, L. S. (1979). Structural analysis of differentiation failure. *Psychiatry: Journal for the Study of Interpersonal Processes, 42,* 1–23. Copyright, William Alanson White Psychiatric Foundation. Reprinted with permission.

ences, clarifying important associations and discrepancies between self and observation-based ratings (Humes & Humphrey, 1994).

For decades, the model and the metric systems have repeatedly been revised and tested by various tests of validity, most often by dimensional ratings and factor analysis (Benjamin, 1974, 1994; Lorr & Strack, 1999; Pincus, Newes, Dickinson, & Ruiz, 1998). Results have indicated that items devised to represent specific interpersonal and intrapsychic states conform to the dimensional assumptions pro-posed by the SASB model. Additionally, researchers and clinicians from a broad range of theoretical perspectives have used SASB-based measures (self-report, other-report, and observation based) for a variety of purposes, including the study of family process and psychological dysfunction (Estroff, Zimmer, Lachicotte, & Benoit, 1994; Florsheim et al., 1996; Grigg, Friesen, & Sheppy, 1989; Humes & Humphrey, 1994; Humphrey, 1989; McGonigle, Smith, Benjamin, & Turner, 1993; Ratti, Humphrey, & Lyons, 1996), married couples (Brown & Smith, 1992), adolescent couples (Florsheim, Moore, Zollinger, MacDonald, & Sumida, 1999), dyadic psychotherapy (Alpher, Henry, & Strupp, 1990; Connolly et al., 1996; Greenberg, Ford, Aldern, & Johnson, 1993; Henry, Schacht, & Strupp, 1990; Talley, Strupp, & Morey, 1990; Wiser & Goldfried, 1998), therapist training (Henry, Schacht, Strupp, & Butler, 1993), individual psychopathology (Ichiyama & Zucker, 1996; Swift, Bushnell, Hanson, & Logemann, 1986; Wonderlich & Swift, 1990), and personality (Pincus, Gurtman, & Ruiz, 1998). Fully validated versions of the SASB-based questionnaires are available in English, German, Nor-wegian, Swedish, and Italian. Interested readers will find further discussion of the development of SASB in Benjamin (1974, 1994, 1996a, 1996b, 1996c).

DESCRIPTION OF THE CODING SYSTEM

The SASB observational coding scheme described here is based on Benjamin's more general model for describing and predicting interpersonal and intrapsychic processes (Benjamin, 1994, 1996a).[1] In the full SASB model, the three circumplexes are each divided into 36 specific points, each of which describes a particular combination of interdependence and affiliation. Because the full SASB model is for too specific for the purposes of process coding, Benjamin and col-leagues developed a simplified model by grouping four to five data points into 24 cluster codes (Benjamin et al., 1981). The cluster model, illustrated in Fig. 8.2, is based on the same set of principles underlying the full model. Specific descriptions and examples of behaviors described by the first two surfaces of the cluster model are provided in Table 8.1 (see pp. 136–137).

The process of SASB coding a unit of interpersonal behavior on the cluster model involves three steps or decisions. First, the coder must decide whether a given interpersonal behavior is self-focused, other focused, or both self- and other focused. Statements that convey a mixed focus (self and other), such as the state-ment "I waited up all night for you to come home," are often among the most diffi-cult to code because it can difficult to tease apart the transitive and intransitive components. On rare occasions, coders may want to consider using the introject

---

[1]Family researchers interested in SASB are encouraged to consider using both the self-report and ob-servation-based measures to study family processes. Readers interested in a summary of clinical and re-search uses of statistical parameters given by the SASB software may find it useful to read: "An Interpersonal Theory of Personality Disorders." by L. S. Benjamin, 1996 in J. F. Clarkin (Ed.), *Major Theories of Personality Disorder,* pp. 141–220, New York: Guilford.

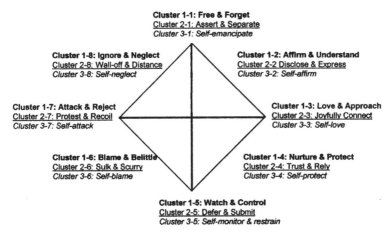

FIG 8.2. Combined versions of the SASB cluster model. From Benjamin, L. S. (1996). *Interpersonal diagnosis and treatment of personality disorder.* New York: Guilford Press, and Benjamin, L. S. (1987). The use of the SASB dimensional model to develop treatment plans for personality disorders: I. Narcissism. *Journal of Personality Disorders, 1,* 43–70. Reprinted with permission. Copyright © 2000, University of Utah.

surface to describe a particular behavior. For example, the statement "You made me feel awful about myself" could be coded as both "other focused" (1–6) and "introject focused" (3–7).

Once the focus of the behavior has been determined, its degree of interdependence is rated on a scale ranging from −5 (highly enmeshed) to +5 (highly differentiated). For example, the other-focused statement "Stop that" would be rated as a −5 on the interdependence scale because it conveys a high level of control. By contrast, the self-focused statement "I'll do as I please" would be rated high on the interdependence scale (+5) because it is highly autonomy taking, conveying interpersonal disengagement. Finally, the degree of affiliation is rated on a scale ranging from −5 (extremely hostile) to +5 (extremely warm). For example, the statement "you make me sick" would be rated as highly disaffiliative (−5), whereas the statement "I love you" would be rated as highly affiliative (+5).

Based on these three coding decisions, a more specific categorical code is assigned to each behavior. For example, the question "Will you help me with this math problem?" posed by a school-age boy to his mother, would be coded as self-focused, moderately warm (+2 or +3), and moderate submissiveness (−2 or −3). Based on these three decisions, the code "trust and rely" would be used to describe this behavior.

Distinguishing Between Simple, Multiple, Complex, and Indirect Communications.   The fundamental assumption of the SASB model is that nearly any interpersonally relevant behavior can be adequately described utilizing the three-step process outlined earlier. In most cases, after completing this process, a

TABLE 8.1

Descriptions of Other-Focused and Self-Focused SASB Cluster Codes

SASB Code	Description	Example
1-1: Free & Forget	Neutral autonomy giving, which includes letting another "be their own person," express their own identity, feelings, or beliefs. This form of behavior is neutral on the affiliative dimension, communicating little warmth or hostility.	"Do whatever you want, it's totally up to you."
1-2: Affirm & Understand	Warm autonomy granting, communicating empathy and understanding of another's experience; includes actively listening and validating the other's perspective or opinion.	"I understand how you must feel."
1-3: Love & Approach	Extreme warmth, which is neither particularly autonomy giving or controlling. This behavior often involves initiating affection.	"I love you."
1-4: Nurture & Protect	Warm, caring control, which may involve taking care of, protecting, teaching, or guiding another person.	"Would you like some help with that?"
1-5: Watch & Control	Behavior that is controlling or monitoring and that conveys little warmth or hostility. This type of behavior may include telling another person what to do or how to think.	"Do as I say."
1-6: Belittle & Blame	Hostile control. This form of behavior communicates criticism or condescension toward another person.	"You never get anything right."
1-7: Attack & Reject	Extremely hostile behavior, which is neither particularly autonomy giving nor controlling. This form of behavior involves destroying or threatening another person (physically or verbally).	"I hate you."
1-8: Ignore & Neglect	Hostile autonomy-giving behavior, which may involve abandoning, neglecting, or ignoring another person.	"Get lost!"

Code	Description	Example
2-1: Assert & Separate	Neutral autonomy-taking behavior, which may involve acting independently and asserting one's own ideas and beliefs. As neutral on the affiliation dimension, this form of behavior is neither particularly warm nor hostile.	"I'm going to do things my way."
2-2: Disclose & Express	Warm autonomy taking; characterized as a friendly, open sharing of ideas, experiences, and feelings with another.	"I am feeling frightened right now."
2-3: Joyfully Connect	Extreme warmth that is neither autonomy taking nor submissive. Involves responding to the other's approach in a receptive, loving, and joyful manner. This communicates enjoyment in being close to the other.	"I love you too."
2-4: Trust & Rely	Warm submissiveness; involves willingly receiving help or learning from another person. This behavior is classically "childlike."	"Would you help me with this?"
2-5: Defer & Submit	Submissiveness that is neither warm nor hostile. This type of submissiveness usually involves giving in, yielding, or complying with expectations.	"Yes, ma'am."
2-6: Sulk & Scurry	Hostile submissiveness, which might include whining, "poor me" statements, defensive self-justification, resentful compliance, and "scurrying" to appease another person.	(In a whiny, defensive tone) "Fine … I'll do what you say—just like I always do!"
2-7: Protest & Recoil	Extreme hostility, which is neither autonomy taking nor deferring. This type of behavior communicates fear, hate, and/or disgust toward another, and may include an attempt to escape from or fight off a perceived attacker.	"I feel disgusted by you."
2-8: Wall off & Distance	Hostile autonomy taking, which may involve shutting others out, isolating oneself, or withdrawing from an interaction.	"Bug off."

Note. The descriptions of these codes are based on summaries found in Humphrey and Benjamin's (1989) SASB observational coding manual.

137

single SASB code is given to a single unit of behavior. However, the coding process becomes more complicated when a particular behavior conveys more than one interpersonally relevant message. There are three situations in which coders might use more than one SASB code to describe an interpersonal behavior.

First, the SASB model recognizes that a single statement or unit of behavior may simultaneously convey two distinct interpersonal components that are packaged together. For example, a father who warmly conveys a story about his own youth for the sake of teaching his child might be coded as both disclosing and nurturing (2–2, 1–4). Likewise, a child who respectfully requests permission to stay out with his friends past his usual curfew (e.g., I really want to go to this party after I've finished my homework, so what do you say?) would be coded both asserting and relying (2–1, 2–4). These forms of behavior are referred to as multiple communications, and are thought to play an important role in families undergoing developmental transitions, when roles are being renegotiated.

The second instance in which a coder may want to assign more than one SASB code to describe a single unit of behavior occurs when a speaker simultaneously conveys two or more distinct but inextricable messages. For example, an exasperated mother who responds to her son's misbehavior by asking "What in the world were you thinking?" conveys two inextricable messages in the same breath, one that is autonomy granting (expressing a genuine interest in his thoughts), and one that is judgmental and condescending. Complex codes are often used to describe communications in which the literal meaning of the words spoken seem at odds with the tone in which they are conveyed, as in sarcastic, sardonic, or otherwise confusing communications ("Nice going, bonehead!"). The SASB coding scheme's capacity to accurately describe these complex communications is particularly important when studying clinical populations, which tend to use more of these mixed messages (Humphrey & Benjamin, 1986). However it is important to note that complex communications are not necessarily pathonomic. For example, a father who warmly responds to his daughter's accomplishment by becoming tearful and saying "I am so proud of you!" is both disclosing how he feels (2–2) and affirming her success (1–2), but the components are inextricable.

The third situation in which a coder may use more that one SASB code to describe a particular behavior involves the use of implied process codes. Implied process codes are used when a family member simultaneously conveys one message to one family member and a distinctively separate message to another family member. The message to the second person is conveyed indirectly. For example, a mother who turns to her husband and says, "I am just so fed up with her," referring to her teenage daughter, is simultaneously expressing (2–2) to her husband (and perhaps seeking his assistance or 2–4) and belittling (1–6) her daughter. This type of code would require the coder to provide more than one set of referents (e.g., wife to husband, mother to daughter).

Because families often communicate important messages indirectly or in ways that seem insincere or duplicitous, enabling coders to assign more than one code to each unit of behavior is one of the most useful features of the SASB coding scheme.

The flexible application of simple, multiple, complex, and indirect codes allows for a more accurate and comprehensive rendering of observed family process.

Process Versus Content.   Related to the issue of complex communications, the SASB model is designed to distinguish between the process and the content of interpersonal communications. When coding interpersonal process, coders are instructed to draw upon a combination of interpersonal cues, including (a) tone and affect, (b) tenor and pitch, and/or (c) the literal meaning of a statement. When coding content, coders focus exclusively on the literal meaning of the words, disregarding the tone, affect, and tenor with which that meaning is conveyed.

Thus far, we have described how the SASB coding scheme assesses interpersonal *process*. Generally, process coding involves the interpretation of both verbal and nonverbal behavior cues. For example, the process-based interpretation of the statement "I don't like the company you've been keeping" would include some consideration of the words that are—at face value—critical, and the tone, which could be either blaming, controlling, or protective. Thus, the final coding decision would depend on *how* this statement was conveyed. Some process codes are based on nonverbal behavior only. For example, a husband who gently touches his wife is communicating affection in a purely nonverbal manner, and would likely be coded as loving (1–3).

In many instances the literal meaning of a statement will match the process through which it is communicated. For example, a person who states "I'm leaving" and then does so, has engaged in an interpersonal process (separation) that mirrors the meaning of his departing words. However, the literal meaning of a statement is not necessarily consistent with its interpersonal meaning. For example, the words "Whatever you say, Mom" may convey a literal message of compliance, but might be said (sarcastically) in way that effectively communicates the message "I will do as I please." In this instance, the interpersonal process could be captured only with a complex code, which combines compliance (2–5) and defiance (2–8).

There is some evidence that process codes provide a more meaningful (e.g., clinically relevant) index of family behavior than content codes. For example, Humphrey (1989) reported that SASB-based *process* codes clearly distinguished between the family interactions of bulimic, anorexic, and normal (nondistressed) adolescent girls. By contrast, no distinctions between these groups could be made on the basis of SASB content codes. These findings suggest that how families engage with one another is far more clinically meaningful than what they say to one another.

THE CODING PROCESS

SASB coders tend to work from both transcripts and videotapes. Once a videotaped family interaction has been transcribed, the first step in the coding process is to segment the transcript into meaningful units of behavior. These thought units may be a long as a complete sentence, or as short as a grunt or gesture. Guidelines for segmenting transcribed data are outlined in Humphrey and Benjamin's (1989) coding manual. After the transcript has been segmented, SASB coders proceed by coding one unit at a time in accordance with the steps described earlier. Coders may choose to code process, content, or both depending on the nature of the research question.

Once completed, a SASB-coded family interaction provides a comprehensive, detailed, and specific rendering of a family interaction. Working backward from a SASB-coded transcript, a skilled coder should be able to articulate a blow-by-blow account of a family's interaction, accurately representing each family member's role in the exchange. Once coded, SASB data can be sorted, condensed, and analyzed using programs available through the Department of Psychology at the University of Utah.

We have a few words of caution for readers considering the using the SASB model for family process research. First, it is difficult and time consuming to become a reliable SASB coder. As we describe in the next section, it may require up to 100 hours of training to achieve interrater reliability. Relative to most coding schemes on the market, the SASB model is more complicated and more difficult to learn, requiring a high degree of patience and persistence. Moreover, we recommend against self-instruction, and strongly suggest that novice SASB researchers receive instruction from someone who has already achieved reliability.

Also, it is important to note that even after reliability has been achieved the tasks of coding, processing, and analyzing SASB data can be extremely time consuming. It typically takes 2–3 hours to transcribe a 10-minute family interaction, and another 2–3 hours to microcode the interaction and enter the data into a SASB data-processing program.

The amount of time required before SASB-based results can be obtained may frustrate researchers eager to quickly reap the fruits of their labor. There are two ways to cut down on time spent coding and processing data. First, a clinically oriented researcher may elect to code "process" only, eliminating the time-consuming task of SASB coding the content of family interactions. Research conducted by Humphrey (1989) suggests that the value of the data obtained from content-coding interactions is not necessarily worth the time spent obtaining it.

Second, coders might consider using the composite system, described next, which saves time but diminishes the level of behavior specificity available to microanalytic coders.

SASB-Composite.   The SASB Composite Coding Scheme is a recently developed variation on the microanalytic scheme described previously (Moore & Florsheim, 1996). There are two primary differences between the global and microanalytic coding schemes. First, rather than assign a code to each specific "speech act," global coders assign summary scores (ranging from 0 to 5) to every 2-minute interval of interaction. These summary scores are based on tallies of specific SASB codes. Because the smallest coding unit is the 2-minute summary score rather than the single unit of behavior, composite coders are able to work directly from videotapes of family interactions. Freed from the necessity of working from both transcriptions and videos, researchers using the composite system are able to avoid the labor-intensive process of transcribing and segmenting their data. The composite coding and data entry process requires about 2–3 hours to complete for each 10 minutes of family interaction, assuming the presence of three family members.

The second difference between the composite and microanalytic systems is that in addition to estimating the frequency of specific codes over each 2-minute period, global coders are asked to provide intensity scores. Intensity refers to the strength with which an interpersonal message is conveyed. For example, a child whose only attempt to assert her or himself consists of a softly spoken statement, such as "I think maybe I'd like to play a different game," might receive a low intensity score on the assert and separate scale. Conversely, a child who boldly shouts, "I am playing a different game now!" would be given a high intensity score for assert and separate. Intensity scores, which range from 1 to 3, are intended to allow for a greater degree of behavioral specificity when assigning summary scores.

The specific steps in composite coding are as follows:

1. The coder watches the videotaped family interaction in 2-minute intervals, focusing on one member of the family at a time.
2. The coder tallies specific simple, multiple, and complex codes and these tallies are converted into frequency scores. Coding sheets for tallying are provided in the composite coding manual, available through the Department of Psychology at the University of Utah.
3. The coder then provides an intensity score for each frequency score, based on the average level of observed interpersonal intensity.
4. For each 2-minute section of interaction, the coder calculates a "summary" based on the product of the frequency and intensity scores given to each SASB cluster.
5. Summary scores for each 2-minute section are then summed to derive a set of total SASB cluster scores.

Although the composite system has been less extensively used than the microsystem, initial results suggest that it functions similarly to the microanalytic system (Florsheim et al., 1999; Moore & Florsheim, 2000).

Although coders using the composite system must be reliably trained as microanalytic SASB coders, composite coding is explicitly designed to help SASB researchers obtain results more quickly and efficiently. The primary disadvantage of the Composite Coding Scheme is that it renders a relatively less detailed and specific account of a family's interaction. Unlike the microsystem, the composite system does not render a blow-by-blow account of a family's interaction. This distinction between the composite and micro system is particularly relevant to researchers interested in sequentially analyzing family process data.

CODER TRAINING

A coding scheme that (a) requires coders to interpret behavior using multiple dimensions, and (b) allows coders to assign multiple codes to a single unit of behavior is difficult to learn. Typically, well-qualified mental health professionals require between 50 and 100 hours of SASB training to achieve reliability. The primary prerequisites for SASB training are as follows: (a) a high level of interpersonal sensitivity (defined as the capacity to accurately interpret interpersonal cues), (b) a working knowledge of interpersonal theory, and (c) a slightly obsessive temperament. Most SASB coders are psychologists, psychiatrists, graduate students of psychology, and a select group of undergraduate psychology students.

It is difficult to overestimate the importance of the "coding group" in training coders. Although the principles of SASB coding are explicitly delineated, the process of deciding how warm or autonomous a statement seems is based on the individual coder's judgment. It is through the process of group coding that a clear fit between a SASB code and an observed behavior is determined. That is, the process of group coding socializes the individual coder to the "markers" of interpersonal behavior. Thus, coders are trained to draw upon consensually derived indicators of affiliation and interdependence.

The coding group also helps manage the problem of individual coder bias, defined as the tendency for coders to drift toward their own idiosyncratic ways of understanding interpersonal process and applying SASB codes. For example, a study participant who lives in the projects, works full-time, and is raising three adolescents on her own may convey her feelings in ways that are not readily understood by a coder who grew up in a two-parent family in the suburbs. Frustration, anger, control, care, and concern may be expressed in ways that are difficult to code because they do not resonate with what is familiar. Novice coders are naturally inclined to read behaviors in ways that are consistent with their own experiences; group coding is intended to have the effect of decentering coders, widening their perspectives, and sharpening their interpersonal acumen. SASB training involves helping coders become more aware of their own subjective perceptions in order to minimize idiosyncratic or ethnocentric interpretations of observed behaviors. Although this form of "objectivity by consensus" is also not free from bias, the process of group coding helps to minimize the potential for bias, in the form of misunderstanding and unmeasured variations in coding. When coding the behavior of ethnically diverse families, establishing construct validity depends, in part, on the inclusion of coders who are aware of the context-bound meanings, interpersonal nuances, and nonverbal cues of the study participants.

Though we have tried to emphasize the importance of training coders to be sensitive to culturally salient interpersonal cues, it is important to note that coders can become *too* caught up in cultural variations in meanings. Becoming oversensitive to cultural differences in behavior can create problems if coders establish different (culturally distinct) sets of criteria for indexing affiliation and interdependence. If coders were to become too relativistic in their application of SASB codes (e.g., well, that was a pretty warm response for *this* guy!), it would be impossible to make meaningful comparisons across groups or even across individual family units. It is important to emphasize that the SASB model is based on well-grounded, clearly defined constructs that are broadly applicable. As such, the model can accommodate variations in meanings without losing its conceptual integrity or empirical utility.

The SASB training process is clearly articulated in Humphrey and Benjamin's (1989) SASB observational coding manual. It is strongly recommended that an experienced and reliable SASB coder supervise the training of novice coders.

RELIABILITY

We recommend that SASB researchers use Cohen's formula for weighted kappa (Cohen, 1968) to calculate interrater reliability when using the microcoding system (Humphrey & Benjamin, 1989). Moreover, we recommend that SASB coders remain blind to families' clinical status, and maintain interrater reliability scores of at least .60 weight kappa (Hartmann, 1982). The standard "kappa" approach to interrater reliability is calculated on a strictly "hit or miss" basis; codes are counted as reliable if and only if they match with one another. Thus, the formula is based on the percentage of agreements, controlling for the likelihood of chance agreements. Weighted kappa is designed to give partial credit for codes that are closely related (e.g., 1–4 and 1–5) and to subtract credit for codes that are quite disparate (e.g., 1–4 and 2–6). Instructions for calculating weighted kappa scores manually were provided by Humphrey and Benjamin. A program for calculating weighted kappa is available from the authors.

When calculating interrater reliability among coders using the composite system, intraclass correlation is recommended (Shrout & Fleiss, 1979; Streiner, 1995). Intraclass correlation is designed to assess for the rate of agreement between two or more raters on a continuous scale or interval data, while controlling for any systematic bias among raters. Intraclass correlations alpha coefficients can be calculated using SPSS, 8.0.

Several research groups using the SASB observational coding scheme to study various types of families have achieved acceptable rates of interrater reliability. Humphrey (1989), who studied the families of bulimic, anorexic, or nondisordered adolescent girls ($N = 74$ mother–father–daughter triads), and used Cohen's (1968) weighted kappa as an index of interrater reliability, reported rates ranging from .63 to .83 (mean = .74) for process codes, and rates ranging form .58 to 1.00 (mean = .79) for content codes. Ratti et al. (1996), who used the SASB coding scheme to study the families of polydrug-dependent, bulimic, and normal adolescent girls ($N = 44$), reported weighted kappas ranging from .60 to .93 (mean = .74). Florsheim et al. (1996) used SASB to study 149 families of African-American and Hispanic boys, and reported weighted kappas ranging from .60 to .82 (mean = .67).

SASB researchers studying couples have also reported on interrater reliability. For example, Brown and Smith (1992) used the SASB model to assess behavior of 45 married couples, and reported a kappa (not weighted) of .60, and percent agreements ranging from 60% to 71%. Also, Florsheim et al. (1999), who used SASB-Composite to code the behavior of 70 pregnant adolescents and their partners, reported intraclass correlations ranging from .80 to .95 (mean = .90). Finally, Benjamin, Cushing, Schloret, Callaway and Gelfand (1999), who conducted an observation-based sequential analytic study of mother–infant dyads, reported kappas ranging from .60 to .85 on the coding of behavioral sequences. As indicated by this selective review of published reliability statistics, SASB-based techniques for coding interpersonal behavior have been reliably used to evaluate family process across several distinct developmental and interpersonal domains.

VALIDITY

The convergent and discriminant validity of the SASB-based observational coding scheme has been independently demonstrated by several research groups. For example, Henry and colleagues (Henry, Schacht, & Strupp, 1986, 1990) found that SASB-coded client-to-therapist behavior correlated with independent indicators of treatment outcome. Brown and Smith (1992) found that increased levels of observed hostility in men (as indexed by SASB observational codes) correlated with increased levels of physiological reactivity (as indexed by changes in systolic blood pressure). Also, Humphrey and colleagues (Humphrey, 1989, 1989; Humphrey, Apple, & Kirschenbaum, 1986) have used SASB observational codes to successfully differentiate between diagnostically distinct clinical groups

As indicated earlier, in addition to the SASB coding scheme described in this chapter, Benjamin (1988) developed a number of associated self-report instruments designed to measure interpersonal and intrapsychic processes. Using these measures, Benjamin (1994) and others (Lorr & Strack, 1999; Pincus, Gurtman, & Ruiz, 1998; Pincus, Newes et al., 1998; Tscheulin & Glossner, 1993) have conducted a series of studies designed to establish the construct validity and internal consistency of the SASB model. Results have confirmed the circumplex structure of SASB, and the existence of the three proposed dimensions. Generally, alpha coefficients for SASB cluster scores have been high. An overview of published studies utilizing SASB-based methods can be found in the introduction to the special section of *Journal of Consulting and Clinical Psychology* on clinical research with the SASB model (Benjamin, 1996c).

STUDIES USING THE SASB

This section focuses on how the SASB observational coding scheme has helped clarify interpersonal in the families of eating-disordered adolescent girls (Humphrey, 1989) and antisocial adolescent boys (Florsheim et al., 1996). Generally, our goal is to highlight the unique strengths of the model for conducting clinically oriented family research. However, it should be noted that in addition to using the SASB to code family processes, researchers have also used SASB to code the interactions of adolescent couples (Florsheim et al., 1999; Moore & Florsheim, 2000), married couples (Brown & Smith, 1992), therapists and clients (Henry et al., 1986, 1993), and mothers and infants (Benjamin & Gelfand, 1992).

Humphrey (1989) has used the SASB model to conduct a series of studies examining the families of anorexic, bulimic, bulimic-anorexic girls, and matched group of normal controls. The overarching goal of these studies was to identify similarities and differences in the family behavior of diagnostically distinct subgroups of eating-disordered girls. Findings indicated that relative to the parents of normal controls and bulimic girls, the parents of anorexic girls engaged in more complex communications when interacting with their daughters, conveying a mix of nurturance and neglect. Their daughters, on the other hand, tended to engage relatively submissive. The parents of bulimic girls were found to be relatively more blaming and belittling toward their daughters, who tended to engage in more sulky and/or counterblaming behavior. The behaviors of the bulimic-anorexic daughters and their parents were not clearly distinguishable from either the anorexic families or the bulimic families. It was also noted that the fathers in all three diagnostic groups tended to be more alike than the mothers, who tended to be more variable across groups. More specifically, the fathers of all three subtypes of eating-disordered girls were more controlling, more blaming, and less nurturing than the fathers of the normal girls. SASB's high level of behavioral specificity contributed to Humphrey's success in clarifying clinically meaningful differences between the families of closely related diagnostic subgroups, and highlighting the interpersonal roles of specific family members across diagnostic groups. This level of specificity greatly facilitates the process of translating research findings into clinical practice (Henry, 1996; Humphrey, 1989).

Florsheim et al. (1996) used the SASB observational coding scheme to examine the relationship between parental control, adolescent autonomy, and the occurrence of antisocial behavior among inner-city boys. In this study, Florsheim et al. focused on boys at high and low risk for antisocial behavior, as indexed by teacher and parent ratings on Achenbach's measure of externalizing behavior (Achenbach, 1991). In summary, they found that compared to low-risk boys, high-risk boys engaged in more submissive behavior and a complex combination of sulky and assertive behavior than low-risk boys, and less trusting behavior. The parents of high-risk boys engaged in more blaming and less nurturing than the parents of low-risk boys. It was also found that the correlation between parental control and child hostile-assertive behavior was significantly higher among low-risk than high-risk families, suggesting that low-risk parents responded more firmly and consistently to their children's negative behavior.

In addition to these differences between families that were based on risk status, Florsheim et al. (1996) found that African-American boys were generally more assertive than Hispanic boys, and that African-American parents tended to engage in a complex form of behavior management that incorporated control and autonomy-giving behavior. Moreover, the correlation between parental control and child assertiveness was significantly higher among the Hispanic families. Generally, these findings suggest that African-American parents seemed more autonomy promoting toward their adolescent sons, whereas Hispanic families are more control oriented. Many of these findings would have been obscured by a less specific approach to behavioral analysis. These results underscore the value of the SASB model for identifying cross-ethnic differences in family process. That is, the specificity of the SASB model helped this group of researchers to identify cross-ethnic differences in how parents and their adolescent sons negotiate issues of control and autonomy.

EXCERPT FROM THE CODING MANUAL

This final section details the step-by-step process involved in SASB coding a brief except from a transcribed, videotaped interaction of a father, mother, and daughter. This excerpt was adapted from Humphrey and Benjamin's (1989) SASB Observational Coding Manual, which provides a more detailed explanation of the steps involved in coding this "normal" family's 10-minute interaction:

SPEAKER	DIALOGUE	EXPLANATION
Mom	(1) O.K. We just kind of wanted to talk to you a little bit because we've noticed you've been kinda withdrawn and not a part of the family. / (2) Is there something in particular that's bothering you?/	(1) & (2) Both these statements from mother (X referent) focus on the daughter (Y referent). They convey warm affiliation, and a moderate degree of influence. In process, they would be coded as cluster 1–4, Nurturing & Protecting. The focus of (1) might seem confusing since the mother says, "We're wanting to talk to you". The thrust of the meaning is not on the mother's experience (i.e., that would be focus on self), but on the parents' "talking" to their daughter (i.e., focus on other).
		In terms of content, there are three codable clauses. The first could be paraphrased as "Parents talking to daughter". It would be focused on daughter, mildly friendly, and somewhat influencing, placing it in cluster 1–4 too. The second clause could be restated as: "Daughter has withdrawn from the family", and coded as daughter focusing on self, somewhat hostile, and fairly autonomous. Cluster 2–8, Walling Off & Distancing, would fit. The third codable clause could be restated as: "Something is bothering you," and coded as an abstract force focused on the daughter, in a moderately hostile and somewhat controlling manner; cluster code 1–6, Belittling & Blaming.

Daughter   (3) Things are just fine./

Daughter (X referent) responds to mother's friendly inquiry with warm reassurance, in process. She's focused on mother (Y referent), is friendly, and somewhat influencing, placing it in cluster 1–4, Nurturing & Protecting. This response might have been coded as a disclosure instead if it were expressive of something significant for the daughter. As it is, the daughter's message is; "No need to worry."

The content is not codable because it is missing a clear Y referent (i.e., things are fine in relation to whom?).

Dad   (4) I guess I feel as parents and as children that we need to … it is very important that we communicate and that is something that we all need to learn./

Father's speech is focused on daughter, warm and influential in process; cluster 1–4, Nurturing & Protecting, would fit.

In content, there are two codable clauses. The first one could be restated as: "We communicate with one another". The verb "communicate" implies a two-way interaction in which each person expresses his/her feelings and listens to the other members. We would suggest coding it as two related messages, technically called a multiple code. Both messages are quite friendly and autonomous, only the focus differs. Expressing oneself is focused on the self, cluster 2–2, whereas listening is focused on the other person, cluster 1–2. The family functions as both the X and Y referents. The next content could be restated as: "We learn from each other". Again, the referents are the family toward itself. Learning from each other is focused on the self, friendly, and interdependent, placing it in cluster 2–4, Trusting & Relying.

REFERENCES

Achenbach, T. M. (1991). *Integrative guide for the 1991 CBCL 4–18 YSF and TRF profiles.* Burlington: University of Vermont Department of Psychiatry.

Alper, V. S., Henry, W. P., & Strupp, H. H. (1990). Dynamic factors in patient assessment and prediction of change in short term dynamic psychotherapy. *Psychotherapy, 27,* 350–361.

Benjamin, L. S. (1974). The structural analysis of social behavior. *Psychology Review, 81,* 392–425.

Benjamin, L. S. (1977). Structural analysis of a family in therapy. *Journal of Consulting and Clinical Psychology, 45,* 391–406.

Benjamin, L. S. (1988). *The short form INTREX user's manual, Part I.* Salt Lake City: University of Utah.

Benjamin, L. S. (1994). SASB: A bridge between personality theory and clinical psychology. *Psychological Inquiry, 5,* 273–316.

Benjamin, L. S. (1996a). *Interpersonal diagnosis and treatment of personality disorders* (2nd ed.). New York: Guilford.

Benjamin, L. S. (1996b). An interpersonal theory of personality disorders. In J. Clarkin (Ed.), *Major theories of personality* (pp.141–220). New York: Guilford.

Benjamin, L. S. (1996c). Introduction to the special section on Structural Analysis of Social Behavior (SASB). *Journal of Consulting and Clinical Psychology, 64,* 1203–1212.

Benjamin, L. S., Cushing, G., Schloret, K., Callaway, K., & Gelfand, D. (1999). *The effect of depression on mother–infant complementarity.* Manuscript in preparation. (Based on a presentation by G. Cushing and L. S. Benjamin at the meeting of the Society for Interpersonal Treatment and Research (SITAR), Madison, WI, May 1999.)

Benjamin, L. S., & Gelfand, D. M. (1992). *Possible transmission of depression through patterns of mother–infant interaction.* Progress report to John D. and Catherine T. MacArthur Foundation Mental Health Research Network on the psychobiology of depression and other affective disorders.

Benjamin, L. S., Giat, L., & Estroff, S. E. (1981). *Manual for coding social interactions in terms of Structural Analysis of Social Behavior.* Distributed by the University of Utah, Salt Lake City.

Brown, P. C., & Smith, T. W. (1992). Social influence, marriage, and the heart: Cardiovascular consequences of interpersonal control in husbands and wives. *Health Psychology, 11,* 88–96.

Carson, R. (1969). *Interaction concepts of personality.* Chicago: Aldine.

Cohen, J. (1968). Weighted kappa: Nominal scale agreement with provision for scaled disagreement or partial credit. *Psychological Bulletin, 70,* 213–220.

Connolly, M. B., Crits-Christoph, P, Demorest, A., Azarian, K., Muenz, L., & Chittams, J. (1996). Varieties of transference patterns in psychotherapy. *Journal of Consulting & Clinical Psychology, 64,* 1213–1221.

Estroff, S. E., Zimmer, C., Lachicotte, & W. S., Benoit, J. (1994). The influence of social networks and social support on violence by persons with serious mental illness. *Hospital and Community Psychiatry, 45,* 669–679.

Florsheim, P., Moore, D., Zollinger, L., MacDonald, J., & Sumida, E. (1999). Adolescent fatherhood in developmental perspective: Does antisocial behavior predict problems in parental functioning? *Applied Developmental Science, 3,* 178–191.

Florsheim, P., Tolan, P., & Gorman-Smith, D. (1996). Family processes and risk for externalizing behavior problems among African American and Mexican-American boys. *Journal of Consulting and Clinical Psychology, 64,* 1222–1230.

Greenberg, L. S., Ford, C. L, Aldern, L. S., & Johnson, S. M. (1993). In-session change in emotionally focused therapy. *Journal of Consulting & Clinical Psychology, 61,* 78–84.

Grigg, D., Friesen, J. D., & Sheppy, M. I. (1989). Family patterns associated with anorexia nervosa. *Journal of Marital and Family Therapy, 15,* 29–42.

Hartmann, D. (1982). Assessing the dependability of observational data. *New Directions for Methodology of Social and Behavioral Science, 14,* 51–65.

Heavey, C., Christensen, A., & Malamuth, N. (1995). The longitudinal impact of demand and withdrawal during marital conflict. *Journal of Consulting and Clinical Psychology, 63*, 797–801.

Henry, W. P. (1996). Structural analysis of social behavior as a common metric for programmatic psychopathology and psychotherapy research. *Journal of Consulting and Clinical Psychology, 64*, 1263–1275.

Henry, W. P., Butler, S. F., Strupp, H. H., Schacht, T. E., et al. (1993). Effects of training in time-limited dynamic psychotherapy: Changes in therapist behavior. *Journal of Consulting and Clinical Psychology, 61*, 434–440.

Henry, W. P., Schacht, T. E., & Strupp, H. H. (1986). Structural analysis of social behavior: Application to a study of interpersonal process in differential psychotherapeutic outcome. *Journal of Consulting and Clinical Psychology, 54*, 27–31.

Henry, W. P., Schacht, T. E., & Strupp, H. H. (1990). Patient and therapist introject, interpersonal process, and differential psychotherapy outcome. *Journal of Consulting and Clinical Psychology, 58*, 768–774.

Henry, W. P., Schacht, T. E., Strupp, H. H., & Butler, S. F. (1993). Effects of training in time-limited dynamic psychotherapy: Mediators of therapists' responses to training. *Journal of Consulting & Clinical Psychology, 61*, 441–447.

Humes, D. L., & Humphrey, L. L. (1994). A multimethod analysis of families with a polydrug-dependent or normal adolescent daughter. *Journal of Abnormal Psychology, 103*, 676–685.

Humphrey, L. L. (1989). Observed family interactions among subtypes of eating disorders using Structural Analysis of Social Behavior. *Journal of Consulting and Clinical Psychology, 57*, 206–214.

Humphrey, L. L., Apple, R. F., & Kirschenbaum, D. S. (1986). Differentiating bulimic-anorexic from normal families using interpersonal and behavioral observational systems. *Journal of Consulting and Clinical Psychology, 54*, 190–195.

Humphrey, L. L., & Benjamin, L. S. (1986). Using structural analysis of social behavior to assess critical but elusive family processes: A new solution to an old problem. *American Psychologist, 4*, 979–989.

Humphrey, L. L., & Benjamin, L. S. (1989). *The Structural Analysis of Social Behavior observational coding scheme.* Unpublished manual, Northwestern University Medical School, Chicago.

Ichiyama, M. A., & Zucker, R. A. (1996). Articulating subtype differences in self and relational experience among alcoholic men using Structural Analysis of Social Behavior. *Journal of Consulting and Clinical Psychology, 64*, 1245–1254.

Kiesler, D. J. (1983). The 1982 Interpersonal Circle: A taxonomy for complementarity in human transactions. *Psychological Review, 90*, 185–214.

Leary, T. (1957). *Interpersonal diagnosis of personality.* New York: Ronald Press.

Lorr, M., & Strack, S. (1999). A study of Benjamin's eight facet Structural Analysis of Social Behavior (SASB) model. *Journal of Clinical Psychology, 55*, 207–215.

Mahler, M. (1968). *On human symbiosis and the vicissitudes of individuation.* New York: International Universities Press.

McGonigle, M., Smith, T., Benjamin, L. S., & Turner, C. (1993). Hostility and nonshared family environment: A study of monozygotic twins. *Journal of Research in Personality, 27*, 23–34.

Moore, D., & Florsheim, P. (1996). *SASB coding manual.* Unpublished manuscript, The University of Utah, Salt Lake City.

Moore, D., & Florsheim, P. (2000). *Interpersonal processes and psychopathology among expectant and nonexpectant adolescent couples.* Manuscript under review.

Murray, H. A. (1938). *Explorations in personality.* New York: Oxford University Press.

Pincus, A. L., Gurtman, M. B., & Ruiz, M. A. (1998). Structural analysis of social behavior (SASB): Circumplex analyses and structural relations with the interpersonal circle and the five-factor model of personality. *Journal of Personality and Social Psychology, 74,* 1629–1645.

Pincus, A. L., Newes, S. L., Dickinson, K. A., & Ruiz, M. A. (1998). A comparison of three indexes to assess the dimensions of Structural Analysis of Social Behavior. *Journal of Personality Assessment, 70,* 145–170.

Ratti, L. A., Humphrey, L. L., & Lyons, J. S. (1996). Structural analysis of families with a polydrug-dependent, bulimic, or normal adolescent daughter. *Journal of Consulting and Clinical Psychology, 64,* 1255–1262.

Schaefer, E. S. (1965). Configurational analysis of children's reports of parent behavior. *Journal of Consulting Psychology, 29,* 552–557.

Schaefer, E. S. (1971). From circular to spherical models for parent behavior and child behavior. In J. P. Hill (Ed.), *Minnesota symposium on child psychology (Vol. 4).* Minneapolis: University of Minnesota Press.

Shrout, P. E., & Fleiss, J. L. (1979). Intraclass correlation: Uses in assessing rater reliability. *Psychological Bulletin, 86,* 420–428.

Streiner, D. (1995). Learning how to differ: Agreement and reliability statistics in psychiatry. *Canadian Journal of Psychiatry, 40,* 60–66.

Sullivan, H. S. (1953). *The interpersonal theory of psychiatry.* New York: Norton.

Swift, W. J., Bushnell, N. J., Hanson, P., & Logemann, T. (1986). Self concept in adolescent anorexics. *Journal of the Academy of Child and Adolescent Psychiatry, 25,* 826–835.

Talley, P. F., Strupp, H. H., & Morey, L. C. (1990). Matchmaking in psychotherapy: Patient–therapist dimensions and their impact on outcome. *Journal of Consulting and Clinical Psychology, 58,* 182–188.

Tscheulin, D., & Glossner, A. (1993). Die deutsche Übertragung der Intrex 'Longform Questionaires': Validität und Answertungsgrundlagen der SASB Fragebogenmethode [The German translation of the Intrex 'Longform Questionnaires': Contribution to the validity of the SASB questionnaire method]. In W. Tress (Ed.), *SASB-Die strukturale Analyse sozialen Verhaltens: Ein Arbeitsbuch* (pp. 123–155). Heidelberg: Asanger.

Wiser, S., & Goldfried, M .R. (1998). Therapist interventions and client emotional experiencing in expert psychodynamic-interpersonal and cognitive-behavioral therapies. *Journal of Consulting and Clinical Psychology, 66,* 634–640.

Wonderlich, S. A., & Swift, W. J. (1990). Borderline versus other personality disorders in the eating disorders. *International Journal of Eating Disorders, 9,* 629–638.

9

Evaluating Coparenting and Family-Level Dynamics During Infancy and Early Childhood: The Coparenting and Family Rating System

James P. McHale
Clark University

Regina Kuersten-Hogan
Bradley Hospital, Brown University Medical Center

Allison Lauretti
Clark University

This chapter describes a system for evaluating several dimensions of coparenting and family process, introducing concepts based on the framework of structural family theory (S. Minuchin, 1974). The Coparenting and Family Rating System (CFRS) and its scales were developed as an alternative to several family-rating approaches that existed at the time of its development (see, e.g., Walsh, 1982) but that tended either to concentrate more focally on family diagnosis than on family process per se, and/or to require a fairly high level of clinical sophistication and inference to evaluate family health. The intent of the CFRS has been to capture variability in observable behavior exhibited during everyday family interactions.

Because its scales have only been applied to community (nonclinical) samples of families with children, its utility with clinically distressed families has not yet been established. Further, the system's emphasis on the exchanges and positioning of adult caregivers during family interaction makes it useful only for families where at least two adults are regularly involved with the children. We have used the scales effectively to evaluate interactions of both married and unmarried, two-parent families and of gay and lesbian parents. We have also used the scales to rate families with cocaregivers who are not intimate partners (e.g., a parent and grandparent) but have very few data on such cases. However, because the focus of the scales is on co*parenting* and not marital relations, we suspect the scales will prove useful in evaluating such family configurations (see, e.g., Tolson & Wilson, 1990).

THEORETICAL FOUNDATIONS

Patterns of behavior among family members within the context of family group interaction (family-level dynamics) often differ from behavior enacted by the same members within the context of family subsystems. For example, in some families fathers who are extremely warm and indulgent toward their sons when the two are alone together appear more distant and removed toward the same sons when parenting in the presence of their involved partner (see, e.g., Gjerde, 1986; Lauretti & McHale, 1997). Piecing together this family-level dynamic from interactional data drawn from each of the two dyadic, parent–child contexts would simply not be possible. Indeed, McHale, Kuersten-Hogan, Lauretti, and Rasmussen (2000) found, literally, *no* association between measures of mother–father parenting "discrepancies" based on data drawn from each, respective parent–child dyad and mother–father parenting discrepancies based on data drawn from family-group-level interactions. Yet it is these latter indices—reflecting, we believe, the family's coparenting dynamic—that show both contemporaneous and longitudinal associations with a variety of important indices of child and family adaptation (Katz & Gottman, 1996; McHale, Kuersten, & Lauretti, 1996).

Much has been written about the family systems tenet that the family "whole" possesses emergent properties that make its gestalt "different" from the sum of its constituting "parts," or subsystems, and pioneering researchers such as Reiss (1981) have proposed what some of these properties might be. Our approach to family measurement is much more modest. We see value in distinguishing "whole-family" from "family-level" concepts—concepts often used interchangeably by family researchers (ourselves included), but actually quite different in certain fundamental respects. Though it is certainly quite possible to construe "coparenting" as an emergent property that derives from marital and parenting processes, to our eyes, one need not invoke the proposition of emergent properties to make the argument that interpersonal dynamics at the level of the family group differ from those occurring within the context of two-person family interactions. Moreover, we concur with P. Minuchin (1985), Cummings and Davies (1996), and others who stress the salience of such family-*group*-level attributes in contributing to young children's socioemotional development.

Based on these considerations, our work has emphasized behavior that can only be glimpsed within the context of the family group (e.g., behavioral competition between partners) or that can look very different in a family-group context than when examined in dyads (e.g., parenting discrepancies). We have also emphasized processes useful in defining all families. Many early, classic papers on family-group process described families using constructs with a clearly pathological bent, including dimensions like marital schism and skew, perverse triangles, enmeshment, and pseudomutuality. Such terminology owed largely to the fact that most families written about by clinicians during the 1950s and 1960s had come to these professionals for help. There was hence a presumption that such families were more troubled than others who had not so self-identified. Several influential accounts of families also blended descriptions of the marriage with characterizations of the family process, obscuring the fact that marital and family dynamics are at least partially distinct—an important consideration for both research and clinical purposes. The measures we use in our work describe typical family processes that are unique to the family-group context, and focus on coparenting and family (as opposed to marital) attributes.

We drew on both family systems theory and research in deriving the CFRS, but did not stray far from the behaviors we were observing in defining constructs of interest. Hence the CFRS assesses (for instance) discrepancies in parental involvement, but not coalitions or boundaries. Similarly, we sought to capture very basic features of coparenting and family commerce to distinguish relatively well functioning families from others that were struggling a bit. Better functioning families show evidence that they enjoy being together, show interest in and attunement to one another's activities (though children's egocentrism leaves them less attuned to adults than adults are to them), and operate so that everyone in the family has free and open access to one another, with interfering and controlling activities at a minimum. With respect to this last supposition, we distinguish guidance from control; adequate structure and "framing" by adults is a necessary prerequisite for organized family functioning, whereas controlling behavior has the effect of interfering with open and autonomous functioning.

The concept of free and open access to all family members is an important one. Our use of the term is similar to that employed by attachment researchers when describing securely attached children's open access to their caregivers; it does not refer in any way to "boundary violation" (family members inappropriately intruding on the space of others, or children getting involved in marital affairs). At the level of the family group, "open access" denotes each family member's psychological freedom to engage spontaneously with any member of the family without feeling controlled or constrained by potential reverberations in other relationships. Recall the family "type" described in the opening paragraph of this section, where fathers are controlled and restrained rather than spontaneous and open with their children in the presence of their wives. The cause for this constraint is not clear; fathers may be excluded from interacting with their children by "gatekeeping" mothers—or by the children themselves; deliberately withdraw as a means of "shutting themselves off" from their wives' manner of interacting with the children, of which they disapprove; or opt not to exhibit the same level of camaraderie they share with their children in private during family group interactions, to keep this aspect of their relationship "hidden" from mothers. Why such fathers do not display the same spontaneity and revelry with their children during family interaction as during dyadic interaction may be unclear, but ultimately an issue of access comes to be reflected in the family dynamic (by virtue of a noteworthy discrepancy in the level of positive engagement shown by mother and by father with the child during family interaction). Problems with open and spontaneous access are also belied when parents thwart their partners' bids to engage the child during family interaction, or when children suddenly revert from approach behavior to solitary play following an interparental spat.

Given our interest in capturing the aforementioned features of family commerce, why would we imagine that we could ask busy couples to bring their very young children to a research lab for an hour or 2, have them engage together in a series of mostly playful, nonthreatening tasks, and expect the resulting data to yield meaningful information about family life? What we rely on in our assessments is family homeostasis (e.g., Zuckerman & Jacob, 1979), consistency, or—more simply put—routine. By routine, we do not mean, literally, the number of times families have engaged in tasks similar to those we present in our lab. Rather, we are referring to something akin to family "procedures" (Reiss, 1989)—for example, the way the family approaches child-related situations when they are all together as a group, or—more important—the way they adapt to new situations that present a number of possibilities for action.

Although infants, toddlers, and preschoolers do not bring a "social desirability" bias with them to the lab, the same is not true for parents. We recognize that families do not, in most cases, precisely mimic their patterns of relating at home. For example, fathers often attempt to take an active role in structuring family activities during the lab tasks—despite the fact that mothers do most "structuring" of child-related activities at home. Notwithstanding the fact that the lab tasks we use involve "play" activities, a domain within which fathers feel comfortable (Parke & Buriel, 1998), it is probably safe to say that paternal "leadership" in family-group activities is not the status quo in many families. If, in the lab setting, father violates standard family practice by asserting leadership in the new situation, mother may choose to build upon his initiative and join in collaboratively, go along with his leads but look for opportunities to reestablish the status quo, or actively resist and counter his initiative. The interplay between coparenting partners is what we believe has been "routinized" sufficiently enough so that the patterns of parenting coordination observed during the session will ultimately reveal meaningful information about the family's dynamics, including the coparental unit's ways of handling things.

DEVELOPMENT OF THE COPARENTING
AND FAMILY RATING SYSTEM

The initial study in which the CFRS was employed is described in McHale (1995). Families of 8 to 11-month-old infants were observed playing together with a series of objects across a modified infant table. Infants show a real thirst for object exploration beginning in the second half of their 1st year, and the tasks used in this study (some of which required problem solving) pulled for both within- and between-family differences in achievement orientation. Such differences are important in discerning parent- versus child-centeredness. The tasks also highlighted differences in parents' propensities to actively collaborate, criticize, and interfere with one another, and allowed for an assessment of differences in parental investment, again both within and between families. In most families, one parent (usually, but certainly not always mothers) tended to be slightly more involved than the other. However, the *degree* of difference in parenting investment proved to be especially telling within this infant sample.

Subsequently, we have used the coding system in samples of families with 2½-year-old toddlers, and with 4½-year-old preschoolers. In these studies, too, we used both tasks calling for a clear, tangible "outcome" (requiring some "framing" and guidance by parents), and tasks allowing families to freelance a bit (see McHale et al., 1996; McHale, Johnson, & Sinclair, 1999). Frustration and mild conflict or disagreement (when it occurs) is more likely in tasks where families are trying to accomplish a certain end, whereas highly charged, positive affect (when it occurs) is more likely when families are not trying to accomplish a particular end. Hence, the tasks researchers assign to families are crucial. A variety of activities allows the family a wide range of situations in which to display their styles of relating, and maximizes opportunities for both cooperative and competitive exchanges. The rating scales can then be used to evaluate collaboration, mutuality, and oppositionality between the coparenting partners, degree of attention to the child's initiatives, and levels of warm, positive engagement among family members, all components of the family-group process that contribute to children's adaptive styles both in and outside the family (McHale & Fivaz-Depeursinge, 1999).

For infants, 10–15 minutes is sufficient to sample family interaction (see, e.g., Fivaz-Depeursinge, Frascarolo, & Corboz-Warnery, 1996; McHale, 1995). Longer periods would be more taxing, and perhaps allow parental behavior to be assessed with children who grow tired or fussy. However, in that it is hard to ensure that every family will get a chance to manage a fussy infant, the family ratings may contain too much "state-related" error variance if families and infants are not all seen at the infant's optimal level of functioning. Conversely, sessions with toddlers and preschoolers should be longer, and contain a requisite "clean-up" period, so that parents and children can be seen both at play and while working at a less pleasant task.

Finally, we note that in every one of our studies to date, we have conducted the family-group interactions toward the very end of a two- or three-visit assessment sequence. Family assessments are always either the final, or the second to last, task completed by the child and her family during the last visit to the lab. As such, children and their parents have become at least somewhat acclimated to the new environment, and we do not intentionally capitalize on the effects of strange surroundings.

DESCRIPTION OF THE COPARENTING
AND FAMILY RATING SYSTEM

Videotaped records of family sessions are evaluated along a series of dimensions including cooperation, coparental competition, verbal sparring, coparental warmth, child (vs. adult) centeredness, discrepancies in parenting, and family warmth. These variables capture both the degree of coordination characteristic of the family's "executive subsystem" (S. Minuchin, 1974) and the quality of the family's affective climate (McHale, 1998). Two new, recently added family codes (assessing range of feelings expressed, and quality of sibling relationships) are not described in this chapter, as fewer data on their reliability and validity are available at the time of this writing. The first five variables are assessed via "global" ratings of the coparental or family unit, whereas the latter variables are "constructed" from data describing dyadic interactions embedded within family-group interaction.

Global Ratings

After watching the full family interaction, coders rate the extent of cooperation, competition, and verbal sparring between the coparenting partners across the session. A rating of overall coparental warmth (used in the formation of the "family warmth" score) is also rendered, as is a rating of who drove the family interaction (adult- vs. child-centeredness). The cooperation, competition, verbal sparring, and coparental warmth variables are rated along 5-point Likert-type scales, where 1 is low, and 5 is high. The child- versus adult-centeredness variable is also rated along a 1 to 5 scale, with 1 signifying a family where the adults structure all activities while ignoring the child's initiatives or preferences, and 5 a family exclusively following the child's interests, quickly abandoning prescribed order of tasks and following the child's lead if she or he does not seem interested. Midrange points reflect varying degrees of these family styles. Most critically, on each scale, every scale point is behaviorally anchored. We strongly advise against the use of simple "high-to-low" rating systems that provide names for scales but leave placement up to the whims of individual raters.

Cooperation.   This variable assesses the degree of active cooperation exhibited by parents during play with their children. Many coders mistake cooperation for absence of antagonism; if adults make it through an entire session without bickering, coders tend to automatically award a high score. In fact, most couples *do* manage to make it through sessions without stepping on one another's toes. However, in and of itself, this "normative" behavior does not warrant a high score; "benign acknowledgment" (parroting one another's suggestions to move on to a new task; saying "it's Mommy's turn") warrants a midrange score. Simply performing the same task at the same time isn't enough; cooperation must be active ("look what Daddy made" [in an effort to orient the child to father's directives]; "can we play too, Mommy?" [in response to the mother's efforts to engage the child]; "hey, we are cooking over here!" [spoken by one parent on behalf of both]). In our samples, multiple, clear instances of facilitating, building, and supporting one another (high-range scores) are relatively rare.

Competition.   This variable, sometimes included as the other end of a competition—cooperation "pole" in other rating systems, is evaluated separately from cooperation in the CFRS. We have encountered many families who are not very competitive, but who also demonstrate very little active cooperation. Moreover, in factor analytic studies, cooperation tends to "hang together" with variables describing family warmth, whereas competition usually loads on factors pertaining to conflict (verbal sparring; see next subsection), and sometimes parent-centeredness (McConnell & Kerig, 1999; McHale, 1995). Competitive coparenting interactions are those in which the partners seem preoccupied with enjoining the child to participate in activities with them, rather than with the other parent. The end result is frequently that the child receives "mixed message" signals—one parent offering one activity, the other suggesting something more enticing. During play sessions, parents may look for opportunities to distract the child away from her other parent, undercut the other parent's efforts to engage the child, or otherwise show evidence of "one-upmanship" toward establishing a superior relationship with the child.

Verbal Sparring.   Coders often confuse this CFRS variable with "competition." Verbal sparring is what most researchers refer to as conflict: disagreements between parents, sarcasm, insults. In laboratory play sessions (as opposed to conflict discussions; see, e.g., chap. 5, this volume; Lindahl & Malik, this volume), it is likely that researchers will never see a family in which parents raise their voice, engage in a prolonged argument, or exhibit any of the behaviors indicative of marital conflict. However, this does not mean that parents do not engage in milder behavior that signifies disapproval or disagreement. Most typically, parents exhibit kidding, ribbing, or "playful" insulting behavior that is unclear in its valence. Although the context of such behavior for any given family needs to be understood (see McHale et al., 1996), we have found, at least in our samples under the age of 5, that there is overlap in parental reports of conflict and disagreement, and enacted "verbal sparring" during family play sessions.

Coparental Warmth.   This variable captures warm, positive connectedness and humor between partners during family play. The key to coding this variable is focusing on what takes place *between partners* and not between parents and child. Many parents are quite warm with children but never look at one another during the session; in fact, in all of our samples, "normative" coparental warmth is actually the absence of warm, engaging interactions. Most parents are polite and respectful, "playing along" with the partner's initiatives, without engaging in a single genuinely warm exchange with one another—a heartfelt laugh, warm smile, truly connecting glance, or affectionate touch. Couples who do connect in this way truly stand out among the families we see.

Child- (Vs. Parent-) Centeredness.   This global rating comes closest to a "family" (as opposed to coparental) descriptor. It describes who "drives" the play session—adults or children. One process captured by this variable is adults' attunement to children's fluctuating interest levels and attention spans, and willingness to structure the environment in a way that accommodates this variability. Families high in child-centeredness may forego the prescribed order of tasks if children demonstrate a lack of interest or boredom with a task. Highly child-centered families are not typically ones with a "dictatorial" child and parents who cater to the child's tyrannical whims. In fact, in most families we see, children's "cheeky" behavior is met by some form of parental resistance (sometimes successful, other times not). A truly child-centered family is one that attends to the child, with adult agendas secondary. Families in which one parent tends toward child-centeredness, while the other tends toward directiveness receive midrange scores. Low-scoring families are those who ignore children's interests and preferences and structure all activities based on their own internal agendas.

"Constructed" Ratings.   We have found success in using two sets of "constructed" variables to accompany the global ratings described earlier. The first are "discrepancy" ratings, signifying the degree of similarity or difference between mothers' and fathers' parenting engagement with the child, and the second is a "family warmth" score. Because these variables are formed largely from ratings of parent-to-child behavior within the context of the family interaction, such ratings of parenting behavior must first be generated. For the CFRS system to work optimally, dyadic, parent-to-child variables should be coded by raters working separately from those providing global ratings, and who received training only on the detection of variability along those dimensions tapped by the parenting variables (see later section).

Parenting Discrepancies.   Our initial studies focused primarily on two parenting discrepancy variables—warmth and investment. In more recent work, following the lead of Katz and Gottman (1996), we have used a composite of five parenting variables to define "positive parenting"—warmth and investment, plus sensitivity and timing of interventions, provision of structure, and (low) negativity—and then formed discrepancy scores reflecting differences in positive parenting during family interaction. The parenting variables themselves are based on similar sets of ratings designed by Block and Block (1980) and adapted by Cowan and Cowan (1990). Warmth includes the use of speech, touch, and active eye contact to convey positive feelings toward the child. Investment describes the level of involvement with the child during the task. Sensitivity and timing of interventions captures the extent to which the parent provides the appropriate level of scaffolding needed by the child, without being intrusive or interfering with the child's activities. Negativity refers to the parent's propensity for making hostile or belittling comments and focusing on the child's shortcomings. The more different parents are in engaging with their child during family interactions (e.g., one parent warm, sensitive, and involved; the other distant, intrusive or critical), the larger the discrepancy score will be.

Family Warmth.   This variable is formed by combining scores for mother–child, father–child, and coparental warmth. Families marked by high warmth in some, but not all family dyads receive lower family warmth scores than families in which high warmth exists within all family dyads. Families in which there is little expressed warmth at all (and we have seen many such families) bring up the rear.

CODER TRAINING

Although the CFRS was developed for use by researchers who may not have had extensive training in family theory and therapy, this does not mean that the system can be used without an extended period of supervised training. Expedience in quickly generating data by using eager but hastily trained undergraduate coders should be avoided at all costs; choosing this route will almost inevitably result in unreliable data of questionable quality and value. Above all, it is important for raters to have had an opportunity to observe and discuss family interaction among a range of families, from engaged to disengaged to conflicted *prior* to using the rating scales.

New raters often bring a positive "halo" effect to rating families and miss some of the nuance built into the scale rating points, focus on the most memorable *individual* within the family and hence fail to pay attention to *interactions* among family members, or allow their positive impressions of an attractive or precocious child to "spill over" into their ratings of the child's family. For this reason, it is important for raters to first observe and discuss videotaped records of a range of families with a senior clinician or researcher. We use tapes of families seen previously in our research studies who exemplify extremes of certain family parameters, as well as unremarkable, midrange families. After raters have studied the rating system, watched, and discussed their beginning impressions of several family tapes with the senior investigator(s), they are then assigned to first rate, and finally to *rank order* 10 to 12 families, with separate rank orderings given for each of the dimensions described in the manual. This provides them with a beginning metric for subsequent coding. The ratings generated by the coders (they are allowed to change them after completing the rank-ordering task) are then compared to ratings made by the senior researchers, and further feedback is provided.

THE CODING PROCESS

Only after an intensive training period do raters begin coding research tapes together. They first render private ratings on each scale, but then immediately conference the ratings for each family before moving on to the next. The senior investigator meets with coders to examine interrater reliabilities (exact agreements) on the initial (private) ratings after they have coded the first several cases to determine whether and where systematic bias remains, and to resolve any discrepancies. From this point on, reliabilities are examined at regularly scheduled intervals to detect and counter observer drift. Raters continue to take careful notes throughout the process (see later discussion), noting especially any cases that do not readily fit the coding scheme so that the correct placement of these families can be conferenced with the senior clinician.

As indicated earlier, for the CFRS to work optimally, dyadic, parent-to-child variables should be rated by separate coders who have received training on just the parenting style variables, or (less optimally) by the family coders on a separate pass after they have rated all other variables. In either case, the same coder should never rate both parents in a single family. There is too much contamination of ratings by comparing one parent with the other. When separate coders are used, it is recommended that (a) three coders be trained, with the early training period conducted identically to that described previously; (b) after the training period, the coders *not* work together; (c) each of the three coders rate one third of the mothers (primary assignment), one third of the fathers (primary assignment), and an additional one sixth of the mothers and one sixth of the fathers (secondary assignments, with data used to establish interrater reliability)—again, ensuring that any one coder never rates both parents in the same family; and (d) recalibration sessions be held at regularly scheduled intervals.

As noted, coders keep notes of critical incidents that capture their attention while watching the tape, and use these notes to inform their own private rating and to resolve discrepancies with their fellow coder(s). Typically, two passes through the tape are made before coders assign and reveal their private ratings. Coders may stop and rewind the tape if need be on the second pass (or third pass, if required). When just a single pass is used, it is common for one coder to miss a very subtle behavior noticed by the other. This is especially true when undergraduate students serve as coders, though it is also sometimes true even when graduate students in family therapy complete the ratings. For example, one coder might take note of a father bouncing a basketball in one part of the room at the same time as a mother is seated at a table, trying to focus their child's attention on completing a puzzle, and record this critical incident. The coder might include this observation when deciding on the rating she or he will assign for the variable "competition." In this case, the coder has correctly noted that the father and mother were (albeit subtly) proffering different choices to the child at the same time (at a different time, when mother and child were not engaged in a collaborative task, father's bouncing the basketball would not have the same meaning). Such subtle goings-on during the family session can be missed by a coder during a single pass, and hence having a detailed record of observations can be very helpful.

When observers disagree, the consensus score is the one used for analyses, whereas the initial, private scores are used to calculate interobserver reliability. With sufficient precoding training, careful monitoring, and feedback on reliabilities at the one-fourth, one-half, and three-fourths marks toward completion of tapes, coders usually achieve very satisfactory interrater agreement. It is rare for coders to fail to come to consensus after discussion and the sharing of notes, but when this happens, the senior clinician should watch the tape independently, take notes, and serve as the "tie-breaking" vote.

Although we do not currently have a collection of training tapes for public dissemination, we do consult with others regarding the CFRS and have offered to watch and rate tapes from other research labs as reliability checks. Currently, several research groups are attempting to use the manual alone to train raters within their labs. Though we do not yet have formal data concerning the success of these in-progress endeavors, preliminary results from one lab (McConnell & Kerig, 1999) have provided substantiating data for both the reliability and validity of the rating scales in a sample of school-age children and their families.

RELIABILITY

Results from several studies now indicate that with adequate, supervised training, both graduate students and astute undergraduate observers can reliably use the CFRS codes. In our prior samples of infants, toddlers, and preschoolers, inter-rater reliabilities for the global coparenting and family ratings have ranged from .64 to .80 (competition), .69 to .83 (cooperation), .71 to .87 (verbal sparring), .73 to .87 (couple warmth), and .63 to .78 (child-centeredness). For the dyadic ratings, inter-rater reliabilities have ranged from .74 to .88 (warmth), .76 to .88 (negativity), .66 to .79 (investment), .62 to .77 (provision of structure), and .69 to .81 (sensitivity). Intraclass correlations are typically a bit higher than are kappas.

VALIDITY

Do CFRS ratings provide a meaningful glimpse into family life? That is, does family variability along the dimensions assessed by our rating scales overlap with similar indices measured by other means? To address this question, we have examined linkages between family indices measured by the CFRS, and how mothers, fathers, and children describe facets of family behavior. We have also studied whether (as would be predicted by systems theory) maritally distressed couples more often manifest difficulties along the coparenting and family dimensions of interest than do nondistressed couples.

In looking for relevant validating criteria, we have found it important to distinguish between dimensions assessed by the CFRS scales, and seemingly related constructs, such as "division of labor" in child care, that on the surface appear to capture similar phenomena. We actually do not believe that the CFRS would be a good indicator of child-care involvement; it seems quite unreasonable to think it possible to observe a couple for 20 or 30 minutes and then expect a resulting "parenting discrepancy" score to accurately mirror the reality of thousands of hours of family life. Moreover, fathers' psychological commitment to child and family can not readily be equated with hours of participation in child care (Hawkins & Dollahite, 1997), and what we measure during the family-group sessions has little to do with feeding, diapering, chauffeuring, or bedtimes. What *does* get captured by the CFRS ratings are the couple's coordination, organization, and affinity as coparenting partners, and the degree to which they seem to be able to "share" their child with one another. Devising relevant validating criteria for these attributes provides a continuing challenge, but we do have evidence that different CFRS dimensions show modest correlations with related variables that they should correlate with.

We have taken a developmental perspective in examining correlates of the CFRS. During the infancy period, father's investment with the baby is a defining feature of the family process. As such, the "constructed" CFRS variable indicating relative levels of mutuality in coparental engagement (size of discrepancy in parents' engagement with the baby) ought to correlate with parental reports of father's family involvement. Such linkages do exist; in families showing more balanced parental involvement during triadic interaction (i.e., smaller parenting discrepancies), fathers report engaging in more hours of play interaction with their baby each week $r = .41, p < .01$), whereas mothers report higher levels of satisfaction with their partners' overall levels of involvement with the baby $r = .31, p < .05$).

By the toddler years, most fathers *are* more actively involved in parenting than they were during infancy (Daniels & Weingarten, 1988). With increasing paternal investment, however, comes the necessity to coordinate coparenting goals and styles. Parental conflicts about handling children may peak during the toddler (and adolescent) years, and hence the CFRS variables capturing interparental disagreement and antagonism (competition and verbal sparring) ought to correlate with parental reports of childrearing differences during this phase of child and family development. In families of 2-year-olds where coders discern more competition and verbal sparring during family play sessions, fathers report larger differences in parenting ideologies between themselves and their wives on Cowan and Cowan's (1990) "Ideas about Parenting" scale $r = .30, p < .05$), and mothers report a greater frequency of weekly coparental disagreements (on a coparenting disagreement measure developed by Jouriles et al., 1991) than is the case in families of 2-year-olds where little competition or sparring takes place during family play sessions $r = .28, p < .05$).

By the preschool period, family cohesion is an important, defining feature of families. The preschool years are the first "peak" for family dissolution, and families vary a great deal in their affective contact and expressed affinity for one another. If parents can be trusted as reliable reporters of their family process, linkages ought to obtain between CFRS variables reflecting warmth and positive contact among family members, and parental reports of family positivity. In families of 4-year-olds showing higher overall levels of family warmth, and smaller discrepancies in the degree of warmth mothers and fathers direct toward their preschool son or daughter, both mothers and fathers describe their families as more positive (more cohesive and expressive, lower in conflict) in the Relationship domain of Moos' (1974) Family Environment Scale $r = .33$ for mothers; $r = .43$ for fathers).

Corroborating evidence also comes from a recent study of toddlers and their families (McHale et al., 2000) linking parents' reports of their own coparenting behavior on McHale's (1997) self-report Coparenting Scale to family ratings on the CFRS. In families showing more balanced levels of positive parental involvement (smaller parenting discrepancies) and a more child-centered family orientation, fathers report engaging in more frequent efforts to promote Family Integrity (inviting their partners to join in with them and the child during play interactions; talking affirmatively about the partner to the child in the partner's absence). In families showing higher levels of competitiveness and verbal sparring on the CFRS, mothers report more interparental conflict in front of the child.

Collectively, these findings suggest that the CFRS codes are tapping into hypothesized dimensions. Modest but significant associations exist between CFRS codes and related measures of interest during infancy, toddlerhood, and the preschool years. Given the difficulties in establishing links between self-report and observational measures of whole-family process (Sprenkle & Bishoff, 1995), and the fact that the "validating criteria" were in the same spectrum as, though not always precisely consonant with, the family constructs assessed by the CFRS, these preliminary investigations suggest that the various scales are approximating family domains of interest. Though work still remains in establishing the construct validity of these measures, research to date with North American samples suggests that the CFRS codes are doing a reasonable job of measuring what they set out to measure.

At the same time, we have insufficient data to evaluate whether the CFRS is of comparable utility for all cultural and ethnic populations. Although the enrollment of Asian-American, African-American, and Hispanic families in our various studies has ranged from 18% to 35%, the actual number of families within each of these three broad subgroups has been too small to allow for meaningful between- or within-subgroup comparisons. We have followed with interest the research of both Gene Brody with two-parent and two-caregiver African-American families in rural Georgia, and Kristin Lindahl with Hispanic families in Miami, each of whom have employed global, family ratings similar to ours to demonstrate the developmental import of family cohesion and harmony for preschool to early adolescent-age children. The broader questions, of course, are (a) whether the "primary triangle" is indeed primary in cultures where virtually all of the day-to-day contact with children is by mothers and other female relatives, but not fathers, and (b) whether topographically similar family behaviors hold similar meanings across different cultures. This is a question of fundamental importance in family studies, one to which our data thus far cannot speak directly.

STUDIES USING THE CFRS

The first study to utilize the CFRS was that of McHale (1995). In a sample of families containing first-born infants, significant, concurrent associations were found between measures of marital distress and three family "composites" derived from factor analyses of seven CFRS codes (competition, cooperation, verbal sparring, child-centeredness, family warmth, investment discrepancies, and warmth discrepancies). Moreover, significant interaction effects were found, such that linkages between marital and coparenting dynamics differed somewhat depending on the gender of the infant. Maritally distressed couples with infant sons (but not daughters) were more likely to display "hostile-competitive" coparenting dynamics during triadic family interaction (more competitiveness and verbal sparring, and a parent- rather than child-orientation), whereas maritally distressed couples with infant daughters (but not sons) were more likely to exhibit larger parenting (warmth and investment) discrepancies, with fathers usually (but not always) being the less involved parent. Links tying marital distress to both hostile-competitive coparenting and to parenting discrepancies were subsequently reported by Katz and Gottman (1996), studying older children and using slightly different measures. Similar gender-related findings were reported by Ablow (1997), again studying older children and using a slightly different measurement approach.

Thirty-seven of the families from the McHale (1995) sample were followed up 3 years later by McHale and Rasmussen (1998). The follow-up study asked whether family variables measured during the infancy period by the CFRS codes showed prospective relationships with later measures of child and family functioning during the preschool years. Findings from this investigation indicated not only that the set of three family process variables showed cross-time correlations with teacher ratings of children's adjustment, but also that these variables accounted for a significant proportion of the variance in these informant ratings, even after accounting for both individual (parental) and marital adjustment. Further, cross-time associations in related family domains were also found. In families where coders discerned higher levels of coparental cooperation and family warmth (family harmony) and more balanced levels of parental engagement with the baby (smaller parenting discrepancies) on the CFRS during the infancy assessments, fathers reported engaging in more behavior in the service of promoting family integrity, and mothers reported less of a propensity to disparage fathers to children, 3 years later. By contrast, in families where coders discerned more competition and verbal sparring, and more of a parent- than child-orientation on the CFRS during the infancy assessments (i.e. higher hostility-competitiveness), mothers reported engaging in *fewer* behaviors in the service of promoting family integrity and a greater propensity for disparaging the father to the child 3 years later.

The CFRS codes were also used to study family process in a second, independent sample of 4-year-olds and their families (McHale et al., 1999). In this study, which involved a full cohort of preschoolers enrolled in a university-based preschool, correlations were examined between CFRS variables and two measures tapping into children's representations of families—discomfort in response to questions posed about family anger in a puppet family, and aggression during spontaneously generated stories told with dolls about families. Results indicated that CFRS variables measuring both coparental support and mutuality (high cooperation, low discrepancies in parental investment) and positive affective contact among family members (high family warmth, small discrepancies between mother–child and father–child warmth) demonstrated statistically significant associations with the two representational measures, *after* accounting for the statistically significant contribution of parenting behavior by mothers and fathers, measured during dyadic play sessions. Further, in families where coders discerned low levels of cooperation and high discrepancies in parental investment using the CFRS, children were more likely to exhibit isolated and withdrawn behavior on the preschool playground (measured via behavioral observations over a 4-month period) than were children from other families. In families where coders discerned lower levels of family warmth and greater discrepancies in mother–father warmth toward the child on the CFRS, children were more likely to exhibit noncompliant and aggressive behavior on the playground than were other children. Evidence supported both direct (CFRS family -> playground) and mediated (CFRS family -> children's family representations -> playground) models linking the family-level dynamics to children's peer behavior.

Most recently, the CFRS codes have been used to evaluate family process in a sample of 30-month-olds and their families. In this study, as in the first two, the CFRS variable capturing the families' overall level of warmth—together with the degree of cooperation between partners (two important components of family cohesion, a concept studied extensively by David Olson and colleagues (Olson, Portner, & Lavee, 1985)—shows a particularly strong relationship with several measures of child adaptation. Family warmth and cooperation are significantly correlated with several indices of toddlers' interpersonal orientation during laboratory tasks with an examiner, including happiness, warmth, and (low) coldness, and with toddlers' comfort levels and approach behavior during a family bear doll play task (Lauretti, Connell, Hill, & McHale, 1999). Moreover, the empirical relationship between family warmth and cooperation and the child lab measures remains after accounting for both maternal and paternal warmth exhibited during dyadic, parent–child interactions (McHale, Krasnow, & Slavick, 1997, in McHale et al., 1996). Similar linkages also remain after controlling for the effects of both concurrent marital distress and mother–child and father–child attachment quality (McHale, Lauretti, & Talbot, 1998).

In summary, several different family process measures, estimated by CFRS codes, have shown both contemporaneous and longitudinal associations with both marital distress and with a range of child outcome measures in samples of families with children ranging from 8 to 54 months of age. Preliminary reports from an independent lab using the CFRS indicate that similar linkages can be found in families with school-age children (McConnell & Kerig, 1999); this is the first work we know of to validate the utility of the CFRS with families of children over the age of 5, suggesting that the system may have broader applicability for evaluating families of children older than the infants, toddlers, and preschoolers who have comprised our samples to date.

Needless to say, much work remains in establishing the construct validity of the CFRS and its various scales. However, existing evidence indicates that its scales can be coded reliably, and that the family process constructs it measures show lawful and conceptually meaningful links to parental reports of related family processes, to marital distress, and to a number of carefully chosen child outcome measures. To date, the CFRS variables that have shown the most reliable associations with child adjustment measures across studies are those measuring positivity in the family group, particularly total family warmth and, secondarily, coparental cooperation (McHale, 1998). However, evidence supporting meaningful associations between "conflict-spectrum" indices (verbal sparring, competition, parent-[as opposed to child-] centeredness) and related measures, and between indices reflecting parenting discrepancies within the triad and related measures, has also emerged in certain studies using the CFRS. At this point, we think it safe to conclude that family-group-level dynamics do vary meaningfully during laboratory-based assessments, and that it does seem possible to capture such variability using behaviorally based rating scales such as the one we have detailed in this chapter.

EXCERPTS FROM THE CFRS CODING MANUAL

We conclude by including two scales from the CFRS (toddler-age and above) to illustrate more fully some of the processes captured by this rating system. The first is a global, coparenting rating; the second, a dyadic, parent-to-child rating:

Coparenting Rating # 1: Active competition between parents.

Competition is a variable that was developed to reflect non-verbal behavior that sends mixed messages to children; parents' verbalizations may help in the assignment of a ranking, but verbal antagonism in and of itself is *not* competition. Most partners show low levels of overt competition; when it occurs, it tends to be subtle. However, a few partners will clearly try to out-do one another during certain games, suggest changing games when it appears the child is enjoying herself in an activity with the other parent, pick up the child and move her physically closer to him or her, respond to the other parent's request to come play a game by suggesting an alternative activity, begin bouncing a ball, clanging a bell, animating a puppet or doll, or engaging in some new behavior as a ruse to distract the child from what she is doing with the other parent (a non-verbal equivalent of "I'm bored, come play with me"), mocking an activity suggested by the other parent, and so on. In most families, within a 30–45 minute play session, such activities may occur once or twice. In such cases, scores of "2" or "3" (not "1", which literally reflects absolutely no instances of competition) are appropriate.

"4"s and "5"s are reserved for families for whom coders are convinced of an underlying theme of competitiveness or desires to be "the most important one" to the child during the play session. Parental agendas clearly seem to be at odds, and parents actively try to sway the session in their direction. Scores of "4" go to parents who demonstrate these tendencies, but occasionally attempt to curb their tendencies by turning activities over to the other parent in a seemingly genuine way ("why don't you and dad play that for a while"). "5"s go to parents who are primarily interested in being the director and relatively uninterested in stepping aside for the other. To be clear: a family receiving a "5" need not jockey for control through an entire session, or even for most of it. However, it is quite clear from the earliest moments of the session that competing agendas are the modus operandi.

1   Absolutely no instances of competition

2   One brief instance of one parent overriding the other, drawing the child's attention away from the other, suggesting a game switch, etc. Otherwise, session is free of competition.

3   Two such instances in an otherwise unremarkable session

4   More than two episodes of jockeying for control, but with some mild awareness and attempts to countermand this proclivity

5   Excessive jockeying with no such insight

Parent-to-Child Rating # 1: Warmth.

This category requires a focus on the behavior of each parent, *individually*, with the target child. The dimension ranges from low warmth, to moderate warmth, to high warmth. While it is usually not possible for a parent to display "excessive warmth" (parents cannot keep up a show of "model parenting" for 30 minutes!), scores of 7 may on rare occasions strike the rater as overly "gushy" (though not ingenuine). More normatively, high scores signify parents who are extremely expressive, and who use speech, touch, and active eye contact to convey warmth throughout the session. Midrange scores go to "average" parents—solid, matter-of-fact men and women who are not overly expressive but who nonetheless provide episodic compliments and praise to the child. Low scores go to emotionless parents who fail to respond with any positive affect even when the child checks in.

7   extremely expressive, uses touch, speech, active eye contact to convey warmth throughout session. Very rare.

6   similar behavior as 7, but not as extensive

5   touch, eye contact, smiles supplement periodic compliments, praise of child

4   solid, matter-of-fact, given to occasional spirited, genuine comments. Normative.

3   matter-of-fact parent; periodically says "good job" or its equivalent without tremendous enthusiasm

2   rather stiff, emotionless parent; on at least one occasion, cracks a smile or nods
     approval when child checks in

1   same as 2, but doesn't smile when child checks in

ACKNOWLEDGMENTS

Work on this chapter was supported in part by Grant MH54250 from the National Institutes of Health. We are grateful to the Psychology Department at the University of South Florida for support received during the writing of this chapter, and to Vicky Phares for her helpful comments on an earlier version of this manuscript.

REFERENCES

Ablow, J. (1997, April). *Marital conflict across family contexts: Does the presence of children make a difference?* Paper presented at the meeting of the Society for Research in Child Development, Washington, DC.

Block, J., & Block, J. (1980). The role of ego-resiliency and ego-control in the organization of behavior. In W. A. Collins (Ed.), *Minnesota symposia on child psychology* (Vol. 13, pp. 39–101). Hillsdale, NJ: Lawrence Erlbaum Associates.

Cowan, P., & Cowan, C. (1990). Becoming a family: Research and intervention. In I. Sigel & G. Brody (Eds.), *Methods of family research: Biographies of research projects* (Vol. 1, pp. 1–52). Hillsdale, NJ: Lawrence Erlbaum Associates.

Cummings, E. M., & Davies, P. (1996). Emotional security as a regulatory process in normal development and developmental psychopathology. *Development and Psychopathology, 8,* 123–139.

Daniels, P., & Weingarten, K. (1988). The fatherhood click: The timing of parenthood in men's' lives. In P. Bronstein & C. Cowan (Eds.), *Fatherhood today: Men's changing roles in the family.* (pp. 36–52). New York: Wiley.

Fivaz-Depeursinge, E., Frascarolo, F., & Corboz-Warnery, A. (1996). Assessing the triadic alliance between mothers, fathers, and infants at play. In J. McHale & P. Cowan (Eds.), Understanding how family-level dynamics affect children's development: Studies of two-parent families. *New Directions for Child Development, 74,* 27–44.

Gjerde, P. (1986). The interpersonal structure of family interactional settings: Parent–adolescent relations in dyads and triads. *Developmental Psychology, 48,* 711–717.

Hawkins, A., & Dollahite, D. (1997). *Generative fathering: Beyond deficit perspectives.* Thousand Oaks, CA: Sage.

Jouriles, E., Murphy, C., Farris, A., Smith, D., Richters, J., & Waters, E. (1991). Marital adjustment, parental disagreements about child-rearing, and behavior problems in boys: Increasing the specificity of the marital assessment. *Child Development, 62,* 1424–1433.

Katz, L., & Gottman, J. (1996). Spillover effects of marital conflict: In search of parenting and coparenting mechanisms. In J. McHale & P. Cowan (Eds.), Understanding how family-level dynamics affect children's development: Studies of two-parent families. *New Directions for Child Development, 74,* 57–76.

Lauretti, A., Connell, A., Hill, A., & McHale, J. (1999, April). *Links between toddlers' non-verbal responses during family doll play and family relationship patterns.* Paper presented at the meeting of the Society for Research in Child Development, Albuquerque, NM.

Lauretti, A., & McHale, J. (1997, April). *Shifting patterns of parenting styles between dyadic and family settings: The role of marital quality.* Paper presented at the meeting of the Society for Research in Child Development, Washington, DC.

McConnell, M., & Kerig, P. (1999, April). *Inside the family circle: The relationship between coparenting and child adjustment in two-parent families.* Paper presented at the meeting of the Society for Research in Child Development, Albuquerque, NM.

McHale, J. (1995). Coparenting and triadic interactions during infancy: The roles of marital distress and child gender. *Developmental Psychology, 31,* 985–996.

McHale, J. (1997). Overt and covert coparenting processes in the family. *Family Process, 36,* 183–210.

McHale, J. (1998, July). *Beyond conflict: Family positivity and young children's adjustment.* Paper presented at the meeting of the International Society for the Study of Behavioral Development, Bern, Switzerland.

McHale, J., & Fivaz-Depeursinge, E. (1999). Understanding triadic and family group interactions during infancy and toddlerhood. *Clinical Child and Family Psychology Review, 2,* 107–127.

McHale, J., Johnson, D., & Sinclair, R. (1999). Family-level dynamics, preschoolers' family representations, and preschool peer behavior. *Early Education and Development, 10,* 373–401.

McHale, J., Krasnow, A., & Slavick, M. (1997, August). *Parenting style, marital quality, and family process as predictors of toddlers' personality styles.* Paper presented at the meeting of the American Psychological Association, Chicago.

McHale, J., Kuersten, R., & Lauretti, A. (1996). New directions in the study of family-level dynamics during infancy and early childhood. In J. McHale & P. Cowan (Eds.), Understanding how family-level dynamics affect children's development: Studies of two-parent families. *New Directions for Child Development, 74,* 5–26.

McHale, J., Kuersten-Hogan, R., Lauretti, A., & Rasmussen, J. (2000). Parental reports of coparenting and observed coparenting behavior during the toddler period. *Journal of Family Psychology, 14,* 220–237.

McHale, J., Lauretti, A., & Talbot, J. (1998, April). *Security of attachment, family-level dynamics, and toddler adaptation.* Paper presented at the International Conference on Infant Studies, Atlanta.

McHale, J., & Rasmussen, J. (1998). Coparental and family group-level dynamics during infancy: Early family precursors of child and family functioning during preschool. *Development and Psychopathology, 10,* 39–58.

Minuchin, P. (1985). Families and individual development: Provocations from the field of family therapy. *Child Development, 56,* 289–302.

Minuchin, S. (1974). *Families and family therapy.* Cambridge, MA: Harvard University Press.

Moos, R. (1974). *Family environment scale.* Palo Alto, CA: Consulting Psychologists Press.

Olson, D., Portner, D., & Lavee, K. (1985). *FACES III.* St. Paul: University of Minnesota, Family Social Science.

Parke, R., & Buriel, R. (1998). Socialization in the family: Ethnic and ecological perspectives. In W. Damon (Ed.), *Handbook of child psychology* (5th ed., Vol. 3, pp. 463–552). New York: Wiley.

Reiss, D. (1981). *The family's construction of reality.* Cambridge, MA: Harvard University Press.

Reiss, D. (1989). The represented and practicing family: Contrasting visions of family continuity. In A. Sameroff & R. Emde (Eds.), *Relationship disturbances in early childhood—A developmental approach* (pp. 191–220). New York: Basic Books.

Sprenkle, D., & Bischoff, R. (1995). Research in family therapy: Trends, issues, and recommendations. In M. Nichols & R. Schwartz (Eds.), *Family therapy: Concepts and methods* (pp. 542–580). Boston: Allyn & Bacon.

Tolson, T., & Wilson, M. (1990). The impact of two- and three-generational Black family structure on perceived family climate. *Child Development, 61,* 416–428.

Walsh, F. (1982). *Normal family processes.* New York: Guilford.

Zuckerman, E., & Jacob, T. (1979). Task effects in family interaction. *Family Process, 18,* 47–53.

10

Measuring Parent–Child Mutuality During Play

Eric W. Lindsey
Texas Tech University

Jacquelyn Mize
Auburn University

The coding system described here was designed to assess patterns of mutuality in observed parent–child and child–peer play interaction. For the purpose of this system, mutuality is defined as a bidirectional process in which partners achieve balance in terms of who determines the direction and course of ongoing play. The coding scheme focuses on event-based assessments of partners' attempts to influence play and responses to influence attempts. From the event-level codes constructs of dyadic mutuality are created based on the balance of partners' influence attempts and compliance to influence attempts. Thus, one strength of the coding scheme is its versatility in providing information on individual partners' interactional style as well as information about the relationship between partners. Although created specifically for use with observations of preschoolers' play interaction with parents and peers, the codes are applicable for use with children of any age and could be adapted for use in coding behavior in a variety of interactional settings. The coding system is most suitable for observations of dyadic interaction, because the addition of a third or fourth partner makes it extremely difficult to identify to whom influence attempts are directed and the responses given to these attempts.

THEORETICAL FOUNDATIONS

The primary focus of the coding system is on parent and child interaction style. In developing the coding system, it was our goal to identify observable characteristics of parent–child interaction style that would be closely linked to children's social skills. This goal was guided by principles of social learning theory (Bandura, 1989; Crick & Dodge, 1994), which postulate that children acquire behaviors from face-to-face interactions within the family, particularly with parents, that then transfer to interactions with peers. Social learning processes, such as modeling and vicarious learning, led to an interest in examining behavior that parents use when interacting with children, which children might in turn use when interacting with peers.

In addition, the coding system was designed to address two major limitations common to current assessments of parent–child interaction style. The first limitation concerns the view of parent–child socialization as a unidirectional process in which parenting behavior influences child behavior in a linear fashion. Research on parent socialization practices demonstrates that children influence their parents' behavior (Bell, 1968; Lytton, 1980; see also Pettit & Lollis, 1997). As a result, bidirectional models of parenting emphasize parents' and children's individual contributions to the quality of their relationship, as well as children's adjustment. Similarly, family systems theory underscores the importance of mutual influences between individuals within a particular relationship. Any given relationship within the family is a product of the behavior that both individuals bring to the relationship, and a relationship is more than the sum of its parts. Thus, both the bidirectional model and family systems theory dictate that in order to understand the parent–child relationship, as well as the influence of that relationship on children's adjustment outcomes, one must consider the behavior that both parent and child bring to the relationship. However, simply assessing the behavior of two individuals does not accomplish the goal of understanding the quality of their relationship; rather it is necessary to create new scores based on both individuals' behavior in order to achieve a relationship perspective (Thompson & Walker, 1982). Only by considering how interactions unfold between partners can researchers obtain a clear picture of the relationship they share (Hinde & Stevenson-Hinde, 1987). Based on this perspective, the present coding system was designed to collect information on the behaviors of both parent and child in order to examine how both contribute to parent–child interaction. That is, the coding system is designed to answer questions concerning the quality of the parent–child relationship by tapping information about the individual behavior of both partners. Computation of the mutuality composites is designed to reflect one aspect of the quality of the parent–child relationship.

The second limitation of many coding systems concerns the use of global descriptions and molar aggregates of parenting behavior to define parenting style. Although global measurements of parenting styles have proven useful in identifying individual differences in developmental outcomes among children, the use of broad dimensions of behavior to characterize parent–child interactions makes it difficult to identify specific behavior—outcome links. Moreover, by focusing on global parenting style, researchers often fail to consider particular attributes of the child that may affect parent–child interaction on a daily basis (Block, 1979). For example, high scores on global assessments of parental control may have different implications for a noncompliant child compared to a child who is more compliant with parental demands (Bates, Pettit, Dodge, & Ridge, 1998; Kochanska, 1992; Kochanska & Askan, 1995). Similarly, parents of boys and girls may appear very similar on global assessments of control and yet differ in the particular strategies they use to control their children (Leaper, Anderson, & Sanders, 1998). In an effort to avoid these limitations and move away from global descriptions of parenting style, the present coding system was designed to focus on specific behavioral indices of parent and child style.

DEVELOPMENT OF THE PARENT–CHILD MUTUALITY CODES

Guided by social learning theory, and keeping in mind our goals of (a) creating a coding system that incorporated a bidirectional view of parent–child interaction and (b) developing codes to overcome the limitation of global descriptions of parenting style, we sought to identify observable parent–child behavioral patterns that would be closely linked to children's social skills. Previous literature on parenting style has identified parental control as an important dimension of parenting behavior that is associated with social outcomes for children (Grusec & Goodnow, 1994: Maccoby & Martin, 1983; Parke & Buriel, 1998; Rothbaum & Weisz, 1994). In particular, parents who share control with their children by engaging in verbal give and take seem to have children with more positive social outcomes (Black & Logan, 1995; Dumas, LaFreniere, & Serketich, 1995). Likewise, research on characteristics of child–peer interaction suggests that the strategies children use to control and influence peers' play behavior are linked to children's social competence. Characteristically, children who are well liked by peers frequently make positive play suggestions rather than bossy commands (Mize & Ladd, 1990), and are responsive to peers' suggestions (Hazen & Black, 1989; Mize & Abell, 1996). Thus, children who display reciprocity in offering play suggestions and accepting the initiations of others seem to be better liked by peers. Based on this body of empirical research, we chose to focus on parent–child control strategies and responses to those strategies in the present coding system because doing so would allow us to operationalize reciprocity in control and responsiveness.

The coding system was developed to assess parent–child interaction patterns in a play context. Play was chosen as the interactional setting based on recent evidence that parent–child play may have special relevance for the development of social skills in early childhood (MacDonald & Parke, 1984; Parke, Cassidy, Burks, Carson, & Boyum, 1992). Play is also the context in which the majority of early child–peer interactions occurs (Brownell & Brown, 1992).

Based on the aforementioned goals of our coding system, an event-based coding strategy was chosen. Specifically, an event-based approach allowed for the coding of both parent and child behaviors in order to elucidate the bidirectional nature of parent–child interaction. In addition, use of an event-based system was in keeping with our goal to move away from global measurement of parent–child interaction style. An event-based strategy offered other advantages as well, such as the potential for sequential analysis of parent and child behavior and greater versatility after the coding is completed. Thus, despite an increased investment in coder training and in the time required to code videotapes of parent–child interaction, an event-level coding strategy seemed most appropriate for our purposes.

Development of the specific behavioral categories for our coding system went through a process of refinement. Initially, we focused on initiation and response strategies shown to be relevant to children's social competence with peers (Hazen & Black, 1989; Mize & Ladd, 1990). After an initial study involving 35 families in which both parents participated, the coding system was modified to include additional behavioral codes to capture a wider variety of parent–child initiation strategies (Kuczynski & Kochanska, 1990; Power, McGrath, Hughes, & Manire, 1994). The changes maintained the integrity of the initial coding system, thus allowing replication of the results from the first sample, while providing greater discrimination among control strategies used by parents and children. The final version of the coding system is described here, although reliability and validity information on the initial coding categories also is presented.

DESCRIPTION OF THE PARENT–CHILD
MUTUALITY CODING SYSTEM

Videotapes of parent–child play sessions were coded using an event-based coding scheme for the occurrence of initiations, and responses to initiations, for both parent and child (Hazen & Black, 1989; Kuczynski & Kochanska, 1990; Power et al., 1994). Coders noted the exact time a statement, question, or other behavior intended to initiate interaction or influence the behavior of the partner was made, who made the initiation, and recorded both the initiation and the play partner's response verbatim.

Initiation and Response Codes

Initiations are coded into one of five categories: *leads*, an initiation that offers the partner a choice of whether to comply or not comply (e.g., "Let's play Batman," "Wanna wrestle?" "Will you sit by me?" "Can you give it to me?"); *requests for permission*, an initiation that is phrased in the form of a question in which the initiator asks the partner's permission to perform some action (e.g., "Should I get the other puppet?" "Do you want me to help?" "Would you like for me to sit in the chair?" "Can I use the bathroom?"); *requests for information,* an initiation that simply asks the listener for information, that provides information to the listener, or that serves as a teaching question (e.g., "What are you building?" "What is this dinosaur called?" "Do you like these blocks?" "Don't you have this toy at home?"); *polite commands,* an initiation that offers the partner no choice but to comply, but is phrased in a polite and courteous way (e.g., "Please hand me the gorilla," "Why don't you get the other bat," "Try not to hit the window," "Pick up the blocks, please"); and *imperatives,* an initiation that offers the partner no choice but to comply and is power assertive (e.g., "You are the baby," "Don't move that truck," "Lower your voice," "Get away from the mirror"). Note that in the initial coding scheme only leads and directives were coded. Leads included requests for permission, whereas directives included both polite commands and imperatives.

Each initiation also is identified as being either a play initiation or nonplay initiation, depending on its intent and the action in which it is embedded. Play initiations are identified as those given with the intent to change or influence a partner's play behavior and those given while the dyad is involved in some play activity (e.g., "Let's play Batman," "Should I get the other puppet?" "Please hand me the gorilla," "Don't move that truck"). Nonplay initiations are identified as those that are not related to ongoing play and/or that are given with the intent to influence the partner's behavior with regard to the furnishings of the room (e.g., "Will you sit by me?" "Can I use the bathroom?" "Pick up the blocks, please," "Get away from the mirror").

In addition to initiations, coders record the responses parent and child made to each initiation they receive. Responses are coded as one of the following: *comply,* partner follows through with or complies with initiation (e.g., child says, "Let's play baseball," parent replies, "Yeah," and picks up bat and ball; parent says, "Build us a house," child replies, "OK," and starts stacking blocks); *comply with turn about,* partner follows through with or complies with initiation and at the same time offers an alternative initiation that elaborates on the play theme (e.g., parent says, "Want to swordfight?" child replies, "Yes, you be Darth Vader"; child says, "Hand me that puppet," parent replies, "Ok, you be a monster"); *reject,* partner refuses to comply with initiation (e.g., parent says, "Let's play with the dinosaurs," child replies, "No"; child says, "Give me that ball," parent gets ball and keeps it); *reject with turn about,* partner refuses to comply with initiation, but offers an alternative initiation (e.g., parent says, "Why don't we play baseball?" child replies, "No, let's build a castle"; child says, "Take that bat," parent replies, "No, I'll pitch"); or *ignore,* partner gives no response to initiation (e.g., parent says, "Get away from that window," child does not move away; child says, "Get that puppet," parent picks up dinosaur) (Hazen & Black, 1989).

Following procedures used by Hazen and Black (1989), an event within a particular interaction sequence may be coded twice, once as an *initiation* and once as a *response.* For instance, in the sequence "Let's play zoo," "OK, will you be a tiger?" "No, I be a monkey," the phrase, "OK, will you be a tiger?" may be coded as a *response* (turnabout) to the initiation "Let's play zoo," and as an *initiation* (play lead) to the response "No, I be a monkey."

From the raw frequencies of the event-level codes, scores are created representing the rate of parent and child play initiations. Specifically, five measures of play initiation type are created for both parent and child (rate of *play leads,* rate of *play information questions,* rate of *play requests for permission,* rate of *polite play commands,* rate of *play imperatives*) by dividing the frequency of each type of play initiation for that individual (parent or child) by the number of minutes in the observation session. In addition, five measures of response types (*comply, comply turnabout, reject, reject turnabout, ignore*) are created by calculating each partner's response types as proportions of that individual's (parent's or child's) total responses.

Variables for Analysis

A variety of approaches may be taken in creating variables to be used in analyses. For example, similar to the approach reported in Lindsey, Mize, and Pettit, (1997b) all four types of play initiations may be summed to form a single *play initiation* score for each partner. Alternatively, each particular initiation strategy may be retained as separate variables, similar the approach reported in Lindsey, Mize, and Pettit (1997a). The approach taken in creating variables should be determined based on the particular goals and questions guiding the research. Regardless of the specific variables used, play initiation rates are computed by dividing the frequency of play initiations by the number of minutes in the observation session. Comply and comply-turnabout proportions are summed to form a single *compliance* score for each partner, whereas reject, reject turnabout, and ignore proportions are summed to form a *negative response* variable. Each partner's total negative response score is redundant with his or her compliance score.

In order to measure patterns of balanced initiation and balanced responsiveness to partners' play initiations, dyadic measures are derived from the individual partners' initiation and compliance scores. The following is a description of the procedure for creating two dyadic measures equivalent to those reported in Lindsey et al. (1997b). First, a *dyadic initiation imbalance* score is created for parent–child pairs by computing the difference between the rate of parent play initiations to child and the rate of child play initiations to parent. From this score an index of *mutual play initiation* is computed as (1 - absolute value of the dyadic initiation imbalance). Thus, the mutual initiation score reflects the relative balance of child and parent attempts to influence play. Second, a *dyadic compliance imbalance* score is created for parent–child pairs by computing the difference between the proportion of parent compliance to child play initiations and the proportion of child compliance to parent play initiations. From this score an index of *mutual compliance* is computed as (1 - absolute value of the dyadic compliance imbalance score). Dyads with more balanced proportions of compliance to initiations have scores closer to 1, whereas less balanced dyads have scores closer to 0. Mutual compliance, therefore, reflects the balance of parent-to-child and child-to-parent play initiation-comply sequences, and as such indexes the degree of mutual responsiveness in parent–child play.

As with the creation of initiation variables, dyadic variables could be created to index a variety of relationship qualities. Using procedures similar to those described earlier, it also would be possible to create balance scores based on specific codes or code combinations, such as mutual play imperatives or mutual compliance to polite commands. As with initiation variables, the approach taken in creating dyadic variables should be determined based on the particular goals and questions guiding the research.

CODER TRAINING

As is likely true of most observational coding, in using the present coding system, graduate students have outperformed undergraduate students in terms of training time and reliability. However, undergraduate students have been trained to use this system reliably. Training for the coding system involved several steps. After familiarizing themselves with the coding manual, coders met to review the event-level codes and discuss instructions contained in the manual. Detailed descriptions of the initiation and response events are provided in the manual, along with numerous examples to aid coders. Once trainees demonstrated familiarity with the manual, as a group, coders viewed four videotapes previously coded by the primary author of the coding system, two of mother–child pairs and two of father–child pairs. Using the manual as a guide, coders noted initiations and responses made by the parent and child. Trainees' codes were compared to those made previously by the author of the coding system and differences were discussed. Next, each coder individually coded three to five tapes that also were coded by the primary author. Upon completion of each tape, coders met individually with the primary author to review differences and resolve disagreements. This process continued until trainees achieved adequate reliability with the primary author (kappa of .80). They then were assigned a list of randomly selected tapes to code, balanced in terms of the number of mothers and fathers observed, and with no mother and father of the same child observed by the same coder. One out of every five tapes on the list was randomly selected for a reliability check, without the coder's knowledge. If reliability dropped below a kappa of .80, the coder was retrained until reliability rose again to that level. Regardless of reliability performance, all coders met for biweekly review sessions to prevent coder drift. For undergraduates, training takes approximately 30 to 36 hours, whereas graduate students require about half that time, approximately 15 to 18 hours. At the beginning of training, it is not unusual for 10 minutes of videotape to require 2 hours of coding time.

Given the event-based focus of our coding system, we are confident that other labs could base training on the coding manual alone. However, the first author is available for consultation in use of the coding system. We do not have training tapes to make available to outside labs, but the first author has offered to consult with others' labs to assist in establishing reliability.

THE CODING PROCESS

Coding is conducted from videotapes of mother–child, father–child, and child–peer play sessions. Because the system is based on events that may occur quickly, and in rapid succession, the system does not lend itself to live coding. Although coding in our lab was conducted by watching videotapes and recording events as they were observed, training time might be reduced and reliability improved if transcripts of the interaction are used. On average, each 10-minute interaction takes a trained coder 1 hour to code. Coders are required to watch each event at least three times, with as many additional viewings as they feel are necessary to ensure accuracy. Upon viewing an event, coders record the time the initiation/response event occurred on the tape to the nearest second. Coders also note who made the initiation or response and record the actual initiation or response as accurately as possible. Statements are written out verbatim, whereas behaviors are described and placed in parentheses. Coders then identify the event as one of four initiation types or one of five response types, and also note whether or not the event was a turnabout (see previous description of codes). Finally, coders identify if the initiation was a play initiation or a nonplay initiation. This process is repeated for each initiation/response event observed on the videotape. For an example of a coding sheet see Table 10.1.

TABLE 10.1
Example of Initiation/Response Code Sheet

				L	RP	R	PC	I	TA	NTA	**P**	NP
03:12	C	**P**	Would you like to play with these blocks?	**1**	2	3	4	5	1	**2**		

				C	CT	R	RT	I
03:17	**C**	P	Yeah (Gets blocks).	**1**	2	3	4	5

				L	RP	RI	PC	I	TA	NTA	**P**	NP
04:22	C	**P**	Want to play puppets?	**1**	2	3	4	5	1	**2**		

				C	CT	R	RT	I
04:24	**C**	P	Ok, you be the monster.	1	**2**	3	4	5

				L	RP	RI	PC	I	TA	NTA	**P**	NP
04:24	**C**	P	Ok, you be the monster.	1	2	3	4	**5**	**1**	2		

				C	CT	R	RT	I
04:27	C	**P**	I'm the monster.	**1**	2	3	4	5

				L	RP	RI	PC	I	TA	NTA	**P**	NP
06:14	**C**	P	Let's build a bridge	**1**	2	3	4	5	1	**2**		

				C	CT	R	RT	I
06:19	C	**P**	Let's make a tower instead.	1	2	3	**4**	5

				L	RP	RI	PC	I	TA	NTA	**P**	NP
06:19	C	**P**	Let's make a tower instead.	**1**	2	3	4	5	**1**	2		

				C	CT	R	RT	I
06:21	**C**	P	Ok, we'll make a tower.	**1**	2	3	4	5

Note. Correct codes for initiations and responses given are underlined and in bold.

RELIABILITY

Coders are judged to have agreed when an event is coded by both observers and the recorded time differs by no more than 10 seconds. Following the procedures of Kochanska (1992), two types of errors are considered: (a) when one coder codes the same event differently than the other coder, and (b) when one coder notices an event and the other coder does not. Thus, the resulting kappa represents a conservative estimate of the overall reliability.

In the initial sample with which the coding system was used, 90% of the recorded times for the same event differed by no more than 5 seconds. Overall reliability for initiations was $k = .95$ and reliability for responses was $k = .89$. In the second sample, for which additional initiation event codes were added to the coding scheme, 86% of the recorded times for the same event differed by no more than 5 seconds. Overall reliability for initiations was $k = .90$ and reliability for responses was $k = .83$. Thus, evidence for good interrater reliability was established and duplicated across two samples, with different sets of coders.

VALIDITY

Evidence for the face validity of the present coding system is provided by existing research on parent–child communication and influence strategies from which the specific behaviors coded in this scheme were drawn. Specifically, the choice of initiation event codes was based on parent–child communication patterns linked to children's social competence (Black & Logan, 1995), as well as control strategies found to characterize parents' and children's use of interpersonal power (Cowan & Avants, 1988; Cowan, Drinkard, & MacGavin, 1984; Dumas et al., 1995). Similarly, response event codes were chosen based on research examining parents' autonomy granting and children's development of autonomy through compliance and noncompliance to control strategies (Kochanska & Kuczynski, 1991; Kuczynski & Kochanska, 1990). The choice of event codes also was guided by research on children's peer-play styles indicating that socially skilled children attempt to influence peers by making positive play suggestions rather than bossy commands (Mize & Ladd, 1990), and are responsive to peers' suggestions (Black & Hazen, 1990; Hazen & Black, 1989).

Evidence for concurrent and construct validity for the initiation/response codes comes from comparisons to more global assessments of parenting style. Specifically, separate independent coders watched the videotapes of parent–child play and coded parent–child interaction for dyadic synchrony and parental control. Synchrony was coded for both samples and represents the extent to which parent and child are engaged in mutually focused, reciprocal, and responsive exchanges (Mize & Pettit, 1997). Synchrony is also a dyadic measure, scored based on raters' impressions of the quality of the parent–child relationship, which not only includes balance in initiations and compliance, but also takes into account behaviors such as eye contact, shared affect, and joint attention. Thus, synchrony includes more than partners' reciprocity of influence. The measure of parental control, adapted from Kochanska and Askan (1995), was used only with the second sample and was designed to reflect the parent's use of power with his or her child. Parental control was expected to be moderately associated with parents' rate of initiation.

In the first sample (Lindsey et al., 1997b) there was a significant association between father–child mutual initiation and father–child synchrony $(r = .46, p < .002)$, and a near significant association between father–child mutual compliance and father–child synchrony $(r = .23, p < .10)$. Mother–child mutual compliance was associated marginally with mother–child synchrony $(r = .26, p < .10)$. Similarly, for the second sample (Lindsey et al., in press), mother–child mutual initiation and mutual compliance were correlated in the expected direction with mother–child synchrony in the appropriate direction $(r = .26, p < .10$ and $r = .21, p < .16)$. Also in the second sample, the correlation between ratings of father control and fathers' rate of initiation was significant $(r = .45, p < .01)$, whereas the rating between mother control and mother's rate of initiation was in the expected direction $(r = .21, p < .18)$, but did not reach significance. Together, these patterns of correlations provide evidence for convergent and construct validity for the parent–child initiation/response variables in that the more subjective judgments of control and synchrony tended to converge with the event-based parent initiations and parent–child mutuality variables.

STUDIES USING THE PARENT–CHILD MUTUALITY CODES

Data based on the original coding system, collected from a sample of 35, predominantly White, middle- to upper-middle-class, mother–father pairs, and their preschool children, is presented in two published articles. The first article (Lindsey et al., 1997b) examined connections between parent–child mutuality during play and preschool children's social competence. Correlations between parent–child initiation/response variables and measures of children's social competence revealed that children who were better liked by peers made more frequent play initiations to their fathers and were more compliant to mothers' play initiations. In addition, children whose fathers complied more often to their play initiations were viewed by teachers as more competent and were better liked by peers. The strongest correlations between parent–child interaction variables and children's social competence were found for parent–child mutuality. Specifically, children in father–child dyads characterized by more balanced levels of compliance between father and child were judged to be more competent by their teachers and were better liked by peers. Similarly, children in mother–child dyads with relatively greater balance of compliance between mother and child were better liked by peers. Moreover, the association between father–child mutual compliance and children's social competence continued to hold even after controlling for individual father and child behavior. This suggests that the mutuality construct reflects more than the behaviors of individual dyad members.

The second article (Lindsey et al., 1997a), examined gender differences in parent–child play patterns of the same sample. Gender of child and gender of parent effects were found in that children were more likely to issue play leads to fathers than to mothers, and fathers were more likely to issue play directives than were mothers. In addition, parent–child initiation and responses were examined using conditional probabilities in order to discern possible gender-based patterns in parent–child interactions. Results of the sequential data suggest that parent were more likely to comply to girls' play leads than to boys' play leads, and that mothers were more likely to comply to children's play directives than were fathers.

Data based on the coding system described in this chapter are presented in an article currently under revision (Lindsey & Mize, in press). Subjects included 33, predominantly White, middle- to upper-middle-class mother–father pairs and their preschool children who attended a university child care center. The study examined connections between parent–child pretense and physical play in relation to children's social competence. Measures of children's social-cognitive functioning, namely emotion knowledge and self-efficacy, were examined as possible mediators linked parent–child play to children's social competence. Within a sample of 33 mother–father pairs, parent–child mutuality was more strongly associated with children's social competence than parent–child involvement in particular play forms. Specifically, mother–child mutuality, in both pretense and physical play contexts, was associated with teacher ratings of children's social competence, whereas father–child mutuality in both pretense and physical play contexts was associated with boys', but not girls', social competence. Tests for mediation revealed that mother–child mutuality contributed directly to children's social competence. The findings of this study replicated those from our previous investigation pointing to the importance of parent–child mutuality to children's social competence with peers.

EXCERPTS FROM THE PARENT–CHILD
MUTUALITY CODING MANUAL

The following information is taken from the introduction of the Parent–Child Initiation/Response Coding Manual:

> Coders will begin by recording the exact time each play session began (pretense and physical play session). Second, coders will record the time the initiation/response event occurred on the tape to the nearest second. Record the time the event began. For instance, the Dad says "Hey, I have an idea, we could play zoo." Record the time displayed when Dad said "Hey." Third, coders will record who made the initiation or response by circling C, M, F, or P. Fourth, coders will record the actual initiation or response as accurately as possible. Statements should be written out verbatim, while behaviors should be described and placed in parentheses. Fifth, coders will record the event as one of 4 initiations or one of 5 responses described below. Sixth, coders will recorded whether or not the event was a turn-about by circling 1 (turn-about) or 2 (non turn-about). Thus, if a response was coded as either a 2 (comply turn-about) or a 4

(reject turn-about) the 1 should be circled in the turn-about/non turn-about column. Furthermore, the turn-about response becomes the next initiation and is also coded as a 1 in the TA/NTA column (for further instructions see description of comply/reject turn-about below). Seventh, coders will identify if the initiation was a play initiation by circling P or a non-play initiation by circling NP. Finally, coders will record the exact time each play session ends.

In order to ensure accuracy, the coder should watch the event when it first occurs. Next, the coder should rewind the videotape to the point just before the event occurred, watch the event again and then code the event. Following the second observation, the coder should rewind the tape to just before event occurred, watch the event again and check codes for accuracy. Thus, coders should watch each event *at least* 3 times, with as many additional viewings as they feel necessary to ensure accuracy. In addition, after each interaction/response episode the coder should rewind tape to just before initiation was made and watch entire episode again to be sure nothing was missed. Note: initiations and events that occur while a researcher is in the room should not be recorded because presence of researcher may have interfered with event.

Initiations. Defined as verbalizations or behaviors designed to influence listener's behavior, initiations will be coded into one of 4 categories. Initiations must involve dyadic interaction. Thus, any statements which individual makes about his/her own behavior without reference to other person should not be coded as an initiation (i.e., "I'm going to play baseball," "Let me look out the window.").

1)   L - *Leads*: Initiations that function to influence or direct the behavior of the listener while offering the listener a choice of whether or not to comply. Includes, questions that imply an action to be performed (e.g., "Wanna play house?" "Wanna sit by me?") requests for compliance which are prefaced by "Will you …?" "Do you … ?" "Can I … ?" (e.g., "Will you pick that up?" "Can you give me that toy?" "Will you play ball with me?" "Do you want this bat?"), and suggestions, which are offered as proposals for the listener to entertain (e.g., "Let's wrestle," "Lets' read a magazine" "We could build a garage," "Let's play basketball," "Let's pretend this is a school."). Also includes open ended questions (e.g., "What do you want to play?" "What toy would you like to play with?" "What are we going to build?" "Who wants to be Darth Vader?" "Do you want to get some more toys to play with?"). Nonverbal behaviors which serve as initiations (see paragraph below) but which offer the observer a choice of whether or not to comply are also included (e.g., sets a toy down near observer while playing with similar toys, using puppet to playfully grab at partner's puppet or using puppet to talk to partner, bringing dolls over to construction partner has built.).

Play leads often serve to change, redirect, expand or elaborate ongoing play (i.e., "Let's make it taller," "Can I bat now?" "Do you want to try?" "What are we going to do next?" individual picks up dinosaur to play with partner building with blocks). However, verbalizations and behaviors which simply facilitate ongoing play should not be coded as a play lead (e.g. "Are you ready?" "Ready?" "Let's try again," handing blocks to partner who is building tower, throwing ball to partner who has already been pitching).

Responses. Defined as a verbal, behavioral or nonbehavior reaction to a partner's initiation, responses will be coded into one of five categories.

1)   CO - *Comply*: A comply response will be coded when the listener verbally or behaviorally follows through or complies with partner's initiation. Compliance may be indicated by a simple one word answer "Ok," "Sure" or by performing behavior in line with the lead or directive given (e.g., "Can you give me that toy?" listener hands partner toy; "Get away from the window," listener moves away from window; "What toy do you want to play with?" listener picks up puppet; "Stop," listener ends activity involved in.). Compliance can also include requests for clarification (e.g., "Where, right here?" "Is this what you meant?" "Like this?" "How?" "With what?").

ACKNOWLEDGMENTS

Research reported in this chapter was supported by grants from the National Institute of Mental Health (MH 49869) and the Alabama Agricultural Experiment Station (10–004) to the second author.

REFERENCES

Bandura, A. (1989). Social Cognitive Theory. In R. Vasta (Ed.), *Annals of child development: Vol. 6. Six theories of child development: Revised formulation and current issues* (pp 1–60). Greenwich, CT: JAI Press.

Bates, J. E., Pettit, G. S., Dodge, K. A., & Ridge, B. (1998). The interaction of temperament and resistance to control and restrictive parenting in the development of externalizing behavior. *Developmental Psychology, 34,* 982–995.

Bell, R. Q. (1968). Reinterpretation of direction of effects in studies of socialization. *Psychological Review, 75,* 81–95.

Black, B., & Hazen, N. L. (1990). Social status and patterns of communication in acquainted and unacquainted preschool children. *Developmental Psychology, 26,* 379–387.

Black, B., & Logan, A. (1995). Links between communication patterns in mother–child, father–child, and child–peer interactions and children's social competence. *Child Development, 65,* 255–271.

Block, J. H. (1979). Another look at sex differentiation in the socialization behaviors of mothers and fathers. In F. L. Denmark & J. Sherman (Eds.), *Psychology of women: Future directions for research* (pp. 29–87). New York: Psychological Dimensions.

Brownell, C. A., & Brown, E. (1992). Peers and play in infants and toddlers. In V. B. Van Hasselt & M. Hersen (Eds.), *Handbook of social development: A lifespan perspective* (pp. 183–200). New York: Plenum.

Cowan, G., & Avants, K. (1988). Children's influence strategies: Structure, sex differences and bilateral mother–child influence. *Child Development, 59,* 1303–1313.

Cowan, G., Drinkard, J., & MacGavin, L. (1984). The effects of target, age, and gender on use of power strategies. *Journal of Personality and Social Psychology, 47,* 1391–1398.

Crick, N., & Dodge, K. R. (1994). A review and reformulation of social information processing mechanisms in children's social adjustment. *Psychological Bulletin, 115,* 74–101.

Dumas, J. E., LaFreniere, P. J., & Serketich, W. J. (1995). "Balance of power": A transactional analysis of control in mother–child dyads involving socially competent, aggressive, and anxious children. *Journal of Abnormal Psychology, 104,* 104–113.

Grusec, J. E., & Goodnow, J. J. (1994). Impact of the parental discipline methods on the child's internalization of values: A reconceptualization of current points of view. *Developmental Psychology, 30,* 4–19.

Hazen, N. L., & Black, B. (1989). Preschool peer communications skills: The role of social status and interaction context. *Child Development, 60,* 867–876.

Hinde, R. A., & Stevenson-Hinde, J. (1987). Interpersonal relationships and child development. *Developmental Review, 7,* 1–21.

Kochanska, G. (1992). Children's interpersonal influence with mothers and peers. *Developmental Psychology, 28,* 491–499.

Kochanska, G., & Askan, N. (1995). Mother–child mutually positive affect, the quality of child compliance to requests and prohibitions, and maternal control as correlates of early internalization. *Child Development, 66,* 236–254.

Kochanska, G., & Kuczynski, L. (1991). Maternal autonomy granting: Predictors of normal and depressed mothers compliance and noncompliance to the requests of five-year-olds. *Child Development, 62,* 1449–1459.

Kuczynski, L., & Kochanska, G. (1990). Development of children's noncompliance strategies from toddlerhood to age 5. *Developmental Psychology, 26,* 398–408.

Leaper, C., Anderson, K. J., & Sanders, P. (1998). Moderators of gender effects on parents' talk to their children: A meta-analysis. *Developmental Psychology, 34,* 3–27.

Lindsey, E. W., & Mize, J. (in press). Parent–child physical and pretense play: Links to children's social competence. *Merrill–Palmer Quarterly.*

Lindsey, E. W., Mize, J., & Pettit, G. S. (1997a). Differential play patterns of mothers and fathers of sons and daughters: Consequences for children's gender role development. *Sex Roles, 37,* 643–661.

Lindsey, E. W., Mize, J., & Pettit, G. S. (1997b). Mutuality in parent–child play: Consequences for children's peer competence. *Journal of Social and Personal Relationships, 14,* 523–538.

Lytton, H. (1980). *Parent–child interaction: The socialization process observed in twin and singleton families.* New York: Plenum.

Maccoby, E. E., & Martin, J. A. (1983). Socialization in the context of the family: Parent–child interaction. In P. H. Mussen (Series Ed.) & E. M. Hetherington (Vol. Ed.), *Handbook of child psychology: Vol. 4: Socialization, personality, and social development* (pp. 1–101). New York: Wiley.

MacDonald, K., & Parke, R. (1984). Bridging the gap: Parent–child play interaction and peer interactive competence. *Child Development, 55,* 1265–1277.

Mize, J., & Abell, E. (1996). Encouraging social skills in young children: Tips teachers can share with parents. *Dimensions, 24,* 1523.

Mize, J., & Ladd, G. W. (1990). A cognitive-social learning approach to social skill training with low-status preschool children. *Developmental Psychology, 26(3),* 388–397.

Mize, J., & Pettit, G. S. (1997). Mothers' social coaching, mother–child relationship style, and children's peer competence: Is the medium the message? *Child Development, 68,* 312–332.

Parke, R. D., & Buriel, R. (1998). Socialization in the family: Ethnic and ecological perspectives. In N. Eisenberg (Ed.) & W. Damon (Series Ed.), *Handbook of child psychology: Vol. 3. Social, emotional, and personality development* (5th ed., pp. 463–552). New York: John Wiley.

Parke, R. D., Cassidy, J., Burks, V. M., Carson, L. J., & Boyum, L. (1992). Familial contribution to peer competence among young children: The role of interactive and affective processes. In R. D. Parke & G. W. Ladd (Eds.), *Family–peer relationships: Modes of linkage* (pp. 107–134.) Hillsdale, NJ: Lawrence Erlbaum Associates.

Pettit, G. S., & Lollis, S. (1997). Reciprocity and bidirectionality. [Special issue]. *Journal of Social and Personal Relationships, 14*(4).

Power, T. G., McGrath, M. P., Hughes, S. O., & Manire, S. H. (1994). Compliance and self-assertion: Young children's responses to mothers versus fathers. *Developmental Psychology, 30,* 980–989.

Rothbaum, R., & Weisz, J. R. (1994). Parental caregiving and child externalizing behavior in non-clinical samples: A meta-analysis. *Psychological Bulletin, 116,* 55–76.

Thompson, L., & Walker, A. (1982). The dyad as the unit of analysis: Conceptual and methodological issues. *Journal of Marriage and the Family, 44,* 889–900.

The Social Events System:
Creating and Coding Focused
Narrative Records
of Family Interaction

Amanda W. Harrist
Oklahoma State University

Gregory S. Pettit
Auburn University

Over the past several decades, as researchers have relied increasingly on naturalistic observation of family interaction to learn about important variations in family functioning (see Grotevant & Carlson, 1987; Jacob & Tennenbaum, 1988), the need to develop and refine family observational systems has become acute. The observational method presented in this chapter—the Social Events System (SES)—addresses that need by reviving an historically important but neglected technique, the narrative record, and rendering it more useful for family researchers than it has been in the past. It was designed to create a data archive that preserves the context and meaning of naturally occurring family interactional episodes. A Social Events Coding System (SECS) also is presented that classifies parent–child interactions into four exhaustive categories (Teaching, Control, Social Contact, and Reflective Listening); however, analysis of data obtained using the SES may be conducted using other coding systems, and may focus on family subsystems other than the parent–child dyad.

THEORETICAL FOUNDATIONS

Framework

The development of this observational method was guided less by a theoretical perspective than by a methodological one, although the theoretical framework most closely aligned with this method is probably an ecological perspective (see Argyle, Furnham, & Graham, 1981; Barker, 1968; Schoggen, 1991). The ecological perspective stresses the importance of studying psychological phenomena in context. The system presented in this chapter was based on the assumption that studying social behavior "in context" means more than conducting observations in natural settings, however. It also has implications for the nature of the data collected: the means by which it is obtained and the form in which it is preserved. Given this assumption, the methodological stance taken here is that complex family interaction patterns are well captured by midlevel, molar descriptions of naturalistic interaction.

When direct observation of families is the method of choice, investigators must make decisions concerning the observational setting, the method to use to record the flow of behavior, and the unit of behavior that is to serve as the basis for the description of family experience. These decisions, of course, are necessarily constrained by the goals of the inquiry. For example, if a goal is to describe how family members attempt to control one another in the home setting, then one might consider several different methodological approaches. If general dimensions of control are of interest, then it might be most sensible to use a method that simply characterizes family members in terms of the presence or absence of control-relevant attributes. Ratings scales often are used for such purposes (e.g., Ladd & Ladd, 1998). The observer's task is then to draw conclusions within or across contexts and make summary judgments. This sort of approach is relatively *global* in the sense that specific contingencies, qualifiers, and mitigating circumstances are not recorded (even though they may be implicit in the ratings given).

An alternative scheme is to focus on discrete acts (e.g., control attempts) and the contingencies associated with them. In this case, either event-based systems (e.g., Kochansha, Kuczynski, Radke-Yarrow, & Welsh, 1987) or interval-based systems (e.g., Patterson, 1976) may be used. This approach—construed as aiming for a more *molecular* level of analysis of family control interactions—allows for the specification of both antecedents and consequences, and complex interactional chains may therefore be reconstructed to depict the flow of family behavior. However, the fact that behaviors of interest must be determined prior to data collection may be considered a limitation in that important contextual details that give meaning to the observed behaviors and sequences are not incorporated into the data record.

A third (and intermediate) approach is to focus on control within the context of its presumed meaning and use among family members. Instead of breaking control down into its key elements and then reassembling these elements via statistical probabilities, an effort is made to retain each controlling episode as an integrated whole.

The observer's task then becomes one of describing the ongoing stream of behavior in terms of naturally occurring episodes, making low-level inferences about contextual features (e.g., where, with whom, over what), noting key verbal and nonverbal behavioral indicators, and taking into consideration previous family interactions that may bear on the event. This approach may be characterized as providing *molar*-level descriptions of family interaction, and is the one employed by the SES.

The relative ease of use and high degrees of predictive utility have made rating scales a popular alternative for family scientists. Molecular approaches, with their precision and objectivity, also have been embraced by a large number of observational researchers, yet many types of social interactions may not be amenable to molecular, reductionistic coding from a prior coding list. Such might be the case, for example, when a mother appears to overreact to a behavioral transgression by her 4-year-old. A sensitive observer might note that the mother had just experienced a frustrating encounter with her spouse and was using the child as a target for her anger. The typical rating system might have difficulty assigning appropriate weight to this kind of exchange, and the typical molecular system would be unable to accurately depict the context of this kind of interactional exchange. However, if the observer were to incorporate the relevant detail into a narrated account of the social episode, then the exchange could become a part of the documented social history of the mother and child.

The SES (Pettit & Bates, 1990) is a system for obtaining and segmenting written, narrative descriptions of familial interactions as they unfold in naturalistic settings. The SES was designed to depict all social activity involving the target child, ranging from brief interactional exchanges (e.g., mother walks by and pats her child on the back) to extended social communication (e.g., a dinnertime conversation about that day's activities). Using this method, the observer records the flow of interaction in a detailed but focused way. Integrative judgments are made about the events as they occur, incorporating a strength of the rating-scale tradition, yet supportive details are included so as to enable an "unpacking" of the event with respect to antecedents, consequences, and other critical qualities. Analyses of family subsystems (parent–child dyads, sibling dyads, parent–child–sibling triads, etc.) and contextual analyses (e.g., analysis of particular types of antecedent events or environmental settings) are particularly well suited to the SES, because the observer includes in the narrative record specific behavioral cues pertaining to all participants interacting with the child, as well as salient surrounding features; furthermore, because of the nature of the data archive created, these analytic decisions may be made after data collection has occurred.

Historical Perspective

Narrative recording methods, where the observer writes a running account of the ongoing behavior of the subject, have been used successfully in early naturalistic research on families and children, particularly in the pioneering work of Barker and Wright (1955). In this tradition, observers create a specimen record that breaks down the stream of behavior into a series of molar behavior units, identified by either structural-dynamic characteristics or by material-content properties (see Barker, 1963). The narrative record provides a detailed description of the molecular behaviors comprising the larger behavior units, as well as a sense of how the behavior units are linked to preceding and succeeding events.

Historically, though providing a potentially rich database, narrative techniques have been found to be difficult to use. Observers attempting to record all activity of the target participants—both nonsocial and social—quickly become fatigued. Also, interobserver reliability tends to be more challenging to demonstrate, likely owing to variations in the precision and comprehensiveness of observers' vocabularies as well as the inherent difficulty of dividing the stream of behavior into units of analysis (see critiques by Gottman, 1991; Green & Gustafson, 1997; McFall & McDonel, 1986). Despite these drawbacks, accumulating evidence suggests narrative records of social interaction provide a highly useful and valid source of information in family interaction dynamics (Baumrind, 1967; Blehar, Lieberman, & Ainsworth, 1977; Hartup, Laursen, Stewart, & Eastenson, 1988; Volling & Belsky, 1992).

DEVELOPMENT OF THE OBSERVATIONAL
AND CODING SYSTEMS

Social Events System

The SES was developed to draw on the strengths of the narrative tradition while seeking to address some of its weaknesses. It streamlines the traditional narrative approach by focusing only on the recording of molar social interactional units, labeled *Social Events*. Observers are taught a descriptive vocabulary to use in recording the Social Events that, in conjunction with the exclusive attention to social interaction, is thought to improve reliability above that obtained using unfocused narrative techniques.

The narrative approaches used by the researchers referred to previously are similar to the SES in that they depict ongoing social interaction in a natural setting, and interactional episodes are delineated by behavioral cues (rather than by time, e.g.). There are some important differences, however. In Blehar et al. (1977), for example, the narrative was a basis for discrete behavior counts (e.g., percentage of initiations made by smiling), and the molar episodes themselves were not analyzed; furthermore, observers were also participants (they purposefully elicited responses from the target children and made note of the children's response), whereas SES observers are nonparticipants. Hartup et al. (1988) and Volling and Belsky (1992) adapted the narrative technique by audiotaping the observed interactions (as a substitute for the written record in Hartup et al.'s case, and as an aid in embellishment of the written record in Volling and Belsky's case), an approach that likely increases reliability but has the constraint that the subject be required to stay in one room or that the observer maintain very close proximity. Hartup's approach also differs from the SES in that observers were told to minimize inferences about the children's motives and, instead, to describe only overt action; SES observers are explicitly trained to record low-level inferences about the meaning of behavior within the Social Event (e.g., determining whether a laugh was sincere or phony, or whether a child ignored her sibling's request as an intentional rebuff or because she didn't hear him). The primary difference between the SES and other narrative systems, though, lies in significance given to the Social Event as a psychologically meaningful (and thus analyzable) entity.

In summary, the development of the SES was driven by the belief that family interactional episodes have an integrity or completeness that necessitates narrative, inferential description, and that analysis of these episodes as complete units may lend an understanding to family process not easily accessed by other methods.

Social Events Coding System

The coding system originally designed in parallel with the SES is labeled the SECS (Pettit & Bates, 1989, 1990). This is a system for analyzing dyadic parent–child interaction and has been used in multiple studies. Each observed Social Event is classified into one of four categories (Control, Teaching, Reflective Listening, and Social Contact, described in detail later) selected to represent hypothetically important dimensions of social interaction. Because these are exhaustive and fairly broad categories, other coding systems can be applied to the Social Events once they have been segmented within the SES.

Early versions of the SES and SECS were used and validated among a sample of 29 mother–child dyads selected from a larger longitudinal to include equal representatives of well-functioning, poorly functioning, and midrange families (classified by multiple measures assessments made during the first 3 years of the children's lives; see Pettit & Bates, 1989). When the children were 4, the dyads were observed by a clinical psychologist or advanced graduate student on 3 separate days for 5.5 total hours and narrative records were made each time. Patterns of occurrence of three types of Social Event (Control, Social Contact, and Teaching) were examined. The observation system was validated by comparing patterns of SES-based ratings to global ratings of family functioning made by observers, and by using the SES-based ratings to discriminate among the three levels of family functioning. A later version of the system included a fourth event type termed Reflective Listening (see Pettit, Bates, & Dodge, 1993), added to allow more refined examination of contingent and responsive forms of parent–child interaction.

DESCRIPTION OF THE SES AND SECS

Description of the SES Narrative Record

The SES observer makes a written narrative record of all social interactions involving the target participant. During the course of recording the interactions in narrative format, the observer segments the narrative record into Social Events (defined in the next subsection). If the flow of events becomes so rapid that the observer can make only brief notes regarding the interaction, the observer returns to these notes during moments of noninteraction (or immediately after the observation) to clarify the description in the usual summary language. It is suggested that observers type their own transcripts within 24 hours of the observation, so that they may add contextual details to make the narration more complete, and also to check their segmenting decisions (e.g., asking themselves, "Is this actually one Social Event or two?").

Definition of SECS Codes

The SECS classifies any parent–child Social Event described in the narrative as one of four types. A *Control* event refers to the attempt of one family member to manipulate, alter, or influence the behavior of another. Control events include attempts to stop or inhibit the behavior of another (inhibitory control, e.g., the child puts her feet up on the table during dinner and the parent tells her to put her feet back under the table) as well as attempts to involve or stimulate another toward desired behavior (instigatory control, e.g., the child talking the parent into putting down the newspaper and playing a board game).

Teaching events refer to protracted, didactic exchanges between a parent and a target child where the parent's intent is to provide an educative experience for the child (e.g., during a discussion about the child's field trip to an aquarium, the parent explains how different fish eat different types of food).

A *Reflective Listening* event refers to a parent's contingent, noncontrolling, and nonteaching responsiveness to a child's verbal initiation or nonverbal cue (e.g., the child is playing with a puzzle and the parent comments on how hard the child is working). The underlying goal or intent of the adult in a Reflective Listening event is judged to be to acknowledge the child's initiation, to reflect upon what the child is doing, or to help the child feel good about his or her actions, thoughts, or feelings.

Social Contact events are interpersonal exchanges that are nonmanipulative, nondidactic, and nonlistening (e.g., the parent is looking in the refrigerator and asks the child whether they had potatoes the other night; the child says that they did, so the child and parent look in the refrigerator together until they find the potato container).

Social Event *descriptors* also are derived from the narrative account of each Social Event. Event descriptor codes include identification of the participants, the initiator, the affect of the participants, and the content of the interaction (e.g., for Control events, the antecedent and type of control, the occurrence and type of countercontrol, the degree of compliance, and the degree of conflict).

CODER TRAINING

SES Observer Training

Graduate and postgraduate research assistants have conducted the majority of SES observations, although some advanced undergraduate students have been able to reliably use the system. Initial observer training consisted of extensive group discussion of Social Events depicted in specially prepared transcripts of families interacting at home (available from the authors). Next, observers practiced making narrative records by observing children's interaction during free play at the university lab school or child-care center. Once they became comfortable with writing the narrative and segmenting it into Social Events, they made a minimum of four practice home visits with nonsubject families where the observer-in-training was paired with a more experienced observer. The two observers typed their narratives separately and interobserver reliability of the Social Events was assessed. This process was repeated until adequate reliability was achieved (see later discussion). In one project (Pettit et al., 1993), observations were conducted at multiple sites, and cross-site training was necessary. This involved (a) conducting training meetings with at least two observers from each of the sites present, (b) mailing pilot narratives across sites for segmenting by each lab, and (c) periodically sending observers to the other sites to collect interobserver reliability data.

SECS Coder Training

Training of coders proceeds as follows: Coders-in-training familiarize themselves with the coding process by reading several (uncoded) narrative records. They then review the coding manual and memorize the definitions of the four event codes. Coding may be done via ACCESS, a computer program developed for this purpose (described later), or coding may be done from the narrative transcripts themselves. If ACCESS is to be used, coders are trained in its use at this point. Next, at least five previously coded narratives are discussed, event by event, with an experienced coder. Coders then work independently until criterion (80% agreement) is reached, with discrepancies between the trainee's and experienced coder's ratings discussed in a group discussion involving all coders. Once criterion has been reached and coders are working independently, tapes are periodically assigned for reliability checks, with the coders blind to which of their tapes are being double coded. Intercoder reliability is checked on approximately 15% of the narratives, with some selected midway through the coding process and some selected toward the end. When coders from other sites were involved, face-to-face meetings were used for training. It is not clear whether coders could be reliably trained using only the manual.

THE CODING PROCESS

Delineating Social Events Within the SES Narrative

The key to using the Social Events System lies in the ability of the observer to divide observed behavior into Social Events. A Social Event is a naturally occurring social interactional episode with a single, continuous goal or purpose. (The term *goal* is used here in the sense that behavior in a Social Event is directed toward an end state, not in the sense that the participants are conscious of working toward that end.) It is defined by structural-dynamic rather thanmaterial-content properties; in other words, the theme around which action revolves, more than the content of the action, defines the event. A Social Event is discernible from preceding and subsequent events based on inherent divisions in the flow of interaction that signify a shift in goal, such as a change in behavioral setting, a change in participants, or a change in participants' focus of attention, affect, topic of conversation, or tempo of activity.

A crucial part of the description of the molar Social Event, then, is the observer's judgment of the goal of the participants during the interaction. When interpreting the intent of the participants, trained observers take into account not only overt cues (such as verbal statements), but also nonverbal signs (e.g., tone of voice, facial expression) and setting characteristics. For example, if an observer were watching a father and child coloring together, the father's original goal (inferred from his affect, etc.) might be to give the child some positive attention; if the focus of the interaction becomes that of teaching the child how to color within the lines, a new Social Event is under way, even though the father and child are still coloring together. The fact that two separate dynamics have occurred ("attention giving" vs. "teaching") overrides the fact of continuity in material-content ("coloring"). Thus, in segmenting the narrative into Social Events, the observer asks questions such as, "Can this episode be characterized by a specific social purpose?", and "Is there a distinguishable affective tone to this episode?", in addition to questions such as "Has there been a change of setting or participants?". Here is an example of a Social Event observed between a mother (M) and target child (TC):

> After she finishes washing her hands upstairs, TC brings some blue hair clips from the bathroom. She takes them over to M and tells M that the clips that are in her hair are all messed up. M asks her what she means by all messed up. TC explains that they aren't in right anymore, adding that the blue look better anyway. M changes the clips for her. TC leans comfortably against M's leg as M changes the clips. When M is finished she helps straighten TC's blouse collar.

The observer's goal in writing the narrative is to record information with as much contextual detail as possible, to provide a framework for interpretation of each event. For each event, observers include the identity of all participants, the apparent cause of the event, as much dialogue as possible (at times, conversation speed precludes verbatim recording), the nonverbal actions of the participants, enough descriptors to convey the affect of the participants, and the outcome of the event.

Observers are trained to use a summary language throughout to convey their low-level inferences about the interaction (e.g., a smile may be sweet, mischievous, or half-hearted). One way to think about the language the observers use is in terms of Ryle's (1968) notion of "thick description." According to Denzin (1989) thick description (a) gives the context of an act, (b) states the intentions and meanings that organize the action, (c) traces the evolution and development of the act, and (d) presents the actions as a text that can then be interpreted. "Thin description," on the other hand, simply records facts. A thick description of a mother–father–child interaction observed in one study follows:

> TC is looking through his backpack when M asks if he has any papers. F suggests TC show M his school papers. TC gladly gathers his school papers and shows them to M. She's interested and teases him about purple broccoli. (Apparently he'd colored the broccoli purple on his worksheet.) M and F look at the papers, commenting on them. They obviously are pleased and proud of his work. TC explains to F how he used a stamp to show the numbers on one page. F says, "Oh, you used a stamp for this." TC smiles and takes the papers to his room.

A thin description of the same event might be: "F asks TC to show M his school papers. TC shows M the papers. F comments. TC leaves the room." Note that the thick description in the first version does not always include verbatim dialogue (e.g., the reader doesn't know exactly what the mother says when she "teases" the child), but the language provides a fairly vivid picture of the interaction: It includes enough detail for the reader to understand what the context was (how the family came to examine the papers), what their intentions or motives likely were (why they were examining the papers, apparently so the parents could show TC their interest), and how the interaction proceeded (who guided the interaction, how the participants responded behaviorally and effectively, how the interaction reached a close, etc.). In providing this level of description, some inferences were made by the observer (e.g., that the parents were proud); however, higher level interpretation—such as classification of the event as "reflective listening"—was not recorded by the observer in the narrative account.

SECS Coding

Coding of the narratives is conducted by nonobservers, blind to any predetermined status of the target participants (e.g., whether they were in high-aggression or low-aggression groups) and, if possible, to the study's hypotheses. The coder chooses a narrative that has already been segmented (i.e., the Social Events have already been delineated) and begins by reading background information about the setting written by the observer at the top of the transcript (time of day, who is present, what the home looks like, etc.). Each Social Event is then coded as a single unit, although in making coding decisions the coder takes into account the preceding Social Events and nonsocial descriptions (labeled "Comment" by the observer; see sample page); this information is conceived as part of the context needed for valid interpretation of the Social Event that is being coded. For each event, information such as participants, setting, number of turns, and affect of participants is coded. The coder then makes the decision as to whether the event is a

Control, Teaching, Reflective Listening, or Social Contact event, and depending on what code is chosen, subsequent coding decisions are required (e.g., antecedents are coded for Control and Reflective Listening events; conflict is coded for Control events) as described in the coding manual.

SECS Coding Software.   To aid in the use of the SECS, a template for use with the computer narrative files called ACCESS (Accessing Computers for Coding Events in Social Systems; Habibi, 1988; Pettit, Raab, & Habibi, 1990) has been created. ACCESS can utilize narratives created via any word-processing program once they have been converted to a standard ASCII file. (Observers prepare the transcript for coding by flagging which paragraphs are Social Events and which are Comments, separating paragraphs by two hard returns, and saving the file in ASCII format.) A decision tree framework dictates the sequence of coding of each Social Event by leading the coder through a number of coding decisions with prompts for appropriate codes. When an event is displayed, it is accompanied by a question about a specific characteristic of that event, a display of valid responses, and a prompt for the coder's response. Responses to the coding questions for each event are saved as data files that can be accessed by statistical software and/or word processors. Coding with ACCESS provides several advantages: It is easy to use and substantially reduces the time required to code a narrative record (to about 3 hours per 2-hour observation); the focus of training efforts can be on interpretive issues rather than the mechanics of coding; coding is more interesting for the coder and more reliable because error detection routines are built into the program; and a separate data entry step is obviated because the ACCESS output file is a computer-language data file that is immediately accessible for data analysis.

Other Coding Systems.   Coding systems other than the SECS may be used with SES data. Researchers may divide Social Events into smaller units or collapse them into larger units before analysis (e.g., Shine & Acosta, 2000, performed a qualitative analysis play sequences of Social Events), or may retain the Social Events and use their own coding schemes (e.g., Harrist & Achacoso, 1994; Harrist, Carrillo, & Foster, 1998; Harrist, Pettit, Dodge, & Bates, 1994) or systems of analysis (e.g., McFadyen-Ketchum, Bates, Dodge, & Pettit, 2000, performed sequential analysis of SES data).

RELIABILITY

Overview

Assessment of reliability of the SES/SECS is a three-step process. Reliability must be demonstrated for (a) the content of the Social Events, (b) the coding of the Social Event types (Teaching, Control, etc.), and (c) the coding of the Social Event descriptors (e.g., antecedent of Control, type of Control).

Interobserver Reliability.   The first step in demonstrating reliability for the SES requires showing that the observed social interactions are being recorded in the same way, in other words, that multiple observers can divide the stream of behavior into analogous Social Events. To assess this type of interobserver reliability, two observers are present and make narrative records for approximately 15% of all observations conducted. Event-by-event concordance between the two independently written narratives is then calculated as follows (see Wright, 1967): Events are judged to be in agreement if, in the judgment of an independent reader, the records' events had the same general content (i.e., were a match); nonmatches were counted when an event described by one observer was not described by the second observer. Agreement was calculated by dividing the number of matches by one half the total number of events seen by the sum of both observers (i.e., the average number of events across the two narratives). Reliability at this level (i.e., reliability of segmenting interactional episodes) is not commonly conducted when narratives are used (e.g., Hartup et al., 1988, and Volling & Belsky, 1992, both reported reliability for coding behavioral event types, but not for segmenting of the events) and is somewhat more conservative than calculating percent agreement (where an episode observed by the second observer but not the first is simply ignored rather than being counted as a mismatch). Interobserver reliability computed in this fashion has ranged from .59 (in the earliest observations) to .83 ($M = .70$) in Pettit and Bates (1989), and from .68 to .83 ($M = .75$) in Pettit et al. (1993).

Intercoder Reliability.   Assessment of intercoder reliability of the SECS involves 15% to 20% of the narratives (randomly chosen) being coded by two separate coders, and then comparing the coders' ratings. Proportion agreement and Cohen's κ can be calculated for event type (agreement on whether a given Social Event is a Control event, a Teaching event, etc.) as well as for event descriptors of interest in the particular study (e.g., agreement on who initiated control episodes). To date, intercoder agreement has been moderate (but significant, with all $ps < .05$). Percent agreement (and κ) for the categorization of Social Events has been 85% for Control (κ = .51), 77% for Teaching (κ = .64), and 56% for Social Contact events (κ = .38) in Pettit and Bates (1989); percent agreement in Pettit et al. (1993), where Reflective Listening events were included) averaged 79% (range = .65 to .90) and κ averaged 64% (range = 45% to 82%).

VALIDITY

Findings from studies utilizing the SECS within the SES have provided evidence of validity, in that SECS codes have been found to be associated with theoretically related variables in an understandable way. For example, in the original validation study (Pettit & Bates, 1989), global summary impression ratings made by observers after spending 5.5 hours with the 4-year-olds' families were compared to SECS codes (made by nonobservers). Rate (i.e., percent of all Social Events observed) of Control events was significantly correlated with observer summary ratings of coercive control ($r = .46, p < .01$) and child noncompliance ($r = .43, p < .01$); rate of Teaching events was associated with observer summary ratings of Teaching ($r = .44, p < .01$); and rate of Social Contact events was significantly related to observer summary ratings of positivity and positive control ($rs = .54$ and $.39, ps < .001$ and $.05$, respectively). In a separate sample of 165 prekindergartners and their parents (Pettit et al., 1993), a similar comparison was made between observers' summary impression ratings and SECS coding (with higher order variables labeled *coercive control, intrusiveness, proactive teaching, social conversation, responsiveness,* and *positive control* operationalized from the original SECS codes). In every instance, the cross-method counterparts were significantly (albeit moderately) related. For example, coercive control was associated with observer summary ratings of coercion ($rs = .47$ and $.41$ for mothers and fathers, respectively, $ps < .001$) and social conversation was associated with observer summary ratings of positive involvement ($rs = .48$ and $.34$ for mothers and fathers, $ps < .001$). These patterns indicate that, although coder's event-based ratings and observers' global ratings diverge somewhat, there is enough overlap to support the validity of the SECS codes.

There also is evidence for the predictive utility of the SECS, in that it appears to capture salient features of family subsystems that reliably relate to (a) earlier family patterns and (b) children's behavior outside the family system both concurrently and prospectively. Additionally, SES-generated data appear to function well as an archive that can be used validly with other (non-SECS) coding systems. Empirical studies evidencing this type of validity are summarized in the following section.

STUDIES USING THE SECS AND SES

The successful use of SECS variables as *outcomes* is illustrated in the Pettit and Bates (1990) sample of 4-year-olds, where families with the highest adaptation scores over the course of the child's first 3 years of life were found to engage in more Teaching than other families, and the low-adaptation group was characterized by children who exhibited more extreme noncompliance and mothers who were more hostile in their control. SECS constructs also have been construed as *predictors* of children's adjustment, such as in the Pettit et al. (1993) study, where elementary school teachers' ratings of externalizing behavior were predicted by earlier SECS-based measures of mother coerciveness and intrusiveness ($rs = .31$ and $.19$, respectively, $ps < .01$ and $.05$ in kindergarten; ($rs = .22$ and $.27, ps < .05$ and $.01$ in first grade) as well as by father responsiveness ($r = -.17, p < .05$ in kindergarten; ($r = -.19, p < .05$ in first grade).

There also is evidence for the validity of data collected with the SES but *not* coded with the SECS. Harrist (1993), for example, rated level of dyadic synchrony for mother– and father–child events delineated with the SES method. High levels of positive synchrony in the prekindergarten home observations were associated with higher levels of children's competence ($r = .23, p < .005$) and lower levels of social withdrawal ($r = -.16$, $p < .05$) and aggression ($r = -.16$, $p < .05$) later in the year, whereas father–child synchrony was associated only with lower levels of aggression ($rs = -.22$, $ps < .01$); mother– and father–child nonsynchrony both predicted child aggression ($rs = .14$ and $.18$, $ps < .05$) and withdrawal ($rs = .25$ and $.18$, $ps < .001$ and $.05$); and mother–child negative synchrony (i.e., coercion) was associated with child aggression in kindergarten ($r = .19$, $p < .01$). Analyses currently under way (Harrist, Carrillo, Pettit, Dodge, & Bates, 2000) suggest that these interaction patterns also predict children's behavior longitudinally, with early mother– and father–child synchrony predicting fewer behavior problems in seventh grade.

Finally, a recent study (Achacoso, 1998) demonstrates the validity of the SES in examining family subsystems other than parent–child dyads, by focusing on sibling pairs. For this study, a sibling interaction checklist was developed and used to classify the Social Events observed among 5-year-old target child/older sibling dyads. The most theoretically significant finding was that children in single-parent families whose older siblings engaged in high rates of coaching and mentoring interactions were buffered from the sociometric rejection their single-parent status put them at risk for (e.g., comparing social preference scores of single-parented children with high levels of sibling coaching and mentoring to scores of children in two-parent families, single-parented children actually had higher social preference scores: $ts = .19$ and 2.42, $dfs = 66$ and 64, $ps < .05$ and $.01$ for coaching and mentoring, respectively).

Enhancing Ecological Validity

Steps can be taken to increase the likelihood that the interaction patterns observed are representative of each family's idiosyncratic pattern of interaction. For example, in our studies, SES data have been collected in the home setting, with observers present for two or three 2-hour sessions spaced approximately 1 week apart. In this setting, we suggest that family members be asked to go about their normal routines and to ignore the presence of the observer as much as possible, and that families be given time (e.g., 15 minutes) to become accustomed to the observer before data collection begins. We also suggest including dinner in the observation period if possible, to maximize the chance that all family members will be present for at least part of the observation.

Limits to Generalizability

Studies using the SES or the SECS have, to date, been conducted among nonclinical populations containing approximately equal numbers of boys and girls. Ages of the target children have ranged from 4 to 6 (although the studies including siblings involved children of other ages, ranging from infancy to adolescence). Ethnic distributions have been fairly representative of the local communities where the sample was drawn, for example, the Pettit et al. (1993) sample came from Knoxville, TN, Nashville, TN, and Bloomington, IN, and included 84% Euro-American and 15% African-American families. SECS coding has only been done by the three labs associated with Pettit, Bates, and Dodge, although other researchers have used the SES to collect data. Validity of the SECS codes has not been examined among a particular ethnic group or among clinical samples; therefore, its generalizability to those populations is not known.

EXCERPTS FROM THE SECS CODING MANUAL

The coding manual contains instructions for (a) conducting SES observations, (b) preparing the narrative transcripts, and (c) coding with the SECS. Following is a sample page from an SES-derived narrative record and an excerpt from the coding manual.

The sample page shows the type of background information recorded at the beginning of the observation, the comments made by the observer (but not coded), and the delineation of the Social Events. This narrative was originally handwritten on a notepad as the observation took place, with the comments written in the margin and Social Events separated as paragraphs. The Social Events were numbered as the narrative was transcribed. This page represents approximately 15 minutes of the 2-hour observation.

The excerpt from the coding manual shows a partial description of one of the four Social Events codes (Control) within the SECS.

SUBJECT ID NUMBER: 22056   DATE: 12-14-88, TIME: 4:50
OBSERVATION: 2   OBSERVER: S.T.T.

PARTICIPANTS: TC = target child, 5-yr-old male; M = mother; F = father; S = sister, approximately 3 years old.

COMMENT: Observation takes place in the home, which has now been decorated for Christmas. M has just returned from work, and F is in the kitchen working on the evening meal. TC and S are roaming around talking with M about their day. However, TC is seen first in the dining are where his father is adjacent to him in the kitchen; M and S are in the den.

EVENT 1: F calls to TC from the kitchen, "Hey, TC, you got a Christmas card!" TC runs into the kitchen. F asks, "Do you want me to read it to you?" TC responds, "Uh-huh.": F reads card and TC looks intently at the card as F reads. When F is finished, TC walks back into the den.

EVENT 2: M walks into the den and asks, "You guys want to put these under the tree?", referring to some packages that have come in the mail. TC and S run to the living room where the Christmas tree is. M and F begin to open a box that has come with presents for them. M wants to show TC to whom the package has been sent. M and F try to get TC to tell them what their address is. TC seems somewhat distracted and says that he doesn't know that their address is. M points to their address and asks TC to name the street numbers in their address. TC does label the ones that M points out, but still doesn't seem to be able to repeat their whole address from memory. F laughs and M says, in an understanding tone, "That's okay."

EVENT 3: M opens a box, and TC asks, "Where's mine?" As TC grabs one package, M asks, "What does it say?" TC looks carefully at the tag and says, "S." M says, "Well, put it under the Christmas tree and we'll open it on Christmas." TC disagrees, "No, let's open it now." M repeats calmly, "No, on Christmas." TC suggests, "Let's open Fonzie's (the dog's)." M and F laugh and say, "No." TC repeats in a whining voice two and three times that he wants to open his package now. M explains calmly that the reason S opened a package today was that she had received it at school and wanted her friend to watch her open it. TC starts to grab his package to open it. F says quickly and firmly, "TC!" TC whines and cries and retorts, "You said that if we got a package from a friend or a teacher…" TC takes the package reluctantly to the tree, crying.

COMMENT: TC is apparently upset over a misunderstanding about a rule that has been made. The family seems to have decided that gifts will be opened on Christmas, except those that are received at school from friends, but TC thinks that any packages from friends can be opened when they are received.

EVENT 4: TC, M, F, and S go back into the dining area. TC, still unhappy, cries and says, "My teacher isn't going to give me a present." F responds, "I bet your teacher will." TC does not seem convinced and M tired to cheer TC with, "What about your Sunday School teacher?" TC disagrees, "Huh-uh."

COMMENT: Sits quietly for a few minutes, pouting. M continues to look through cards as F entertains S.

Sample SECS Code

Event # 3 would be coded as a Control event, described in the SECS coding manual as follows:

Control events. Control refers to the attempts of one family member to influence or alter the behavior of another. Thus, any family member can be the initiator of a Control event. Control attempts may refer to a family member's immediate behavior or to incidents that happened in the pat with an implied intent to influence future behavior. Included in Control events are attempts to stop or inhibit the behavior of another (Inhibitory Control) as well as attempts to involve or stimulate another toward desired behavior (Instigatory Control). Control may be manifested in both positive ways (e.g., giving simple instruction, encouraging, redirecting, reasoning) and negative ways (scolding, criticizing, yelling, whining, threatening, punishing physically, etc.).

These attempts may be direct and obvious, or covert and subtle; they may be successful or unsuccessful (i.e., the target of the control may or may not comply). Also, Control episodes may be quite brief (e.g., parent instructs, child complies; or parent instructs, child ignores, parent doesn't follow through), or they may evolve into more lengthy interactions that contain elements of coerciveness or counter-control (as when two family members have different purposes or goals). Varying degrees of conflict may be involved.

It is important to remember that the underlying intent of the initiator of Control events is to manipulate, modify, or influence the actions of another person. Thus, simple instructions (either isolated or embedded in other events) or simple requests for assistance are not coded as Control events (e.g., at dinner, a brief, neutral request such as "Please pass the salt," would not be considered a Control event). When writing the narrative, remember to include the antecedent of the Control event, the initiator of Control, the type of Control used, the affective tone of the participants, an indication of the number of exchanges between the participants or of the amount of coerciveness, and the outcome.

Note: The manual also provides several examples of Social Events that are and are not coded as Control.

Description	*Control Codes*
Antecedent Event Type	1 = antecedents of other initiated (usually parent-initiated)control to stop or inhibit target child (i.e., inhibitory control)
	2 = antecedents of other-initiated control to involve/stimulate target child (i.e., instigatory control)
	3 = antecedents of target child-initiated control to stop/inhibit other (i.e., inhibitory control)
	4 = antecedents of target child-initiated control to involve/ stimulate other (i.e., instigatory control)
	5 = antecedent not observable
Antecedent Event Subtype	Subtypes for *other-initiated inhibitory* control:
	01 = Target child actively engages in behavior that is counter-productive to other's goal or to demands of setting (e.g., child plays with food during mealtime; child continues to play when parent is ready to go inside; child disturbs parent who then seeks end to intrusion)
	02 = Target child accidentally commits immature act (e.g., spills)
	03 = Target child intentionally commits immature or irresponsible act or approaches "trouble" (produces behavior with the potential for threat of mild danger to objects or persons or approaches violation of household rules)
	04 = Target child gets into "real" trouble (produces behavior that is dangerous or violates a household rule; excludes aggression toward people or objects)
	05 = Target child behaves aggressively toward a person or object (e.g., hitting, kicking, pushing, destroying objects)
	Subtypes for other-initiated instigatory control:
	06 = Other seeks to stimulate child toward responsible or self-help behavior (e.g., washing hands before dinner)
	07 = Child refuses to participate in demands of setting with passive resistance (e.g., passively refuses to eat dinner)
	08 = Other requires service or physical help from child
	09 = Other seeks to involve child in play or activity (with either the parent or another adult or a child)

Description	Control Codes
	Subtypes for *child-initiated inhibitory* control: 10 = Other presents barrier to immediate child goal with active interference (may be play or finishing activity) 11 = Child is being disturbed and seeks an end to intrusion 12 = Child seeks independence by requesting/demanding to do task on own
	Subtypes for *child-initiated instigatory* control: 13 = Other presents barrier to short-term goal with passive interference(e.g., from child's perspective, dawdling) 14 = Child requires physical help or simply wants something 15 = Child seeks to involve other in play or activity 16 = Child seeks attention (use only when it is certain that 13, 14, or 15 is not appropriate)
	Subtypes for *antecedent not observable*: 19 = parent is being arbitrary, capricious; control unrelated to ongoing events) 20 = cannot be determined
Initial Control	1 = positive 2 = negative
Initial Control Subtype	Subtypes of *adult positive* control 01 = tells (gives simple directive) 02 = engages in verbal give and take, suggests, negotiates, reasons, explains, encourages, initiates discussion 03 = offers positive incentive 04 = positive anticipatory guidance 05 = provides physical guidance 06 = other
	Subtypes for *adult negative* control: 07 = tells, negative (e.g., "Don't do that.") 08 = demands 09 = criticizes, scolds, shames 10 = yells, screams 11 = withdraws love or affection 12 = threatens, warns, gives negative incentive 13 = power assertive (e.g., restrains, takes away an object) 14 = gives physical punishment (e.g., restrains) 15 = other

Note: The remainder of the Control codes include: Subtypes for Child Positive Control; Subtypes for Child Negative Control; Subsequent Control used by initiator; Subsequent Control Subtype; Counter-Control; Counter-Control Subtype; Compliance of Controllee, Compliance of Counter-Controllee; and Conflict.

ACKNOWLEDGMENTS

Research reported in this chapter was supported in part by Research Grant MH-42498 from the National Institute of Mental Health to Kenneth A. Dodge, Gregory S. Pettit, and John E. Bates, and Research Grants SRG-264 and R-149 from the University Research Institute of the University of Texas to Amanda W. Harrist.

REFERENCES

Achacoso, J. A. (1998). *Complementary and reciprocal sibling interactions: Differential predictors of peer relations in single- and two-parent families.* Unpublished doctoral dissertation, University of Texas, Austin.

Argyle, M., Furnham, A., & Graham, T. A. (1981). *Social situations.* Cambridge, England: Cambridge University Press.

Barker, R. G. (1963). The stream of behavior as an empirical problem. In R. G. Barker (Ed.), *The stream of behavior* (pp. 1–22). New York: Appleton–Century–Crofts.

Barker, R. G. (1968). *Ecological psychology: Concepts and methods for studying the environment of human behavior.* Stanford, CA: Stanford University Press.

Barker, R. G., & Wright, H. F. (1955). *Midwest and its children: The psychological ecology of an American town.* Evanston, IL: Row, Peterson.

Baumrind, D. (1967). Childcare practices anteceding three patterns of preschool behavior. *Genetic Psychology Monographs, 76,* 43–88.

Blehar, M. C., Lieberman, A. F., & Ainsworth, M. D. S. (1977). Early face-to-face interaction and its relation to later infant–mother attachment. *Child Development, 48,* 182–194.

Denzin, N. K. (1989). The interpretive point of view. In L. Bickman & D. J. Rob (Series Eds.), *Applied social research methods series: Vol. 16. Interpretive interactionism* (pp. 10–34). Newbury Park, CA: Sage.

Gottman, J. M. (1991). Finding the roots of children's problems with other children. *Journal of Social and Personal Relationships, 8,* 441–448.

Green, J. A., & Gustafson, G. E. (1997). Perspectives on an ecological approach to social communicative development in infancy. In C. Dent-Read & P. Zukow-Goldring (Eds.), *Evolving explanations of development* (pp. 515–546). Washington, DC: American Psychological Association.

Grotevant, H. D., & Carlson, C. I. (1987). Family interaction coding systems: A descriptive review. *Family Process, 26,* 49–74.

Habibi, A. (1988). ACCESS: A Turbo-Pascal interactive computer program for coding Social Events [Computer software]. Nashville, TN: Vanderbilt University.

Harrist, A. W. (1993, March). *Family interaction styles as predictors of children's competence: The role of synchrony and nonsynchrony.* Paper presented at the biennial meeting of the Society for Research on Child Development, New Orleans, LA. (ERIC Document Reproduction Service No. PS 021 772)

Harrist, A. W., & Achacoso, J. (1994, February). *Complementarity and reciprocity in sibling interaction: Interactional qualities related to dyads' age, sex, and birth interval.* Paper presented at the biennial meeting of the Southwestern Society for Research on Human Development, Austin, TX.

Harrist, A. W., Carrillo, S., & Foster, I. R. (1998, March). *The naturalistic occurrence of parent's social teaching in conversation.* Paper presented at the annual meeting of the biennial meeting of the Southwestern Society for Research on Human Development, Galveston, TX.

Harrist, A. W., Carrillo, S., Pettit, G. S., Dodge, K. A., & Bates, J. E. (2000). *Mother- and father–child interaction style and children's social competence and behavior problems over time.* Manuscript in preparation.

Harrist, A. W., Pettit, G. S., Dodge, K. A., & Bates, J. E. (1994). Dyadic synchrony in mother–child interaction: Relation with children's subsequent kindergarten adjustment. *Family Relations, 43,* 417–424.

Hartup, W. W., Laursen, B., Stewart, M. I., & Eastenson, A. (1988). Conflict and the friendship relations of young children. *Child Development, 59,* 1590–1600.

Jacob, T., & Tennenbaum, D. L. (1988). *Family assessment: Rationale, methods, and future directions.* New York: Plenum.

Kochanska, G., Kuczynski, L., Radke-Yarrow, M., & Welsh, J. D. (1987). Resolutions of control episodes between well and effectively ill mothers and their young children. *Journal of Abnormal Child Psychology, 15,* 441–456.

Ladd, G. W., & Ladd, B. K. (1998). Parenting behaviors and parent–child relationships: Correlates of peer victimization in kindergarten? *Developmental Psychology, 34,* 1450–1458.

McFadyen-Ketchum, S. A., Bates, J. E., Dodge, K. A., & Pettit, G. S. (2000). *Understanding the development of aggression: Sequential analysis of mother–son and mother–daughter interactions.* Manuscript in preparation.

McFall, R. M., & McDonel, E. C. (1986). The continuing search for units of analysis in psychology: Beyond persons, situations, and their interactions. In R. O. Nelson & S. C. Hayes (Eds.), *Conceptual foundations of behavioral assessment* (pp. 201–24). New York: Guilford.

Patterson, G. R. (1976). The aggressive child: Victim and architect of a coercive system. In E. J. Mash, L. A. Hamerlynck, & L. C. Handy (Eds.), *Behavior modification and families: Vol. 1. Theory and research* (pp. 267–316). New York: Brunner/Mazel.

Pettit, G. S., & Bates, J. E. (1989). Family interaction patterns and children's behavior problems from infancy to 4 years. *Developmental Psychology, 25,* 413–420.

Pettit, G. S., & Bates, J. E. (1990). Describing family interaction patterns in early childhood: A Social Events perspective. *Journal of Applied Developmental Psychology, 11,* 395–418.

Pettit, G. S., & Bates, J. E., & Dodge, K. A. (1993). Family interaction patterns and children's conduct problems at home and school: A longitudinal perspective. *School Psychology Review, 22,* 403–420.

Pettit, G. S., Raab, M. M., & Habibi, A. (1990). *ACCESS: An interactive computer program for coding narrative records of complex social events.* Unpublished manuscript.

Ryle, G. (1968). *The thinking of thoughts* (University Lectures No. 18). Saskatoon, Canada: University of Saskatchewan.

Schoggen, P. (1991). Ecological psychology: One approach to development in context. In R. Cohen & A. W. Siegel (Eds.), *Context and development* (pp. 281–301). Hillsdale, NJ: Lawrence Erlbaum Associates.

Shine, S., & Acosta, T. Y. (2000). *Parent–child social play in a children's museum.* Manuscript submitted for publication.

Volling, B. L., & Belsky, J. (1992). The contribution of mother–child and father–child relationships to the quality of sibling interaction: A longitudinal study. *Child Development, 63,* 1209–1222.

Wright, H. F. (1967). *Recording and analyzing child behavior.* New York: Harper & Row.

12

Assessing Changes in Family Interaction: The Structural Family Systems Ratings

Michael S. Robbins
Olga Hervis
Victoria B. Mitrani
José Szapocznik
Center for Family Studies, University of Miami School of Medicine

The Structural Family Systems Ratings (SFSR; Hervis, Szapocznik, Mitrani, Rio, & Kurtines, 1991; Szapocznik et al., 1991) were developed to assess changes in family interactions that result from family interventions. Based on structural family theory and therapy (Minuchin, 1974, 1976; Minuchin & Fishman, 1981) and our own program of clinical research (Szapocznik et al., 1997; Szapocznik & Kurtines, 1989), the SFSR identifies patterns of family interaction that are theoretically parallel to the clinical conceptualizations of structural family therapists. Besides assessing changes in interactional patterns, the SFSR also provides descriptive information about the form or process of family relationships.

The SFSR reveals the interactional processes that govern the family system and rates them as to their relative level of functionality. Specific patterns of family interaction are identified by trained raters from videotapes of family members completing standardized interaction tasks (Wiltwick Family Tasks; Minuchin, Rosman, & Baker, 1978). The SFSR was originally developed to assess changes in patterns of interaction in families with a behavior problem youth. More recently, the SFSR is also being used to assess changes in family interactions in the families of child (e.g., diabetes) and adult medical and psychiatric populations (e.g., HIV, dementia, schizophrenia).

THEORETICAL FOUNDATIONS OF THE SFSR

The SFSR (Hervis et al., 1991; Szapocznik et al., 1985, 1991) was developed to systematically identify aspects of family functioning and pathology that are consistent with structural theory and the structuralist approach to assessment and therapy (Minuchin, 1974; Minuchin & Fishman, 1981; Minuchin et al., 1978). As an offshoot of communications theory, structural family theory is based on the understanding that patterns of communication are what create family structures. The structuralist approach understands human phenomena from a "relational" perspective, that is, a belief that an important source of information about individuals is obtained by understanding how family members "relate" to each other and to the whole family. Repetitive patterns of relating evolve into the transactional operations that regulate the family experience. The members of a family system organize their relationships according to the requirements of the functions and tasks that the system has selected to complete. A family's adjustment, whether "good" or "bad," and the consequent well-being of its members, is determined, in part, by the manner in which the family system organizes itself in relation to these functions. The repertoire of interactional patterns that the family develops in its attempts to carry out its ongoing functions gives the family its unique character or form. Therapists detect the family's underlying structure by observing who speaks to whom and in what way. The SFSR conforms to this principle in that trained raters (rather than therapists) are used to identify dominant interaction patterns on which most of the family operations are based.

The structural family therapy field (Minuchin, 1974, 1976; Minuchin & Fishman, 1981; Minuchin et al., 1978) has identified criteria for judging healthy or maladaptive functioning along certain basic dimensions of family interaction. These dimensions are measurable and observable in five areas of family functioning (Szapocznik & Kurtines, 1989): Structure, Developmental Stage, Resonance, Identified Patienthood, and Conflict Resolution.

DEVELOPMENT OF THE SFSR

In addition to establishing the effects of an intervention on primary outcomes (e.g., depression, drug use), psychotherapy research also includes an explicit focus on identifying critical variables that mediate outcome (e.g., self-object relations in psychodynamic therapy, maladaptive cognitions in cognitive therapy) as well as an emphasis on identifying specific in-session mechanisms (i.e., therapeutic interventions, relationships) that are related to or that engender changes in these mediators. However, to accomplish any of these goals, it is necessary to have valid and reliable measures of outcomes, mediators, and in-session mechanisms.

One challenge we encountered early in our program of research was the need to assess the types of family functioning that we specifically targeted in structural family therapy (Szapocznik et al., 1997). The measures that were available were not sensitive to these specific aspects of family functioning, and consequently were limited in their ability to demonstrate structural family functioning as a mediator of behavioral outcomes. Thus, to conduct our research it was essential to develop a measure that was—as recommended by Kazdin (1986)—theoretically appropriate and clinically relevant for assessing structural family changes that we identified as significant in our work, and that had psychometric properties adequate for use in research settings.

To launch this work, we borrowed from the work of Minuchin and his colleagues with the Wiltwick Family Tasks (Minuchin et al., 1978; Rosman, 1978). The tasks were useful as standard stimuli, but the scoring of these tasks presented problems of standardization and reliability. For this reason, we reorganized the scoring procedure into broad, theoretically and clinically important dimensions of structural family functioning; standardized the administration procedure; developed a detailed manual with anchors and examples to enhance reliability and replicability of the scoring procedure (Hervis et al., 1991); and obtained validational evidence for the usefulness and nonreactivity of the measure when used in treatment outcome studies (Santisteban et al., 1996; Szapocznik, Kurtines, Foote, Perez-Vidal, & Hervis, 1983, 1986; Szapocznik, Rio et al., 1989; Szapocznik, Santisteban et al., 1989). The SFSR has been further revised to a) reduce subjective judgment by the raters by operationalizing "dysfunctionality" in more concrete terms, b) increase the raters' focus on identifying dysfunctional behaviors, c) weight behaviors according to their level of dysfunctionality, and d) separate the scoring functions of the SFSR from the rating functions (Hervis et al., 1991).

DESCRIPTION OF THE SFSR

Administration Instructions

Prior to administration, set up chairs so that family members can talk to one another. Do not line chairs up in a row. Position videocamera so that all family members appear on screen. The Family Tasks should be introduced in a standardized manner to reduce bias and increase comparability across families. Instructions are found in the SFSR manual (Hervis et al., 1991). Once every member of the family understands the instructions, turn on all video equipment and begin recording. Verbally identify all family members present (e.g., "from left to right are the youth referred for treatment, his mother, father ... "). Also, make a written record of all of the family members who participated. Family members should be identified by role, age of children, and any other relevant information (e.g., youth or adult referred for treatment - 13 years old, mother, mother's sister).

Play the instructions on an audio player to ensure a standard stimulus. If an audio player is not available, instructions may be read. Ask the family if they understood the instructions. If family members ask for an explanation, play the tape again and tell the family to "do the best you can." No elaboration, explanation, or examples should be given. When the family acknowledges that they have understood the task, leave the room. Allow approximately 5 minutes for the family to complete each task (add 2 or 3 minutes for larger families).

It is preferable to view the interaction task from a separate observation room. If this is not possible, stay behind the camera and remain unobtrusive. If family members speak softly, wait until between tasks to prompt them to speak louder. Do not provide feedback to families about their performance on any task (e.g., don't say, "That was fast." or "That was great.").

Family Tasks

The instructions for the three tasks are as follows:

- Task I: Planning a menu

    Suppose all of you had to work out a menu for dinner tonight and would all like to have your favorite foods for dinner, but you can only have one meat, two vegetables, one drink, and one dessert. Talk together about it, but you must decide on one meal you would all enjoy that has one meat, two vegetables, one drink, and one dessert. Remember you must end up agreeing on just one meal that everyone would enjoy. Okay, go ahead.

- Task II: Things others do in the family that please or displease you

    Each of you tell about the things everyone does in the family: the things that please you the most and make you feel good, and also the things each one does that make you unhappy or mad. Everyone try to give her or his own ideas about this. Go ahead.

- Task III: A family argument

    In every family things happen that cause a fuss now and then. Discuss and talk together about an argument you had, a fight or argument at home that you can remember. Talk together about it, like what started it, who was in on it. See if you can remember what it was all about. Take your time. Go ahead.

Description of the Structural Family Functioning Rating Scales

The SFSR organizes the information on repetitive interactional patterns within the family along five interrelated dimensions of family functioning: Structure, Resonance, Developmental Stage, Identified Patienthood, and Conflict Resolution. A composite of the five scales (dimensions) yields a Total score measuring overall family functioning. Table 12.1 presents variables and anchors for each dimension.

TABLE 12.1
Structural Dimensions, Variables Assessed, and Anchors

Dimension	Variable	Anchors
1. Structure	*Leadership* a. hierarchy b. behavior control c. guidance *Subsystem Organization* a. alliances b. triangulations c. subsystem membership *Communication Flow* a. directness b. gatekeeper-switchboard operator c. spokesperson	A5" Highly Functional Structure A4" Good Structure A3" Average Structure A2" Dysfunctional Structure A1" Very Dysfunctional Structure
2. Resonance	*Differentiation* a. undifferentiated b. semidifferentiated c. differentiated *Enmeshment* a. mind readings, mediated responses, personal control, joint affective reactions b. simultaneous speeches, interruptions, continuations c. loss of distance *Disengagement* a. absence of communication, affective relating, alliances, participation b. desire for distance	A5" Well-defined yet permeable boundaries A4" Moderately well defined yet permeable boundaries A3" Somewhat defined and/or somewhat permeable boundaries A2" Poorly defined or slightly permeable boundaries A1" Nonexistent or impermeable boundaries
3. Developmental Stage	a. parenting roles and tasks b. child/sibling roles and tasks c. extended family roles and tasks	A5" Excellent Developmental Performance A4" Good Developmental Performance A3" Average Developmental Performance A2" Dysfunctional Developmental Performance A1" Very Dysfunctional Developmental Performance
4. Identified Patienthood	a. negativity about IP b. IP centrality c. overprotection/nurturance of IPhood d. denial of other problems e. other IPhood	A5" Very Flexible IPhood A4" Moderately Flexible IPhood A3" Somewhat Flexible IPhood A2" Moderately Rigid IPhood A1" Very Rigid IPhood
5. Conflict Resolution	a. denial b. avoidance c. diffusion d. emergence without resolution e. emergence with resolution	A5" Excellent Handling of Conflicts A4" Good Handling of Conflicts A3" Average Handling of Conflicts A3" Average Handling of Conflicts A1" Very Poor Handling of Conflicts

Brief definitions for each of the rating variables are presented in the sections that follow. The rating manual contains a more detailed description of these variables (Hervis et al., 1991).

Structure

Structure refers to the organizational aspects of patterns of interaction within the family. Three categories of family organization are examined: leadership, subsystem organization, and communication flow.

Leadership.   Leadership assesses the distribution of authority and responsibility within the family, including: (a) *hierarchy* (Who takes charge of the family's directorship? Is leadership in the appropriate hands? Is it shared? Is hierarchy appropriate with respect to age, role, and function?), (b) *behavior control* (Who keeps order, if anyone? Are attempts to keep order successful?), (c) *guidance* (Who provides advice and suggestions? Does the advice provided have an impact?).

Subsystem Organization.   Subsystem Organization assesses the formal and informal organization of the family system, including: (a) *alliances* (Who supports whom? Are dyad members closer to each other than to the rest of the family? Are alliances appropriate?), (b) *triangulations*, defined as an interference by family member C in a conflict between family members A and B, where C acts as an intermediary between A and B and where such interference causes a detour away from the original conflict, (c) *subsystem membership* (Who is a member of which subsystem? Are subsystems appropriate with respect to age and function? Are subsystem boundaries clearly defined?).

Communication Flow.   Communication Flow assesses the quality, quantity, and direction of communication, including: (a) *directness of communication* (Do individuals communicate directly with each other?), (b) *gatekeepers - switchboard operators* (Does someone control, direct, or channel communications between family members?), (c) *spokesperson* (Is there a family member who speaks for others in the family or for the whole family?).

Resonance

Resonance is a measure of subsystem differentiation that takes into account the threshold of each family member's sensitivity to one another. Ratings assess the permeability of boundaries and differentiation between individuals in the family. At one extreme, boundaries can be too rigid and impermeable, resulting in a lack of connectedness or disengagement among family members. At the opposite extreme, boundaries can be too open or permeable resulting in overconnected or enmeshed family interactions.

Disengagement.   Disengagement includes ratings that identify the absence of key aspects of family interaction, such as communication, affective relating, alliances, and participation in the task.

Enmeshment.   Enmeshment includes ratings that identify the extent to which family members speak for one another, mind read, interrupt or continue each other's speeches, speak simultaneously, or imply one family member's personal control over other family members.

Developmental Stage

Developmental stage refers to the appropriateness of family members' interactions with respect to roles and tasks assigned to various family members, taking into consideration their age and position within the family. The following sets of roles and tasks are rated.

Parent Figure Roles and Tasks.   Are parent figures parenting at a level consistent with the age of the children? For example, are controlling and nurturant functions in accordance with child's age and stage of psychological development? Are parent figures parenting at cooperative and equal levels of development?

Child/Sibling Roles and Tasks.   Do the children function competently for their age and have appropriate rights and responsibilities? Are parent expectations for children too high or is the child taking on a position in the family that is below her or his abilities?

Extended Family Member's Roles and Tasks.   In extended families, are parent figures able to assume proper parental position relative to their children in light of the role of their own parents and other relatives? Do extended family members interfere with or usurp the authority of parent figures?

Identified Patienthood

Identified Patienthood refers to the extent to which a) the family is convinced that their primary problem is *all* the fault of the person exhibiting the symptom (Identified Patient-IP), and b) the family organizes itself around this person, so that the IP is largely at the center of the family's interactions. There are five signs indicative of strong Identified Patienthood: (a) *negativity about the IP,* personal attacks or criticisms directed at the IP, (b) *IP centrality,* the IP is frequently the center of attention and topic of conversation and interactions, (c) *overprotection of the IPhood*, family avoids confrontation with IP dysfunction by excusing it, explaining it away, minimizing it, or feeling that there is nothing that can be done about it ("That's just the way she or he is."), (d) *nurturance of IP hood*, the IP dysfunction is supported or abetted by other family members (e.g., a sibling does the homework for an IP who skips school), and (e) *denial of other problems,* statements suggested that the IP is seen as the sole cause of family pain and unhappiness.

Conflict Resolution

Conflict Resolution assesses the family's style in managing disagreements. Five conflict resolution styles are identified: (a) *denial,* disagreements are not allowed to emerge and situations are structured or redefined to prevent the emergence of conflict, (b) *avoidance*, disagreement begins to emerge but is stopped, masked, or strongly inhibited in some way, (c) *diffusion,* moving from one disagreement to another without letting any emerge fully or making personal attacks that are not essential to the conflict issue, (d) *emergence without resolution,* separate accounts and opinions regarding one disagreement are clearly expressed but no solution is negotiated, and (e) *emergence with resolution,* separate accounts and opinions regarding a single disagreement are clearly expressed and a single final version or solution acceptable to all family members is negotiated.

CODER TRAINING

Coders

Although the SFSR was developed initially to be rated by experienced structural family therapists, subsequent revisions to the manual have made the SFSR more user friendly for coders with less clinical sophistication. Ideally, coders should have some training and experience with structural family theory and therapy. However, graduate student coders with no family therapy experience have been trained to successfully identify structural family interactions using the SFSR.

Training

Because of the complexity of the SFSR, a great deal of practice and preparation is necessary to ensure the production of valid ratings. The training goals of the SFSR are to develop a full understanding of the five structural dimensions and to learn to reliably identify which types of behavior meet rating criteria. Training typically lasts approximately 3 months. During this time, coders are expected to devote approximately 6 hours per week to SFSR training. Three hours are spent in a weekly meeting with the training group, and 3 hours are spent conducting weekly homework assignments. We have found that it is best to train coders in groups because they are able to work together to discuss and calibrate their ratings. Training groups should be led by an experienced structural family therapist who has extensive knowledge and experience with the SFSR.

Initial meetings (2 to 3 weeks) are focused on introducing coders to basic structural family theory and to the rating dimensions of the SFSR. Coders are expected to complete selected readings to gain a thorough understanding of basic structural family concepts, and become familiar with the procedures, definitions, and examples in the SFSR manual. Subsequent meetings (4 to 12 weeks) are focused on rating practice family tasks and reviewing ratings. During Weeks 4 to 6, videotapes of family tasks are presented during the weekly meeting to demonstrate rating procedures and to facilitate the identification of structural family interactions. In subsequent weeks (7 to 12), coders are expected to independently complete one rating per week. During the weekly meeting, discrepancies between the independent ratings are discussed and the videotape is reviewed by the group leader to clarify disagreements. By reviewing tapes in this manner, the group leader can identify and correct any individual coder tendencies that are contributing to invalid ratings. Training should always include review of videotapes and ratings by the group leader. The group leader should also rate the family tasks in order to compare the training group to a "gold standard."

It is possible for coders to be trained primarily from the manual. However, the training group leader must be familiar with structural family theory and concepts. We recommended that the coders trained in this manner compare their ratings to a gold standard, endorsed by the authors to ensure that their ratings adhere to the manual. Previous groups have contacted the authors and asked to have gold standard comparisons conducted. The authors can also make several training tapes available to facilitate the training of new groups.

THE CODING PROCESS

To conduct ratings, coders must be able to identify each member of the family. This information should be easily obtained from the introductions of family members on the videotape and the written record of Family Task participants. The coder should have no further information. Ratings should be based on what occurs in the interaction task. Sometimes families go on to talk about matters not related to the task after they have indicated that they have completed the task. If this occurs, such discussions should not be rated even if they occur within the allotted (5 to 7 minutes) time. Each task is rated on four of the five SFSR scales (see Hervis et al., 1991).

The rating process should proceed task by task rather than scale by scale. In other words, coders should begin with Task I and rate it on its four relevant scales before proceeding to Task II or III. Beginners will need to view each task once without doing any rating to become familiar with the content of family discussions, and then view each task at least one time for each scale being rated. Thus, each task should be viewed at least four times. As coders become more experienced, they typically bypass the step of viewing the tape without rating, and will even be able to rate more than one scale per viewing of a task. Experienced coders may view the videotape more than once, scoring two or three scales each time. The rating process is generally highly efficient, requiring no more than 30 minutes for a highly experienced coder. The coder uses a detailed SFSR Rating Form (see Table 12.2 in Excerpts From Coding Manual section) for a sample of the form) when conducting ratings. The SFSR Rating Form is a convenient way for the coder to record their observations prior to making the actual ratings.

RELIABILITY

Interrater Reliability

Excellent interrater reliabilities for the SFSR were obtained in a prior study (see Szapocznik et al., 1991). For example, examination of raw data for 24 families show that complete agreement was achieved in 52% of the ratings, and that the coders were within 1 point on 40% of the ratings. Thus, the coders either completely agreed or were within 1 scale point of each other in 92% of the comparisons. In this study, interrater reliability coefficients were also calculated using intraclass correlations (Lahey, Downey, & Saal, 1983; Shrout & Fleiss, 1974). Reliabilities for the dimensions were as follows: Structure (.76), Resonance (.86), Developmental Stage (.46), Identified Patienthood (.86), Conflict Resolution (.63), and Total score (.84). These reliabilities are excellent, with the exception of Developmental Stage.

In this initial study, the low interrater reliability for Developmental Stage may have been due to the lack of sufficient clarity in the manual regarding the age and role appropriateness of behaviors for different family members. Subsequent revisions to the manual have improved the description of the Developmental Stage items (as well as the variable descriptions for the other rating dimensions). More recent examinations of interrater reliability coefficients among raters using the revised manual range from .65 to .95, with an average reliability of .86 (Resonance = .65; Conflict Resolution = .67; Identified Patienthood = .79; Structure = .94; Developmental Stage = .95; Total = .92). Thus, the revisions to the manual improved the reliability for the Developmental Stage dimension. It is important to note that these latter comparisons involved graduate student coders, whereas the original comparisons involved experienced structural family therapists. Thus, less clinically experienced coders can be trained to reliably identify family interactions using the revised SFSR rating manual.

Internal Consistency

Internal consistency for the Total score as estimated by the alpha coefficient is .87, indicating that the SFSR has high internal consistency. The interdimension correlation coefficients range from .69 to .89 (see Szapocznik et al., 1991).

VALIDITY

Evidence for the validity of the SFSR has been collected as part of our ongoing program of research. We have used the SFSR as a treatment outcome measure in a number of large clinical research studies involving over 1,000 families in treatment.

Content Validity

Because the SFSR is theoretically based, content validity refers to the degree to which the measure is consistent with the structural framework in which it is based. Several factors provide support for the content validity of the SFSR. First, the Family Tasks used to make the ratings of family functioning were adopted from the developmental work of the Minuchin group (Minuchin et al., 1978; Rosman, 1978) and were specifically designed to elicit interactions relevant to structural family functioning. Second, the guidelines and the instructions in the rating manual were derived from extensive structural-based observational work with clinical families (Szapocznik et al., 1983; Szapocznik & Kurtines, 1989, 1986; Szapocznik, Rio et al., 1989; Szapocznik, Santisteban et al., 1986, 1989). Third, the five dimensions of structural family functioning included in the SFSR ratings clearly correspond to relevant structural family therapy and theory concepts (Minuchin, 1974, 1976; Minuchin & Fishman, 1981; Szapocznik & Kurtines, 1989).

STUDIES USING THE SFSR

The development and refinement of the SFSR played a key role in the evolution of our research program because the SFSR made it possible to test basic assumptions about structural family therapy (Szapocznik & Kurtines, 1989; Szapocznik, Kurtines, Santisteban, & Rio, 1990;). The following section summarizes research that provides evidence for (a) the nonreactivity of the SFSR when used in treatment outcome research, (b) the utility of the SFSR in assessing the impact of structural family intervention versus alternative interventions, and (c) the utility of the SFSR in assessing the impact of different types of structural family intervention modalities. This section also includes recent studies extending the SFSR into work with new clinical and nonclinical populations, and into examinations of changes in family interaction in the treatment context.

Nonreactivity of the SFSR in Treatment Outcome Research

Szapocznik, Santisteban et al. (1989) examined the nonreactivity of the SFSR using a Solomon Four Group Design to test for the effects of repeated testing. For this study, half of the families were randomly assigned to a family intervention condition and half of the families were assigned to a no treatment/wait list control condition. Within each modality, half of the families were assigned to receive the SFSR at pretest, and half of the families were assigned to a "no pretest" condition. All families were posttested with the SFSR at the end of 13 weeks. Results demonstrate that there were no significant effects due to repeated testing under either the treatment or no-treatment condition (Szapocznik, Santisteban et al., 1989). Thus, the SFSR is nonreactive in that its application shows no significant effect due to repeated testing.

Structural Family Therapy Versus Alternative Interventions

Structural Family Therapy Versus Individual Child Psychodynamic Therapy.   Szapocznik, Rio et al. (1989) provided data on the utility of the SFSR in assessing the impact of a structural family intervention condition relative to an individual psychotherapy intervention. Subjects were 69 Hispanic-American boys, ages 6 to 12, who were clinic referred due to behavioral or emotional problems. Youth were randomly assigned to three conditions: structural family therapy, individual psychodynamic child psychotherapy, or recreational activity group. SFSRs were administered at pre, post, and 1-year follow-up.

The results of this study provided evidence for the utility of the SFSR in discriminating between the effects of family versus individual psychotherapy interventions. Although there were no significant differences at posttest on the SFSR between all three conditions, there were significant differences favoring structural family therapy on the Total score and three dimensions of family functioning (Structure, Resonance, and Developmental Stage) at the time of the 1-year follow-up. Moreover, the pattern of findings indicated that although family functioning in structural family therapy improved significantly from post to follow-up, families in the recreational activity group remained at the same level, and families in the individual child psychodynamic psychotherapy condition deteriorated significantly.

Structural Family Therapy Versus Group Therapy.   Santisteban et al. (1996) provided data on the utility of the SFSR in assessing the impact of structural family therapy versus a group therapy control condition. Subjects were 79 Hispanic-American youth (77% boys; 23% girls), ages 13 to 17, who were referred for treatment for behavior problems or family conflicts. Youth were randomly assigned to structural family therapy (with or without specialized engagement procedures) or a group therapy control condition. SFSRs were administered at pretreatment and termination.

Analyses were conducted on a subset of cases ($n = 49$) to examine if changes in family functioning mediated the observed changes in behavior problems. The results of this study demonstrate that family functioning improved slightly (although not significantly) from pretreatment to termination, whereas in the control condition a significant deterioration in family functioning was observed. To determine if these results were influenced by pretreatment levels of family functioning, the 49 cases were partitioned into two groups: good family functioning and poor family functioning based on a median split on pretreatment SFSR scores. Results of analyses of families with poor family functioning demonstrate that family functioning improved significantly in the structural family therapy condition, but did not change in the group therapy condition. The results of analyses of families with good family functioning demonstrated that families in the structural family condition showed a nonsignificant deterioration, whereas families in the group therapy control condition show statistically significant deterioration.

Structural Family Therapy Versus No Treatment/Wait List Control.   Szapocznik, Santisteban et al. (1989) provided data on the utility of the SFSR in assessing the impact of a structural family intervention condition versus a no treatment/wait list control condition. Subjects were 79 Hispanic-American boys, ages 6 to 12, who were clinic referred for the treatment of behavior problems. Youth were assigned to a 13-week family effectiveness training intervention (which was based on structural family theory and included a structural family therapy component) or to a no-treatment/wait list control condition. In the control condition, youth were placed on a wait list for 13 weeks. All families were posttested at 13 weeks, and families in the control condition were then offered the opportunity to enter the family effectiveness training.

The results of this study demonstrated a significant time by condition interaction favoring the family effectiveness training condition over the no treatment/wait list control condition for all but one of the SFSR dimensions, Identified Patienthood.

Assessing the Impact of Different Types of Structural Family Intervention Modalities.   Szapocznik, Kurtines (1983, 1986a) examined the utility of the SFSR in assessing the impact of different types of structural family intervention modalities. For this study, 76 Hispanic-American families with a drug-abusing youth were randomly assigned to Conjoint Family Therapy or One Person Family Therapy. Both conditions were based on structural family therapy. However, the entire family participated in therapy in the conjoint condition, whereas only one family member was seen in the one-person condition. Family members completed the SFSR at intake, termination, and 6-month follow-up. Results show significant improvements in family interaction for both treatment conditions, with no significant differences between the conditions. Taken together with findings comparing structural family therapy to individual child psychodynamic therapy (Szapocznik, Rio et al., 1989), these results demonstrate the utility of the SFSR in discriminating the impact of family-based (conjoint or one person) andnon-family-based interventions on family functioning.

Recent Studies

Our program of research at the Center for Family Studies has expanded considerably in the past 10 years. Prior to 1991, our research focused almost exclusively on intervention studies with Hispanic-American families of behavior problem youth. More recently, however, our studies with behavior problem youth have expanded to include African-American youth and their families, which has elicited considerable discussion about the utilitization of the SFSR across cultures and, more specifically, with African-American youth and their families. In addition to expanding our work with behavior problem youth, the Center for Family Studies has also initiated new programs of research with populations other than behavior problem youth. Presently the SFSR is being used to assess family interaction patterns in families of (a) HIV+ African-American women, (b) adult caregivers of mentally retarded Hispanic-American adults, (c) adult caregivers of dementia patients, (d) families with a diabetic child, and (e) families with an adult diagnosed with schizophrenia. We are currently in the process of collecting data to examine family interaction patterns in each of these new populations. In some instances, we have had to make minor revisions to the rating manual to ensure that the data we are collecting identify appropriate processes relevant to these families. For example, in the families of caregivers of developmentally disabled adults, we added a rating for positive statements about the IP because our experiences working with these families suggested that IP-hood is often maintained in very supportive and nurturing ways rather than with high levels of negativity.

We are also in the process of developing an interactional measure that assesses family interactions in the therapeutic context that are theoretically consistent with the five dimensions of the SFSR. As we have noted, the SFSR has been very useful in assisting us in demonstrating the mediating role of family interactions in the successful treatment of behavior problem youth. However, this research has focused on pre- to posttreatment changes, and has not shed light on the process of change over the course of therapy. For this reason, we have adapted the SFSR to rate family interactions as they occur in the treatment context. This new measure, the Family Therapy Structural Systems Ratings (Robbins, Mitrani, Hervis, Zarate, & Szapocznik, 1998), will allow us to answer critical questions about how family interactions change over the course of therapy, and how these changes are linked to changes in family interaction and the youth's behavioral problems that occur outside of treatment. In a small pilot study using the Family Therapy Structural Systems Ratings, we were able to successfully demonstrate improvements in family interactions over the course of family therapy among cases in which the adolescent demonstrated clinically significant improvements in conduct disorder, and no improvements in family interactions among cases in which the adolescent's conduct disorder did not improve (Robbins, Mitrani, Zarate, Coatsworth, & Szapocznik, 1996).

EXCERPTS FROM CODING MANUAL

The SFSR Rating Form is used by coders to summarize their observations of family interactions. The SFSR Rating Form organizes information from the rating manual, and includes brief operational definitions of relevant rating categories. Table 12.2 is an excerpt from the SFSR Rating Form. In particular, Table 12.2 presents the rating categories for the Leadership subcategory of the Structure scale.

TABLE 12.2
Sample of SFSR Rating Form

STRUCTURE

1. LEADERSHIP

A. Hierarchy

Note how often each family member gives a task opinion on Task I or III by making a checkmark in the appropriate space on the lines provided.

Task I:	M	/F	/IP	/Sib1	/Other
Task III:	M	/F	/IP	/Sib1	/Other

Check the corresponding box next to each item listed below if it is true for Task I or III.

TASK I	TASK III	
☐	☐	1. Either parent gives no task opinions.
☐	☐	2. One parent gives more than twice as many task opinions as the other parent.
☐	☐	3. Any non-parent surpasses either parent in the number of task opinions given.

B. Behavior Control

Note each parent's effective (+) and ineffective (−) behavior control attempts on Tasks I and III by making a checkmark in the appropriate space on the lines provided.

Task I:	M+	/M−	/F+	/F−
Task III:	M+	/M−	/F+	/F−

Check the corresponding box next to each item listed below if it is true for Task I or III.

TASK I	TASK III	
☐	☐	1. Parents fail to control children's uncooperative behavior, causing miscompletion of the Task.
☐	☐	2. More than half of either parent(s)' behavior control attempts are ineffective.
☐	☐	3. Parents are unable to persuade a child to participate in the Task.
☐	☐	4. Parents allow a child to be disrespectful towards an adult.

(Continues)

TABLE 12.2 (Continued)

STRUCTURE

I. LEADERSHIP

C. Guidance

Note how often each family member gives guidance on Task I or III by making a checkmark in the appropriate space on the lines provided.

Task I:	M	/F	/IP	/Sib1	/Other
Task III:	M	/F	/IP	/Sib1	/Other

Check the corresponding box next to each item listed below if it is true for Task I or III.

TASK I	TASK III	
☐	☐	1. Parent(s) misinterpret the Task causing miscompletion of the Task.
☐	☐	2. Any nonparent surpasses either parent in the number of guidance behaviors performed.

ACKNOWLEDGMENTS

This chapter was supported in part by National Institute on Drug Abuse grants (DA 10574, Jose Szapocznik, Principal Investigator; DA 11328, Howard Liddle, Principal Investigator).

REFERENCES

Hervis, O. E., Szapocznik, J., Mitrani, V. B., Rio, A.T. & Kurtines, W. M. (1991). *Structural family systems ratings: A revised manual* [Tech. Rep.]. Miami, FL: University of Miami School of Medicine, Department of Psychiatry, Spanish Family Guidance Center.

Kazdin, A. E. (1986). Comparative outcome studies of psychotherapy: Methodological issues and strategies. *Journal of Consulting and Clinical Psychology, 54,* 95–105.

Lahey, M. A., Downey, R. G., & Saal, F. E. (1983). Intraclass correlations: There's more there than meets the eye. *Psychological Bulletin, 93,* 586–595.

Minuchin, S. (1974). *Families and family therapy.* Cambridge, MA: Harvard University Press.

Minuchin, S. (1976). Structural family therapy. In G. Caplan (Ed.), *American handbook of psychiatry* (Vol. 2, pp. 178–192). New York: Basic Books.

Minuchin, S., & Fishman, S. (1981). *Family therapy techniques.* Cambridge, MA: Harvard University Press.

Minuchin, S., Rosman, B. L., & Baker, L. (1978). *Psychosomatic families: Anorexia nervosa in context.* Cambridge, MA: Harvard University Press.

Robbins, M. S., Mitrani, V., Hervis, O., Zarate, M., & Szapocznik, J. (1998). *The family therapy structural systems ratings*. Unpublished manuscript, University of Miami School of Medicine, Miami, FL.

Robbins, M. S., Mitrani, V. B., Zarate, M., Coatsworth, D. & Szapocznik, J. (1996, June). *Linking process to outcome in structural family therapy with drug using youth: An examination of the process of family therapy in successful and unsuccessful outcome cases.* Paper presented at the 27th annual meeting of the Society for Psychotherapy Research, Amelia Island, FL.

Rosman, B. L. (1978). *Family tasks and scoring.* Unpublished manuscript, Philadelphia Child Guidance Clinic.

Santisteban, D. A., Szapocznik, J., Perez-Vidal, A., Kurtines, W., Murray, E. J., & LaPerriere, A. (1996). Efficacy of interventions for engaging youth/families into treatment and some variables that may contribute to differential effectiveness. *Journal of Family Psychology, 10,* 35–44.

Shrout, P. E., & Fleiss, J. L. (1974). Intraclass correlations: Uses in assessing rater reliability. *Psychological Bulletin, 86,* 420–428.

Szapocznik, J., Hervis, O., Rio, A., Faraci, A. M., Foote, F., & Kurtines, W. (1985). *Manual for the structural family systems ratings.* Miami, FL: University of Miami School of Medicine.

Szapocznik, J. I., & Kurtines, W. M. (1989). *Breakthroughs in family therapy with drug-abusing and problem youth.* New York: Springer.

Szapocznik, J., Kurtines, W. M., Foote, F. H., Perez-Vidal, A., & Hervis, O. (1983). Conjoint versus one person family therapy: Some evidence for the effectiveness of conducting family therapy through one person. *Journal of Consulting and Clinical Psychology, 51,* 889–899.

Szapocznik, J., Kurtines, W. M., Foote, F. H., Perez-Vidal A., & Hervis, O. (1986). Conjoint versus one person family therapy: Further evidence for the effectiveness of conducting family therapy through one person with drug-abusing adolescents. *Journal of Consulting and Clinical Psychology, 54,* 395–397.

Szapocznik, J., Kurtines, W., Santisteban, D. A., Pantin, H., Scopetta, M., Mancilla, Y., Aisenberg, S., McIntosh, S., Perez-Vidal, A., & Coatsworth, J. D. (1997). The evolution of structural ecosystemic theory for working with Latino families. In J. Garcia & M. C. Zea (Eds.), *Psychological interventions and research with Latino populations* (pp. 166–190). Boston: Allyn & Bacon.

Szapocznik, J., Kurtines, W. M., Santisteban, D. A., & Rio, A. T. (1990). The interplay of advances among theory, research, and application in treatment interventions aimed at behavior problem children and adolescents. *Journal of Consulting and Clinical Psychology* [Special series: Research on Therapies for Children and Adolescents], *58*(6), 696–703.

Szapocznik, J., Rio, A. T., Hervis, O. E., Mitrani, V. B., Kurtines, W. M., & Faraci, A. M. (1991). Assessing change in family functioning as a result of treatment: The Structural Family Systems Rating Scale (SFSR). *Journal of Marital and Family Therapy, 17,* 295–310.

Szapocznik, J., Rio, A., Murray, E., Cohen, R., Scopetta, M., Rivas-Vasquez, A., Hervis, O., Posada, V., & Kurtines, W. (1989). Structural family versus psychodynamic child therapy for problematic Hispanic boys. *Journal of Consulting and Clinical Psychology, 57,* 571–578.

Szapocznik, J., Santisteban, D., Rio, A., Perez-Vidal, A., Kurtines, W., & Hervis, O. (1986). Bicultural effectiveness training (BET): An experimental test of an intervention modality for families experiencing intergenerational/intercultural conflict. *Hispanic Journal of Behavioral Sciences, 8,* 303–330.

Szapocznik, J., Santisteban, D., Rio, A., Perez-Vidal, A., Santisteban, D. A., & Kurtines, W. M. (1989). Family effectiveness training: An intervention to prevent drug abuse and problem behaviors in Hispanic adolescents. *Hispanic Journal of Behavioral Sciences, 11*(1), 4–27.

13

Meso-Analytic Behavioral Rating System for Family Interactions: Observing Play and Forced-Compliance Tasks With Young Children

Annette Mahoney
Amy Coffield
Terri Lewis
Samuel L. Lashley
Bowling Green State University

The purpose of the Meso-Analytic Behavioral Rating System for Family Interactions (MeBRF) is to assess the behavior of young children and parents during family interactions involving play or forced-compliance activities. The system involves observational ratings of child and parent functioning on a 5-point scale for each minute of a family interaction. The term *meso-analytic* refers to the unit of measure which is neither microanalytic, where the presence/absence of discrete behaviors are coded during brief time intervals (e.g., 6–10 seconds, speaker turns), nor macroanalytic, where behaviors are rated once for an entire interaction period. Instead, the unit of measure is "midlevel" and focuses on each participant's behavior for each minute of a family interaction. The term *rating* highlights the fact that

225

coders generate summary evaluations of behavior rather than code the yes/no occurrence of discrete behaviors. The constructs directly assessed by the MeBRF reflect social learning and developmental theories, with an emphasis on parent and child behaviors hypothesized and/or previously found to be related to child externalizing behavior problems. Parent ratings include positive attention, involvement, hostility, controllingness, coercive control, ambiguous control, and permissiveness toward the child. Child ratings consist of noncompliance, antisocial and prosocial behavior.

THEORETICAL FOUNDATIONS

In the past two decades, the importance of studying triadic family interactions has been increasingly recognized (Hinde & Hinde, 1988; Kerig, 1995; Vuchinich, Emery, & Cassidy, 1988). In particular, theory and research suggests that children are affected by how effectively couples forge a coparenting alliance (Abidin, 1992; Abidin & Brunner, 1992; Gable, Belsky, & Crnic, 1992; Mahoney, Jouriles, & Scavone, 1997). The MeBRF was created to assess both parents' child management skills as well as child behavior during commonplace, developmentally appropriate family activities. As is described later in the chapter, the MeBRF ratings of individual family members can be used in concert to study triadic processes highlighted by family systems theories, such as coparenting alliances. As is reviewed in the following discussion, the MeBRF ratings directly assess theoretical constructs proposed by social learning and developmental theories to be linked to child externalizing behavior problems.

Social learning theory highlights modeling processes to account in part for children's behavior (Bandura & Walters, 1963). Because children learn how to behave through the observation and imitation of adult models, antisocial and prosocial child behavior should mirror analogous behavior by parents. In addition, children's behavior reflects the degree to which parents appropriately use reinforcers and punishers. Skillful parents selectively attend to and immediately reinforce desirable child behavior (e.g., compliance) and ignore or swiftly punish misbehavior (e.g., whining). Unskilled parents often reinforce negative behavior with attention, and inadvertently ignore or punish appropriate behavior (Chamberlain & Patterson, 1995; Patterson, 1982; Snyder et al., 1988). The quality of antecedents used to elicit child behavior, particularly the clarity of parental commands, is also an important influence on the probability of gaining child compliance (Chamberlain & Patterson, 1995). Finally, coercion theory (Patterson, 1982; Snyder, Rains, & Popejoy, 1988) suggests that antisocial child behavior results from a complex learning history where parents and children engage in increasingly coercive behavior to "win" compliance struggles. Parents undermine their effectiveness by being excessively repetitive but indirect and vague when issuing commands, and negatively reinforcing child resistance by failing to punish noncompliance. Children, in turn, realize they can often avoid complying by ignoring parents or escalating obnoxious behavior.

Whereas social learning theory emphasizes specific parent and child behaviors, developmental models of parenting styles emphasize traitlike and affect-laden constructs to account for child behavior (Baumrind, 1971, 1989; Darling & Steinberg, 1993; Maccoby & Martin, 1983). Parents presumably foster close attachment bonds with their children when they exhibit high levels of involvement marked by warmth and responsiveness. In turn, children who experience a strong sense of emotional security with parents are hypothesized to be cooperative and motivated to conform to expectations (Darling & Steinberg, 1993; Maccoby & Martin, 1983). Developmental theories also emphasize an appropriate balance of parental control and child autonomy. Optimal parenting consists of exerting firm, unambiguous control when necessary (i.e., authoritative style) while being neither overly tolerant (i.e., permissive style) nor punitive (i.e., authoritarian style; Baumrind, 1971, 1989). Notably, the affective tenor of parents' actions greatly shapes which parenting style is manifested. Parents send different nonverbal messages when they deliver commands in a firm, matter-of-fact tone of voice as opposed to an ambivalent, pleading, lax tone, or a threatening, harsh tone. Likewise, efforts to praise children can vary considerably in warmth, depending on the tone of voice and nonverbal signals. Children respond less positively when the affective messages embedded in parents' statements are negative or ambiguous rather than positive (Dix, 1991).

In sum, based on social learning principles and developmental theory, parental positive attention, hostility, involvement, permissiveness, and degree and quality of controllingness (e.g., ambiguous, coercive) are critical constructs associated with child noncompliance as well as child anti- and prosocial behavior. As is described later, the MeBRF codes assess these aspects of triadic parent–child interactions.

Development of the MeBRF

The MeBRF was developed to assess two standardized, brief family interactions in a laboratory setting: a play activity and a forced-compliance task. Notably, these types of triadic interactions tend to elicit child-focused behavior by parents, with few direct interchanges between parents. Thus, the MeBRF emphasizes parenting practices and child misbehavior. This sharply contrasts coding systems designed to assess marital dialogue and child reactions to witnessing and/or taking part in marital problem-solving discussions (e.g., Cummings & Davies, 1994; Gordis, Margolin, & John, 1997; Lindahl, Clements, & Markman, 1997).

Another important consideration in the development of the MeBRF system was our desire to assess aspects of triadic family interactions that are difficult to capture using microanalytic observation techniques. By definition, microanalytic coding systems do not easily assess the absence of behavior (e.g., parent not responding to a child's bid for attention or misbehavior) or the qualitative nature of behavior (e.g., parent tone of voice during a command). Though one may infer the degree to which parents fail to respond to child behaviors with sequential analyses, an alternative approach is to ask raters to assess directly the degree to which parents are disengaged and/or do not take appropriate action given the context of the situation. Ratings systems are also well suited to assess the intensity and affective tone of behavior. For example, the literal question "Did you hear what I said?" could represent (a) a forceful, clear control strategy despite its lack of precision and directness as a command, (b) a simple, innocuous question, or (c) an indirect, weak plea for child compliance, depending on preceding events between a child and parent, and the parent's voice tone and inflection.

The development of the MeBRF was also prompted by the various benefits of a coding system that taps into midlevel, dimensional constructs. First, MeBRF's 1-minute ratings are sufficiently distinct and variable to be analyzed separately. In contrast, mutually exclusive and sharply focused microanalytic codes often have to be collapsed into global, summary categories to ensure sufficient variability (e.g., "positive" and "negative" parenting; Lobitz & Johnson, 1975). This represents a loss of potentially important conceptual distinctions among codes and wastes the initial effort needed to generate microanalytic data. Second, meso-analytic ratings inherently capture a range of frequency and intensity in behavior, whereas highly detailed, categorical microanalytic codes may need to be excluded from analyses due to low base rates (e.g., Lemanek, Stone, & Fishel, 1993). Third, MeBRF encompasses several parenting constructs rather than focusing primarily on the frequency of specific parental commands. Fourth, by using minute-by-minute ratings rather than global, macroanalytic ratings, the MeBRF increases the likelihood of obtaining reliable ratings and maintains the option of analyzing changes in participants' behavior over time. However, it should be noted that dimensional ratings cannot provide insight into immediate sequential contingencies among family members' specific actions (e.g., probability of parent praise following child compliance).

Another drawback of the MeBRF is that directly interpreting dimensional ratings can be more difficult than comprehending the frequency of discrete events (e.g., number of vague commands). Ideally, the means, standard deviations and standard errors of measurement of data generated by any observational system would be available from large, nationally representative sample, and for clinic-referred and non-clinic-referred parents. Such normative data would facilitate the interpretation of MeBRF ratings and help clarify individual differences due to cultural and ethnic backgrounds. Currently, research on the MeBRF is limited to White families from a suburban-rural community in the Midwest with middle-class backgrounds.

DESCRIPTION OF THE MeBRF

Parent Ratings

The MeBRF includes seven parent ratings. Each parent's behavior toward the child is assessed separately on a 5-point scale for each minute of the family interaction.

Positive Attention.   This rating measures the frequency and intensity with which the parent proactively communicates warmth and support toward the child via nonverbal (e.g., physical affection, enthusiasm and sincerity in tone of voice) and verbal behavior (e.g., compliments, specific praise, spontaneous or enthusiastic comments about child's activity, empathic statements reflecting an appreciation for child's point of view).

Hostility.   The frequency and intensity with which the parent communicates disapproval, irritation, and displeasure toward the child via nonverbal (e.g., accusatory, angry, or sarcastic tone of voice; eye rolling; disapproving facial expressions; obvious withdrawal or ignoring; provocative touching or spanking) and verbal behavior (e.g., statements of criticism, displeasure, rejection, impatience, etc).

Involvement.   The frequency and intensity of parent involvement, interest in, and engagement with the child, regardless of quality (e.g., positive or negative) or content (e.g., commands, praise or criticism) of behavior, is assessed by this rating. This rating reflects the total amount of nonverbal (e.g., eye contact, physical proximity) and verbal behaviors the parent directs toward the child.

Controllingness.   This rating measures the frequency and intensity of *all* nonverbal and verbal efforts the parent puts forth to control the child, regardless of skill and effectiveness. Controlling verbalizations involve indirect suggestions, requests, or questions ("Are you going to get started?") and direct, declarative commands ("I want you to do it now"). Both classes of directives can vary in precision or clarity (e.g., specific to global/vague) and in firmness (e.g., coaxing to matter of fact to threatening). The context of the situation and nonverbal cues (e.g., facial expressions, hand movements, tone and loudness of the parent's voice) paired with verbalizations help determine the degree of controllingness. Purely nonverbal behavior may also reflect controllingness (e.g., taking object away from child, physical restraint, or raising hand in air). Ratings increase as a function of the frequency of directives and/or intensity with which the parent communicates insistence for compliance.

Ambiguous Control.   This rating measures the frequency and intensity with which the parent relies on indirect and ambiguous methods to assert control, and communicates that the child has a choice in deciding how to behave. The number of indirect or vague suggestions and requests, and tone of voice when issuing directives (ranging from polite and solicitous to coaxing and pleading) determines the level of ambiguous control. Lower ratings indicate the parent is underplaying his or her authority (which can be appropriate); higher ratings indicate the parent has handed over an inappropriate degree of choice to the child, and is unable or unwilling to make clear, firm demands as an authority figure.

Coercive Control.   The frequency and intensity with which the parent relies on coercive methods to back up efforts to control the child, and communicates that the child should feel fearful, guilty or bad about his or her behavior is assessed by this rating. The degree to which the parent uses unnecessary commands, punitive or guilt-inducing remarks, and threatening or hostile nonverbal cues (e.g., raising voice) determines level of coercive control. Lower ratings indicate unnecessary use of directives (e.g., nagging), impatience, and mild blaming or critical remarks to reinforce parental authority. Higher levels reflect a more threatening, harsh, and punitive stance toward the child.

Permissiveness.   This rating measures the extent to which the parent ignores inappropriate behavior and communicates a tolerant and permissive stance toward the child. Verbal behavior includes statements that distract the child or change the focus of the interaction without directly commenting on child misbehavior. Nonverbal behavior includes backing down easily from a directive, exerting little effort to impose structure or redirection, and avoidance of issuing a directive when child is being resistant, noncompliant, or antisocial. Lower ratings reflect potentially reasonable use of selective ignoring. Higher ratings reflect an unwillingness to issue commands or reprimand the child.

Child Ratings

The MeBRF includes three child ratings, briefly described next.

Overt Noncompliance.   This rating measures the frequency and intensity with which the child fails to respond in a desired manner to parental control efforts, assuming the child has been given the opportunity to comply (e.g., parent[s] has not taken over for child) and the child understands what is expected. How often and intensely a child refuses to comply with parent directives in a prompt manner (within 6 seconds of a directive) is taken into account.

Antisocial Behavior.   The frequency and intensity with which the child exhibits defiant, oppositional, hostile, and/or disruptive behavior is measured by this rating. Persistent or spontaneous off-task and noncompliant behaviors that do not directly follow a specific parent command are included in this rating. Other examples include whining, complaining, interrupting parent, engaging in backtalk or babytalk, name calling, using annoying tone of voice, screaming or yelling, issuing bossy demands, breaking rules, and engaging in excessive motor activity or destructive behavior.

Prosocial Behavior.   This rating measures the frequency and intensity with which the child exhibits prosocial behavior, and is likable, cooperative and pleasant. It helps capture the degree of a child's cooperativeness in situations where parents issue few directives, as well as the child's frustration tolerance and sociability (e.g., smiling and laughing, physical affection). Other examples include being persistently on-task, compliant, or patient; delaying gratification; taking turns and sharing; and doing what is appropriate given the context of family interaction.

Overall, the MeBRF child ratings represent direct samples of child externalizing behavior problems (noncompliance, antisocial ratings) or lack thereof (prosocial rating). The child ratings *do not* represent direct samples of child internalizing behavior problems. Also, we decided against making separate child-to-mother and child-to-father ratings because children often exhibited behaviors without intentionally excluding one parent over the other. For example, children would often voice complaints or play cooperatively without appearing to target a specific parent. In retrospect, we realized that it may be useful to rate child noncompliance toward mothers and fathers separately for some research purposes, but we believe the overall noncompliance rating is a valid reflection of general resistance to parental control efforts.

CODER TRAINING

We recommend that three coders be placed on a team with a supervisor who understands the hypotheses of the study for which the coding is being done and who is experienced with observational coding. Coders should remain blind to the hypotheses. Undergraduate psychology majors who possess a high grade point average have been excellent MeBRF coders. Commitment to the coding task is the key issue in determining the ease of training, which should take about 6 weeks (total of 25–30 hours). The coders should first carefully read the coding manual. Team meetings can then be scheduled to teach coders the coding process, which is as follows.

Each family interaction is rated each minute, starting with the 1st minute. A 1-minute segment of the tape is watched once through without coding. The segment is then watched a second time, and the first family member is rated. The segment is reviewed a third time to code a second family member, and a fourth time to code the third family member. If necessary, the tape can be stopped and started, or reviewed repeatedly to assign ratings. The order in which family members are rated is counterbalanced across 10-minute interactions, and all three family members are coded before going to the next 1-minute segment. Coders *do not* observe the entire 10-minute interaction prior to doing ratings because the MeBRF relies on judgments on the context of behaviors, and salient events at the end of tapes may unduly influence early ratings.

During the first stage of training, the supervisor and coders should meet together to code five tapes. Team members should code all three family members and compare scores. Absolute agreement between team members on each code is not necessary to reach adequate reliability in the long run. If each coder is within 1 point of another coder for a particular MeBRF rating, no discussion would usually be necessary about that rating for that minute. An exception is when one particular coder systematically gives ratings for several minutes that are 1 point lower or higher for a given MeBRF rating than one or both of the other coders. This indicates that the coder in question is using a different threshold for assessing the behaviors in the rating. Such discrepancies should be identified and discussed. Discussion should also occur when one coder displays a 2-point difference from both of the other coders, or a pair of coders is 3 or more points apart. If necessary, the minute of tape can be reviewed again for coders to find support for their ratings and to come within 1 point of each other.

In the second stage of training, the supervisor and team of coders should individually rate seven tapes in the same order. Team meetings should continue to take place to discuss coding discrepancies for each tape. When everyone has finished a given tape, the supervisor should also compute an intraclass correlation coefficient (ICC) based on the 1-minute ratings of the three coders across *all* codes for that particular tape. After all seven tapes have been rated, an ICC can be computed based on the coders' 1-minute ratings for *all* codes and for *each* code collapsed across all seven tapes. These figures forecast the team's internal reliability across all tapes.

When using the MeBRF, we recommend that a team of three coders rate all of the triadic interactions in the data set, and the average ratings yielded by the team for each code be used as the best estimates of "true scores." We also recommend using ICCs to assess interrater reliability on the ratings generated by three coders, rather than computing Pearson correlations on ratings from pairs of coders. For many research questions, the appropriate data points for analyses would be the team's 1-minute MeBRF ratings for each family member averaged across all 10 minutes (exceptions would include questions about changes in behavior over time). To evaluate the reliability of such data points, ICCs should be computed to reflect the level of consistency between the three team members' average 10-minute ratings for each of the codes (i.e., seven mother, seven father, and three child ratings) across the *total* sample of families. However, during training, the number of families available will not be sufficient to yield stable reliability figures based on coders' average 10-minute figures. Thus, as mentioned previously, to assess initial levels of reliability on a family-by-family basis, ICCs can be calculated based on the 1-minute ratings rather than on the 10-minute averages of separate codes. During training, coders should attain ICCs at .65–.70 or higher for 1-minute ratings of each MeBRF code across seven tapes before moving to the coding of "actual" data. Final ICCs for each code are calculated on the 10-minute averages of all families in the study.

Overall, we suggest that 12 tapes be used for training purposes. If a limited number of families can be recruited for a study, the following strategy can be used to minimize the number of tapes dedicated only to training purposes: (a) recruit two teams of three coders to do coding; (b) set aside five tapes for all coders to use in the first stage of training, thereby losing these five tapes for use as "actual" data; (c) divide the other cases in the database into two sets of tapes, and assign one set to each team to code later as "actual" data; (d) randomly assign seven tapes from one team's set of tapes to the other team for use in the second stage of training, and vice versa; and (e) have each team use the selected seven tapes in training before moving to coding of "actual" data. If one team does not reach adequate reliability after with the seven tapes, additional tapes could be selected from the other team's set for more training. Ideally, the same supervisor would oversee both teams. Reliability between teams of raters could also be assessed by overlapping their assigned tape sets. At this time, we do not have tapes to release for training to people outside our lab. A detailed MeBRF manual is located on the web page. We would be available for consultation.

THE CODING PROCESS

We recommend the MeBRF be used only with videotaped triadic interactions to allow for repeated viewing of tapes. Given the age of the children, nature of tasks, and type of ratings used, transcripts are not relevant. The coding process of tapes is described in detail in the preceding section—coders watch each minute of interaction, once without coding, and three additional times to code each of the three family members. Once coders are well trained, however, reliable ratings can often be made of less complex intervals without watching the tape four times. Thus, the coding of one 10-minute interaction usually takes between 25 and 45 minutes. During the coding process, coders should continue to attend a weekly meeting to maintain interrater reliability. A final issue to emphasize is that a different random order of tapes should be assigned to each coder during the coding of actual data. If all coders on a team are assigned the same tapes in the same order, undetectable drift could occur across time in the criteria coders use to rate families as they become more experienced and exposed in the same order to different types of families. For reliability to be systematically assessed throughout the coding process, however, every fifth tape assigned should be the same so that ICCs can be calculated at regular intervals.

RELIABILITY

Satisfactory interrater reliability has been found for raters' average rating of each MeBRF code across a 10-minute interaction. The following ICC values emerged for ratings of mothers and fathers, respectively: .85 and .83 for positive attention, .72 and .61 for hostility, .88 and .92 for involvement, .95 and .94 for controllingness, .80 and .77 for ambiguous control, .75 and .72 for coercive control, and .81 and .81 for permissiveness. For child ratings, the ICC values were .95 for overt noncompliance, .94 for antisocial behavior, and .84 for prosocial behavior. Notably, these reliability figures are restricted to a sample of White families with middle-class backgrounds; different reliability indices may occur with families from other backgrounds.

VALIDITY

The validity of the MeBRF is supported by several sets of findings from a research project we conducted with 76 families who were randomly assigned to a 10-minute family interaction where parents either conjointly played with their child (19 boys and 19 girls) or supervised their child in a difficult clean-up task (19 boys and 19 girls). To facilitate an understanding of these findings, the protocol used to collect data is now described in more detail. Prior to the triadic family interaction, parents completed questionnaires while their child went to a playroom with a research assistant (RA) who interviewed the child and then ensured that a standardized "mess" was created with preselected toys. Immediately before parents joined their child, the RA opened a large cabinet containing other attractive toys. For the forced-compliance task only, the RA also turned on a computer game just before the parents entered the room. Parents assigned to the triadic play task were asked to play with the child as they would at home. Parents assigned to the forced-compliance task were asked to get their child to pick up and sort the 400 plastic chips into four colored boxes while the computer game intermittently made distracting noises.

Construct Validity: Coparent Alliance

The ratings generated by the MeBRF can be used to test hypotheses about triadic processes from a whole-family system perspective. As one illustration, we offer the following preliminary finding about coparenting alliances for the 38 families involved in the clean-up task.

Although ratings of mothers' and fathers' use of ambiguous control (e.g., indirect commands, coaxing) increased as child antisocial behavior increased, these associations obviously do not reveal how maternal ambiguous control may influence the link between paternal ambiguous control and child antisocial behavior, or how paternal ambiguous control may influence the link between maternal ambiguous control and child antisocial behavior. Such questions about coparent alliances, however, are of great importance according to whole-family system perspectives on child functioning. Both structural (Colapinto, 1991) and strategic (Madanes, 1991) models of family system therapy posit that dyadic interactions are profoundly influenced by how a third party in the family system acts. Thus, one could expect that one parent's behavior would moderate the link between the other parent's behavior and the child's behavior. One example of the effect of the coparent alliance can be seen from a hierarchical regression analysis where child antisocial behavior serves as the dependent variable, and mothers' and fathers' ambiguous control are used as predictors. We have found that the interaction term of maternal and paternal ambiguous control adds substantial variance (14%) to the prediction of child antisocial ratings after accounting for the variance due to the main effects of maternal and paternal ambiguous control (31%; Mahoney, Coffield, Lewis, & Lashley, 1998).

This finding illustrates that the interplay between each parent and the child's behavior can vary as a function of the other parent's behavior. Specifically, for families in which fathers exhibited little effort to control the child, higher levels of mothers' use of ambiguous control (i.e., parental "splitting") were clearly linked to more child antisocial behavior. Whereas, in families where fathers displayed high levels of ambiguous control, higher levels of mothers' use of ambiguous control (i.e., coparent alliance) were not linked to greater child antisocial behavior. Of course, the significant interaction term also means that maternal behavior moderated the link between father–child associations in the same manner. In sum, despite the fact that higher use of ambiguous control by a parent tends to be associated with increased child misbehavior, this parenting technique appears to be increasingly effective as two parents echo and amplify each other's use of indirect, ambiguous directives.

STUDIES USING THE MeBRF

Group Differences: Play Versus Forced-Compliance Tasks

We evaluated the ability of the MeBRF to discriminate between the triadic play activity and the forced-compliance task. In the latter condition, parents were expected to exhibit lower levels of positive attention and involvement, and higher levels of hostility, controllingness, ambiguous control, and permissiveness, and children were expected to exhibit higher levels of noncompliance and antisocial behavior, and lower levels of the prosocial behavior. Three one-way, between-group (play vs. forced compliance) MANOVAs (multivariate analyses of variance) were computed and significant multivariate effect for condition emerged for mother ratings, Wilks' lambda = .20, F, $(7, 68) = 38.23$; $p < .0001$; father ratings, Wilks' lambda = .20, F, $(7, 68) = 39.79$; $p < .0001$; and child ratings, Wilks' lambda = .55 F, $(3, 72) = 19.49$ $p < .0001$. Using follow-up one-way ANOVAs (analyses of variance), all codes differed in the expected direction, with the exception of parent positive attention where fathers showed no difference and mothers had higher ratings in the clean-up task. These findings indicate that the type of activity families engage in has a marked effect on behavior patterns. Forced-compliance tasks elicit higher rates of undesirable child behavior as well as more parental negativity and control efforts than play activities (Mahoney, Coffield, & Lashley, 1998).

Associations Between MeBRF Parent and Child Ratings

The pattern of associations between parent and child ratings offer another means to assess the construct validity of an observational system. According to theories reviewed earlier, higher ratings of parental hostility, controllingness, coerciveness, ambiguous control, and permissiveness should be related to higher ratings of child noncompliance and antisocial behavior, and lower prosocial behavior. The MeBRF yields associations that are consistent with these expectations for both mothers and fathers (Mahoney, 1999). Contrary to expectations, however, higher levels of maternal positive attention were associated with more negative child behavior, suggesting that mothers may inadvertently increase positive attention as negative child behavior increases.

Associations Within MeBRF Parent
and Within MeBRF Child Ratings

Ideally, an observational system should yield variables that are interrelated in meaningful ways, but not completely redundant. The MeBRF ratings for mothers and fathers appear to meet this criterion (Mahoney, 1999). For example, parental positive attention exhibited low to moderate positive associations with parental involvement and efforts to exert more control over the triadic situation. This suggests that parents can use multiple, but distinct, techniques to gain dominance in a triadic family interaction. Higher parental hostility was not associated with lower positive attention, but was moderately linked with higher control ratings. This finding is compatible with the notion that greater parental irritation co-occurs with increased demands to impose more structure on child behavior (Dix, 1991). Not surprisingly, moderate to high associations emerged for controllingness and the two subtypes of control (ambiguous and coercive control), but the two subtypes of directives were only moderately associated (Mahoney, 1999). Finally, higher permissiveness was moderately associated with higher overall controllingness and ambiguous control efforts (Mahoney, 1999). This pattern is consistent with the idea that parents who issue higher rates of directives may be triggering and/or responding to higher rates of child noncompliance as well as intermittently tolerating more child misbehavior.

The pattern of correlations within the child ratings indicated that ratings of child antisocial behavior were fairly redundant with ratings of overt noncompliance and prosocial behavior. However, the ratings of child noncompliance and prosocial behavior maintained some distinctiveness (Mahoney, 1999).

Associations Between MeBRF Ratings
and Analogous Microanalytic Codes

Although incorporating raters' judgments about the context, frequency, and intensity of behavior into observations of family interactions can be viewed as an advantage of a dimensional rating system like the MeBRF, it is important to know whether the ratings *only* reflect subjective opinions of observers. To evaluate this issue, we have conducted preliminary analyses on the degree of association between MeBRF ratings and analogous variables from a traditional microanalytic coding system (Mahoney, Coffield, & Lashley, 1998). At a minimum, we expected to find moderate associations between variables from the two systems that tap the same construct domain. The microanalytic system involved yes/no coding within each 10-second interval of the occurrence of three specific child behaviors: noncompliance, misbehavior, and on-task behavior; and eight specific parent behaviors: approval statements, disapproval statements, empathic statements, clear commands, vague/confusing commands, and general conversation, other negative statements, and other attending statements. The validity of this microanalytic coding system has been demonstrated in prior research (Jouriles & Farris, 1992; Mahoney, Boggio, Jouriles, 1996). Comparisons of the two coding systems yielded moderate to high associations between the MeBRF ratings and conceptually parallel microanalytic codes of child noncompliance, antisocial behavior, and social behavior. Moderate to high associations also emerged across the two systems for parent positive attention, hostility, involvement, controllingness, and ambiguous control (Mahoney, Coffield, & Lashley, 1998). Analogous microanalytic codes were not available for coercive control and permissiveness. Thus, the MeBRF provides a fairly efficient way to assess constructs traditionally assessed with microanalytic systems while capturing constructs not easily amenable to microanalytic methods.

Associations Between MeBRF Ratings and Parent Reports of Child Behavior Problems

Associations between observations of family interactions and parent reports of general child behavior offer another source of evidence of the validity of an observational assessment system. In particular, child behavior and parenting practices observed during a difficult forced-compliance task should be linked to parent reports of children's general level of oppositional and defiant behavior to lend external validity to an observational system. For families assigned to the forced-compliance task, maternal reports of child externalizing behavior problems were significantly associated at $p < .05$ in the expected direction with MeBRF child ratings of noncompliance, antisocial behavior, and prosocial behavior, and with MeBRF parent ratings of ambiguous control and permissiveness for mothers and fathers (Mahoney, Coffield, Lewis, & Lashley, 1998). With the exception of child noncompliance, similar links did not emerge between behavior exhibited by family members in the play condition and maternal reports of child externalizing behaviors. For both conditions, paternal reports of child externalizing behavior problems were not associated with observed child or parenting behavior. Overall, these results offer some evidence for the external validity of the MeBRF codes, and suggest the system would be sensitive to pre- and posttreatment differences in child and parent behavior.

EXCERPTS FROM THE MeBRF CODING MANUAL

Excerpts from the MeBRF on parent ambiguous control and child antisocial behavior are included to give the reader a better sense of the nature of the manual and coding system.

Parent Rating: Ambiguous Control

Definition. This rating reflects a dimension of the quality of parents' control efforts—namely, the degree to which parents have difficulty sending clear, unambiguous messages to the child that he or she is expected to comply to expectations (regardless of whether or not the child might want to perform a task). Indirect/confusing messages often take the form of commands to start or stop behavior that are phrased as indirect requests or questions. Tone of voice may range from polite and solicitous to coaxing and pleading. As a group, these commands send the message to the child that he or she has some degree of choice in deciding whether or not to comply. At low to moderate levels, such requests and questions may reflect a parent who wants a child to do something, but he or she is underplaying his or her authority. At moderate to high levels, the parent communicates a lack of confidence, tentativeness or lack of assertiveness about whether to push for compliance (i.e., wimpiness), and is handing over an inappropriate degree of control and power to the child. Overall, these indirect and confusing commands can come across as sending "mixed messages" to the child (i.e., I want you to do something you don't want to do, but I want you to choose to do it and figure out the details, so I don't have to make a clear demand as an authority figure and risk triggering a conflict or having to back up my authority).

Likert scale. Lower scores reflect low levels of intensity and/or frequency. Higher scores reflect high intensity or/and frequency of indirect commands.

1	2	3	4	5
None	Low	Mod	Mod-High	High

Examples for moderate to high scores. (a) Indirect, vague suggestions

"Do you think you could be quiet"; "Maybe you can do that yourself"; "Let's don't do that anymore, please"; "Do you think it is time for you to clean up?"; (b) Question/Request commands (may sound polite, may imply a choice on part of child, may sometimes facilitate child cooperation) "Why don't you make it higher?"; "Can you tell me what color this is?"; "Why don't we sit here?"; "Would you like to hand me the car?"; "Can you pick up the pieces for me?"; "Would you come here?"; "Can you put them all away in the boxes they go in?" (c) Coaxing/begging—is determined mostly by tone of voice and context of situation

Child Rating: Antisocial Behavior

Definition. This rating reflects the degree to which a child exhibits active verbal and nonverbal defiant, obnoxious behavior, uncooperativeness, resistance, hostility, complaints, whining, smart talk, and disrespect. This category includes behavior more severely inappropriate than playing or being inattentive (i.e., daydreaming) instead of attending to parent or being on-task. This category also includes off-task and noncompliant behavior that is independent of a specific command.

Likert scale. Lower scores reflect low levels of intensity and/or frequency. Higher scores reflect high intensity or/and frequency of coercive commands.

1	2	3	4	5
None	Low	Mod	Mod-High	High

Examples for moderate to high scores. Whining; Using annoying tone of voice; Making unusual or odd noises; Babytalk or other forms of inappropriate talk; Screaming or yelling; Bossy demands (as opposed to matter-of-fact questions about activity); Crying or Fake crying; Complaints; Back-talk; Name calling; Throwing things; Standing on furniture; Breaking rules; Rude behavior (intentional belching, farting, sticking out tongue); Interrupting parent when he or she is clearly attempting to give a clear command or request; Excessive motor activity (i.e., hyperactive, running around room); Off-task & nonspecific noncompliance—instances where child is not engaged in activity that parent has clearly or strongly requested the child perform, and presumably would still want child to continue. Raters will have to make a judgment call from the context of situation as to whether parent would want the child to be "on task".

Examples for low to moderate scores. If it is ambiguous about what the parent wants the child to do, or is unclear if the parent wants the child to persist in a given activity, then give lower scores when the child is "off task" for the context of the situation. Thus, lower scores are given to a noncompliant child who is engaged in behavior other than what is called for by the situation (e.g., play or clean up) simply because the parent has never imposed structure or delivered unambiguous commands about what the child was supposed to do.

ACKNOWLEDGMENTS

Prior to 1993, Annette Mahoney published under the name Annette M. Farris. This research was funded, in part, by grants to the first author from a Bowling Green State University (BGSU) Faculty Research Committee and a State of Ohio Academic Challenge Grant. The authors would like to thank Frank Floyd for his helpful review of the chapter, and BGSU students who assisted with this research including Sameera Ahmed, Margaret Barham, Mariah Cornwell, Stan Edwards, Ty Fowler, Angie Gentile, LeaAnn Lape-Brinkman, Julie Geers, Adela Guterriez, Julie Hach, Kelly Huffman, Liz Logee, Maria Pamblanco, Katie Riley, Lisa Query, Anita Rundell, Amy Seiter, Jodi Spencer Jamie Wieber, and Gina Yanni.

REFERENCES

Abidin, R. R. (1992). The determinants of parenting behavior. *Journal of Clinical Child Psychology, 21,* 407–412.

Abidin, R. R., & Brunner, J. F. (1992). Development of a Parenting Alliance Inventory. *Journal of Clinical Child Psychology, 24,* 31–40.

Bandura, A., & Walters, R. H. (1963). *Social learning and personality development.* New York: Holt, Rinehart & Winston.

Baumrind, D. (1971). Current patterns of parental authority. *Developmental Psychology Monograph, 4*(1, Pt. 2).

Baumrind, D. (1989). Rearing competent children. In W. Damon (Ed.), *Child development today and tomorrow* (pp. 349–378). San Francisco: Jossey-Bass.

Chamberlain, P., & Patterson, G. R. (1995). Discipline and child compliance in parenting. In M. H. Bornstein (Ed.), *Handbook of parenting: Vol. 4 Applied and practical parenting* (pp. 205–226). Hillsdale, NJ: Lawrence Erlbaum Associates.

Colapinto, J. (1991). Structural family therapy. In A. S. Gurman & D. P. Kniskern (Eds.), *Handbook of family therapy* (Vol. 2, pp. 417–443). New York.: Brunner/Mazel.

Cummings, E. M., & Davies, P. T. (1994). *Children and marital conflict: The impact of family dispute and resolution.* New York: Guilford.

Darling, N., & Steinberg, L. (1993). Parenting style as context: An integrative model. *Psychological Bulletin, 113,* 487–496.

Dix, T. (1991). The affective organization of parenting. *Psychological Bulletin, 110,* 3–25.

Gable, S., Belsky, J., & Crnic, K. (1992). Marriage, parenting, and child development: Progress and prospects. *Journal of Family Psychology, 5,* 276–294.

Gordis, E. B., Margolin, G., & John, R. S. (1997). Marital aggression, observed parental hostility, and child behavior during triadic family interaction. *Journal of Family Psychology, 11,* 76–89.

Hinde, R. A., & Hinde, J. S. (1988). *Relationships within families: Mutual influences.* Oxford, England: Clarendon:.

Jouriles, E. N., & Farris, A. M. (1992). Effects of marital conflict on subsequent parent–son interactions. *Behavior Therapy, 23,* 355–374.

Kerig, P. K. (1995). Triangles in the family circle: Effects of family structure on marriage, parenting, and child adjustment. *Journal of Family Psychology, 9,* 28–43.

Lemanek, K. L., Stone, W. L., & Fishel, P. L. (1993). Parent–child interactions in handicapped preschoolers: The relation between parent behaviors and compliance. *Journal of Clinical Child Psychology, 22,* 68–77.

Lindahl, K., Clements, M., & Markman, H. (1997). Predicting marital and parent functioning in dyads and triads: A longitudinal investigation of marital processes. *Journal of Family Psychology, 11,* 139–151.

Lobitz, G., & Johnson, S. M. (1975). Normal versus deviant children: A multimethod comparison. *Journal of Abnormal Child Psychology, 3,* 353–374.

Maccoby, E., & Martin, J. A. (1983). Socialization in the context of the family: Parent–child interaction. In E. M. Hetherington (Ed.)., *Handbook of child psychology: Vol. 4. Socialization, personality, and social development* (4th ed., pp. 1–102). New York: Wiley.

Madanes, C. (1991). Strategic family therapy. In A. S. Gurman & D. P. Kniskern (Eds.), *Handbook of family therapy* (Vol. 2, pp. 396–416). New York: Brunner/Mazel.

Mahoney, A. (1999). *The reliability and validity of the Meso-Analytic Behavioral Rating System for Family Interactions.* Unpublished manuscript.

Mahoney, A., Boggio, R., & Jouriles, E. N. (1996). Effects of verbal marital conflict on subsequent mother–son interactions in a child clinic sample. *Journal of Clinical Child Psychology, 25,* 262–271.

Mahoney, A., Coffield, A., & Lashley, S. L. (1998, November). *A meso-level behavioral rating system for triadic interactions with young children: Reliability, validity, and cost compared to a microanalytic approach.* Symposium conducted at the 32nd annual meeting of the Association for the Advancement of Behavior Therapy, Washington, DC.

Mahoney, A., Coffield, A., Lewis, T., & Lashley, S. L. (1998, November). *A "meso-level" behavioral rating system for observing triadic family interactions with young children.* Paper presented at the 32nd annual meeting of the Association for the Advancement of Behavior Therapy, Washington, DC.

Mahoney, A., Jouriles, E. N., & Scavone, J. (1997). Marital adjustment, marital discord over childrearing, and child behavior problems: Moderating effects of child age. *Journal of Clinical Child Psychology, 26,* 415–423.

Patterson, G. R. (1982). *Coercive family process.* Eugene, OR: Castalia.

Snyder, J., Rains, J., & Popejoy, J. (1988). Assessing aggressive and violent parent–child interaction. In P. Karoly (Ed.), *Handbook of child health assessment: Biopsychosocial perspectives* (pp. 579–607). New York: Wiley.

Vuchinich, S., Emery, R. E., & Cassidy, J. (1988). Family members as third parties in dyadic family conflict: Strategies, alliances, and outcomes. *Child Development, 59,* 1293–1302.

14

Measuring Triadic Coordination in Mother–Father–Child Interactions

Michael A. Westerman
New York University

This chapter describes a set of scales for measuring "triadic coordination" processes. The instrument provides a method for examining how each parent coordinates his or her behavior with the other parent's bids toward their child as mother, father, and child engage in triadic interactions. It offers an approach to operationalizing whether a child is "caught in the middle" of marital discord, a family process that is of considerable interest to researchers and clinicians. More generally, it provides a way to study interesting new questions about the organization of interaction in family triads.

To date, this instrument has been employed to study interactions in mother–father–child triads including children 5 to 12 years of age as they engaged in a structured building-block task (Westerman & Massoff, 1995, 2000). Its applicability probably extends to a wide range of interaction contexts and to mother–father–child triads including children ranging in age from the toddler years through adolescence.

THEORETICAL FOUNDATIONS

Findings from a large number of studies have established that marital discord is associated with difficulties in children's functioning. Most of these investigations have examined relations between marital discord and behavior problems in children (see reviews by Emery, 1982; Reid & Crisafulli, 1990). Other studies have found associations with a range of other aspects of children's functioning as well, including, for example, attachment in toddlers (Goldberg & Easterbrooks, 1984), adolescent identity exploration (Grotevant & Cooper, 1985), and academic achievement (Westerman & LaLuz, 1995).

One hypothesis regarding the mechanisms underlying these associations derives at least in a general way from family systems theory ideas about such processes as "triangulation" (Bowen, 1981; S. Minuchin, Rosman, & Baker, 1978) and "divided loyalties" (Boszormenyi-Nagy & Ulrich, 1981). These clinical formulations have led several investigators to suggest that the crucial mechanism may be whether children are caught in the middle of interparental discord (Emery, 1988; Emery, Joyce, & Fincham, 1987; Westerman, 1987).

The rationale for the Triadic Coordination Scales was based on the belief that in order to investigate this hypothesis, it is necessary to create new methods of investigation that make possible a shift to a triadic level of analysis (see Emery et al., 1987; P. Minuchin, 1985). It is not sufficient to study interactions involving three family members using methods for examining the behavior of individuals or dyads. As I have discussed elsewhere (Westerman, 1987; Westerman & Massoff, 1995, 2000), attempts to operationalize the "caught in the middle" idea in terms of such constructs as interparental consistency in childrearing (e.g., Block, Block, & Morrison, 1981), disagreements over childrearing (e.g., Jouriles et al., 1991), problematic coalition patterns (e.g., Gilbert, Christensen, & Margolin, 1984), or how husband and wife act toward one another in the presence of the child (e.g., Cummings, Zahn-Waxler, & Radke-Yarrow, 1981) have been limited because they employ a dyadic level of analysis. For example, consider families in which one parent's childrearing style is permissive and the other's is authoritarian. Although the score on interparental consistency (Block et al., 1981) would be low, in some families with this profile the parents may have developed an integrated, coordinated way of interacting with their children on a moment-to-moment basis. Conversely, two parents who share a common approach to childrearing (high score on interparental consistency) may oppose each other's bids toward their child quite routinely—for example, if the specific occasions on which mother takes a restrictive stand always differ from the specific times when father is restrictive, even though the two have similar scores on restrictiveness in their dyadic relationships with the child.

The Triadic Coordination Scales represent an attempt to provide a more adequate way to operationalize the "caught in the middle" phenomenon. Triadic coordination refers to *how each parent coordinates his or her contributions with the spouse's bids toward their child as mother, father, and child interact together* (Westerman, 1987; Westerman & Massoff, 1995, 2000). These are specifically triadic processes. This approach provides a way to operationalize whether a child is "caught in the middle" because we can examine whether one parent fails to agree with and/or opposes the other parent's bids toward their child on a moment-to-moment basis as the three interact. It should be noted that the triadic coordination approach differs from several recent efforts to investigate what has been called "coparenting" (e.g., McHale & Rasmussen, 1998), because most of those approaches mix together a focus on triadic coordination processes with processes concerning parents' behavior toward one another in the presence of the child (see Westerman & Massoff, 2000).

The rationale for the Triadic Coordination Scales also included another goal in addition to creating a way to investigate the role played by whether a child is caught in the middle of interparental discord. Once we begin to think about how the contributions of one parent relate to his or her spouse's bids toward their child, it becomes possible to consider new questions about the organization of triadic mother–father–child interaction in general. For example, the scales provide a way to examine whether a parent typically gets involved at all in exchanges between the other parent and their child. Also, there are issues about specific ways in which one parent relates his or her bids to the other parent's behavior toward the child (e.g., when the parent supports the other parent, does this take the form of simple agreements or elaborations). The scales also make it possible to assess separately mothers' and fathers' contributions to triadic coordination. Therefore, they provide a way to examine such questions as whether these contributions differ by gender in general or whether they differ in a particular family.

DEVELOPMENT OF THE TRIADIC COORDINATION SCALES

Three major decisions were made in the course of developing the instrument. The first decision was to base the system on ratings by judges on Likert-type scales rather than codings of discrete behaviors. In measurement systems based on coding discrete behaviors, questions frequently come up about how to take into account the larger context in which particular behaviors occur. Although these issues can be challenging, usually they can be resolved when the focus is on individual behaviors, for example, "self-disclosures." By contrast, when one is interested in relational processes such as whether the behavior of one parent "opposes" the other parent's efforts or "elaborates" on what the other parent is doing, issues concerning how the participants' behavior should be viewed in the overall context become central. For example, a particular comment by one parent may appear to contribute to the other parent's efforts, if one considers how that comment relates to what the other parent just said in the immediately preceding turn (e.g., the comment "why don't you find the blocks to build the chimney now" following "what do you think we should build next?"), but the comment may actually be in clear-cut opposition to the other parent's efforts if one takes into consideration how that parent set the stage for the larger exchange of which the turns in question are a part (e.g., if at the outset the other parent made a big point of saying that the child should add the chimney last). The decision was made to employ ratings instead of discrete behavior codes, because raters can make judgments about such complex processes. Hence, the instrument is based on ratings, but these ratings are not about global dimensions (e.g., warmth). Rather, they are assessments of the extent to which a given person's contributions to the interaction conformed to certain clearly defined patterns.

Turning to the second key decision: In general, the construct directs attention to how the contributions of one parent (who I refer to as the "second" parent) relate to the other parent's (the "first" parent's) behavior toward their child. The first parent's behavior is what we might call the "starting point" for an assessment of coordination. How should we think about starting point behaviors? In an early stage in the development of the scales, we attempted to examine separately whether the second parent's contributions were coordinated with respect to positive and negative bids by the first parent to the child. We found that this made the resulting system too complex. As a result, the decision was made to take as the starting point contributions by the first parent directed to the child in general. Hence, assessments of whether the second parent opposed or supported the first parent's contributions do not distinguish between different types of bids by the first parent. In the future, it probably would be possible to revisit this feature of the scales and develop a procedure that is more differentiated in this regard.

The third decision concerned the assessment context. As noted at the outset of this chapter, to date the scales have been employed to study interactions during a structured building-block task (see Westerman & Schonholtz, 1993 for a description of the task). This context ensures comparability between assessments of different families. It also offers a delimited universe of possible behaviors and goals, which makes it easier to assess how any given behavior by one person during the interaction relates to the contributions by the other participants. No doubt, assessments of triadic coordination could be made in other contexts, although this might require modifying the scales in some ways.

DESCRIPTION OF THE TRIADIC COORDINATION SCALES

The instrument is comprised of a total of 14 items. Seven scales focus on how fathers coordinate their contributions to the interaction with their wives' behavior toward the child (mother is the first parent, father is second parent). The other seven items are identical to these scales except they substitute "mother" for "father" and vice versa. They focus on how mothers coordinate their behavior with their husbands' bids toward the child (father is first parent, mother is second parent). The items are rated on 20-point unipolar Likert-type scales anchored at points 1 ("almost never"), 4 ("rarely"), 7 ("occasionally"), 10 ("slightly less than half the time"), 11 ("slightly more than half the time"), 14 ("often"), 17 ("very frequently"), and 20 ("almost always").

What follows is a basic description of the scales. The actual instrument includes additional specification of the processes indexed by each scale. Also, there is a set of "Guidelines" that indicate how judges should apply the scales in certain complicated situations. The seven items in which mother is the first parent and father is second parent are presented in entirety at the end of this chapter.

The first item is a measure of the extent to which the first parent *participated* in the exchange by directing contributions toward the child. The second item assesses the extent to which the second parent *attempted to involve* the first parent when he or she was not participating. The third item is a rating of the extent to which the second parent was *uninvolved* when the first parent was participating. The fourth item assesses the extent to which the second parent *agreed with or supported* the first parent when he or she was participating. The fifth item measures the extent to which contributions by the second parent were *elaborated* when he or she agreed with or supported the first parent. The sixth scale assesses the extent to which the second parent *disagreed with or opposed* the first parent when he or she was participating. The final item, Scale 7, is a rating of the extent to which contributions made by the second parent were *constructive* when he or she disagreed with or opposed the first parent.

The rationale for Scale 1, the starting point, was presented in the previous section. Items 4 (agreement/support) and 6 (disagreement/opposition) are included because they are related conceptually to the "caught in the middle" hypothesis. It is necessary to include both of these scales because failing to provide support does not have the same psychological meaning as disagreeing/opposing. Further, many family interaction studies have found empirically that measures of positive and negative behaviors are not simply the inverse of one another and that they typically have different, but not just opposite, relations to third variables. Scale 3 (uninvolved) is included because one thing the second parent might do is remain uninvolved in an interaction between the first parent and the child. This aspect of triadic interaction is interesting to study in its own right as part of an effort to learn about the organization of mother–father–child exchanges in general. Note that pilot work showed that in the context of the building-block task, Scales 3, 4, and 6 exhaustively covered possible responses by the second parent to the first parent's participation. In other contexts, it might be necessary to include a scale for contributions by the second parent that are neither agreements or disagreements. Like Scale 3, Scale 2 (attempts to involve) is included because whether the second parent attempts to involve a spouse who is not participating is an interesting triadic phenomenon to assess in its own right. Items 5 (extent to which agreement/support is elaborated) and 7 (extent to which disagreement/opposition is constructive) offer more differentiated views of processes of support and opposition.

Note that with the exception of the first item, all of the scales measure the extent to which a participant in the interaction behaves in a certain manner *when* something else occurs. The main reason for this follows directly from the focus on triadic coordination processes, that is, what does the second parent do when the first parent directs bids to the child. It should be pointed out that although items build upon one another, scores on the respective items are independent. For example, if the first parent seldom participates, but the second parent opposes these efforts whenever the first parent does participate, the first parent would receive a low score on Item 1 and the second parent would receive a high rating on Scale 6. Along the same lines, if the second parent very frequently supports his or her spouse but only a small proportion of these agreements are elaborated, the second parent would receive a high score on Scale 4 and a low score on Scale 5.

CODER TRAINING

The Triadic Coordination Scales can be used by raters who are undergraduate students. Several criteria should be kept in mind when selecting raters. Raters should be careful observers so that they can track interaction patterns over time. Also, raters should have good conceptual skills so that they can understand subtleties in the definitions of the scale items and the independence of ratings of items that build upon each other (i.e., an item concerns what a family member does "when" something assessed by another item occurs).

The first step in rater training involves familiarizing the raters with the scales, guidelines, and the use of worksheets (see next section). Following this introduction, the person doing the training shows the raters how to use the scales by going through several tapes with them. For the core of the training, raters are assigned several tapes to assess independently, their ratings are reviewed, and problems and questions are discussed at length. Raters work on about six tapes in this final part of the training process. The complete training process takes a total of about 18 hours devoted to meetings and practice ratings over a period of about 3 weeks.

A manual including the scales, guidelines, worksheets, and instructions for using the worksheets is available (Westerman, 1991). Researchers interested in employing the instrument in their own projects are also welcome to contact this author by telephone to discuss any questions that may come up regarding use of the scales. The manual supplemented by phone consultations should provide sufficient guidance for successful use of the instrument.

THE CODING PROCESS

The core of the rating process involves making assessments using one of the two versions of the seven basic scales, which treat either mother or father as the first parent and the other parent as second parent. The seven items are assessed in three phases with each phase requiring another viewing of the complete interaction. In the first viewing, the rater focuses on the first parent to assess the extent to which he or she participated (Item 1). Raters typically view the tape in real time, although they are permitted to stop the tape if they choose to do so. At the end of the first viewing, the rater makes a rating on Scale 1 and depicts the extent of the first parent's participation graphically on a worksheet as a proportion of a rectangular box (e.g., if the rating was 15 on the 20-point scale, the rater would draw a line marking off three fourths of the box).

In the first phase, the rater also assesses the extent to which the second parent tried to involve the first parent when he or she was not participating (Item 2). Use of the worksheet can be quite helpful when it comes to making actual ratings on this item and all subsequent items. For example, the first parent may have participated a great deal so that there was little time when he or she was not participating. Nevertheless, the second parent may have attempted to involve the first parent almost all those times when the first parent was not participating. This situation would be represented by marking off a large part of the original rectangle to reflect the extent to which the first parent was participating (Item 1). This leaves the small remaining segment of the box as a representation of the extent to which the first parent was not participating. Then, the rater would mark off a large portion of this small box to reflect the fact that the second parent almost always attempted to involve the first parent on those few occasions when he or she was not participating (Item 2). This representation would make it clear that the rater should assign a high score on Scale 2.

The rater then views the interaction a second time. In this phase, the rater focuses on what the second parent did when the first parent directed contributions to the child. The rater assesses the extent to which the second parent remained uninvolved (Item 3), agreed with/supported the first parent (Item 4), and disagreed with/opposed the first parent (Item 6). The rater makes notations on the worksheet to graphically depict assessments of Items 3, 4, and 6 within the part of the original box marked off in the first phase as representing the extent of participation. Note that because these three items are considered to exhaustively describe possible responses by the second parent, ratings assigned to these items are required to sum to 20.

The rater views the tape a third time to assess the extent to which the second parent elaborated on the first parent's contributions when the second parent agreed with/supported the first parent (Item 5) and the extent to which the second parent was constructive when he or she disagreed with/opposed the first parent (Item 7). Use of the worksheets is often quite helpful here to keep track of the relevant "universe" of events under consideration (e.g., those times when the second parent agreed with/supported the first parent is the universe for assessing Item 5).

The part of the rating process just described (completing ratings on the seven items with one parent treated as first parent and the other as second parent) can be completed in about three times the actual duration of the interaction. Note that this is a good deal less time than would be required by coding systems that involve preparing transcripts or stopping and starting the videotape in order to code discrete behaviors.

Because the rating process calls for making judgments about complex processes, multiple raters should be used so that one can enhance reliability by pooling scores across judges. In our research, assessments were made by six raters (Westerman & Massoff, 1995, 2000). For future studies, it probably would be sufficient to have a team of four raters.

In the complete rating procedure, each rater is assigned a different randomized order of the full set of tapes. He or she assesses the whole corpus following this order. Half of the raters do this using the version of the seven basic scales in which mother is the first parent and father is the second parent, whereas the other raters use the other version of the scales. After completing this first set of ratings, each rater makes assessments on the complete corpus of videotapes again using the other version of the scales. Hence, some of the raters begin by focusing on mothers as first parent and fathers as second parent and then switch, whereas other raters proceed in the opposite order. Note that ratings on the two versions of the scales are conceptually independent. For example, if a given mother almost always supports her husband when he directs bids toward their child, her husband may or may not support his wife's bids toward the child.

RELIABILITY

Interrater reliability was examined in the research conducted by Westerman and Massoff (1995, 2000). Reliabilities were estimated using Pearson correlations averaged across all pairs of raters and stepped up using the Spearman–Brown prophecy formula, because all families were assessed by all raters and the data points employed in the substantive analyses were average scores pooled across judges.

With the exception of the two "attempts to involve" variables ("mother tried to involve father when he was not participating" and "father tried to involve mother when she was not participating"), the reliabilities were acceptable notwithstanding the complexity of the interaction processes measured. Raters agreed that the "attempts to involve" pattern occurred rarely across all families both when mothers and fathers were viewed as the second parent who might try to involve the other parent when he or she was not participating. The poor reliabilities for these variables were a consequence of the lack of variability across subjects. The reliabilities for the other variables were as follows: .96 for mother participates, .97 for father participates, .88 for mother remains uninvolved when father is participating, .90 for father remains uninvolved when mother is participating, .80 for mother agrees with/supports father, .77 for father agrees with/supports mother, .63 for mother elaborates when she agrees with/supports father, .68 for father elaborates when he agrees with/supports mother, .84 for mother disagrees with/opposes father, .82 for father disagrees with/opposes mother, .81 for mother is constructive when she disagrees with/opposes father, .55 for father is constructive when he disagrees with/opposes mother.

In future research, it would be useful to examine test–retest reliabilities. It would be interesting to determine the stability of these triadic coordination measures over time.

VALIDITY

Note that questions about the validity of the Triadic Coordination Scales should not be considered in the same way one would approach this issue regarding a measure that purports to index a unitary construct. The Triadic Coordination Scales assess multiple aspects of triadic interactions and they separately assess the roles played by mothers and fathers. Moreover, although the scale items related to agreement/support and disagreement/opposition were viewed a priori as having potential relevance to the "caught in the middle" phenomenon, we have treated it as an empirical question whether and how specific items from the instrument serve to index this general notion.

Westerman and Massoff (1995, 2000) investigated a number of issues related to the validity of the scales. One of these issues, which bears on convergent validity, concerned relations between the triadic coordination measures and a behavioral outcome measure of family performance on a building-block task, which was employed as an index of joint parental support (see next section for more information about this measure). Convergent validity was also studied by examining relations between the triadic coordination measures and reports of marital adjustment by mothers and fathers. In addition, predictive validity was investigated by examining associations with child behavior problems as reported by teachers and parents. Here, I present a summary of findings regarding the behavioral outcome measure of parental support, which illustrate some of the conclusions related to the issue of validity.

We found significant associations between both measures of maternal disagreement/opposition (extent to which mother disagreed with/opposed father, extent to which mother disagreed with/opposed father in a constructive manner) and the joint parental support index. These relations were in the directions one would expect—greater disagreement/opposition was associated with poorer family performance, more constructive disagreement/opposition was related to better family performance. Furthermore, the associations were large in magnitude.

Two other features of the findings merit comment here. First, there were no significant associations between the measures of agreement/support and the joint support index. This aspect of the findings suggests that the processes measured by the disagreement variables play the key role. The other noteworthy feature of the findings was that the results for fathers were quite different from the findings for mothers. In fact, the measures of disagreement/opposition by fathers were significantly related to the behavioral index of family functioning in the opposite directions from what was found for the parallel measures for mothers. I return to this feature of the results later.

These results about relations with the joint parental support index coupled with findings about associations with the other criterion measures (marital adjustment, child behavior problems) suggested that the measures from the Triadic Coordination Scales concerning whether and how mothers disagree with/oppose their husbands play an important role. These measures may index important family processes related to the "caught in the middle" phenomenon.

In future research, it would be useful to investigate the cross-situational consistency of the Triadic Coordination Scales. It is likely that there will be considerable overlap between measures of a given variable (e.g., the extent to which mother disagrees with/opposes father in a constructive manner) assessed in the building-block task and in other structured contexts, but there probably will be some systematic differences between assessments made in different contexts as well. Assessments based on multiple contexts probably would have even stronger relations with criterion variables.

STUDIES USING THE TRIADIC COORDINATION SCALES

The research conducted on the scales to date (Westerman & Massoff, 1995, 2000) was a follow-up investigation to a study conducted by Westerman and Schonholtz (1993). That earlier study included the outcome measure of family performance, which was considered to be an *indirect* measure of how effectively mothers and fathers worked together as they interacted with their child. In particular, this index of joint parental support was defined as the degree to which family performance on a building-block task exceeded or fell short of what would be predicted based on the child's individual performance on a similar block task. The study by Westerman and Massoff used the Triadic Coordination Scales to build upon this by examining actual interaction patterns from the videotapes made in the previous study of the family triads as they engaged in the family block task.

It should be noted that the sample was small. It included 16 family triads. Volunteer families were recruited from two schools and a few after-school programs. The sample was heterogeneous with respect to ethnicity. The children ranged from 5 to 12 years of age and included 12 boys and 4 girls.

As noted earlier, Westerman and Massoff examined associations between triadic coordination processes and the parental support index, marital satisfaction, and child behavior problems. Several issues about the triadic coordination processes themselves were investigated as well. For example, findings indicated that, across parents, agreement/support scores were significantly higher than scores for both disagreement/oppose and uninvolved, and that parents remained uninvolved significantly more than they disagreed with/opposed their spouse. We also examined interrelations among the triadic coordination scales both within and between spouses and found a number of interesting results. In particular, measures of activity, disagreement/opposition, and constructive disagreement/opposition by one parent were related inversely to those measures for his or her spouse. Note that these results are consistent with the findings briefly discussed in the previous section about differences in how maternal versus paternal disagreement/opposition scores related to the measure of parental support.

This summary of some of the findings shows how the triadic coordination scales provide a useful way to examine (a) how mothers and fathers coordinate their behavior with their spouses' bids to the child during triadic exchange, (b) relations between maternal and paternal contributions to coordination, and (c) how these behaviors relate to criterion variables of interest.

EXCERPTS FROM THE CODING MANUAL

The material that follows is part of the manual for the Triadic Coordination Scales. It presents the seven scales that treat mother as the first parent and father as the second parent. The instrument also includes another seven scales in which father is treated as the first parent and mother is the second parent. In addition, as explained earlier, the manual also includes a set of guidelines, worksheets, and instructions for using the worksheets. The items that follow are rated on 20-point Likert-type scales (see rationale in the section Development of the Triadic Coordination Scales). These scales are anchored at several points as described previously in the section Description of the Scales. Each item is followed by hypothetical, illustrative examples of exchanges that would receive a score of 17, which corresponds to "very frequently," and a 4, which corresponds to "rarely." Note that these descriptions are simplified illustrations. In practice, various combinations of behaviors can lead to the same score, because ratings are based on rather large samples of behavior. The examples describe different exchanges. They are *not* all meant to describe one single family exchange across the set of items.

1. *Mother's Participation.*

To what extent did mother participate in guiding the child on the task? This should include indirect attempts at guiding the child through interaction with the father. If mother is simply observing what is taking place without engaging in any interaction with family members or offering any suggestions, she is not participating in guiding the child. Solitary efforts on the task are not counted as participating in guiding the child unless they are meant as a bid to someone else, that is, not actually solitary. Note that mother can be participating in guiding the child even if she is only communicating with gestures. For this scale, your rating should also include mother's attempts to participate as participating, even if she did not get through to the child (e.g., because father interrupted or because the child couldn't hear her).

> *Example "4"-* Most of the time, mother sat back and observed as father interacted with child. For part of this time, she casually manipulated some of the puzzle pieces, but this was simply a way of spending time; it was not meant as a suggestion or contribution to what father and child were doing. On a few occasions, mother commented on child's efforts or handed the child a block to use on the next step.

> *Example "17"-* Mother was actively involved guiding the child in the task. She gave many suggestions and directions, sometimes verbally and sometimes with gestures, and only refrained from doing so for a brief span of time. During a longer period of time, both mother and father attempted to guide the child, although the child actually worked on the project independently without taking their suggestions into account.

2. *Father's attempts to involve mother.*

When mother was not participating in guiding the child, to what extent did father try to involve her?

> *Example "4"-* Mother participated a considerable amount of the time, but there were many points when she was not engaged in the exchange. On one of those occasions, father asked for her opinion about what to do next and, on another, he asked if she agreed with an idea of his. Otherwise, father directed his efforts to the child and did nothing about the fact that his wife was not participating.

Example "17"- Although mother participated most of the time, father tried to involve her by asking for her suggestions on almost all occasions when she was not participating.

3. *Father remains uninvolved.*

When mother was participating in guiding the child, to what extent was father uninvolved in the mother–child exchanges? Father is uninvolved in the mother–child exchanges if he does nothing whatsoever or if he simply watches while mother and child interact. Also, father is uninvolved in the mother–child exchanges if he is pursuing task-related activity in parallel to the mother that does not compete with her bids or clearly distract the child from responding to mother. Note that if father ignores mother's direct attempts to involve him, this does not count as being uninvolved. This will contribute to scale 6, disagree/oppose. Also, if father pursues task-related activity in parallel to the mother that does directly compete with her bids or clearly distract the child from responding to mother, then this does not count as being uninvolved. This too contributes to scale 6, disagree/oppose. Note that it is not necessarily "good" or "bad" if father was uninvolved in mother–child exchanges.

Example "4"- Almost all the time when mother attempted to direct the child, father offered his opinion on her suggestions or told the child how to complete the step in question.

Example "17" - Father spent most of the time observing mother and child interact. For a few minutes, he put together a few of the blocks and then took them apart. This was not intended as a contribution to the task, but just a way of passing the time. A few times, father made comments about mother's suggestions.

Note that items 3, 4, and 6 must add up to a total of 20.

4. *Father agrees with/supports mother.*

When mother was participating in guiding the child, to what extent did father agree with or support mother's bids? Note: Include all responses that indicate explicit agreement with what mother said (e.g., says yes, concurs) as well as any responses directed toward child or mother that promote, encourage, build on, or help to clarify mother's bid. Include any instances where father helps mother nonverbally by doing what she asks or doing something to help her in her efforts (e.g., arranging the blocks into separate piles or looking for pieces of a certain size in response to mother's suggestion to the father or child).

Example "4"- Father seldom supported mother's efforts to guide the child because on most occasions when mother directed the child, father remained uninvolved and on a few occasions he interrupted her by suggesting his own ideas. On a few occasions, he voiced approval of mother's suggestions by saying something like, "Good idea."

Example "17"- Almost all the time when mother attempted to guide the child, father assisted her by clarifying her suggestions for the child or by helping the child follow the suggestions. There were a small number of times when father sat back and simply watched as mother made suggestions.

5. *Father's agreements are elaborated.*

When father agreed with or supported mother's bids, to what extent were his responses elaborated? Note: an elaborated response is one which adds to or builds upon mother's bid rather than simply affirming it.

> *Example "4"*- On almost all occasions when mother guided the child, father agreed with her, but with very few exceptions, these agreements were simple affirmations like "okay" or "good."

> *Example "17"*- Father did not agree with mother's suggestions very often, but almost whenever he did, he showed the child the correct block to use to take the step his wife had suggested.

6. *Father disagrees with/opposes mother.*

When mother was participating in guiding the child, to what extent did father disagree with or oppose mother's bids? Note: include all responses directed to child or mother that indicate discouragement or disapproval of mother's bid as well as explicit disagreement or suggestion of a different approach. Also include those times where father interrupted mother, prevented mother from participating, ignored mother when she directly tried to involve him, or pursued his own strategy in a way that directly competed with the mother's strategy or clearly distracted the child from responding to the mother.

> *Example "4"* - On almost all occasions when mother attempted to guide the child, father simply observed. On a few occasions, he interrupted her.

> *Example "17"*- On only a few occasions when mother attempted to guide the child, father agreed with her. On the other occasions, he suggested different ways of proceeding or he interrupted his wife.

7. *Father's disagreements are constructive.*

When father disagreed with or opposed mother's bids to what extent did he do this in a constructive vs. nonconstructive manner? In order for his disagreement to be constructive, he must respond directly to what mother said and his bid must be respectful, not negative, in tone. If father responds directly to mother's bid but in a disrespectful way, his disagreement is not constructive. Also, his disagreement is not constructive if he interrupted mother, prevented mother from participating, ignored mother when she directly tried to involve him, or pursued his own strategy in a way that directly competed with mother's strategy or clearly distracted the child from responding to the mother.

> *Example "4"* - Almost every time father disagreed with mother, he did so by commenting in a disrespectful tone or by interrupting her.

> *Example "17"* - Almost without exception, when father disagreed with mother, he did so by explaining in a polite tone why he thought it would be best for child to proceed in some other way than what mother had suggested.

REFERENCES

Block, J. H., Block, J., & Morrison, A. (1981). Parental agreement–disagreement on child rearing orientations and gender related personality correlates in children. *Child Development, 52,* 965–974.

Boszormenyi-Nagy, I., & Ulrich, D. N. (1981). Contextual family therapy. In A. S. Gurman & D. P. Kniskern (Eds.), *Handbook of family therapy* (pp. 159–186). New York: Brunner/Mazel.

Bowen, M. (1981). The use of family theory in clinical practice. In R. J. Green & J. L. Framo (Eds.), *Family therapy: Major contributions* (pp. 265–311). New York: International Universities Press.

Cummings, E. M., Zahn-Waxler, C., & Radke-Yarrow, M. (1981). Young children's responses to expressions of anger and affection in the home. *Child Development, 52,* 1274–1282.

Emery, R. E. (1982). Interparental conflict and the children of divorce. *Psychological Bulletin, 92,* 310–330.

Emery, R. E. (1988). *Marriage, Divorce and child adjustment.* Newbury Park, CA: Sage.

Emery, R., E., Joyce, S., & Fincham, F. D. (1987). The assessment of child and marital problems. In K. D. O'Leary (Ed.), *Assessment of marital discord: An integration of research and clinical practice* (pp. 223–262). Hillsdale, NJ: Lawrence Erlbaum Associates.

Gilbert, R., Christensen, A., & Margolin, G. (1984). Patterns of alliances in nondistressed and multiproblem families. *Family Process, 23,* 75–87.

Goldberg, W. A., & Easterbrooks, M. A. (1984). The role of marital quality in toddler development. *Developmental Psychology, 20,* 504–514.

Grotevant, H. D., & Cooper, C. R. (1985). Patterns of interaction in family relationships and the development of identity exploration in adolescence. *Child Development, 56,* 415–428.

Jouriles, E. N., Murphy, C. M., Farris, A. M., Smith, D. A., Richter, J. E., & Waters, E. (1991). Marital adjustment, parental disagreements about child rearing, and behavior problems in boys: Increasing the specificity of the marital assessment. *Child Development, 62,* 1424–1433.

McHale, J. P., & Rasmussen, J. (1998). Coparental and family group-level dynamics during infancy: Early family precursors of child and family functioning during preschool. *Development and Psychopathology, 10,* 39–58.

Minuchin, P. (1985). Families and individual development: Provocations from the field of family therapy. *Child Development, 56,* 289–302.

Minuchin, S., Rosman, B. L., & Baker, L. (1978). *Psychosomatic families: Anorexia in context.* Cambridge: Harvard University Press.

Reid, W. J., & Crisafulli, A. (1990). Marital discord and child behavior problems: A meta-analysis. *Journal of Abnormal Child Psychology, 18,* 105–117.

Westerman, M. A. (1987). "Triangulation," marital discord and child behavior problems. *Journal of Social and Personal Relationships, 4,* 87–106.

Westerman, M. A. (1991). *Manual for assessing triadic coordination.* Unpublished manuscript, New York University, New York.

Westerman, M. A., & LaLuz, E. J. (1995). Marital adjustment and children's academic achievement. *Merrill–Palmer Quarterly, 41,* 453–470.

Westerman, M. A., & Massoff, M. (1995, August). *Triadic coordination, marital adjustment, and child behavior problems*. Paper presented at the meeting of the American Psychological Association, New York.

Westerman, M. A., & Massoff, M. (2000). *Triadic coordination: An observational method for examining whether children are "caught in the middle" of interparental discord.* Manuscript submitted for publication.

Westerman, M. A., & Schonholtz, J. (1993). Marital adjustment, joint parental support in a triadic problem-solving task, and child behavior problems. *Journal of Clinical Child Psychology, 22,* 97–106.

15

Observing Families Through the Stories That They Tell: A Multidimensional Approach

Barbara H. Fiese
Syracuse University

Arnold J. Sameroff
University of Michigan

Harold D. Grotevant
University of Minnesota

Frederick S. Wamboldt
*National Jewish Medical Research Center and University of Colorado
Health Sciences Center*

Susan Dickstein
Bradley Hospital and Brown University

Deborah Lewis Fravel
Indiana University

This is a tale about how a group of family researchers came to study family stories. We were brought together under the auspices of the MacArthur Foundation to develop systematic methods to evaluate family processes associated with child outcome. Our focus was on how family meaning is transmitted across generations. We believed that families are faced with many challenges in raising children as well as continuing the socialization of the adults. As a group, they must make sense of personal experiences and define what it means to be a member of their family. Although there is an extensive literature documenting generational effects on children (e.g., Benoit & Parker, 1994; Downey & Coyne, 1990), many of the existing methodologies focused on structural aspects of the family without considering family process variables that may be a part of family genealogy. We felt that family process could be tapped directly by observing how individuals make sense of their family of origin experiences that in turn influences how they make sense of current family experiences. Several areas seemed ripe for investigation: the study of family traditions, the planned preservation of family of origin strengths, the deliberate avoidance of family of origin weaknesses, and the transmission of family values and belief systems through family stories. We took as our starting point the study of family stories and established the Family Narrative Consortium (FNC).

As a group, we were interested in developing a system for understanding narratives that would be multidimensional. As researchers, we were frustrated with existing coding schemes that could essentially be distilled into two poles reflecting the relative "goodness" or "badness" of families. We felt that diversity in family life extends into how families create coherent accounts of experiences, how families work together in telling their stories, and how relationships are depicted in personal accounts. Therefore, we aimed to develop a system that could be used to generate different profiles of family adaptation using data that were collected with a variety of techniques from studies with a variety of goals.

Finally, we wanted to take into account the family's perspective and how they struggled with the meaning-making process. We started our venture by examining four existing data sets that differed in content and focus (for details regarding the individual data sets see Fiese et al., 1999). The data sets had in common family interviews in which the family members were asked to make sense of family experiences, but the content of the interviews differed. Three of the four data sets focused on how couples made sense of family experience such as psychiatric illness (Dickstein, St. Andre, Sameroff, Seifer, & Schiller, 1999), adopting a child (Grotevant, Fravel, Gorall, & Piper, 1999), or becoming a couple (Wamboldt, 1999). The fourth data set included families with school-age children and parents telling stories directly to their children (Fiese & Marjinsky, 1999).

Scales developed by the Family Narrative Consortium may be used with individual or multiple family members where there is an interview or task that calls for the family to make sense of personal experiences. The consortium defined family stories as the verbal accounts of personal experiences that are important to the family, and typically involve the creation and maintenance of relationships, depict rules of interaction, and reflect beliefs about family and other social institutions.

THEORETICAL FOUNDATIONS

There has been a burgeoning interest in the study of narratives over the past 10 years. Some have gone so far as to propose that narratives are a new paradigm for psychology (Howard, 1991) and clinical practice (cf. White & Epston, 1990). In reality, however, the study of narratives has a long history in both. Indeed, Freud's case studies are accounts of individual narratives and the struggle to make sense of personal experience. A focus on narratives necessitates a focus on experience and meaning.

Much of the current interest in narrative psychology stems from using talk as a window into cognitive processes of the individual (Bruner, 1987). How the individual puts together the pieces of his or her life story may reflect important aspects of individual identity (McAdams, 1993). As individuals recount personal experiences, they are creating their autobiographies. But this is not necessarily a factual accounting of person, place, and time. Rather, it is a constructive process where past events are viewed in light of current context (Riessman, 1993). Whereas there has been considerable focus on narratives and the creation of an individual's autobiography, there has been less attention paid to how narratives may be constructed among family members and reflect family relationship functioning. Some aspects of the study of individual narratives may be directly applicable to the study of family narratives such as the struggle with meaning making and the organized structure of the narrative. There are additional dimensions, however, to the study of family narratives that include the exchange of information among family members and the regulation of close relationships.

Although the vitality of meaning making in the family has been recognized, reliable and ecologically valid methods for ascertaining meaning in the family have been scarce. An examination of family narratives highlights the process of meaning making and takes as its core the interpretation of experiences from the family's perspective. The Family Narrative Consortium was organized to devise a research methodology that could capture some of the richness of family narratives along reliable dimensions that could be related to family interaction patterns, marital satisfaction, and child adjustment.

The Deep Structure of Family Narratives

The consortium began its efforts by identifying a number of components we believed central to the study of family narratives. These are: narrative coherence, narrative interaction, and relationship beliefs. On the individual level, the relative coherence of each family member's narrative may be related to his or her individual identity and life history. As a group activity, constructing a narrative reflects how the family works together and is linked to each member's relationship history. As a set of beliefs, family narratives reflect how much trust can be placed in relationships within and outside the family.

Although narratives are clearly communications, they have rarely been studied along the multiple dimensions that characterize other communication forms such as language. Language is typically considered a multidimensional phenomenon, broken into syntax, semantics, and pragmatics. We are proposing that family narratives include three analogous dimensions: (a) *Narrative Coherence* reflects the ways in which individuals considered separately and together organize the narrative, or the syntax of the narrative; (b) *Narrative Interaction* reflects the ways in which two or more family members construct the story, or the pragmatics of the narrative; and (c) *Relationship Beliefs* reflects the implicit beliefs about the trustworthiness of relationships, or the semantics of the narratives. These three dimensions are proposed to reflect the "deep structure" of family narratives and may make unique contributions to the understanding of family process.

Narrative Dimensions.   The first component we identified was the Coherence of the narrative. Coherence refers to how well the individual is able to construct and organize a story. The ways in which an individual's story makes sense, how clauses and thoughts are organized, the willingness of the individual to consider differing perspectives, and the match between affect and content are all considered part of the coherence of an individual's story or narrative.

Whereas the coherence of the story may be linked to the individual's struggle with meaning making, narratives also include important markers of relationship functioning and the meaning of an interaction between two or more people. We labeled this second component Narrative Interaction. Narrative Interaction refers to how the couple or family works together in putting together their story, the *act* of storytelling.

The third component of family narratives we identified was Relationship Beliefs. These beliefs include themes about the trustworthiness of the social world and expectations for rewarding relationships. Narratives are not only told by someone about some event but also told to someone. Qualities of the narrative reflect beliefs about the "telling" relationship as well as the family. Family belief systems reflect the family's shared value system and provide meaning to family interactions (Reiss, 1981). As narratives deal with the "vicissitudes of human intention" (Bruner, 1990), family narratives serve to verify beliefs about family members' intentions and actions. Implicit in many family stories are beliefs about the trustworthiness of relationships. The ways in which family members describe each other often include whether there is an expectation for reward and satisfaction or whether there is an expectation to be disappointed or even harmed.

These stories also include family beliefs about the workings of the social world. Some families are very secure in their interactions with the social world and embrace the opportunity to "tell their story." Other families, however, are reticent to share either with each other or with the social world. Reiss (1981) proposed that families differ in their perceptions about the relative safety of relationships within the family and relationships with the outside world. The relative trustworthiness of relationships has been found to be related to engagement in psychotherapy and psychiatric status (Costell, Reiss, Berkman, & Jones, 1981). The distinction between inside and outside the family has also been noted in the narratives described by Bruner (1987). According to Bruner, the "psychic geography of the family" (p. 25) is evident in narrative accounts of one family's perception of the relative safety of the home in contrast to the unpredictable nature of the "real world." The stories constructed by the family must also mesh with their beliefs about the social world.

Ultimately, the narrative must include an understanding of what it means in the context of the community and culture in which it takes place (Polkinghorne, 1988).

DEVELOPMENT OF THE FAMILY NARRATIVE CONSORTIUM CODING SYSTEM

We chose to create several scales to capture different aspects of each dimension. The scales were developed over a 4-year period and underwent four major revisions. We felt that because the scales were somewhat subjective in nature and involved considerable judgment on the part of the rater, it was critical to provide as many behavioral markers (verbal and nonverbal) as possible on a 5-point scale. Each revision of the coding scheme was aimed at providing more precise behavioral markers to clearly identify the different levels of each scale. It is unlikely that the scales are completely linear. However, for most empirical cases, they can be summed, in most cases, within each dimension to provide summary scores of Coherence, Narrative Interaction, and Relationship Beliefs.

Initially, the principal investigators from each site met as a group on several different occasions. We began the process by sharing transcripts and tapes of interviews conducted at each site. We reviewed the interviews and made careful notes regarding content and process that cut across studies. Once we felt that we had a foundation to work from we called in two consultants to help refine the measures. We relied on the expertise of David Reiss in clarifying our thoughts about family relationship beliefs and how families interact with the social world and on Howard Markman in understanding how couples interact with each other along dimensions of confirmation or disconfirmation of each other's opinions.

Once we could agree on scale definitions and composition of the codebook, we conducted a 2½-day training workshop for raters from each of the four principal sites. During the workshop we reviewed each scale in detail, provided audio- and videotaped examples, and engaged in coding exercises. Subsequently, interrater reliability was established at each site between the coder and principal investigator of that site.

We decided to use verbatim transcripts along with the video- or audiotape for coding purposes. There are drawbacks in using transcripts because of the extensive amount of time involved in formulating adequate written records. Transcription rules must be made (Mishler, 1991), including but not limited to how to punctuate, whether affect is noted (e.g., laughter), what to do with unintelligible speech, and checking for accuracy by someone other than the transcriptionist. There are several advantages, however, in using a transcript while coding. Transcripts aid in the expediency of training, as they are hard copies of what was actually said rather than relying on coders' perception and/or memory of what was heard. This may be particularly important when coding long interviews. Transcripts are also important when coding narrative coherence. It is much easier to detect contradictions, stumbles in speech, and perspective taking when the actual words are in front of you. Current projects are experimenting with coding without transcripts and may better inform this time-consuming issue.

DESCRIPTION OF THE FAMILY NARRATIVE CONSORTIUM CODING SYSTEM

The three dimensions of the Family Narrative Consortium Coding system are scored from subsets of scales. The Narrative Coherence dimension is comprised of four scales, the Narrative Interaction dimension is also comprised of four scales, and the Relationship Beliefs dimension is made up of two scales. A description of each scale follows.

Narrative Coherence

Narrative Coherence refers to how well the individual is able to construct and organize a story. Four distinct qualities are incorporated in Narrative Coherence: (a) Internal Consistency, (b) Organization, (c) Flexibility, and (d) Congruence of Affect and Content.

Internal Consistency.   Internal consistency of the narrative reflects its completeness and how well the different parts of the individual's theory of relationships form a cohesive whole. Narratives range from a disconnected theory full of discrepancies with little rationale to a well-developed and integrated theory. Referents noted for internal consistency include unrecognized contradictions, recognized contradictions, explained contradictions, personalized examples, and synthesizing explanations.

Organization.   Organization refers to the respondent's management of the narrative, with particular attention to statements that convey information as to how points are made within the narrative. An organized narrative provides the listener with a sense of orientation to context and flows smoothly with completed thoughts. Referents for disorganization include scattered comments with no transition, incomplete thoughts, ambiguous referents for who, what, or where, overelaboration, repetitive language, stops and starts, and lack of orienting statements.

Flexibility.   Flexibility refers to the respondent's ability to explore new ideas and alternatives. The flexible respondent is able to view issues as others might see them. Positive referents for flexibility include elaboration of alternatives with possibility of action, whereas negative referents for flexibility include rigid statements of conviction.

Congruence of Affect and Content.   This scale assesses the fit between reported actions or thoughts and the emotion expressed in regard to them. Narratives scored high on this scale show a good match between descriptions of events or actions and corresponding emotions, both in the type of affect expressed and the level of intensity. Tone of voice, facial expressions, and emotional content are major indicators of congruence. Referents for lack of congruence include inappropriate laughter, inappropriate crying, nervous laughter, inappropriate bland or flattened affect, and inappropriate intensity of affect.

Narrative Interaction

The Narrative Interaction scales rate how the couple works together in constructing the narrative and are only used when there is a joint interview. We drew on existing marital coding schemes such as the Rapid Couple Interaction Scoring System (RCISS; Gottman, 1983) and Interactional Dimension Coding System (IDCS: Julien, Markman, Lindahl, Johnson, & Van Widenfelt, 1987) to aid in forming definitions and to be consistent with previous couple interaction schemes. There are four scales to the Narrative Interaction dimension: Couple Narrative Style, Coordination, Husband Confirmation/Disconfirmation, and Wife Confirmation/Disconfirmation. The Couple Narrative Style and Coordination scales score the couple as a unit. The Husband and Wife Confirmation/Disconfirmation scales are scored separately for each spouse.

Couple Narrative Style. This scale is designed to capture the style and character of the narrative conjointly produced by the couple or family. This code requires attention both to the *content* of the story as well as to the couple's storytelling *process*. Negative referents for couple narrative style include discrepancies, differences of opinion, parallel stories, and occasions of anger. Positive referents include additions to the partner's story and synthetic interaction.

Coordination. Coordination is the assessment of how the couple or family works together and the ability and willingness to develop shared solutions and perceptions. Negative referents include disconfirming opinions and exclusions. Positive referents include polite turntaking, confirmation of opinions, asking for others' opinions, asking for clarification, and "we" statements.

Confirmation/Disconfirmation. The scale is scored separately for husbands and wives. The scale assesses the degree of confirmation or disconfirmation from each partner in the dyad to the other. In a dyad, individuals differ in conveying a message that the partner and his or her ideas are important, or alternatively, that the partner and his or her ideas are inferior and unimportant. Negative referents include invalidating behaviors or statements, statements or behaviors that convey indifference, and behaviors or statements that are restrictive of the other's opinion. Positive referents include validating behaviors or statements and behaviors or statements that convey interest.

Relationship Beliefs

The Relationship Beliefs codes represent the way a family's construction of the social world is reflected in the narrative content and style of the interview. There are two scales in the Relationship Beliefs dimension: Relationship Expectations and Interviewer Intimacy.

Relationship Expectations.   The Relationship Expectations scale assesses whether the family views relationships as manageable, reliable, and safe. The husband and wife are scored separately for expectations about relationships in their current family and also for expectations associated with their family of origin. Family of origin relationship expectations are coded for how the husband or wife reports relating to his or her family of origin at the time of the interview. Negative referents include statements that relationships are dangerous and unfulfilling, interaction with the social world is avoided, and the family dichotomizes relationships into good or bad. Positive referents include statements that relationships are safe, satisfying, understandable, and opportunities are made to interact with the social world.

Interviewer Intimacy.   The Interviewer Intimacy scale assesses the degree to which the family is open and willing to share personal and affectively sensitive material with the interviewer. Families scoring higher on this scale will characteristically engage the interviewer in a way that leaves the interviewer feeling as if he or she were an old friend of the family. Referents to this scale include hostile comments, an unexplained referent (e.g., naming a person without clarifying relationship), sensitive material mentioned but not elaborated, sensitive material elaborated, and family invites interviewer to participate in conversation.

CODER TRAINING

It is important to carefully select individuals who will be responsible for coding. We have found that individuals who have some clinical or life experience that has sensitized them to the subtle nuances of language are good candidates. It is crucial that the coders understand that establishing reliability is a *process* and that disagreement does not need to lead to personal defensiveness. It is helpful to interview potential coders to determine their ability to handle complex coding decisions, detect subtle aspects of affect, and willingness to be open to multiple perspectives.

Training has been conducted in a variety of ways. Most recently, we have found it helpful to first discuss narrative approaches in general before training on individual scales. Representative readings (e.g., Bruner, 1987; Cohler, 1991; McAdams, 1993) may be discussed to familiarize coders with the theoretical framework of narrative analysis. Each dimension is presented separately. Coders are presented with videotaped examples of relatively high or relatively low scores on each scale. Once the coder has become familiar with each of the scales within a dimension, practice coding ensues for each dimension. Coders are typically trained in groups of two or more. During practice coding, coders discuss the basis for their scores and must reach a verbal consensus on each scale. Once the coders are comfortable with each dimension, training tapes are coded for reliability of each dimension. Verbal consensus is reached for any disagreements. Typically five cases are assigned in the early stages of establishing reliability. Additional cases are assigned until acceptable reliability is reached. Training to reliability has ranged from 30 to 40 hours.

It is important that the principal investigator is very familiar with the data set and has a good sense of the expectable range of responses within the sample under study. For example, a psychiatric population may have more pronounced affect incongruencies than a community-based sample. However, the scales are not meant to be used as norming devices, and judgments about subtle differences in affect and verbal behavior need to be made for each study. Coding can proceed from the manual. Although the coding system and manual were intentionally made to be appropriate for a wide variety of family interviews, its "one size" is unlikely to "fit all." Indeed, it may be necessary to make adjustments based on the interview and sample. Consultation by members of the FNC is available and may be arranged by contacting the first author or the web page listed in this chapter.

THE CODING PROCESS

At minimum, a three-step process is used in coding. First, the coder reviews the transcript, often marking passages that relate to a particular scale. Second, the coder reviews the audio- or videotape while following along with the transcript. At this point, particular attention is paid to affect and nonverbal communication. Third, the coder returns to the transcript and completes a note-taking sheet designed for each individual scale. Often a repeat viewing of the tape is needed to resolve remaining questions. Once the coder has made and verified notes documenting behavioral markers, the points of the scale are considered and a score is assigned. Coders may rereview the audio- or video tape as necessary. In the beginning stages of coding, it may take between 60 and 90 minutes to code an interview that lasts between 20 and 45 minutes. Once the coder is proficient, coding time is decreased by approximately half.

RELIABILITY

Interrater reliability was determined at each site in the FNC based on paired ratings of 10–27 cases. Cohen's kappa's ranged from .57 to .96, with an average of .83. In three of the four sites, the interrater reliability was based on interviews conducted with the couple. At the Minnesota site, two sets of interrater reliability estimates were calculated. The first set was calculated according to interviews conducted with the husband or wife alone, and the second set was calculated according to conjointly conducted interviews. Across all sites, interrater reliability estimates were in the good-to-excellent range (Fleiss, 1981).

Internal consistency was calculated for each dimension for each site. Three of the four sites reported acceptable alpha levels ranging from .53 to .99, with an average of .74. The one exception was the Washington, DC, site where the wives' narrative coherence was well below acceptable levels. We reasoned that because the couples in this sample were in the formative stages of constructing their story that the individual parts did not yet "hang well" together. Further research is needed to document this phenomenon.

VALIDITY

We tested the dimensional structure of the scales through a confirmatory factor analysis. We found that the scales identified a priori for Narrative Coherence and Narrative Interaction fit a two-dimensional model with the two factors moderately related to each other. The Relationship Beliefs dimension was proposed to be more content based and was not included in the analysis. Details regarding the factor analysis and differences between husbands and wives can be found in Fiese and Sameroff (1999).

Validity of the measures was also calculated within each site through correlations with other family and outcome measures. In regard to Narrative Coherence, it was found that mothers with major depression and currently experiencing psychiatric symptoms created less coherent accounts than nonill mothers (Dickstein et al., 1999). In another study, parents who had undergone open adoptions created more coherent accounts than parents who had undergone closed adoptions (Grotevant et al., 1999). In terms of Couple Narrative Style, couples who worked together in collaboratively telling their stories expressed more positive affect at the dinner table than couples whose narrative interactions were characterized by disconfirming statements and put-downs (Dickstein et al., 1999; Fiese & Marjinsky, 1999). Couples' self-report of their relationship satisfaction was related to how they interacted in the narrative construction (Wamboldt, 1999). Couples' relationship beliefs expressed about their family of origin were related to self-report measures of family of origin experiences (Wamboldt, 1999) and family functioning (Dickstein et al., 1999). Relationship beliefs expressed about the current family were related to positivity at the dinner table (Dickstein et al., 1999; Fiese & Marjinsky, 1999) and parent report of child behavior problems (Fiese & Marjinsky, 1999)

STUDIES USING THE FAMILY NARRATIVE
CONSORTIUM CODING SYSTEM

In addition to the empirical analysis conducted with the four original sites of the FNC, several studies are ongoing or have already been completed. The findings from these studies demonstrate moderate stability of narrative coherence over time (Curry-Bleggi, 1998) and moderate correlations with verbal intelligence (Chance, 1998; Curry-Bleggi, 1998). However, the relation between maternal narrative coherence and child behavior problems remained when effects of verbal intelligence were partialed out (Curry-Bleggi, 1998).

Several projects are under way that use the FNC scales to code family interviews. These studies include a longitudinal investigation of outcomes for adopted adolescents (Grotevant & McRoy, PIs—Principal Investigators), the impact of illness on family life (Fiese & Wamboldt, PIs), stability and change in dinnertime stories over 4 years (Fiese, PI), narrative coherence of children's family stories (Bickham, PI), and a longitudinal study of family functioning and maternal psychiatric illness (Dickstein, Seifer, & Sameroff, PIs).

To date, the FNC scales have been applied to interviews of primarily middle-class families. Future efforts are warranted to include more economically and ethnically diverse families in the interview process. Because the FNC scales were devised to be used by a variety of researchers with different interests in family process, it will be important to consider the feasibility and desirability to use all the scales. Researchers are advised to contact members of the FNC should they have questions about the applicability of the codes to their particular project.

EXCERPTS FROM THE FAMILY NARRATIVE CONSORTIUM CODING SYSTEM MANUAL

An excerpt from the Narrative Coherence dimension, Organization subscale is presented. Complete manuals may be obtained by contacting the first author or through the web site.

Organization	
SCALE LEVEL	*INDICATORS*
1. Poor Organization	**Rater has no clear picture of story.** Individual does not put pieces of narrative together. Many/mostly markers of disorganization; especially stops and starts, scattered with no transitions, thought blockage, and ambiguous referents.
2. Moderately Poor Organization	**Rater understands most of narrative, with effort or assistance from interviewer or other family member.** Individual puts some of story together but not all of story. Some markers of disorganization, typically stops and starts, or incomplete thoughts.
3. Moderate Organization	**Rater can understand story but there may still be some markers of disorganization.** Individual does put together story but with some difficulty.
4. Moderately Good Organization	**Rater can understand story clearly with rare incidence of markers of disorganization.** Individual puts together story and self-corrects.
5. Good Organization	**Individual puts story together in succinct and direct fashion.** Use of orienting statements.
8. Can't code due to mechanical problems.	
9. Unclear/Can't Code	

ACKNOWLEDGMENTS

Preparation of this chapter was supported, in part, by a grant from the National Institute of Mental Health to the first author.

REFERENCES

Benoit, D., & Parker, K. C. H. (1994). Stability and transmission of attachment across three generations. *Child Development, 65,* 1444–1456.

Bruner, J. (1987). Life as narrative. *Social Research, 54,* 11–32.

Bruner, J. (1990). *Acts of meaning.* Cambridge, MA: Harvard University Press.

Buehlman, K. T., Gottman, J. M., & Katz, L. F. (1992). How a couple views their past predicts their future. *Journal of Family Psychology, 5,* 295–318.

Chance, C. (1998). Stories of personal change and narrative coherence. *Dissertation Abstracts International, 59* No. 08B (1998): 4497.

Cohler, B. J. (1991). The life story and the study of resilience and response to adversity. *Journal of Narrative and Life History, 1,* 169–200.

Costell, R., Reiss, D., Berkman, H., & Jones, C. (1981). The family meets the hospital: Predicting the family's perception of the treatment program from its problem-solving style. *Archives General Psychiatry, 38,* 569–577.

Curry-Bleggi, E. (1998). The day you were born: A longitudinal study of maternal birth narratives. *Dissertation Abstracts International, 59* No. 08B (1998): 4498.

Dickstein, S., St. Andre, M., Sameroff, A. J., Seifer, R., & Schiller, M. (1999). Maternal depression, family functioning, and child outcomes: A narrative assessment. In B. H. Fiese, A. J. Sameroff, H. D. Grotevant, F. S. Wamboldt, S. Dickstein, & D. Fravel. *The stories that families tell: Narrative coherence, narrative interaction, and relationship beliefs. Monographs of the Society for Research in Child Development, 64,* (2, Serial No. 257). Malden, MA: Blackwell.

Downey, G., & Coyne, J. C. (1990). Children of depressed parents: An integrative review. *Psychological Bulletin, 108,* 50–76.

Fiese, B. H., & Marjinsky, K. A. T. (1999). Dinnertime stories: Connecting family practices with relationship beliefs and child adjustment. In B. H. Fiese, A. J. Sameroff, H. D. Grotevant, F. S. Wamboldt, S. Dickstein, & D. Fravel. *The stories that families tell: Narrative coherence, narrative interaction, and relationship beliefs. Monographs of the Society for Research in Child Development, 64,* (2, Serial No. 257). Malden, MA: Blackwell.

Fiese, B. H., & Sameroff, A. J. (1999). The Family Narrative Consortium: A multidimensional approach to narratives. In B. H. Fiese, A. J. Sameroff, H. D. Grotevant, F. S. Wamboldt, S. Dickstein, & D. Fravel. *The stories that families tell: Narrative coherence, narrative interaction, and relationship beliefs. Monographs of the Society for Research in Child Development, 64,* (2, Serial No. 257). Malden, MA: Blackwell.

Fiese, B. H., Sameroff, A. J., Grotevant, H. D., Wamboldt, F. S., Dickstein, S., & Fravel, D. (1999). *The stories that families tell: Narrative coherence, narrative interaction, and relationship beliefs. Monographs of the Society for Research in Child Development, 64,* (2, Serial No. 257). Malden, MA: Blackwell.

Fleiss, J. L. (1981). *Statistical methods for rates and proportions.* New York: Wiley.

Gottman, J. M. (1983). *Rapid couples interaction coding system.* Unpublished manuscript, University of Illinois, Champaign.

Grotevant, H. D., Fravel, D. L., Gorall, D., & Piper, J. (1999). Narratives of adoptive parents: Perspectives from individual and couple Interviews. In B. H. Fiese, A. J. Sameroff, H. D. Grotevant, F. S. Wamboldt, S. Dickstein, & D. Fravel. *The stories that families tell: Narrative coherence, narrative interaction, and relationship beliefs. Monographs of the Society for Research in Child Development, 64,* (2, Serial No. 257). Malden, MA: Blackwell.

Howard, G. S. (1991). Culture tales: A narrative approach to thinking, cross-cultural psychology, and psychotherapy. *American Psychologist, 46,* 187–197.

Julien, D., Markman, H. J., Lindahl, K., Johnson, H. M., & Van Widenfelt, B. (1987). *Interactional dimensions coding system: Researcher's manual.* Unpublished manuscript, University of Denver, Colorado.

McAdams, D. P. (1993). *The stories we live by: Personal myths and the making of the self.* New York: Morrow.

Mishler, E. G. (1991). Representing discourse: The rhetoric of transcription. *Journal of Narrative and Life History, 1,* 255–280.

Polkinghorne, D. E. (1988). *Narrative knowing and the human sciences.* Albany: State University of New York Press.

Reiss, D. (1981). *The family's construction of reality.* Cambridge, MA: Harvard University Press.

Riessman, C. K. (1993). *Narrative analysis.* Newbury Park, CA: Sage.

Wamboldt, F. S. (1999). Co-constructing a marriage: Analyses of young couples' relationship narratives. In B. H. Fiese, A. J. Sameroff, H. D. Grotevant, F. S. Wamboldt, S. Dickstein, & D. Fravel. *The stories that families tell: Narrative coherence, narrative interaction, and relationship beliefs. Monographs of the Society for Research in Child Development, 64,* (2, Serial No. 257). Malden, MA: Blackwell.

White, M., & Epston, D. (1990). *Narrative means to therapeutic ends.* New York: Norton.

16

The Young Family Interaction
Coding System

Blair Paley
*University of California–Los Angeles Neuropsychiatric Institute
and Hospital*

Martha J. Cox
University of North Carolina–Chapel Hill

Korrel W. Kanoy
Peace College

The Young Family Interaction Coding System (YFICS) is an observational coding system that was designed to assess family interactions beyond the dyadic level—that is, to assess verbal and nonverbal behavior among multiple members of a family. In particular, the YFICS was designed to examine interactions among new parents and their 24-month-old child. This system is most appropriate for family interactions with young children (2 to 3 years of age) because it attempts to capture interactions around regulation of emotion and support for autonomy within a family context, issues that are important developmentally for 2- to 3-year-old children. The YFICS is used with a family play task in which parents are asked to build something together as a family. When the task is complete, parents are asked to have the 2-year-old clean up. This task elicits information about the affective quality of family exchanges, the parents' strategies for approaching the task (whether they promote autonomous functioning in the child), and the extent to which the parents assist the child in regulating emotion and maintaining a positive and enthusiastic approach to the task.

To date, the YFICS has been used with a primarily White, lower- to lower-middle-class sample, and thus its generalizability to families of other ethnic groups or socioeconomic statuses is not yet known. We expect the qualities of family interaction assessed by the YFICS to be important across different ethnic and socioeconomic groups because of their relevance for the developmental tasks faced by children and their families. However, it would clearly be important that any efforts to extend this coding system to more diverse samples be accompanied by piloting and other strategies to ensure its appropriate application. These strategies may include training coders of relevant ethnic/cultural groups and examining the coding system for cultural equivalence across different groups (see Cauce, Coronado, & Watson, 1998).

THEORETICAL FOUNDATIONS

Development of the YFICS was largely guided by two theoretical frameworks: family systems theory and attachment theory. Central to family systems theory is the notion that a family is a "complex, integrated whole" (P. Minuchin, 1988, p. 8), wherein individual family members continually and mutually influence one another. The family system is both comprised of smaller subsystems (e.g., parental, marital, sibling), but also embedded in larger systems (e.g., communities). Families interact within and across these various levels. From a systems perspective, any individual family member is inextricably embedded in the larger family system, and can only be truly understood in the context of that larger system (Cox & Paley, 1997; Kreppner & Lerner, 1989; P. Minuchin, 1985; Sameroff, 1994).

In line with these notions, family therapists and systems theorists (Hoffman, 1981; P. Minuchin, 1985; S. Minuchin, 1974) have long recognized the importance of studying family interactions at multiple levels, and in particular, of moving beyond the dyad—traditionally the unit of analysis in much of family research—in order to develop a better understanding of family processes and disturbances. However, empirical efforts at this level have lagged behind. Until recently, there was some acceptance of the notion that assessments of dyadic interactions sufficiently capture the important features of family life. However, this notion of family relationships as largely dyadic is, at least in part, an artificial construction of researchers. Indeed, P. Minuchin noted that many of our conclusions about childrearing are based on studies that focus on only one caregiver (usually mothers) and that regard that caregiver as providing all necessary information about patterns of parenting in the family. Yet observations of triadic and whole-family interactions may be particularly informative with regard to family processes that are not discernible in dyadic interactions.

Structural family theory highlights a number of such processes, including the formation of coalitions within the family and difficulties regulating boundaries between subsystems (S. Minuchin, 1974). Indeed, the reorganization that is required by young families as they accommodate to a new child in the family may represent a challenging developing period for some families. In families in which parents have not established a strong marital or coparenting alliance, one parent may attempt to coopt the child into an alliance against the other parent. S. Minuchin and Fishman (1981) further noted that:

> As the child begins to move around and talk, the parents must establish controls that give them space while maintaining safety and the parental authority. Adults who have established patterns of nurturance must now modify those patterns, developing appropriate methods of maintaining control while encouraging growth. (p. 24)

As the child enters toddlerhood, one or both parents may react to the child's attempts at independence by either being quite intrusive with, or alternatively, being quite detached from the child. Thus, the YFICS was in part designed to capture those aspects of family life that may be most salient when multiple members are interacting with one another, including *alliances* between two family members, the extent to which family members *intrude* on one another, or alternatively, the extent to which they are *detached* or disengaged from one another.

The development of this coding system was also significantly influenced by attachment theory (Bowlby, 1969, 1973, 1980), and in particular, the notion that a critical feature of the parent–child relationship is the parent's ability to foster the child's capacity for emotional regulation (Carlson & Sroufe, 1995). Learning to regulate one's own affective states is seen as a central task of development and highly influenced by the quality of early caregiving (Sroufe, 1995). Sroufe noted that young children who trust in the responsiveness of their caregiver are more likely to explore their environment and to experience and share a wide range of emotional states. In the event that they become dysregulated, such children can turn to caregivers for support in regaining their emotional equilibrium. Thus, children must be allowed to explore independently, yet be provided with sufficient support in such exploration. Consequently, healthy development requires that families strike a balance between fostering independence while maintaining connectedness, without sacrificing one for the other (Emde & Buchsbaum, 1990; Sroufe, 1995).

Much of attachment research has focused on examining the quality of the affective bond between parent and child (and typically between mother and child), and parents' ability to promote emotional regulation in their child in the context of dyadic relationships. However, mothers and fathers most likely to foster their child's emotional regulation skills are likely to respond not only to their child's emotional states sensitively and supportively, but to each other's as well. Not surprisingly then, researchers (Cowan, 1997; Marvin & Stewart, 1990) have increasingly emphasized the need to expand our perspective on attachment relationships to the larger family system. In particular, there is a need to explore how a child's emotional development is supported (or not) in the context of the larger family system. That is, a child's emotional development may not only be shaped by how parents interact with him or her, but how they interact with one another. Mothers and fathers may support or undermine one another's efforts to provide sensitive parenting, or may directly model poor emotional regulation skills in conflicts with one another. Thus, the YFICS was designed in large part to assess a number of aspects of family functioning that attachment theorists have identified as critical to children's emotional development. For example, the YFICS assesses whether parents respond in a *sensitive,* "child-centered" manner to their child's emotional needs. Studies suggest that children who develop secure attachments and a corresponding ability to self-regulate are more likely to have caregivers that respond to their emotional distress in a sensitive, supportive manner (Ainsworth, Blehar, Waters, & Wall, 1978). The YFICS also evaluates whether family members are emotionally *detached* from one another. Attachment studies have documented that some parents may have difficulties tolerating their children's expressions of distress, and may ignore or disregard their children's bids for support (Ainsworth et al., 1978). The YFICS also assesses the extent to which parents may intrude upon their children's emotional experiences, and are, in essence, unable to differentiate their own emotional experiences from their children's. Bretherton (1990) proposed that parents who are consistently "overattuned" to their children's affective states may be committing a "form of emotional theft," wherein they "model for their infants how and how intensely they ought to feel, as opposed to affirming how the infants do feel" (p. 87). The extent to which *positive* and *negative affect* characterize exchanges among family members is also coded.

Although the extent to which families promote the development of autonomous, emotionally regulated functioning was the main focus of the YFICS, one other aspect of family interaction was assessed as well. A considerable body of literature has documented (a) the influence of enriched environments on intelligence (e.g., Campbell & Ramey, 1994), and (b) the importance of adult sensitivity and responsiveness for child exploration (e.g., Belsky, Goode, & Most, 1980; Clarke-Stewart, 1973). In particular, we were interested in the degree to which whole-family processes might make an independent contribution, beyond that made by dyadic parent–child processes, to children's cognitive development. Thus, the YFICS assesses the extent to which families *stimulate* the *cognitive development* of their child.

DEVELOPMENT OF THE YOUNG FAMILY INTERACTION CODING SYSTEM

The YFICS was developed as part of a larger longitudinal study aimed at examining the transition to parenthood and the development of young families. The sample consisted of 138 couples recruited from a largely rural part of the southeastern United States. In this sample, 97% of the couples were White, with the remaining 3% being African-American, as is representative of this rural area, and most couples were of lower- to lower-middle-class socioeconomic status. Couples were initially assessed prior to their birth of their first (the target) child, and then reassessed at several subsequent time points, with the final assessment occurring during the year the target child entered kindergarten. Assessments were made of individual, dyadic, and whole-family functioning. Of interest here, families were videotaped during a 15-minute family play task in which they were presented with Legos® and instructed to build anything of their choosing. Parents were further instructed to request that their child clean up the toys at the end of the task. For most families, this task included father, mother, and the target child. However, for a minority of families who had had another child within the 24 months since the initial assessment, the new sibling was also included in the family interaction task.

The nature of the family interaction task was guided by a number of factors. First, the task of family members engaging in play together is likely representative of interactions that occur with some regularity in the lives of young families, particularly given the developmental stage of the child (24 months) at the time of assessment. Second, the inclusion of both play and "clean-up" segments were thought to have the potential to elicit a range of both positive and negative experiences for family members, and to elicit interactions that would require parents to read and respond to their children's (and likely to each other's) emotional signals. Indeed, some families exhibited quite sensitive and supportive responses to one another's emotional needs, whereas in other families, members were either quite affectively disengaged from one another, or alternatively, imposed their own emotional experiences on other family members. Third, the need to transition from a "free-play" segment to a "clean-up" segment might be particularly challenging for a 24-month-old, who is likely experimenting with independence and the need to assert oneself. The inclusion of both of these segments in the family interaction task would ideally provide the opportunity to view the various capacities of families to balance a child's need for autonomy with the need to socialize a child and teach them to cooperate and follow rules. Finally, we opted to leave the task relatively unstructured in order to allow parents the opportunity to impose whatever degree of structure on the task they desired or felt necessary. We felt this approach was likely to elicit a range of behaviors in family members as they attempted to negotiate how the play task would proceed. That is, in some families, parents entirely dictated the course of interaction with little regard for the child's autonomy. In other families, parents allowed both their child and one another some independence, yet provided support and assistance when needed. In still other families, parents were extremely passive and detached, providing the child and one another with little or no guidance or support.

Although the YFICS was designed for use with families with children ages 2–3 years old, it may be possible to adapt this system for use with families with children of other ages. Obviously, the interactional task selected for use with the YFICS should be age-appropriate, but the aspects of family functioning assessed by the YFICS are likely to be relevant for other developmental periods as well. Regarding the range of family constellations for which the YFICS might be appropriate, this coding system has been applied to families with a target 24-month-old child, and in some cases, a younger sibling. Again, we expect that the dimensions of family functioning captured by the YFICS would characterize a variety of family configurations. In both cases, the YFICS should be piloted in order to ensure its generalizability to other kinds of interactional tasks (e.g., problem discussion task) and other family configurations (e.g., extended).

DESCRIPTION OF THE YOUNG FAMILY INTERACTION CODING SYSTEM

The purpose of the YFICS is to assess interaction at the triadic (mother–father–child) or family level. Thus, in developing the various dimensions of this coding system, it was important to describe such dimensions in a way that would characterize the quality of interactions among all family members, rather than exclusive to any individual or dyad, even if such interactions were largely directed toward one particular family member. For example, in developing the code of sensitivity, we intended that this dimension would reflect *the child's experience of sensitivity within the family* rather than the mother's level of sensitivity and the father's level as two separate codes. That is, children sometimes interact with their parents separately, but they also have experiences within the family that cannot be adequately represented by the summation of mother and father scores.

The YFICS contains seven family codes and three child codes.[1] Although the primary focus of the YFICS is to assess various aspects of family-level interactions, this system also consists of individual child codes designed to reflect the child's emotional and behavioral responses during these family interactions. That is, it was deemed important to not only assess the various patterns of interaction among multiple family members, but also to examine the adaptations that children make in the context of such interactions. Each family and child dimension is coded on a 7-point Likert scale ranging from 1–7, with 1 representing little or no evidence of the dimension and 7 representing a high degree of the dimension. The Family codes include *Sensitivity/Child-Centeredness, Positive Affect, Negative Affect, Detachment, Intrusiveness/Adult-Centeredness, Family Alliances,* and *Stimulation of Cognitive Development. Sensitivity/Child-Centeredness* reflects the extent to which families are child centered in their interactions, provide stimulation that is situationally appropriate, respond contingently to the child's needs, and provide responses that are "in sync" with the child. Families displaying *Positive Affect* seem to enjoy being together and are warm, affectionate, relaxed, and comfortable with each other. *Negative Affect* assesses conflict, hostility, disagreement, and criticism within the family. Families exhibiting *Detachment* are not involved with each other, reserved in their interactions with one another, and appear to be unaware of or uninterested in each other's needs. *Intrusiveness/Adult-Centeredness* reflects the extent to which families are adult centered and overcontrolling, impos-

---

[1]It should be noted that some descriptions of constructs and examples in the YFICS were adapted from the dyadic coding system developed for the NICHD Study of Early Child Care. That is, some processes that characterize dyadic parent–child interactions were also expected to be important in whole-family interactions (e.g., sensitivity, intrusiveness). Such codes were of course revised to assess interactional patterns at the broader family level rather than between a particular parent and the child.

ing their own agenda on the child. Often, the child's autonomy will be compromised because of one or both parents' need to remain in control of the situation and/or because of their inflexibility. Family *Alliances* are evident whenever two family members interact to the exclusion of the third member. *Stimulation of Cognitive Development* assesses the degree to which families engage in a variety of behaviors that facilitate development, such as expanding on the child's verbalizations, suggesting more sophisticated play activities, or focusing the child's attention on perceptual qualities of objects.

The Child codes include *Enthusiasm, Compliance,* and *Anger. Enthusiasm* reflects the extent to which the child responds with interest, confidence, and eagerness during the family play task; a child high in enthusiasm takes an active interest and invests effort and energy in his or her activities, and takes pleasure in his or her own successes. *Compliance* assesses the extent to which the child shows a willingness to listen to parents' suggestions and responds to parental requests and commands in a cooperative and pleasant manner. *Anger* reflects the amount of anger shown by the child during the interaction regardless of its source or target (e.g., parent, toy).

CODER TRAINING

The coding team for the original coding of the 24-month whole family interaction task was composed of two professionals with doctoral degrees. No undergraduates have been trained to date, but based on their ability to learn other coding systems within our project, they may be acceptable coders. They would likely perform better as coders if they had some understanding of family dynamics and appropriate developmental expectations for 24-month-old children, as well as frequent supervision. Graduate students, especially those in developmental or clinical programs, generally make excellent coders.

Training typically involves two joint sessions between a trainer and trainee, followed by subsequent independent sessions in which trainer and trainee code additional sets of tapes separately and then compare and discuss their respective scores. Training begins with a trainee studying the manual for the YFICS. In the first training session, the trainee watches two to three tapes with a reliable coder. These tapes are carefully selected because of the range of behaviors seen on the tapes. The trainer identifies key behaviors that would be considered in coding various dimensions. After watching each tape twice, the trainer and trainee discuss the various codes and jointly arrive at scores for the family and child. This initial session typically requires approximately 4 to 6 hours.

In the second session, the trainer and trainee jointly watch another set of two to three tapes, but do not discuss the codes this time as they are viewing the tapes. Both the trainer and trainee independently take notes from the tape and write a justification for each code. Trainees are instructed to write down specific behaviors and verbal exchanges as opposed to general impressions. Based on their notes and multiple viewings of the tapes, the trainer and trainee independently score each dimension and then discuss their respective scores. Mistakes in coding are discussed with the trainee and final scores for each code are determined. This second training session also typically requires 4 to 6 hours, but may vary depending on the facility of the trainee in using the coding system.

After the initial two joint training sessions, the trainer and trainee view another set of two to three tapes separately. The trainee is again instructed to take written notes and provide justifications for his or her scores. The trainee and trainer then meet to compare their scores and to discuss and clarify any discrepancies. This process should continue until interrater reliabilities of .80 or above between the trainer and trainee have been achieved for all family and child codes on a set of 30 independently coded tapes.

After a trainee is deemed reliable and begins to code independently, the trainer conducts reliability checks on a random sample of the tapes. Typically, the trainer or reliability coder will code 20% of the total number of tapes in the set. These reliability checks should occur at regular intervals (e.g., weekly) to prevent drift in the use of the coding system and to ensure that reliability remains high. Weekly reliability meetings are scheduled to discuss specific problems. These meetings are critical to maintaining reliability. No training tape exists for training new coders. Any new coders who are trained must work with a reliable coder.

THE CODING PROCESS

Coders should allow 1 to 1½ hours to review and code each 15-minute interaction. Each tape is reviewed three to four times, and coders may frequently start and stop the tape to take notes about specific behaviors. The first time coders review a tape, they should simply watch the tape through, noting specific behaviors and interactions relevant to the codes. On the second viewing, coders should take extensive notes about the interaction and start and stop the tape as necessary to make notes about specific behaviors relevant to the codes. On the third viewing, the coder refines his or her notes on the whole-family categories and arrives at scores for each whole-family category. On the fourth viewing, the coder refines notes on the child category and arrives at scores for each child category. A fifth viewing can be used to confirm codes. Each final score is justified by examples of behavior from the tape.

RELIABILITY

Reliability of the 24-month YFICS has been determined using data from the 138 families participating in our larger longitudinal study of the transition to parenthood. Pearson correlations between the scores of two trained coders coding a subset of tapes independently indexed the following reliabilities: Sensitivity ($r = .87$), Positive Affect ($r = .96$), Negative Affect ($r = .80$), Detachment ($r = .74$), Intrusiveness ($r = .64$), Stimulation of Cognitive Development ($r = .90$), Child Enthusiasm ($r = . 84$), Child Compliance ($r = .80$), and Child Anger ($r = .89$).[2]

Correlations among the various family and child codes were also examined as it was expected that many (although not all) of these dimensions would be related to one another. For example, consistent with our expectations, Sensitivity was positively correlated with Positive Affect ($r = .61, p < .001$), Child Enthusiasm ($r = .60, p < .001$), and Child Compliance ($r = .39, p < .001$), and negatively correlated with Negative Affect ($r = -.65, p < .001$), Detachment ($r = -.63, p < .001$), Intrusiveness ($r = -.69, p < .001$), Family Alliances ($r = -.57, p < .001$), and Child Anger ($r = -.52, p < .001$).

VALIDITY

To investigate the concurrent validity of the YFICS, we examined the correlations between various dimensions of the YFICS and similar dimensions assessed during 24-month *dyadic* parent–child interactions. We expected some degree of correspondence between similar dimensions of the dyadic and whole-family interactions. However, it is important to note that we did not necessarily expect extremely high correlations across these different levels of interactions, as a system perspective would suggest that there may be some unique processes that unfold when an entire family comes together, processes that cannot be derived simply by adding or averaging that which occurs in various dyadic interactions. Consistent with these expectations, a number of dimensions were moderately correlated across dyadic and whole-family interactions. For example, Whole Family Negative Affect was positively correlated with both Dyadic Mother–Child Negative Regard ($r = .53, p < .001$) and Dyadic Father–Child Negative Regard ($r = .36, p < .001$); Whole Family Detachment was positively correlated with both Dyadic Mother–Child Detachment ($r = .42, p < .001$) and Dyadic Father–Child Detachment ($r = .37, p < .001$); Whole Family Child Enthusiasm was positively correlated with both Dyadic Mother–Child Enthusiasm ($r = .30, p < .001$) and Dyadic Father–Child Enthusiasm ($r = .31, p < .001$).

We also examined the construct validity of the YFICS system by assessing whether dimensions of this coding system related to other constructs in a theoretically expected manner. A wealth of literature has documented linkages between marital adjustment and dyadic parent–child relationships (for reviews, see Cox, Paley, & Harter, in press; Erel & Burman, 1995), and similarly, we predicted that marital adjustment would also relate to whole-family interactions. To evaluate this prediction, we examined the extent to which a self-report measure of marital adjustment completed by mothers and fathers in our larger longitudinal study both prior and subsequent to the birth of their first child related to whole-family interac-

---

[2]The reliability of the Alliances code is currently being established, as this code was added to the YFICS after reliability for the other family and child codes had already been established.

tions when the child was 24 months old. Two subscales of the Four Factor Scale of Intimate Relations (Braiker & Kelley, 1976) were administered to assess spouses' commitment to their relationship (Ambivalence) and feelings of positive regard for their partner and their relationship (Love). Analyses revealed that whole-family interactions were related to self-reported marital adjustment assessed both prenatally and 24 months following the birth of the couple's first child. For example, mother's report of Ambivalence about the marriage prenatally was negatively related to Family Sensitivity ($r = -.19, p < .01$), Positive Affect ($r = -.25, p < .01$), and Stimulation of Cognitive Development ($r = -.21, p < .01$), and positively related to Detachment ($r = .25, p < .01$) and Alliances ($r = .23, p < .01$) at 24 months. Father's report of Ambivalence about the marriage prenatally was positively related to Family Detachment ($r = .27, p < .01$) and Alliances ($r = .19, p < .01$) at 24 months. Family Sensitivity, Positive Regard, and Stimulation of Child Development were also negatively related to both mother's and father's reports of Ambivalence about the marriage at 24 months ($rs = -.19 -.33, ps < .05$), whereas Family Detachment and Alliances were positively related to mother's and father's report of Ambivalence at 24 months ($rs = .25-.30, ps < .01$). Similar correlations were obtained between mother's and father's reports on the Love factor and several of the Family interaction dimensions as well.

STUDIES UTILIZING THE YOUNG FAMILY INTERACTION CODING SYSTEM

Paley, Cox, Kanoy, Harter, and Margand (1999) examined the role of mother's and father's attachment stance and of the quality of the couple's marriage in predicting the quality of whole-family interaction 24 months later. Using the Adult Attachment Interview (George, Kaplan, & Main, 1984), mothers and fathers were classified as having either a secure or insecure attachment stance with regard to their own childhood attachment experiences. Marital quality was assessed in the context of a 15-minute problem-solving interaction task. These marital interactions were coded for negative escalation (the extent to which spouses reciprocate one another's negative behavior) and withdrawal. Results indicated that husband's prenatal marital withdrawal was predictive of less Positive Affect, more Negative Affect, and greater Detachment in family interactions at 24 months. Additionally, families with insecure fathers were characterized by less Positive Affect and more Negative Affect at 24 months, but only when there were higher levels of negative escalation in the marriage prenatally.

A study by Frosch, Caskie, Cox, Morrison, and Goldman (1999) also utilized the YFICS to examine the extent to which whole-family interactions made an independent contribution to the prediction of children's cognitive development, beyond the contribution made by dyadic parent–child interactions. Ratings were made of mothers and fathers interacting (separately) with their 24-month-old children in a dyadic task during which children were presented with a challenging puzzle task and parents were instructed to provide children with whatever assistance they required. Children were also observed at 24 months interacting with both parents together (and younger siblings in some cases) in the whole-family interaction task previously described here. A subsequent assessment was made of these families just prior to the target child entering kindergarten. At this time, children were administered the Peabody Picture Vocabulary Test–Revised (PPVT–R; Dunn & Dunn, 1981), a measure of children's receptive vocabulary. Analyses revealed that Family Stimulation of Cognitive Development was a significant predictor of children's prekindergarten PPVT scores, even after accounting for the contributions of mother's dyadic Stimulation of Cognitive Development and mother's dyadic Intrusiveness.

EXCERPTS FROM THE YOUNG FAMILY INTERACTION CODING SYSTEM MANUAL

Two codes, Sensitivity and Detachment, are excerpted below in detail. It should be noted that behavioral anchors are provided for every other point on the rating scale (1,3,5,7); however, all points on the scale are used when rating families on the various dimensions of the YFICS.

Sensitivity/Child-Centeredness

The defining feature of family systems that are sensitive to the child's needs is that they are child-centered. Sensitive parents are tuned in to the child and manifest awareness of the child's needs, mood, interests, capabilities, and allow this awareness to guide their behavior with the child. In preschoolers, this includes sensitivity to the child's own agenda, needs for autonomy, independence, mastery, and individual self-regulatory abilities, including needs for control. The sensitive parents of a preschooler structure the child's physical and social environment so that the child's preferences can be honored within reason, and so that the child can remain effectively engaged in playful or goal-directed activities. Sensitive parents offer the right mix of support and independence so that the child can experience mastery, success, pride, and develop effective self-regulatory skills.

If the child appears disengaged, sensitive parents take time to reengage the child in a manner that demonstrates awareness of and sensitivity to the child's mood and preferences for play style and content. When the child is bored or frustrated, sensitive parents offer toys, activities or other engaging opportunities, help the child decide what to get involved with, or help the child make the transition to a new activity. When the child is interested and involved, sensitive parents allow him/her time to independently explore. Sensitive parents do not demand participation in activities at all times, nor do they ignore an aimless child.

In child-centered families, as much as possible, the child is given choices for how to do the activity. This includes providing choices of the pieces to use, how to combine them, and what to make. How and what is built is geared to whether or not the child seems to be enjoying the activity. The parents do not persist with an activity that the child is obviously not enjoying; rather the parents try to engage the child's interest by appealing to the child. The sensitive parent permits the child as much choice, control, and autonomy as possible while enforcing necessary rules, regulations, and constraints.

Sensitive parents provide stimulation that is situationally appropriate. They acknowledge the child's interest, efforts, affect, and accomplishments. Sensitive parents need not spend all the time engaged with the child, but the difference between them and detached parents is that the sensitive parent seems to be actively taking an interest in the child's activities, as evidenced by comments, embellishments, or redirection when the child loses interest, achieves success or does something new and interesting. It is at these times that the difference between the sensitive and the detached parents is most easily seen; detached parents don't respond, respond in a listless or perfunctory manner, or respond with developmentally inappropriate comments and behaviors. Insensitive parents also could be over-stimulating/intrusive and might continue in their attempts to engage the child even when the child is providing clues that he/she is seeking to end the interaction.

Sensitive interactions are well-timed and paced to the child's response, a function of their child-centered nature. Such an interaction appears to be "in sync." If the child initiates interaction with the parent or makes demands, desires, or requests known, the sensitive parent responds appropriately, based on the child's behavior and speech. The parents pace activities to keep the child engaged and interested, but also allow him/her to disengage if interest is lost, and generally shape the nature of the involvement.

During the preschool years, sensitivity also can be inferred on the basis of how the parents manage disciplinary encounters. Sensitive parents are neither over-controlling nor detached, but rather are attentive to child behaviors that need sanctioning and respond in a way whereby the sanction fits the misdeed. Sensitive discipline involves an indication by parents that they are aware of what motivates the child and the offering of an explanation or rationale for why the discipline is taking place. To be noted, however, is that excessive explanations and rationales can reflect insensitive-intrusive parenting rather than sensitive parenting. Long-winded speeches and lectures often reflect the parents' lack of awareness of the child's developmental level.

Sensitivity also can be manifested in the parents' response to the child's distress, anger, or frustration. Sensitivity may involve speaking sympathetically to the child, approaching the child, redirecting the child's activities, hugging, patting, or holding the child in one's lap and comforting when distressed.

Markers of sensitivity include (a) acknowledging the child's affect; (b) caregiver conversation that is responsive to the content of the child's talk and/or activity; (c) facilitating, but not over-controlling the child's play with objects; (d) appropriate timing of activities to reflect children's interest; (e) changing the pace when the child appears understimulated, overexcited, or tired; (f) picking up on the child's interest in the toys present during the task; (g) shared positive affect; (h) providing an appropriate level of stimulation and appropriate range and variety of activities; (i) timely discipline that matches the nature of the violation under consideration and the child's ability to understand and benefit from whatever reprimand is offered; and (j) general flexibility in handling compliance and autonomy issues, including not over-reacting to noncompliance and supporting autonomy while permitting dependence.

Ratings on this scale should be based on both quality and quantity of caregiver behavior.

1 = Not at all characteristic. There is little evidence of parent sensitivity. The parents rarely, if ever, respond appropriately to the child's cues, or manifest an awareness of the child's needs. Interactions are characteristically ill-timed or inappropriate.

3 = Minimally characteristic. This rating should be given to families in which parents display infrequent or weak sensitivity/responsivity. While the parents are sometimes sensitive, the balance is clearly in the direction of insensitivity to the child's needs.

5 = Moderately characteristic. This rating should be given to families in which parents are predominantly sensitive/responsive. The parents demonstrate sensitivity in many interactions, but not all, or may show some insensitivity while being predominantly sensitive (e.g., available and responsive to child's needs, but some responses are more adult-driven than child-driven, or adult is somewhat more detached than is optimal).

7 = Highly characteristic. This rating should be given to caregivers who are exceptionally sensitive and responsive. Insensitivity is rare. Interactions are characteristically well-timed and appropriate, meeting the child's developmental needs. If the child is busy, engaged, and happy, then a caregiver need not directly interact with the child. However, if the parents are preoccupied or detached, then he or she is not sensitive even if the child is engaged.

Detachment

This rating reflects the extent to which family members seem uninvolved and reserved with each other as opposed to emotionally engaged. Detachment can be seen in family members who appear emotionally uninvolved or disengaged and unaware of each other's needs. This is especially evident when parents are unaware of children's needs, and fail to facilitate involvement with the task or with people. The parents do not react contingently to the children's vocalizations or actions, and do not provide the "scaffolding" that children need to explore the task objects. Simply allowing other family members to play or work on the project by themselves is not necessarily a sign of detachment; this can be appropriate when a family member is clearly happy and contented to be doing that and other family members seem aware of that. The detached family shows passivity and lacks the emotional involvement that the engaged family shows. The family members appear uninterested in each other.

Detachment can be seen in family members: (a) facing away from each other as they work on the task without visually checking in; (b) presenting objects to each other without first engaging the other person; (c) rarely making eye contact or talking with each other; (d) not responding to others' vocalizations, smiles, or other behaviors; (e) ignoring the interesting things other family members are doing. Detached members may not pay attention to others' bids for attention or they pay more attention to their own activities rather than those of family members, or they appear distracted. A family that interacts with each other consistently but does so in a perfunctory or indifferent manner with little or no emotional involvement would be rated as high on detachment. The scale reflects both qualitative and quantitative components.

1 = Not at all characteristic. This rating should be given to families who display almost no signs of detachment or underinvolvement. Their interactions show clear involvement with each other.

3 = Minimally characteristic. This rating should be given to families who display minimal detachment. While the family members are sometimes emotionally uninvolved, they are clearly more involved than not.

5 = Moderately characteristic. This rating should be given to families who are predominantly detached. The members are relatively more uninvolved than involved, but the detachment is not so prevalent that it is worrisome.

7 = Highly characteristic. This rating should be given to families who are so detached that it is worrisome. The child lies or sits without parental attention almost all of the time, even when the parent is within a suitable distance for interacting. When family members do interact, the behaviors appear mechanical and perfunctory. The family members are clearly not emotionally involved with each other and appear to be "just going through the motions".

ACKNOWLEDGMENTS

Support for the development of the Young Family Interaction Coding System, for the collection of data for our longitudinal study of couples across the transition to parenthood, and for preparation of this chapter was provided in part by a grant from the National Institute of Mental Health (R01MH44763) to Martha Cox.

REFERENCES

Ainsworth, M. D. S., Blehar, M. C., Waters, E., & Wall, S. (1978). Patterns of attachment: A psychological study of the strange situation. Hillsdale, NJ: Lawrence Erlbaum Associates.

Belsky, J., Goode, M. K., & Most, R. K. (1980). Maternal stimulation and infant exploratory competence: Cross-sectional, correlational, and experimental analyses. *Child Development, 51,* 1163–1178.

Bowlby, J. (1969). *Attachment and loss: Vol. 1. Attachment.* New York: Basic Books.

Bowlby, J. (1973). *Attachment and loss: Vol. 2. Separation: Anxiety and anger.* New York: Basic Books.

Bowlby, J. (1980). *Attachment and loss: Vol. 3. Loss, sadness, and depression.* New York: Basic Books.

Braiker, H., & Kelley, H. (1976). Conflict in the development of close relationships. In R. Burgess & T. Huston (Eds.), *Social exchange and developing relationships* (pp. 79–102). New York: Academic Press.

Bretherton, I. (1990). Open communication and internal working models: Their role in the development of attachment relationships. In R. A. Thompson (Ed.), *Nebraska Symposium on Motivation: Socioemotional development* (pp. 57–113). Lincoln: University of Nebraska Press.

Campbell, F. A., & Ramey, C. T. (1994). Effects of early intervention on intellectual and academic achievement: A follow-up study of children from low-income families. *Child Development, 65,* 684–698.

Carlson, E. A., & Sroufe, L. A. (1995). Contribution of attachment theory to developmental psychopathology. In D. Cicchetti & D. J. Cohen (Eds.), *Developmental psychopathology: Vol. 1. Theory and methods* (pp. 581–617). New York: Wiley.

Cauce, A. M., Coronado, N., & Watson, J. (1998). Conceptual, methodological, and statistical issues in culturally competent research. In M. Hernandez & M. Isaacs (Eds.), *Promoting cultural competence in children's mental health services* (pp. 305–329). Baltimore: Brookes.

Clarke-Stewart, K. A. (1973). Interactions between mothers and their children. *Monographs of the Society for Research in Child Development, 38* (6–7, Serial No. 153).

Cowan, P. A. (1997). Beyond meta-analysis: A plea for a family systems view of attachment. *Child Development, 68,* 601–603.

Cox, M. J., & Paley, B. (1997). Families as systems. *Annual Review of Psychology, 48,* 243–267.

Cox, M. J., Paley, B., & Harter, K. S. M. (in press). Interparental conflict and parent–child relationships. In J. H. Grych & F. D. Fincham (Eds.), *Child development and interparental conflict.* New York: Cambridge University Press.

Dunn, L. M., & Dunn, L. M. (1981). *Peabody Picture Vocabulary Test–Revised.* Circle Pines, MN: American Guidance Service.

Emde, R., & Buchsbaum, H. (1990). "Didn't you hear my mommy?" Autonomy with connectedness in moral self-emergence. In D. Cicchetti & M. Beeghly (Eds.), *The self in transition* (pp. 35–60). Chicago: University of Chicago Press.

Erel, O., & Burman, B. (1995). Interrelatedness of marital relations and parent–child relations: A meta-analytic review. *Psychological Bulletin, 118,* 108–132.

Frosch, C. A., Caskie, G. I. L., Cox, M. J., Morrison, F. J., & Goldman, B. D. (1999). *Early aggression and the development of verbal skills in pre-kindergarten children.* Manuscript submitted for publication.

George, C., Kaplan, N., & Main, M. (1984). *The attachment interview for adults.* Unpublished manuscript, University of California, Berkeley.

Hoffman, L. (1981). *Foundations of family therapy: A conceptual framework for systems change.* New York: Basic Books.

Kreppner, K., & Lerner, R. M. (1989). Family systems and life span development: Issues and perspectives. In K. Kreppner & R. M. Lerner (Eds.), *Family systems and life span development* (pp. 1–33). Hillsdale, NJ: Lawrence Erlbaum Associates.

Marvin, R. S., & Stewart, R. B. (1990). A family systems framework for the study of attachment. In M. T. Greenberg, D. Cicchetti, & E. M. Cummings (Eds.), *Attachment in the preschool years* (pp. 51–86). Chicago: University of Chicago Press.

Minuchin, P. (1985). Families and individual development: Provocations from the field of family therapy. *Child Development, 56,* 289–302.

Minuchin, P. (1988). Relationships within the family: A systems perspective on development. In R. A. Hinde & J. Stevenson-Hinde (Eds.), *Relationships within families: Mutual influences* (pp. 7–26). Oxford, England: Clarendon.

Minuchin, S. (1974). *Families and family therapy.* Cambridge, MA: Harvard University Press.

Minuchin, S., & Fishman, H. C. (1981). *Family therapy techniques.* Cambridge, MA: Harvard University Press.

Paley, B., Cox, M. J., Kanoy, K., Harter, K. S. M., & Margand, N. A. (1999, April). *Adult attachment stance and marital quality as predictors of whole family interactions*. Paper presented at the biennial meeting of the Society for Research in Child Development, Albuquerque.

Sameroff, A. J. (1994). Developmental systems and family functioning. In R. D. Parke & S. G. Kellam (Eds.), *Exploring family relationships with other social contexts* (pp. 199–214). Hillsdale, NJ: Lawrence Erlbaum Associates.

Sroufe, L. A. (1995). *Emotional development: The organization of emotional life in the early years*. Cambridge, England: Cambridge University Press.

Author Index

Curry-Bleggi, E., 268, 270
Cushing, G., 144, 148
Cutrona, C., 35, 53

D

Damon, W., 239
Daniels, P., 162, 168
Darling, N., 227, 240
Davies, P. T., 7, 20, 79, 90, 113, 124, 152, 168, 227, 240
Davis, B. T., 17, 20, 114, 124
Demorest, A., 148
Denmark, F. L., 183
Dent-Read, C., 204
Denzin, N. K., 194, 204
Dickinson, K. A., 133, 150
Dickstein, S., 12, 20, 259, 260, 268, 269, 270
Dishion, T. J., 34, 37, 54, 55, 60, 74, 61, 74
Dix, T., 227, 236, 240
Dodge, K. A., 101, 107, 172, 173, 183, 191, 196, 199, 203, 205
Dollahite, D., 162, 168
Downey, G., 260, 270
Downey, R. G., 216, 222
Drinkard, J., 179, 183
Dumas, J. E., 173, 179, 184
Dunn, L. M., 282, 287

E

Easterbrooks, M. A., 114, 124, 244, 256
Eastenson, A., 190, 205
Elder, G. H., 34, 35, 45, 46, 47, 49, 53, 54, 55, 56, 57
Elliot, S. N., 96, 107
Emde, R. N., 114, 124, 275, 287
Emery, R. E., 61, 75, 114, 125, 226, 241, 244, 256
Epston, D., 260, 271
Erel, O., 113, 124, 281, 287
Estroff, S. E., 127, 134, 148

F

Falloon, I. R. H., 60, 74
Faraci, A. M., 223

Farris, A. M., 168, 236, 240, 256
Fauber, R., 113, 124
Feder, T., 109
Fetrow, R., 61, 74
Fiese, B. H., 3, 6, 12, 14, 28, 29, 95, 107, 259, 260, 268, 269, 270
Fincham, F. D., 7, 20, 115, 125, 244, 256, 287
Fishel, P. L., 228, 240
Fishman, H. C., 208, 217, 222, 275, 287
Fishman, S., 207, 222
Fitzpatrick, M. A., 52, 75
Fivaz-Depeursinge, E., 9, 20, 155, 168, 169
Fleeson, J., 8, 22
Fleiss, J. L., 27, 32, 43, 56, 119, 125, 143, 150, 216, 223, 267, 270
Flor, D. L., 7, 19
Florsheim, P., 3, 10, 14, 15, 16, 25, 26, 127, 131, 134, 140, 141, 143, 144, 145, 148, 149, 150
Foote, F. H., 209, 223
Forbes, C., 3, 6, 14, 15, 25, 28, 29, 59
Ford, C. L., 134, 148
Forehand, R., 14, 20, 113, 124
Forgatch, M. S., 37, 53, 60, 61, 74
Foster, I. R., 196, 204
Foster, S. L., 60, 75
Framo, J. L., 256
Frascarolo, F., 9, 20, 155, 168
Fravel, D., 12, 259, 260, 270, 271
Friesen, J. D., 134, 148
Frosch, C. A., 282, 287
Furnham, A., 188, 204

G

Gable, S., 226, 240
Gardener, K., 53, 61, 74
Gatherum, A., 67, 75
Ge, X., 35, 43, 44, 46, 47, 54, 55
Gelfand, D. M., 145, 148
George, C., 282, 287
Ghosh, C., 121, 125
Giat, L., 127, 148
Gibbins, F., 35, 53
Gilbert, R., 112, 124, 244, 256
Ginsberg, B. G., 101, 107
Gjerde, P. F., 7, 8, 20, 113, 124, 152, 168
Gleser, G. C., 26, 31

Subject Index